States, Ideologies and Social Revolutions

A Comparative Analysis of Iran, Nicaragua, and the Philippines

Between 1979 and 1986 Iran, Nicaragua, and the Philippines underwent dramatic political and social revolutions. This book examines the
conditions and processes that give rise to revolutions and their outcomes, through an in-depth analysis of economic and political developments in these countries. The book studies the background to revolution
provided by state formation and development, economic intervention,
the states' vulnerabilities, and the social consequences of their development policies. Extensive primary data are used to analyze the impact of
the collective actions and ideologies of the major social groups involved
– students, clergy, workers, and capitalists – and how they affected the
potential for a successful revolutionary outcome. Parsa challenges prevailing theories of social revolution and develops an alternative model
that incorporates variables from a wide variety of perspectives. His book
provides a valuable framework within which to understand the causes of
revolutions, their mechanics and development, and their outcomes.

MISAGH PARSA is Professor of Sociology at Dartmouth College, New
Hampshire. He is the author of *Social Origins of the Iranian Revolution*,
cited in the American Historical Association's 1995 *Guide to Historical
Literature* as one of the finest books on Iran and an "important revision-
ist" work.

States, Ideologies, and Social Revolutions

A Comparative Analysis of Iran, Nicaragua, and the Philippines

Misagh Parsa

CAMBRIDGE
UNIVERSITY PRESS

CAMBRIDGE UNIVERSITY PRESS
Cambridge, New York, Melbourne, Madrid, Cape Town, Singapore, São Paulo

Cambridge University Press
The Edinburgh Building, Cambridge CB2 2RU, UK

Published in the United States of America by Cambridge University Press, New York

www.cambridge.org
Information on this title: www.cambridge.org/9780521773379

First published 2000
Digitally reprinted (with minor corrections) 2006

A catalogue record for this publication is available from the British Library

Library of Congress Cataloguing in Publication data

Parsa, Misagh, 1945–
   States, ideologies, and social revolutions: a comparative analysis of Iran,
Nicaragua, and the Philippines / Misagh Parsa.
      p.   cm.
   ISBN 0 521 77337 7 (hb) – ISBN 0 521 77430 6 (pb)
   1. Revolutions – Case studies. 2. Iran – Politics and government – 20th
century. 3. Iran – Economic conditions – 20th century. 4. Nicaragua – Politics
and government – 20th century. 5. Nicaragua – Economic conditions – 20th
century. 6. Philippines – Politics and government – 20th century. 7. Philippines
– Economic conditions – 20th century. I. Title.

JC491.P36 2000   303.6'4–dc21   99-087457

ISBN-13 978-0-521-77337-9 hardback
ISBN-10 0-521-77337-7 hardback

ISBN-13 978-0-521-77430-7 paperback
ISBN-10 0-521-77430-6 paperback

For Susan and Arlen

Contents

Tables

Preface

This book presents both a new theoretical framework for the study of social revolutions and new evidence about the revolutionary processes in Iran, Nicaragua, and the Philippines. To my knowledge, this is the first comparative work on the revolutions in these countries. The three cases proved to be appropriate choices for a comparative analysis because, despite some similarities, they experienced different outcomes. While Iran and Nicaragua underwent social revolution, the Philippines experienced a political revolution only. This is also the first study to analyze the structure of both the state and the economy, which are critical components in the study of revolutions. At the same time, this work analyzes the collective actions by the major participants in the revolutionary struggles, namely students, clergy, workers, capitalists, and challenging organizations. The book examines in depth the demands and ideologies of these actors during the revolutionary processes. Based on detailed examination of extensive primary data, the book challenges the prevailing theories of social revolution that attribute sweeping powers to ideology.

I would like to thank the Nelson A. Rockefeller Center for Public Policy at Dartmouth College for providing the grant that made this research possible. I am grateful to my research assistants, Susan Rosales Nelson and Fiona Paua, for their meticulous work during data collection.

I was fortunate to have insightful critiques from a number of scholars who read all or parts of the manuscript. My deepest thanks go to Ervand Abrahamian, William Lee Baldwin, John Foran, Gene R. Garthwaite, John L. Hall, Douglas E. Haynes, Howard Kimeldorf, David Morgan, Jeffery Paige, A. Kevin Reinhart, Ken Sharpe, Marc Steinberg, Charles Tilly, and Stanley H. Udy, Jr. I owe special thanks to my colleague, John L. Campbell, who read the manuscript twice and provided very valuable suggestions. The support of my colleagues Denise Anthony, Eva Fodor, Christina Gomez, Raymond Hall, and Deborah King has been very helpful throughout the process of preparing the book.

A number of individuals graciously agreed to be interviewed for this book, and to them I extend my sincere gratitude. Dr. Oscar Arias, former president of Costa Rica, supplied valuable insights on the conflicts in Nicaragua and commented on the manuscript. Stephen W. Bosworth, US ambassador to the Philippines during the revolutionary struggles, provided very useful information about the conflicts there. Sedfrey A. Ordoñez, former Philippine ambassador to the UN, generously supplied much material about the workings of the Marcos regime and the opposition. Others who gave of their time and insights included A. K. Hakkak, A. Y. Khosrowshahi, A. Lebaschi, J. Majidi, R. Moghadam, H. Nategh, F. Negahdar, N. Pakdaman, M. Shaneh-chi, and Tahmasebi-Pour. I have privately thanked a number of individuals who agreed to be interviewed but wished to remain anonymous, and I take this opportunity to express my gratitude to them.

My deepest thanks go to John Haslam of Cambridge University Press for his unswerving support of my manscript. I greatly appreciate the contributions of Paula Starkey and Susan Rosales Nelson, who made valuable editorial comments, and Kim Albanese, who proofread the entire manuscript. N. Adel, S. Behdad, S. Pourdejanfeshan, and M. H. Zarrabi provided friendship throughout this project. My son, Arlen, remained patient with me despite my preoccupation most of the time. For their support and understanding, I dedicate the book to Susan and Arlen.

Part I

Theory and structural background

1 Toward a theory of revolution: linking structure and process approaches

Introduction

Popular mobilization and collective action overthrew three long-standing regimes between February 1979 and February 1986 in Iran, Nicaragua, and the Philippines. In Iran, the revolution put an end to 2,500 years of monarchy, dissolved the Pahlavi dynasty, and established an Islamic theocracy. In Nicaragua, the revolution uprooted the Somoza dynasty, which had dominated the country since the early 1930s, and enabled the socialist Sandinistas to seize power. In the Philippines, popular mobilization resulted in the expulsion of Ferdinand E. Marcos, who had ruled the country for twenty years, well beyond the two terms to which he had been elected. These political conflicts also had international consequences, especially for the United States inasmuch as some segments of the population and elite in these countries opposed US policies and interventions.

The uprisings and their outcomes in Iran, Nicaragua, and the Philippines provide remarkable cases for comparative analysis. Broadly speaking, the three countries shared certain similar experiences and structural features. Economically, all three pursued capitalist development strategies, which had been quite successful by international standards. For years, they succeeded in generating high levels of growth, development, and industrialization that were impressive by any measure. Politically, each of the regimes governed by means of authoritarian mechanisms and coercive apparatuses, which for years had been successful in controlling or repressing opposition and dissent. In fact, all three had survived earlier challenges: Iran in the early 1950s and again in the early 1960s; Nicaragua in the late 1960s and early 1970s; and the Philippines in the early 1970s. In addition, none of the regimes had been weakened or defeated in external war or had experienced state breakdown prior to the insurgencies. Finally, all three governments had long enjoyed the economic, political, and military support of the United States. Thus, the emergence of the conflicts in the three countries is itself perplexing.

Despite these similarities, the immediate political outcomes of the conflicts in each of the three countries differed widely. Significantly, in all three cases, unlikely challengers were able to seize power. In Iran, power was seized by Ayatollah Khomeini, who ideologically enjoyed only a very small following among primarily low-ranking clergy. Neither Khomeini, who had opposed the Shah for years, nor his clerical supporters were the originators of the conflicts of 1977. Rather, secular intellectuals, members of the Writers' Association, liberal-nationalists, organized in the National Front, and leftist students initiated the opposition and mobilized against the government. Despite the claims of some scholars that a strong Islamic movement had emerged by the early 1970s, Khomeini and his supporters failed to mobilize the population in June 1975, scarcely two years before the rise of insurgency. Nevertheless, by 1978, Khomeini headed a revolutionary coalition that succeeded in overthrowing the Pahlavi dynasty. But the new Islamic regime resorted to unprecedented violence in order to maintain power. Khomeini not only repressed liberal-nationalists and leftists, he had some of his own closest advisors and allies expelled from politics or killed. Although, during the revolutionary struggles, Khomeini advocated freedom, independence, and social justice, he ultimately established a theocracy, which denied basic human freedoms to the Iranian people.

The immediate political outcome of the conflict in Nicaragua was unexpected as well. Although the moderate opposition initially had the support of large segments of the population in the struggle against Somoza, it failed to maintain hegemony in the revolution. In the final stage of the revolutionary struggles, a small group of Marxists, the Sandinista Liberation Front, or the FSLN, led the coalition, seized power, and then initiated socialist policies to transform Nicaraguan society. The FSLN victory was surprising because, although they had struggled since the early 1960s to overthrow the Somozas and had gained the support of segments of the peasantry in some parts of the country, they had failed to gain control over any part of the countryside. Nor had the FSLN garnered much support among the major social classes in urban Nicaragua where the bulk of the revolutionary insurgencies were carried out. Indeed, the Sandinistas themselves had been the targets of severe repression in the years immediately preceding the inception of the popular insurgency. But, in 1979, they succeeded in overthrowing the state and introducing some major changes in Nicaraguan society.

In the Philippines, the most likely candidate for power was the Communist Party of the Philippines, which had struggled against the government for years. The Communist Party possessed a powerful nationwide political organization and enjoyed the support of segments of the population through the National Democratic Front, established to unite the people against the Marcos regime. The armed wing of the Communist Party, the New People's Army (NPA), was a large, capable guerrilla army that operated throughout much of the country. Though nowhere was it actually in control, the NPA was the *de facto* government, collecting taxes and providing health and sanitation services in many parts of the countryside. In 1985, Marcos even threatened to use foreign troops to fight the NPA. Yet, surprisingly, the communists failed to seize power when the Marcos regime was overthrown. Rather, the elite emerged victorious, and formal democratic institutions were restored. The new president, Corazón Aquino, came from one of the wealthiest families in the Philippines and, strikingly, had no history of prior political involvement.

These puzzling developments in the three countries constitute the basis for this unique comparative research. This is the first in-depth work to explain the causes and immediate outcomes of the conflicts in these three countries, using primary data. First, the analysis will focus on both the structures and the processes that culminated in social revolutions in Iran and Nicaragua, and political reforms in the Philippines. This dual approach is essential because both the structures and the processes exert influence on the outcome of the conflicts. Second, in order to understand the revolutionary processes, this research presents and analyzes extensive, primary data about the collective actions of major social groups and classes, including students, clergy, workers, capitalists, and alternative challengers in these countries. Collective actions by specific actors are at the heart of revolutionary struggles but are often given short shrift by analysts who examine mainly the ideology of the successful challengers. This research will uncover much about the specific social and political conflicts, which is a significant contribution to scholarship on revolutions because there remain some lingering misconceptions about the insurgencies and outcomes in these cases. In particular, the Iranian revolution, despite a wealth of scholarship, is still not completely understood. Third, the current research is unique in its analysis of the interests and ideologies of major social actors. It disaggregates the revolutionary conflicts into their distinct collectivities, which acted together to bring about social change, and analyzes the particular interests and ideologies of each group, along with any shifts that occurred during the struggles. Without analyzing the demands and ideologies of each of these groups in detail, no study can present a complete explanation of the causes and outcomes of the conflicts.

Finally, the goal of this research is to contribute to a comprehensive theory of social revolution in developing countries and a framework within which to understand and explain other revolutions. A comparative analysis of the three cases will illuminate our understanding of the roles of state structures, social classes, and ideologies in large-scale social conflicts. Furthermore, a key element in the examination of revolutionary outcomes presented in this work is the comparative analysis of the similarities and differences between Iran and Nicaragua, where ideologically driven challengers assumed power, and the Philippines, where power was restored to the elite. The inclusion of the Philippines is central to the analysis because this country shared many of the structural characteristics of Iran and Nicaragua and possessed even stronger revolutionary challengers than either of the two other cases; yet, unlike them, it did not experience social revolution. In addition, as part and parcel of this analysis of successful processes, the current research will also attempt to explain the failure of earlier insurgencies in these countries. A comparative-historical analysis reveals that prior to the successful removal of these powerholders, all three countries experienced insurgencies which culminated in defeat. Revolutionary success and failure may belong to the same category, as Tilly reminds us, and it may be equally important to explain the failures as well as the successes of revolutionary movements and conflicts. "If a theory purports to tell us when and why a society is ready for rebellion, it also ought to tell us which sectors of the society will resist the rebellion, and why. Exceptions prove the rule. Counter-revolutions test our explanations of revolution" (Tilly 1963:30). The following will present the theoretical framework used in this research.

Linking structures and processes

Most scholars define social revolutions as rapid, basic transformations of a society's state and class structures that are carried through class-based revolts from below (Skocpol 1979:4). Although this tends to be a very demanding definition, it is very useful in distinguishing social revolutions from other political conflicts and outcomes. According to this definition, the ousters of the Shah and Somoza in Iran and Nicaragua qualify as social revolutions, while the removal of Marcos in the Philippines does not. While debates[1] over the definition of revolutions continue, the crucial task undertaken here is to explain what happened in the three cases and why.

Although several generations of social scientists have attempted to explain the causes and origins of social revolutions (Goldstone 1980), no general theoretical consensus has emerged. In the past few decades,

---

[1] For other perspectives on the definition of revolution see Walton (1984:7–13) and Aya (1990:11).

structural models of revolution have greatly advanced our understanding of revolutions in developing countries. Several influential works, focusing on variables such as the nature of the state, economy, classes, and international conditions, have gone a long way toward explaining social revolutions (Goldstone 1991b; Moore 1966; Paige 1975; Skocpol 1979). Structural analyses of states' vulnerabilities within the world system, their internal structures, and their relations to economy and society have proved very fruitful in studying large-scale social conflicts and revolutions.

Yet, despite great advances, structural models by themselves cannot explain the complexity of social revolutions in developing countries. Although structural conditions set the stage for conflicts, they do not determine the revolutionary process or outcome. Thus, if a structural analysis of revolutionary conflicts and their outcome is to be comprehensive, it must rely on additional variables. Furthermore, models that rely on the role of class conflict are insufficient to account for social revolutions. Although some degree of class antagonism characterizes most revolutions, class conflict by itself does not produce social revolution in contemporary developing countries. In fact, intense class conflict may actually reduce the likelihood of revolutions because, in the absence of state breakdowns, class coalitions have been crucial for the overthrow of the state. Marx's theory of revolution focused primarily on social classes and assumed that class conflict in the economic sphere would inevitably find expression in the political sphere. The central argument of Marx's analysis was that class exploitation in the context of economic crisis would result in rebellion and revolution (Boswell 1993). The present work will demonstrate that, contrary to Marx's theory, a high level of working-class militancy and an ideological shift against the capitalist class and system may actually impede the formation of broad coalitions, which are necessary for revolutions. Because revolutions in the twentieth century have occurred only where major social classes succeeded in forming broad coalitions, any theory of revolution must also focus on the state, its nature, and its vulnerability to revolutionary conflicts (Goldfrank 1979:141; Goldstone 1980, 1986; Parsa 1985, 1989; Rueschemeyer and Evans 1985; Skocpol 1979).

Skocpol's influential work (1979) makes an important contribution and shifts the focus of analysis back to the state and allows for its potential autonomy. She maintains that the social-revolutionary conflicts involve a struggle over the forms of state structures (Skocpol 1979:29). But Skocpol's formulation is somewhat problematic because it relies heavily on the relationship between the dominant class and the state. It locates the center of the conflicts around the capitalist class and the state. It is true that, as the present work will show, the capitalist class often joins the insurgency primarily to change the power structure. But, as Skocpol has argued, revolutionary struggles always involve multiple conflicts and multiple actors with diverse interests, and cannot be reduced to merely one set of conflicts. Furthermore, many states in developing countries do not rule in alliance with the upper classes. Thus, the simple withdrawal of support by the capitalist class from the state may increase state vulnerability but may not result in revolutions. Skocpol's analysis also suffers from the fact that her formulation does not take into account the role of other classes and actors. Working-class insurgency may threaten the capitalist class and prevent them from opposing the state even in the face of rising conflicts. Thus, capitalists' attacks against the state are affected by the intensity of class conflict and threats posed by other classes. Labor radicalism, particularly in the presence of powerful, revolutionary challengers, may prevent capitalists from attacking the state.

Some theorists of social revolutions also criticized Skocpol's structural formulation for failing to take into account the role of ideology in social revolutions. To redress the shortcomings, a number of analysts brought ideology to the forefront of the analysis of revolutions.[2] Many of these theorists attributed independent power and dynamics to ideology. In an analysis of the French revolution, Sewell argued that ideology had a central role in the social structure and its transformations. He stated that if societies are ideologically constituted, "then adding ideology to the account will also mean rethinking the nature, the interrelations, and the effects on the revolution of state, class, international, and other structures" (Sewell 1985:61). Goldstone argued that once the institutional constraints have collapsed, ideology and culture develop their own momentum and play a leading role in revolutions (Goldstone 1991b:418). Moaddel went even further and in his analysis of the Iranian revolution turned ideology into an independent actor. He argued that although foreign capital and the state had adversely affected the bazaaris and workers, the conflicts of these classes were not inherently revolutionary. Rather, he argued, Shiite revolutionary discourse transformed social discontent into revolutionary crisis (Moaddel 1993:153–163). Even Skocpol (1979:17), who had claimed that revolutionary movements rarely begin with revolutionary intentions, in her analysis of the Iranian revolution, argued that ideas played an important role in the revolution. In fact, she assigned sweeping powers to ideology.

---

[2] Some of the important works that have paid greater attention to ideology include Foran (1993, 1997a), Foran and Goodwin (1993), Hobsbawm (1973), Migdal (1974), Scott (1979), Moaddel (1993), Arjomand (1981, 1986), Farhi (1990), Colburn (1994), and Burns (1996).

Skocpol asserted that the Shiite culture of martyrdom inspired devout Iranians to oppose the Shah in the face of repression and death (1982:275).

Despite significant contributions in understanding the role of ideology in social revolutions, some of the works that assign primacy to ideology in revolutions still suffer from a number of shortcomings. To begin, some of these works suffer from methodological reductionism. These analyses often focus primarily on the ideology of the successful revolutionary challengers and thus assume that those who participated in the conflicts actually adhered to the challengers' ideologies. Furthermore, such explanations tend to be circular because they use the outcome of the revolution to account for its causes. This method of reasoning tends to ignore the complexity of revolutions and to simplify the revolutionary process. The problem is that revolutionary challengers do not always present all aspects of their ideology to the public and at times modify or even conceal their ideologies to ensure the participation of privileged social groups that may be threatened by their radical tendencies. Furthermore, in repressive situations, ideological debates are very limited, and ideologically driven challengers may be unable or unwilling to reveal the precise nature of their ideology.

Although an understanding of the ideology of challengers is essential, a sound analysis must also convincingly demonstrate that the principal actors were both aware of such an ideology and actually supported it. If participants line up behind certain challengers, this does not necessarily imply ideological conversion. Rather, such support may come about because of political causes and tactical considerations. Therefore, an analysis of challengers' ideologies cannot be a substitute for an understanding of the ideologies of the specific collectivities that carry out most of the collective actions during conflicts. Where substantial variation exists in both the timing of the collective actions of various groups and the articulated demands of the actors, it is reasonable to suspect that the outcome cannot be due to ideological causes. A complete explanation of the role of ideology in revolutionary conflicts requires a thorough analysis of the demands and ideologies of all major social actors.

Most importantly, analyses that attribute sweeping powers to ideology fail to account for the social origins of ideologies and their relation to the social structure. Ideologies do not emerge in a vacuum and should always be understood in the social and historical context. Furthermore, because ideologies have social structural consequences, they should be analyzed in relation to the existing social actors. Although some scholars have noted the role of ideology in different phases of revolutionary conflicts (Arjomand 1986:384; Goldstone 1991b:418), no contemporary work has yet presented a comprehensive analysis of the ideology of the various actors in Third World revolutionary situations. As will be seen in the three cases, different social groups have different propensities toward revolutionary ideologies. In highly differentiated, stratified societies, various collectivities not only have different interests but also differ in their propensities toward different ideologies about the social order. A sound analysis must provide systematic, empirical data on the ideologies of major participants and their ideological preferences. Such an analysis must present systematic and comprehensive evidence about the demands and slogans of all social actors during large-scale conflicts. Only a systematic analysis of all the major participants in their actual social and historical context will reveal the impact of ideology in large-scale social conflicts. This work will attempt to make such a contribution.

Social revolutions are complex, rare processes and, as such, are extremely difficult to predict (Keddie 1995b:3; Stinchcombe 1965:169).[3] The following discussion presents a preliminary sketch of the variables that may be useful in guiding the analysis. The analysis draws and extends variables from the structural model of revolution, resource mobilization theory, and the political process model. As we shall see, certain state structures are more likely than others to generate the conditions that favor large-scale social conflicts. For example, states that form exclusive polities and states that intervene highly in capital accumulation tend to become very vulnerable to challenge and attack. Prolonged exclusion from the polity predisposes the excluded toward radical measures and insurgency. State intervention in capital accumulation also affects state vulnerability to challenge and attack. Highly interventionist states can readily become targets of attack during social conflicts. In addition, levels of state intervention also affect the nature of class conflict. But structural variables mainly set the stage for conflicts. They are inadequate to explain the dynamics of mobilization and collective action. Thus, it is important to analyze the process of insurgency and the dynamics that encourage or discourage coalition formation. In the absence of prior state breakdown or military victory by insurgents, broad coalitions are crucial to the removal of powerholders. Finally, it is essential to analyze the role of revolutionary challengers and ideology in social revolutions. The following discussion elaborates on the constellation of structures and processes that culminate in social revolution in developing countries.

---

[3] Because of the complexities, Stinchcombe (1965:169) has proposed that sociologists attempt to explain the occurrence of a revolutionary situation, rather than actual revolutions.

Exclusive rule: centralization and repression

States that are characterized by exclusive rule tend to become vulnerable to challenge and attack in times of crisis. Such states contract the scope of the polity and block access to the state and the centers of political power. They often tend to eliminate or render irrelevant formal democratic institutions. In extreme cases, highly exclusive states may develop an exceedingly personalistic rule, which excludes virtually the entire population, even the economic elite, from decision making and government resources. "Sultanic" regimes (Linz 1975:259–263) and "autonomous personalist" regimes (Midlarsky and Roberts 1986:24–27) are extreme examples of exclusive rule. Under such regimes, rule is based on personal characteristics (Chehabi and Linz 1998:7). Such regimes also tend to minimize or eliminate accountability to the public and rule independently of the underlying population (McDaniel 1991:6). Centralized, dynastic regimes are especially vulnerable because they restrict elite access to the polity and remain exclusive for prolonged periods without providing any option for change (Foran 1997a:229; Goodwin 1994:758; Snyder 1998:56).

When exclusive rule and centralization of power come about in the context of large-scale social conflicts, they often have several crucial consequences. First, in such conditions, states may have to continually resort to violence and repression to demobilize or eliminate their opponents or insurgents. The continuous use of repression may reduce social support for the regime and force it to become dependent on both the military and external support to maintain power. State reliance on military coercion may enable governments to hold on to power in the short run, but such reliance may prove to be inadequate in the long term. When challenged by broad coalitions that disrupt the social order, governments may not enjoy the loyalty of the armed forces, particularly if rulers do not completely control the military or if it lacks cohesion. In times of crises, preexisting divisions may render the military vulnerable to schisms and defection. For example, armies that are based on conscripts are often vulnerable especially because they may retain regular contact with the civilian population. Second, government repression may weaken or eliminate elite or moderate challengers and consequently polarize the opposition in favor of the hegemony of radical or revolutionary challengers. Thus, government repression may well affect mobilization options in future rounds of conflict.

States that are highly exclusive may attempt to rely on external support to remain in power (Snyder 1998:58). The external dependence of such states also renders them vulnerable, as such reliance can be a double-edged sword. Although such relations may protect dependent states in the international state system, shifts in international alignments may expose them to unfavorable political decisions made beyond their borders. Support may be eroded during times when major powers are preoccupied with war or urgent internal conflicts, or are seeking to balance one another's allies. Additionally, the dependent states are at an obvious disadvantage when they receive less external support than do the armed rebel groups within their borders seeking to overthrow them (Goldfrank 1979:149). External support may even be withdrawn in the face of a forceful internal opposition, especially when continued support for the existing regime could potentially spawn a more radical alternative that may pose a greater threat to the old regime's external allies. Thus, a high level of dependence on external sources may prove distinctly detrimental in times of conflicts and crisis.

Social theorists have long maintained that states which are characterized by exclusive rule and extreme centralization of power are highly vulnerable to challenge and attack (Goodwin and Skocpol 1994). Moore has suggested that centralization of power in China rendered that state more vulnerable to peasant rebellion than India (Moore 1966:458–459). Tilly argued that "Perhaps the largest single factor in the promotion of revolutions and collective violence has been the great centralization of power in national states" (Tilly 1973:445–446). Skocpol (1979:47) presented a similar analysis of the French, Russian, and Chinese states, which were centralized and relatively autonomous from the dominant classes and geared toward extracting greater surplus. All three states were overthrown by revolutions.

State intervention and target of social conflicts

The relationship between the state and economy has crucial consequences for social conflicts. Although virtually ignored by structural theorists of revolution, state intervention in capital allocation and accumulation has profound consequences in such situations. Skocpol's analysis of the "rentier state" (1982) does capture an aspect of state intervention, but it is a concept that is too narrow and thus fails to explain revolutions in non-oil-producing countries. Basically, state intervention in capital accumulation converts the government into a major economic actor and thus affects the nature of social conflicts by providing a visible, concrete target for challenge and attack. State intervention has an impact on social and political conflicts by affecting the interests of various social classes and collectivities and thus setting the stage for conflicts. Furthermore, the level of state intervention affects the nature and likelihood of class conflict. These variables in turn affect the outcome of social conflicts.

The degree of state intervention in the economy can be analyzed by means of a simple typology categorizing the level of government involvement in the process of capital accumulation. Based on such criteria, three types of states can be distinguished: regulative states, administrative states, and hyperactive states.[4] Regulative states intervene minimally in the economy, limiting their activities to enforcing rules and assuring "efficient" operation of the market, often through fiscal and monetary policies. Administrative states intervene moderately in economic matters. In addition to regulative activities, they initiate planning, pursue corporatist policies, and may provide economic incentives to certain sectors. Hyperactive states intervene extensively in capital allocation and accumulation, thus limiting the scope of the market's operation. In addition to extensive regulating and planning, hyperactive states often own and control vast economic resources and, consequently, become major economic actors.

In general, social conflicts may lead to revolution only when contending collectivities and classes target the state. Although many factors contribute to struggle over state power, certain state structures seem to be more vulnerable to social conflicts than others. The level of state intervention affects the nature and outcome of social conflicts. In general, a low level of state intervention in capital accumulation, as exists in regulative states, reduces the probability that the state will become the direct target of collective action and thus, in turn, diminishes the likelihood of revolutionary conflicts. In this case, capital allocation and accumulation are determined by an abstract, decentralized, depoliticized, and "self-regulating" market system, which tends to defuse and privatize conflicts, confining them to the civil society. Because it is abstract, decentralized, and depoliticized, the market cannot be attacked or overthrown. As a result, the regulative state is unlikely to attract direct attacks or challenges because class conflict remains confined within the economic sphere and the civil society. Should such conflicts escalate, aggrieved groups may clamor for the state to intervene on their behalf against their adversaries. Because aggrieved groups solicit help from the state, rather than attacking it, they are far more likely to be reformist than revolutionary. Furthermore, when state intervention is low, the regulative state tends to be perceived as an autonomous entity that serves general, societal interests. In such cases, the state may become an integrative, rather than a divisive, force. Finally, a low level of state intervention in capital accumulation may increase the likelihood and intensity of class conflict. Intensification of class conflict, in turn,

---

[4] I have borrowed the first two terms from the work of Zysman (1983), although he may not agree with my definitions.

removes the state from being the principal target of attack and thus reduces the likelihood of revolution.

In contrast, states that intervene to a great extent in the economy render themselves more vulnerable to challenge and attack. Hyperactive states tend to become major economic actors, control a great deal of economic resources, and intervene extensively in capital allocation and accumulation. As loci of accumulation, hyperactive states may become direct producers and financiers. In extreme cases, a hyperactive state may even become the single largest entrepreneur, industrialist, banker, and landowner in its domain. These states also tend to institute regulative mechanisms, which intervene extensively in multitudinous aspects of the economy in order to promote economic development.

High levels of intervention entail significant political consequences for the interventionist states. High state intervention replaces the abstract, decentralized, and depoliticized market mechanism with a visible, concrete, social entity, which can be targeted for attack during conflict or crisis (Parsa 1985, 1989; Rueschemeyer and Evans 1985:69). High state intervention expands the extent of political conflicts because of the convergence of economic and political conflicts in the political arena. In addition to ordinary political conflicts, states also become the center for economic conflicts. Thus, at times of economic crisis, the state, rather than market forces, will be held accountable for failure and mismanagement, once again making the government vulnerable to challenge and attack. Furthermore, hyperactive states in developing countries often pursue development strategies that serve narrow and particular, rather than general societal, interests. Such strategies are often accompanied by rapid accumulation of resources in some sectors in contrast to others, thus widening social, economic, and regional inequalities. State power in such conditions becomes visibly and directly linked to privilege and disprivilege and inevitably politicizes the development process. If inequalities and disadvantages were generated by the market mechanism, adversely affected groups would not blame the state; rather, aggrieved segments of the population would demand state intervention to redress their grievances. But when rising inequality is directly and visibly linked to state policies, politicization may be inevitable and the hyperactive state cannot escape liability.

Finally, a high level of state intervention affects the nature of economic and political conflict. Hyperactive states that employ sizable segments of the workforce inevitably tend to become the target of workers' economic conflicts. Workers' attacks against the state may reduce the intensity of class conflict. Reduction in the intensity of class conflict, in turn, increases the likelihood of coalition formation and revolutions.

Following World War II, state intervention expanded dramatically in many dimensions. Although it is impossible to quantify this variable, an approximation of the degree of intervention may be obtained by examining the government's share of total fixed capital expenditure within the national economy. Table 1 presents the public share of fixed capital formation, that is, expenditures on infrastructure and public enterprises, for a number of non-socialist, developed and developing countries between 1978 and 1980. As the table illustrates, governments in developed countries did not intervene highly, but those in developing countries were highly interventionist. The share of fixed capital formation in Western Europe and North America was modest, ranging from 8.3 percent in Spain and 8.5 percent in the United States to a high of 18.4 percent in Ireland. Among developed countries, Japan and New Zealand had the highest ratio, 31.3 and 33.5 percent respectively. In contrast, most states in developing countries seemed to play a much greater role in fixed capital expenditures. Most developing countries had exceedingly high levels of state contribution, with some African countries, such as Burundi and Morocco, reaching upwards of 95 percent. Indeed, perhaps the most significant characteristic of states in developing countries is that they were at the center of economic activity and development, in contrast to Western European and North American states.

Although European governments played a crucial role in economic growth in the initial stages of their development,[5] developing countries in the decades following World War II until at least the early 1980s pursued highly interventionist approaches. The many economic factors that influence government intervention in developing countries include the absence of a strong and resourceful entrepreneurial class; high risk and large investment; the need to provide support for the private sector by developing basic industries; stiff competition from powerful transnational corporations; and the rising cost of capital and advanced technology in the twentieth century. In some cases, the departure of foreign capital led to an increased number of state-owned enterprises, which at times represented a significant share of the economy.[6] Political factors, too, can bring about government intervention, such as the rise of nationalist movements and the nationalization of foreign assets; pressures from below to nationalize

[5] Although the state performed certain necessary functions in the economic development of Western European countries, its activities were limited in comparison with contemporary Third World countries. For the European experience see Hall and Ikenberry (1989), Supple (1980), Tilly (1990), Weiss and Hobson (1995).
[6] State enterprises accounted for 75 percent of the total sales by firms in developing countries, compared with 10 percent for public enterprises in developed countries (Kirkpatrick 1984:152). On the issue of public enterprises see also the following works: Gillis (1980), Shepherd (1976), and Short (1984).

Table 1   *Public share of fixed capital expenditure in comparative perspective,
1978–1980*

Developing countries	Percentage	Developing countries	Percentage
Morocco	95.59	India	45.42
Burundi	95.20	Fiji	45.03
Zambia	82.99	Argentina	44.65
Togo	75.59	Venezuela	44.51
Gambia	73.23	Congo	43.28
Malawi	70.33	Botswana	43.22
Seychelles	67.10	Kenya	43.03
Central African Republic	65.67	Mexico	42.24
Benin	63.66	Brazil	40.81
Pakistan	62.46	Uruguay	40.60
Swaziland	62.29	Papua New Guinea	40.54
Cape Verde	59.62	Saudi Arabia	40.26
Cameroon	59.18	Ecuador	38.33
Lesotho	58.94	Rwanda	38.29
Liberia	58.74	Egypt	38.27
Tunisia	58.66	El Salvador	38.02
Bolivia	57.76	Honduras	37.37
Sri Lanka	57.68	Chile	36.98
Yemen	55.92	Colombia	36.40
Jordan	55.69	Senegal	36.20
Sierra Leone	51.74	Chad	36.11
Haiti	51.67	Nepal	36.07
Zaire	51.28	Malaysia	35.82
Jamaica	51.26	Costa Rica	34.93
Uganda	51.07	Gabon	34.91
Nigeria	50.59	Mauritius	34.16
Turkey	50.56	Guatemala	34.07
Trinidad-Tobago	49.52	Thailand	31.79
Ghana	49.32	Dominican Republic	29.33
Taiwan	47.02	Somalia	27.07
Bangladesh	46.28	Singapore	26.52
Mali	45.96	Paraguay	23.40
Indonesia	45.85	Peru	22.86
Panama	45.80	South Korea	19.11

Table 1   (*cont.*)

Developed countries	Percentage	Developed countries	Percentage
New Zealand	33.58	Netherlands	15.15
Japan	31.30	Iceland	14.87
Ireland	18.41	United Kingdom	14.05
Switzerland	17.99	France	13.33
Denmark	17.81	Australia	13.08
Sweden	17.45	Finland	12.81
Austria	17.20	Italy	12.79
Belgium-Luxemburg	16.44	Canada	11.93
Norway	15.89	United States	8.58
Germany	15.86	Spain	8.32

Source: World Bank (1991)

or expand employment; and antagonism against out-of-favor entrepreneurs linked to outsiders.

Governments in many developing countries own some of the most important economic assets, such as basic industries or oil and other minerals, which are significant sources of revenue. Such states may also control most of the country's financial capital. During the Cold War, many such states were the recipients of foreign aid and development assistance, which transformed them into major financial players. They also borrowed massive amounts of capital from international banks to promote economic development. An important consequence of state capital allocation is the increasing potential for the financial system to become politicized, especially where preferential treatment excludes segments of the business community. Many governments in developing countries also became direct producers and owned the largest industrial enterprises in their countries. The 500 largest industrial corporations outside the United States in 1979 included 52 corporations in developing countries. Of these, 34 were owned by the state (*Fortune*, August 13, 1979).

Governments in developing countries also used a variety of regulatory mechanisms. In pursuit of import substitution industrialization after World War II, many governments in developing countries erected steep tariff barriers, issued limited licenses, and allocated foreign exchange on the basis of quotas to restrict domestic competition. To promote industrial development and obtain vital technology, these states sometimes overvalued their currency, thus adversely affecting the agricultural sector. Sometimes they also controlled wages and prices, which severely undermined the market mechanism. More importantly, states often intervened in industrial relations as well, restricting or banning labor organizations and strikes in order to speed up capital accumulation.

Although a number of countries in Asia and other parts of the world have successfully used state power to promote industrialization (Japan, South Korea, Taiwan), in general, high state intervention increases the likelihood that social conflicts will become politicized and, given the appropriate conditions, target the state. High levels of state intervention in capital accumulation in developing countries often have negative consequences for many social groups and classes, thereby weakening political support for the regime across the board and setting the stage for social conflict. For example, state intervention during the 1960s and 1970s adversely affected the agricultural sector in many developing countries that pursued import-substitution industrialization. These governments either ignored the agrarian sector or failed to carry out substantial reforms to improve the condition of the peasantry. In fact, in most cases, government intervention served the interests of large producers at the expense of smaller ones. State intervention in the industrial sector may also adversely affect working-class interests when hyperactive states promote capital accumulation by banning strikes, keeping wages down, and restricting or prohibiting working-class organizations. Although ordinarily workers may accept these policies, in times of crisis these policies constitute grounds for working-class mobilization. The likelihood of workers' politicization increases, particularly in conditions where state intervention is high and the government is the principal employer. In such cases, the state will become the direct target of workers' attacks.

High levels of state intervention may also negatively affect the capitalist class, splitting its interests. While state intervention may protect and promote nascent industries, some capitalists may oppose regulative activities, for example, limited licensing and high protective tariffs, which may reduce potential entry into such sectors. While these policies may prove highly lucrative for a small segment of capitalists who are protected from competition and the vagaries of the market, the vast majority of small and medium-sized capitalists may oppose such privileges because they may be compelled to operate without protection and advantages. Capitalists may likewise oppose state intervention in capital allocation, which often politicizes the financial process, because segments of the capitalist class are likely to be excluded from government resources. Although large, favored enterprises may be granted access to state resources, small and medium-sized businesses may be excluded, placed in precarious circumstances, and may turn to bribery to gain advantage. These capitalists often condemn corruption because it imposes an additional cost on their businesses. Exclusion of these smaller entrepreneurs from the most favorable loans and subsidies may reduce the hyperactive state's base of social support, making it vulnerable in times of conflict.

Such high levels of state intervention may inevitably result in the exclusion of segments of the capitalist class from preferential treatment by the government because of the relatively large size of the class in developing countries. This class remains sizable in developing countries in contrast to industrialized countries, where capitalism and market competition have reduced its size. As shown in table 2, employers and self-employed segments of the population constitute 38.09 percent in Bangladesh, 25.67 percent in Brazil, 67.7 percent in Ghana, 30.55 percent in Iran, 29.93 percent in Nicaragua, and 36.33 percent in the Philippines. In contrast, the corresponding figures are only 8.1 percent of the workforce in the United States, 7.57 percent in the United Kingdom, 8.36 percent in West Germany and 14.29 percent in Japan. Where the capitalist class is large, as it is in developing countries, it may be inevitable that significant segments of this class will find themselves excluded from preferential treatment and government resources.

Where high levels of state intervention adversely affect the interests of all major social classes, this may encourage coalition formation among various social groups. Although these social groups and classes may have conflicting interests, in times of crisis they may coalesce against a common enemy, that is, the interventionist state.

Finally, the hyperactive state may also become a target of attack if it pursues inappropriate economic and financial policies that increase the country's economic vulnerability in the world market.[7] States that heavily rely on external sources of capital and technology may become vulnerable during unfavorable economic conditions and experience a debt crisis (Foran 1993, 1997; Walton 1989:299). Of course, government mismanagement of resources often intensifies the debt crisis. The vulnerability is especially acute for developing countries that rely heavily on exports of a few raw materials and primary commodities. An economic downturn may produce falling prices for these goods and a decline in demand on the world market. Monocrop economies can be devastated by such world market fluctuations, and even oil-rich countries are susceptible. A decline in the world market can negatively affect those segments of the population that produce the single export and may even threaten broad segments of the population. In the context of declining resources, a highly indebted country may experience a balance of payments crisis and may be

---

[7] Dependence may generate economic difficulties and render Third World countries vulnerable to political conflicts; see Eckstein (1989), Foran (1993, 1997a), Wolf (1969), Paige (1975), Walton (1989), and Boswell and Dixon (1990).

Table 2 *Percentage of employers and self-employed in the total labor force, in comparative perspective*

Developing countries	Percentage	Developed countries	Percentage
Togo	70.28	Ireland	19.01
Malawi	69.88	Israel	18.29
Ghana	67.70	Italy	17.94
Nigeria	65.39	Spain	17.92
Cameroon	60.24	New Zealand	15.98
Sudan	57.95	Japan	14.29
Haiti	51.48	Australia	13.96
Pakistan	48.17	France	13.96
Mali	45.84	Finland	13.43
Guatemala	42.19	Singapore	12.72
Bangladesh	38.09	Austria	10.09
Ecuador	37.27	Denmark	8.90
Philippines	36.33	Norway	8.82
Greece	32.53	Sweden	8.66
Iran	30.55	Netherlands	8.64
Nicaragua	29.93	Canada	8.49
El Salvador	28.24	Germany	8.36
South Korea	28.11	United States	8.10
Venezuela	27.40	United Kingdom	7.57
Morocco	27.08		
Mexico	27.00		
Colombia	26.94		
Taiwan	26.92		
Egypt	26.51		
Chile	26.47		
Turkey	26.10		
Brazil	25.67		
Tunisia	25.06		
Portugal	24.71		
Sri Lanka	24.57		
Malaysia	24.20		
Costa Rica	24.00		

Source: ILO, *Yearbook of Labor Statistics, 1989–90.* Geneva: ILO.

required to initiate "structural adjustment" and currency devaluation, often with adverse effects on the country's entire economic structure.

To sum up, the high level of intervention characteristic of hyperactive states can reduce the operation of the market mechanism and politicize the process of capital allocation and accumulation, making the state a target for aggrieved social groups. Exclusionary state policies may affect various interests adversely and diminish support for the state. If such exclusion is coupled with external economic adversities and pressures, hyperactive states may become increasingly vulnerable to crisis and challenge.

But structural vulnerabilities by themselves do not inevitably produce social conflict, let alone revolution. The history of the world is replete with examples of states that were highly centralized and interventionist and also excluded and adversely affected large segments of the population. Many of these states had only limited social support, yet only a few actually experienced social revolution. In short, structural theories by themselves are inadequate to explain the eruption, nature, timing, and outcome of social conflicts (Aya 1990; Kim 1991:10; Walton 1984). Although structural factors set the stage for conflict and restrict certain options by affecting the interests and capacities of different collectivities for mobilization and action, they cannot determine the complex revolutionary processes and actual outcomes. There is always more than one potential outcome present in any conflictual situation (Kimmel 1990:185–186). Similar structural conditions may give rise to different outcomes (Selbin 1993:29). Thus, any analysis of revolution must also take into account the revolutionary process and the role of revolutionary challengers in order to explain the outcome of social conflicts.

Collective action and coalition formation

All social structures generate conflicting interests. But such conflicts do not usually translate into mobilization and insurgency in the short run. Thus, analyses of social revolutions must go beyond structural theories and examine the process of mobilization and collective action. It is essential to explain the revolutionary process by focusing on variables such as opportunities, organization, threats, vulnerabilities and coalition formation (Tilly 1978).

In highly repressive situations, large-scale insurgencies are initiated only when favorable opportunities emerge, that is, when the balance of power favors disadvantaged groups and classes (McAdam 1982:40–41; McAdam and Snow 1997:34). "The major power of movement is exerted when opportunities are widening, elites are divided and realignments are occurring," as Tarrow (1994:150) has noted. Favorable opportunities may arise when the state becomes vulnerable due to external pressures, schisms within the state, or state reforms that reduce repression against insurgents (Jenkins 1985; Jenkins and Perrow 1977). External pressures may render the state vulnerable particularly when the state is highly dependent on external powers in the world system. State vulnerability may lead well-organized collectivities to challenge the state.

External pressures may also prompt the state to introduce certain reforms that could reduce repression and facilitate opposition mobilization
and collective action. Finally, repressive measures in the context of political polarization may also generate popular mobilization and collective
action and render the state vulnerable. Regimes that are threatened by
large-scale challenges may resort to sudden repressive measures to intimidate the opposition. Ironically, repressive measures undertaken by
the government against leading challengers may render the state vulnerable by generating at least a short-term coalition among broad segments
of the population and various collectivities. Unfortunately, political opportunity theorists have not studied the complex role and impact of
repression on opportunities in the context of political polarization.[8]

Once favorable opportunities emerge, collectivities and classes that are
organized have a greater potential to engage in collective action than
those that are unorganized. "Individuals are not magically mobilized for
participation in some group enterprise, regardless of how angry, sullen,
hostile or frustrated they may feel. Their aggression may be channeled to
collective ends only through the coordinating, directing functions of an
organization, be it formal or informal . . . otherwise, the unhappy merely
brood passively on the sidelines" (Shorter and Tilly 1974:338). Organizations provide communication networks essential for collective action,
adopt tactics and strategies, and coordinate the actions of large numbers
of people (Morris 1984:282). Most significantly, organizations are most
effective when they can mobilize preexisting solidarities and stimulate
larger publics into collective action (Tarrow 1994:150). Such organizations, of course, must be independent of the structures they attack. For
this reason, those alternative channels of mobilization that are not restricted by government repression may have a decisive impact on the outcome
of the conflicts.

In the absence of prior state breakdown or military victory by insurgents, various social classes and collectivities must form broad coalitions
to neutralize government repression and overthrow the regime. But coalition formation is often a difficult process because of the existence of
disparate interests and ideologies in any society at any point in time. The
nature of the state and level of state intervention affect the likelihood of
coalition formation. A high level of state intervention encourages the
likelihood of coalition formation because it tends to become the target of
attack for every major social class and collectivity. The nature of the
political system may also affect coalition formation. Exclusive rule also
tends to limit options for change and weaken or repress the moderate

[8] Charles Kurzman (1996) has criticized political opportunity theorists for ignoring
subjective perceptions in the analysis of revolutions.

opposition. As a result, it may encourage the moderates to form an alliance with radical forces.

The dynamics of conflicts also affect the process of coalition formation. The likelihood that broad coalitions will be formed increases during times of crisis. Economic crises generally have a sweeping impact, negatively affecting large segments of the population, imposing new costs, creating new losers, and generating distributional conflicts (Haggard and Kaufman 1995:6–10, 28–32, 45–46). These conditions, in turn, set the stage for the formation of broad coalitions. Political crises make coalition formation likely by activating third parties that come under pressure to take sides (Gamson 1975:118). The likelihood of coalition formation also increases where there is a low level of class conflict. In contrast, coalition formation is unlikely where ideologically driven challengers become very powerful and threaten the privileges of the upper class.

In the absence of a political compromise, coalition allies may have to escalate the conflicts and disrupt the social structure to overthrow the regime. Disruptive collective action can make the state extremely vulnerable (Jenkins 1985; McAdam 1982; Cloward 1977; Schwartz 1976). Prolonged structural disruptions may have a serious impact, especially on societies that are characterized by an urban economy. When production, distribution, and services are interrupted, the social structure may be destabilized to the point of economic crisis, which may deprive the state of revenues and resources necessary for its continued operation. A state's inability to prevent sustained, large-scale disruptions may itself signal political instability, which may, in turn, intensify the crisis and precipitate mobilization by groups that have not yet engaged in collective action.

State impotence in the face of growing conflict may lead dissatisfied members of the polity to defect. Such defections reduce support for the state at the same time that they augment the opposition's resources. The most dangerous defections at this stage are those from the armed forces, which can paralyze the coercive apparatus. Preexisting divisions within the armed forces may widen and result in breakdown. The probability of defection increases if relatively close links exist between members of the armed forces and the civilian population. Armies largely staffed by conscripts are especially vulnerable to defection because the recruits maintain contact with the rest of the population. In contrast, armies composed of professional soldiers who remain segregated from civilians are less susceptible to defections. As defections increase, the armed forces may become paralyzed, declare neutrality, or even join insurgents to allow a transfer of power. Finally, the armed forces may be defeated by insurgents who initiate an armed struggle that is combined with large-scale disruptive actions, even if the military is not entirely shut down.

Increased external support and resources for insurgents combined with a decline of support for the state increases the likelihood that a transfer of power will occur.

Ideology and social revolution

Whether large-scale social conflicts will end in political change only or eventually transform the entire social structure depends, at a minimum, upon the challengers that ultimately seize power. If the new leaders are moderate with ties to the upper class, the revolution will result only in changes in the political system, accompanied perhaps by limited social reforms. If, on the other hand, the new leaders are radical revolutionaries, the outcome may be a large-scale social transformation of the class structure. Thus, the ascendancy of ideologically driven challengers, i.e., revolutionaries, is critical in determining whether the conflicts will culminate in social revolution.

In theory, challengers who possess crucial resources, who are well organized and unconstrained by repression are in a better position to lead the insurgency and seize power. Thus, moderate challengers have a greater potential than do revolutionaries to gain power. They have greater economic resources, which can be used offensively in times of conflicts. They are often mobilized because they are permitted to form occupational or economic organizations to defend their interests, which also serve to enhance their capacity for collective action. They may be less restricted by repression because they do not advocate fundamental change in the social structure. Finally, elite challengers may have allies within the government with whom they can form coalitions to advance their cause. But it is important to note that such challengers, by definition, do not mobilize to bring about social revolutions. At most, they may advocate the expansion of the polity and democratization.

In contrast, radical challengers who advocate social revolutions often lack adequate resources and are forced to operate underground to escape repression. Furthermore, ideologically driven challengers generally do not have allies within the government to advance their interests. If revolutionary challengers become very powerful and attract allies among the working classes, they may threaten privileged social classes and collectivities and reduce the likelihood of coalition formation, an important factor in overthrowing repressive regimes whose armed forces remain intact. Under such conditions, moderate and upper-class organizations may withdraw from disruptive collective action and rely upon the state to block radical challengers from power. Thus, revolutionary challengers are not, under ordinary conditions, in an advantageous position to succeed in gaining power. As a result, many revolutionary challengers emerge, but only a few succeed.

Radical challengers may be successful, however, under certain conditions. Revolutionary challengers gain strength under exclusive regimes that repress the moderate opposition. They may be able to seize power where the elite opposition has broken away from the existing regime but has failed to remove the powerholders. In this case, the elite opposition and the rulers must have already rejected compromise by means of an electoral contest, which would have limited options in favor of the elite and isolated the radicals. In addition, revolutionary challengers may succeed in seizing power where they can forge a coalition with moderate challengers or obtain their implicit support by reducing the intensity of class conflict so that the upper class is not threatened. They are more likely to succeed in forming such coalitions if they tone down their radical platform and modify their exclusive claim to state power. If an implicit or explicit coalition is formed, revolutionary challengers are more likely to come to power. Once a broad coalition is formed, the likelihood of success increases if revolutionary challengers simultaneously combine popular uprising, disruptive collective action in the form of general strikes, and armed attacks on the coercive apparatus of the regime.

Conclusion

The model of Third World social revolutions presented in the current research draws on various aspects of the structural, resource mobilization, and political process theories. Based on this analysis, states that form exclusive polities and are hyperactive appear to be most vulnerable to challenge and attack. Although structural variables set the stage for conflicts, they do not determine the occurrence, timing and the process of conflict. Because similar structural conditions may give rise to dissimilar processes and outcomes, it is important to analyze the actual dynamics of revolutionary conflicts by analyzing the role of opportunities, organization, mobilization options, the likelihood of coalition formation, and disruptions of social structure.

The three case studies of Iran, Nicaragua, and the Philippines will be used to illustrate precisely how the variables discussed above can be used to explain large-scale Third World social conflicts and their outcomes. The methodology of comparative analysis is especially revealing here because these countries had developed, broadly speaking, similar social structures, experienced massive, popular opposition, and ultimately emerged with very different outcomes. To explain these different outcomes, the current research will present and analyze extensive primary data about the structures of the state, the economy, and how state intervention affected the economic development of each country. Furthermore, the research analyzes a great deal of primary data on the frequency, timing, and nature of the collective actions and the demands and ideologies articulated by major collectivities involved in the struggles. These include students, clergy, workers, capitalists, and alternative challengers. The research will also present similar analyses on the conflicts of farmers, peasants and the new middle class that joined the struggles in all three cases, largely in their final stages.

This research will demonstrate that although classes are crucial in political development, intensified class conflict may actually prevent the formation of broad coalition. In the absence of prior state breakdown or military victory by insurgents, broad coalitions play a very significant role in social revolutions. Thus, intensification of class conflicts and the absence of broad coalitions may reduce the likelihood of social revolutions. This research will also show that, in general, different collectivities have different propensities toward revolutionary ideologies, despite differences in the three countries' histories and cultures. Students reveal by far the greatest propensity toward adopting revolutionary ideologies and closely follow the lead of dissident intellectuals. The current research will attempt to present a new understanding of the role of students, a group that has been virtually ignored by scholarship on revolutions.

This research will also analyze the role of revolutionary challengers and their success or failure in overthrowing the existing regimes. An important conclusion is that the presence of powerful revolutionary challengers may actually impede the formation of broad coalitions that are essential in the overthrow of the state in the absence of a military defeat or prior state breakdown. Powerful revolutionary challengers may threaten radical transformation of the social structure and thus increase upper-class dependence on the state for stability. This likelihood may be reinforced if revolutionary challengers have strong working-class allies who also threaten the capitalist class. Finally, this work will demonstrate that the dynamics of conflicts and mobilization options available in the final stages of the conflicts are critical in affecting their immediate outcome.

To summarize briefly, in Iran, during successive periods of conflicts in the 1950s and 1960s, the Shah eliminated opponents and constructed an exclusive polity. The government severely repressed and banned the moderate opposition, preventing them from any organizing whatsoever. At the same time, with increased resources, the state expanded intervention in capital allocation and accumulation and limited the extent of the market mechanism. State power was used effectively to promote economic development and accumulation of capital. Aided by increased oil revenues, state intervention succeeded in generating spectacular economic growth and development. But government policies also increased social and economic inequalities. Political mobilization and conflicts began in 1977 when the government became vulnerable through very mild external pressures and a limited reduction of repression in the country. Different social groups and classes mobilized and initiated collective action at different times and made different claims. As the process unfolded, the opposition had to mobilize through the mosque because government repression had eliminated all other mobilization options. Eventually, a coalition of various social groups and classes with disparate interests and ideologies succeeded in overthrowing the monarchy. In the end, a small segment of the clergy, who had been poorly organized in the initial stage of the struggles, seized power, repressed their coalition partners, and established a theocratic state.

In Nicaragua, the Somozas also constructed a centralized state that excluded broad segments of the population from the polity. Although moderate opposition was rendered ineffective in Nicaragua, they were not as severely repressed as in Iran. In the decades prior to the revolution, the state also expanded its intervention in the economy and, particularly, in capital allocation. Although relatively successful in terms of economic growth, the intervention resulted in rising national debt and increased social and economic inequalities. While a small segment of the population benefited greatly from state intervention, the majority were left out of the process. Segments of the population, including students, workers, and elements in the Catholic Church, mobilized against the government after the 1972 earthquake in Managua. Mobilization and collective action terminated at the end of 1974 when the government imposed a state siege. A new round of mobilization emerged in the fall of 1977 when external pressures led the state to reduce repression. In the context of rising mobilization, the assassination of Chamorro in January 1978 resulted in the intensification of conflict. Eventually, as in Iran, a broad coalition composed of different social groups and classes overthrew the state in 1979. The coalition was led by the Sandinista Front for National Liberation, or FSLN, and it had to resort to armed struggle because the government closed all other options for change. In the end, the result was the ascendancy of the Sandinistas who seized state power and ushered in socialist transformations.

Unlike Iran and Nicaragua, the Philippines' political system was characterized by formal democratic institutions until 1972. At this time, in response to political conflicts, President Marcos imposed martial law, repressed the moderate opposition, and restricted access to the polity. This resulted in the centralization of power and the formation of exclusive rule. As in Iran and Nicaragua, Marcos also expanded state intervention in the economy. Although the country experienced spectacular growth for several years, the growth could not be sustained. Soon the country faced rising national debt and had to devalue its currency several times. It also experienced rising social and economic inequalities. In 1981 in response to external and internal pressures, President Marcos lifted martial law, but he removed only some of the repressive aspects of his rule. Thus, political mobilization did not emerge until August 1983 when the state was rendered vulnerable and targeted for attack as a result of the assassination of Benigno (Ninoy) Aquino, a leading opponent of Marcos. But, for more than two years, the opposition could not remove Marcos from power because, despite strong popular opposition and mobilization, a broad coalition was not formed. The opposition remained divided and Marcos succeeded in deepening the divisions by encouraging moderates to participate in the 1984 elections for the National Assembly. In the end, a stalemate emerged after a presidential election and led to a schism in the armed forces. A complex set of processes resulted in the ascendancy of the elite-led opposition. Thus, unlike in Iran and Nicaragua, the outcome of the Philippines conflict was a political rather than a social revolution.

Aside from these general patterns, as the following chapters will demonstrate, there were important similarities and differences between the three cases. In particular, Iran and Nicaragua had greater similarities in their structures and both experienced social revolutions. Although the Philippine political structure also underwent similar experiences and trends, these changes often differed in intensity from the other two cases. More importantly, the revolutionary process generated different dynamics that ultimately produced a different outcome. As will be seen, these similarities and variations provide a fruitful comparative analysis.

Chapter 2 will analyze the making of exclusive polity and the issues of centralization of power in the three cases. Chapter 3 will discuss such economic variables as state intervention in the economy, increased dependence on the world market, and economic mismanagement and decline, all of which set the stage for conflict and rendered the states structurally vulnerable to challenge and attack. Chapters 4 through 7 will examine the conflicts and insurgencies of major social groups and classes, including students, clergy, workers, and capitalists, and their roles in the revolutions. Chapter 8 will analyze the formation of coalitions, the rise of new challengers, and the overthrow of the old regimes. The final chapter will summarize the analysis and return to theoretical issues.

2   Conflict and the making of exclusive rule

In chapter 1, discussion focused on the varying degrees to which certain states were rendered structurally vulnerable to conflict and challenge. States in Iran, Nicaragua, and the Philippines shared many of those traits. These regimes had emerged or solidified their power during earlier rounds of social and political conflicts that were largely nationalist in nature. During these conflicts alternative challengers had arisen and gained the support of some segments of the population, who mobilized and demanded certain changes. All three regimes succeeded in eliminating or weakening these challengers and repressing their supporters. Following the repression, all three regimes increasingly centralized their power structure and constructed polities that excluded broad segments of the population, including segments of the privileged classes. The regimes also eliminated or weakened formal democratic institutions and political parties. Thus, the three powerholders rendered elections and democratic procedures irrelevant. Once secure after the power struggle, these states were free to pursue policies likely to undermine the power and at times the privilege of at least segments of the upper classes and groups that had previously been part of the polity. As a result, the rulers were not accountable to any internal social or political forces. Under these conditions, the regimes in Iran and Nicaragua built dynasties that lasted for several decades. Although Marcos could not construct a dynasty in the Philippines, he managed to stay in power long after his two presidential terms had expired.

Given their narrowed social base, these regimes increasingly relied on the coercive apparatus and external support. To retain power, these rulers expanded the size and resources of the armed forces, which had little or no involvement in external conflicts. The regimes also relied on support from the United States in economic, political, and military matters. Specifically, the armed forces in all three countries obtained military training, arms, and equipment from the United States.

In the short run, external support and repressive measures compensated for limited social bases of support for these regimes. But in the long run, the exclusion of broad segments of the population from the polity rendered these regimes vulnerable to challenge. As a result, when large-scale social conflicts broke out in the final days of these regimes, each of them could count on support only from segments, at times very small, of the population. The following analysis will focus mostly on internal developments, specifically the rise of exclusive rule, which in part generated the conflicts in the three countries.

The Pahlavi state and exclusive rule in Iran

Although the Shah faced challenges twice during the early period of his rule, both times he succeeded in weakening or eliminating his opponents and establishing an exclusive rule. By the early 1960s, power became highly centralized in the hands of the Shah who rendered the formal political institutions irrelevant. With a powerful army, a secret police, and support from the United States, he ruled Iran with an iron fist. Despite rapid economic development and the rise of new challengers, the monarch kept power centralized and the state remained under his exclusive rule. Eventually, however, these state structures rendered his regime vulnerable to challenge and overthrow.

The rule of Mohammad Reza Pahlavi, the last king of the Pahlavi dynasty, opened with the expansion of the polity and the formation of some democratic institutions in Iran. Initially, political parties were able to organize and mobilize their supporters to participate more widely in the political sphere and press for social change. But soon conflicts broke out and enabled the Shah to eliminate some of his opponents. The conflicts emerged within the state in the early 1950s between liberal-nationalists, led by Prime Minister Dr. Mosaddegh, and by the monarchists, under the leadership of the Shah himself. The two camps clashed over issues such as control of the state apparatus and the army; the extent of power exercised by the royal family and the monarch himself; nationalization of oil, economic inequality, and land reform; and civil liberties, democratic rights, and election laws.

Backers of the monarch included the landed upper class, most of the politically active clergy, a significant number of old guard politicians, and the upper echelon of the army. The opposition camp consisted of the vast majority of the urban population, the emerging middle class, students, and nascent industrial workers, most of whom were organized by the Tudeh Party, the official Communist Party. Perhaps the most significant opposition sector was composed of merchants, shopkeepers, and artisans, known collectively as bazaaris. With the exception of the communists, much of the opposition, including bazaaris, steadfastly supported Prime

Minister Mosaddegh, even after the highest religious leaders had defected from him and his National Front Party. Major segments of the population repeatedly engaged in collective action on Mosaddegh's behalf during the early 1950s (Parsa 1989).

A showdown in 1953 resulted in the elimination of the liberal-nationalists. On August 16, after a failed military *coup d'état* against Mosaddegh, the Shah was forced to flee the country. In his absence, another military *coup*, this time engineered by the American CIA, arrested the prime minister. By employing harsh repressive measures, the *coup* leaders were able to secure the country for the monarch's return a few days later.

While the *coup* succeeded in removing Mosaddegh, it could not eliminate his supporters. These supporters attempted to defend Mosaddegh and resist the *coup*, but eventually failed. In particular, bazaaris, whose loyalty to the ousted prime minister was unswerving, protested against Mosaddegh's arrest by closing their shops (*New York Times*, August 21 and 22, 1953). They took this action even in the face of public support for the Shah by the highest clerical leaders, headed by the most preeminent Marja'a Taghlid, Ayatollah Boroujerdi (*Ettelaat*, August 25 and September 1, 1953; Nategh 1982). Despite government assurances that they would not be jailed, bazaaris refused to reopen their shops. They were soon obliged to do so under continued government duress (*New York Times*, August 25, 1953). Bazaaris' support for Mosaddegh and the National Front eventually resulted in their expulsion from the polity and their exclusion from state resources and policies.

Yet the Shah did not have total control over a population that had been politically mobilized for years. Thus, he imposed martial law in Tehran for four years and ruled the country by intense repression. These measures enhanced the Shah's powerful position over the liberal-nationalists and effectively eliminated the Communist Party from the political scene. In 1957, he established the SAVAK, the secret police, to ensure the repression of the opposition.

The Shah's regime survived these struggles, in large part because of the CIA involvement and assistance from the United States. Following the *coup d'état* President Eisenhower sent a message of congratulation to the Shah, and United States officials, who had refused to provide aid to Mosaddegh, announced that America would favor extending aid to Iran, if it were requested. Ten days after Iran did just that, the United States government responded: the existing aid was raised to $23.4 million and augmented by an additional $45 million in emergency funds. Throughout the following years, Iran continued to receive a massive amount of foreign aid from the United States (Gasiorowski 1991:90–95).

Following the removal of liberal-nationalists and the exclusion of ba-zaaris, the government attempted to expand social support through a development strategy to industrialize the country. But government efforts toward development sowed the seeds of eventual economic decline and financial crisis, which set the stage for conflicts. As domestic and interna-tional credit expanded rapidly, so did the state's expenditure on the second Seven-Year Development Plan (1955–1962). These policies, coupled with poor harvests, boosted the cost-of-living index by 35 per-cent between 1957 and 1960 (Abrahamian 1982:421–422). The state also eased monetary and fiscal controls, freely issued import permits, and imported foreign goods on an enormous scale. By 1959, Iran's imports had jumped more than six-fold from their 1954 level (Katouzian 1981:206). The overly ambitious Seven-Year Plan, combined with in-creasing military expenditures, forced the state to resort to deficit financ-ing and borrowing from abroad. The rapid growth of imports, along with the necessity of repaying foreign loans, created a trade imbalance and reduced foreign exchange to zero.

On the recommendation of the International Monetary Fund, the state implemented a stabilization program that forbade the import of luxury items, raised import tariffs on nonessential goods, and restricted both bank credit and the sale of foreign exchange. These policies had negative effects on the private sector, resulting in a number of bankruptcies and bank failures. Tight credit controls raised the unofficial interest rate within the business sector to 30 percent. Urban land values dropped drastically by 500 percent (Katouzian 1981:229). At the same time, the stringent economic measures stabilized the economy to the point of complete stagnation for nearly three years and all these conditions fa-vored the emergence of conflict.

Meanwhile, the Iranian government was also under pressure to reform and thereby avoid the trajectory of processes that changed regimes in Iraq in 1958 and Cuba in 1959. The United States encouraged the Shah to bring about some measure of ameliorative social change. The Iranian Majles, or parliament, even heard an address by President Eisenhower in December 1959, in which he declared, "military strength alone will not bring about peace with justice. The spiritual and economic health of the free world must be likewise strengthened" (Alexander and Nanes 1980:247).

In response to internal economic conditions and external political pressures, the Shah announced a program of political liberalization that set the stage for conflicts. In early 1960, he stated that he would permit opposition groups to participate in upcoming elections. He planned to control the Majles and undermine the position of the landed upper class by introducing two new parties with connections to the royal court. The August elections were obviously rigged, with the state interfering everywhere to insure the victory of its favored candidates. Public outcry overwhelmingly repudiated the results and obliged the Shah to nullify the outcome, while the prime minister was forced to resign.

At the same time, the Shah was increasingly pressured by the new Kennedy administration in the United States to install a reformist government. According to former United States ambassador Armin Meyer,

the Kennedy administration was very concerned about Iran and immediately set up a task force . . . The result of that task force was to instruct our ambassador that we would provide $35 million in aid in return for which we would expect from the Iranians various steps which we considered necessary for progress, including even suggestions as to the prime ministerial candidate we considered best qualified to administer the proposed reforms. (quoted in Bill 1988:143)

In response to US pressure and growing internal protests, notably a teachers' strike which garnered a great deal of support from other social groups, the Shah appointed Ali Amini, a reformer, as prime minister. Amini quickly initiated a series of reforms. The government dissolved the newly elected Majles, exiled the head of the secret police, granted freedom of the press, and allowed the National Front to resume public activities.

Most importantly, the Shah appointed a radical advocate of land reform, Hassan Arsanjani, as Minister of Agriculture to carry out a land reform. The Shah's decision to accept land reform was extraordinarily complex, both economically and politically. Three major groups were likely to oppose both the principle and practice of land reform. First was the royal family itself, the country's largest landowner, which would be significantly affected by any reforms that might reduce its holdings and resources (Lambton 1969:49–50; Alexander and Nanes 1980:248–259). Another group sure to resist land reform was the landed upper class, which had regained its politically dominant position following Mosaddegh's removal. Of the representatives to the Majles in 1959, 61 percent were drawn from the landed upper class; two years later, 58 percent still came from this landed class (Shaji'i 1965:173). The third group certain to be alienated by any land reform program was the politically powerful members of the clergy, who also controlled extensive land holdings.

At the same time, the Shah stood to reap distinct benefits from implementing agrarian reform. First, he would be able to cast himself as a reformer heedful of his people's welfare. Second, the land reform would create a new base of support for him among the peasantry. Third, land reform would be favorably received by the Kennedy administration, which was pushing Third World land reform (Hooglund 1982:50). Fourth, land reform would boost production by dismantling precapitalist agrarian relations and enlarging monetary relations (Najmabadi 1987:9–10). Finally, the Shah wanted to present any land reform program in a way that would make sure he received credit for it (Bill 1988:145).

In light of these considerations, and in the midst of an economic decline and rising social conflicts, the Shah finally moved toward reform. In May 1961, he ordered the government to introduce a comprehensive package of reforms, including land reform. He dissolved the landlord-dominated Majles to facilitate the process. Soon, he presented a reform package, labeled the White Revolution, which also later became known as the "Revolution of the Shah and the People." Initially, the reforms were contained under six headings:

(1) land reform,
(2) nationalization of pastures and forests,
(3) public sale of state-owned factories to finance land reform,
(4) profit-sharing in industry,
(5) enfranchisement of women, and
(6) establishment of a literacy corps.

The reforms had several major consequences. First, they reduced the economic power of the landed upper class in rural areas. This, in turn, eliminated its control over the peasantry and its ability to use peasants for political gains. Second, the reforms dissolved the alliance between the landed upper class and the monarchy. They also expanded the role of the state in the rural economy and in class relations. More importantly, the reforms changed state–clergy relations. Most clergy had opposed the reforms since they would considerably reduce the holdings of both mosques and some individual clerics. The clergy also particularly objected to measures that permitted women's suffrage as well as some other issues (Bakhash 1984:24).

Clerical opposition and economic decline, combined with the Shiite mourning month of Muharram, resulted in the politicization of religious ceremonies in May and June 1963. During the Ashura processions, held on June 3, participants shouted anti-Shah slogans as the marchers reached the Marble Palace (Chehabi 1990:178), although organizers tried to block such slogans. On June 5, the day after the culmination of the mourning ceremonies, Ayatollah Khomeini was arrested along with a number of other clerics throughout the country. Within a few hours of Khomeini's arrest, popular protests erupted in Tehran, Qom, Mashhad, Isfahan, Shiraz, Tabriz, and Kashan. This uprising lasted for three days, from June 5 through June 7, and was met by decisive repression.

In the end, the uprising failed to dislodge the regime; in fact, decisive repression solidified the power of the government and the Shah. But the price was the breakup of the loose alliance that had existed between the monarch and the clergy since the Shah first came to power during World War II. Similarly, with the reforms, the landed upper class also lost its political power and influence. Thus, the end result was the narrowing of the social basis of support for the monarchy.

Soon the Shah ruled exclusively. As the oil revenues increased and the state became the determinant of the shape of the social structure, power and privilege, the Shah controlled all major power centers in the country, including the cabinet, parliament and political parties, the judiciary, the state bureaucracy, and the army. He personally made every important political and economic decision, with no accountability to any person, group, or institution. To carry out his development projects the Shah increasingly relied simply on his own bureaucracy.

The shifting power of major social groups and classes can be seen in a comparison of the occupational backgrounds of Majles deputies in 1943–1961 and 1975–1979. Whereas landowners constituted 40.4 percent of the deputies in the earlier period, their representation had declined to 9.8 percent by the latter period. The proportion of clergy in the Majles also slipped from 2.8 percent to 0.3 percent. Bureaucrats and professionals gained, constituting the two largest blocs in the Majles, representing 40.8 and 21.3 percent, respectively. The Shah insured that classes with economic resources would not become very powerful. Modern entrepreneurs, who were elected to 10.2 percent of the seats in the twenty-fourth Majles (1975–1979), still lagged far behind bureaucrats and professionals (Ashraf and Banuazizi 1992:678). It is important to note that the gain by capitalists in the last election of the monarchy involved no corresponding increase in substantive powers and was not welcomed by the Shah, who warned: "The affluent candidates who have managed to get elected to the Majles and the Senate are by no means allowed to misuse their political office in order to protect the interests of capitalists and plunder the people" (quoted in ibid.:680).

The extreme centralization of power and formation of an exclusive polity rendered formal political institutions and elections irrelevant for the population. As a result, on the eve of the eruption of popular insurgency, voter turnout was extremely low. For example, in the 1977 election for the Majles, the capital city of Tehran had approximately four million inhabitants, of whom roughly half were eligible to vote. Only 61,000 people registered to vote, and of these only 18,275 actually cast ballots (*Kayhan*, September 24 and 25, 1977).

With the establishment of exclusive rule, the Shah relied increasingly on the coercive apparatus to maintain power. To carry out his plans and control the population, the Shah forged a powerful army and the notorious secret police known as the SAVAK. The size of the armed forces multiplied from 185,000 in 1941 (Afshar 1985:177) to 454,000 by the monarch's ouster (Amuzegar 1991:161). The state's annual military expenditures absorbed an average of approximately one-third of the total national budget in the 1970s (Abrahamian 1982:435; Boroujerdi 1996:28). The SAVAK's full-time personnel grew from roughly 2,000 in the early 1960s to between 7,000 and 10,000 by the end of the monarchy. In addition, the secret police employed a large number of part-time informers (Gasiorowski 1991:152–153). Together, these forces provided stability for the regime. This shift toward governmental centralization, combined with increased oil revenues and the formation of a well-trained and -equipped modern army, made the polity a highly exclusive institution.

In addition, the Shah continued to receive a great deal of support from the United States. Between 1953 and the early 1970s, Iran obtained massive amounts of military and economic assistance from the United States. Iran became the largest single purchaser of American arms, with military hardware purchases increasing from $524 million in 1972 to $3.91 billion in 1974. Because Iranian military personnel lacked the training and expertise to operate such sophisticated equipment, thousands of Americans were hired to operate the weapons and instruct Iranian soldiers in their use.

With increased oil revenues, there also came an expansion of economic ties between Iran and the United States. In November 1974, the two countries established the United States–Iran Joint Commission, headed by US Secretary of State Henry Kissinger and Iranian Minister of Economic Affairs and Finance Houshang Ansari. Its purpose was to broaden and intensify economic cooperation and consultation on economic policies. The following March, the two countries agreed to cooperate on various projects that were budgeted to cost $12 billion.

In sum, by the time the revolutionary conflicts erupted, the Shah had constructed a state that excluded the vast majority of the population from the polity. As a result, the social basis of support for the state had narrowed to consist of the army, the SAVAK, the higher echelon of the bureaucracy, and a small group of wealthy capitalists who had emerged in the modern sectors of the economy. The Shah also had to rely heavily on the external support of the United States. But, ultimately, these conditions rendered the regime vulnerable to challenge and attack in the final round of the conflicts.

The Somozas' exclusive rule in Nicaragua

Like the Shah of Iran, the Somozas of Nicaragua also centralized power and constructed a state and a polity that excluded broad segments of the population. In fact, the Somoza rule has been labeled "sultanic" (Paige 1989:107; Shugart 1989:259). As "sultanic" rulers, the Somozas exercised governmental authority as though it was their personal prerogative or private property. Under this system, they made use of both the state and the subjects to enrich the chief and his associates. The Somozas achieved a remarkable continuity in Nicaragua through a combination of external support and use of repressive measures. During a reign lasting forty-two years, the Somozas allowed only five nonfamily members to assume power for a total of scarcely three-and-a-half years (Weber 1981:18). Obviously, the Somozas were very successful in constructing a dynasty and an exclusive polity.

The Somozas rose to power in the context of intense conflicts between the two Nicaraguan political factions, the Liberals and the Conservatives. Although in 1927 both factions accepted terms to end the conflict, General Augusto César Sandino rejected the US-negotiated peace and vowed to fight until the last American soldier left Nicaragua. After four years of warfare against Sandino's guerrilla army, the USA did decide to quit the country. Sandino signed a peace agreement with the United States on February 2, 1933, one month after the last US marine left the country, and his army of some 2,600 fighters laid down their arms. Soon, however, Sandino was assassinated by order of Anastasio Somoza Garcia, head of the National Guard (Paige 1997:174). By killing Sandino, Somoza Garcia also succeeded in demobilizing his followers and seizing their farms and assets. As the head of the National Guard, Somoza was officially above politics, but by 1936 it became clear that he had his sights on the presidency. Civil war broke out on May 31, 1936, and eight days later Somoza controlled Nicaragua. He and his two sons then ruled Nicaragua, with only brief interruptions, until 1979.

With limited social support, the Somozas, throughout their rule, remained highly dependent on American support and always took care to cultivate a favorable relationship with the United States, which played a more direct role in Nicaraguan history than in Iran. The Somozas gained and maintained their political power and exclusive rule almost entirely because of their tight association with and dependence on the United States, which also fostered such a policy. In fact, it was during the American military occupation that Somoza Garcia became the commander of the National Guard. President Franklin D. Roosevelt summarized this well when he stated: "Somoza may be a son of a bitch, but he is our son of a bitch" (Black 1981:174; Lernoux 1980:81).

Over the years, the Somozas became very dependent on American support. With the onset of the Cold War after World War II, the Nicaraguan government received substantial economic and military aid from the United States. In the 1960s, the United States contributed millions of dollars to Nicaragua through the Alliance for Progress (LaFeber 1984:162–163). Militarily, more officers from Nicaragua were trained at the School of the Americas in the Panama Canal Zone in the 1950s and 1960s than came from any other Latin American nation (ibid.:164). Somoza Garcia's son, Somoza Debayle, claimed that over the years, Nicaragua sent more than 14,000 men to the United States for military training. In 1972, the United States sent $32 million for the reconstruction of Managua after an earthquake. Furthermore, as the Nicaraguan National Guard proved incapable of keeping order in the aftermath of the quake, the United States sent 600 US military personnel from the Canal Zone to help the government maintain control (ibid.:227). US diplomats stationed in Nicaragua were widely known to be close to the Somozas. US ambassador Turner Shelton, a Nixon appointee who served from 1970 to 1975, visited Somoza Debayle almost daily (Kinzer 1979:13). The US embassy was adjacent to the president's residence, and the ambassador was considered the second, or even the most powerful individual in Nicaragua (LaFeber 1984:160).

In return, Nicaragua unfailingly adhered to North American international politics and rendered assistance to the United States (Christian 1985:35; Close 1988:27–28). According to one US foreign policy expert, "No regime in the world cooperated more fully with the United States than did the Somozas between 1930 and the late seventies" (LaFeber 1984:11). Somoza Debayle himself boasted that, because of the close association with the United States, "Nicaragua was often referred to as the little USA of Central America" (Somoza 1980:262). Somoza Debayle cultivated good relations with the American Congress, executive, military, and the business community through provision of gifts, hunting and vacation trips to Nicaragua, and joint ventures (Booth 1998:144).

In addition to relying on the support of the United States to stay in power, the Somozas also used the National Guard to maintain control. The National Guard, a near-personal army of the Somozas, initially had been established, financed, and trained by the United States (Paige 1985:94; Sholk 1984:254; Wickham-Crowley 1991:221). A succession of three Somoza rulers expanded the size of the Guard by more than 250 percent, from roughly 2,900 in 1937, when Anastasio Somoza Garcia became president (Millett 1977:191) to approximately 8,000 by 1978. In the wake of the September 1978 insurrection, the then president, Anastasio Somoza Debayle announced his intention to bolster the National Guard's strength even further by expanding its forces to 15,000 and increasing defense expenditures from 10 to 20 percent of the national budget (*La Prensa*, October 7, 1978). According to one account, by the end of Somoza rule, this expansion of National Guard strength had been reached (Black 1981:178).

To ensure absolute control, the Somoza family administered the National Guard through a combination of paternalism, corruption, and division (Millett 1977:192, 199; Weber 1981:31). The Guard was given a large number of tasks through which it affected and controlled Nicaraguan society. It operated Nicaragua's telephone, telegraph, and postal services, radio, customs, the railway, the national health care, and the tax collection systems (Booth 1998:139). The members of the National Guard were kept isolated from the rest of the population to ensure that the ruling family could control and deploy them against all others. Guard personnel were provided with separate medical care, schooling, and preferred access to housing, food, and clothing. Officers were not subject to the same taxes and duties as ordinary citizens, nor could they be tried in civil courts when accused of crimes against civilians (Millett 1977:256–257). Officers close to Somoza Debayle embarked on a variety of business pursuits, which even penetrated the educational institutions. These businesses received handsome government subsidies and licenses denied to others (*La Prensa*, February 24, 1978).

Total, direct command of the National Guard enabled the Somozas to check all opposition through intimidation and repression. The National Guard was effectively used to repress the opposition during the popular protests in 1944. Following Somoza Garcia's assassination in 1956, segments of the Conservative Party and other opposition groups initiated a number of unsuccessful armed attempts to overthrow the government, including one attempt led by Pedro Joaquin Chamorro. Anastasio Somoza Debayle, the commander of the Guard, stated that in the five years following the death of Somoza Garcia, the Guard repulsed twenty-six revolts (Close 1988:26). In the 1960s, the Guard was used to demobilize the reformist opposition. In 1967, the opposition made one more attempt to check the arbitrary nature of the Nicaraguan rulers. When the Conservative Party reasserted its oppositionist stance and organized a march of 40,000 people to protest against the upcoming election of Anastasio, the National Guard opened fire on the protesters, killing an estimated 600 persons, and arrested the organizers and Conservative Party leaders, including Chamorro and Agüero Rocha.[1]

The Somozas used their political power to weaken their opponents, enrich themselves, and strengthen their own political power (*La Prensa*, November 11, 1977; February 19, 1977). For example, in the 1930s, Somoza Garcia seized farms and gold claims belonging to followers of his rival, Sandino. He also collected a tribute of one-and-a-half cents per pound on exported cattle and received contributions from numerous industries, including $400,000 in one year from US mineral companies in exchange for tax exemptions. In addition, during World War II, Somoza Garcia acquired the cattle farms and coffee plantations owned by German *émigrés* (Black 1981:34; Booth 1982:67; Wheelock 1978:165–166). On occasion, prominent families were forced to relinquish land by the threat of imprisonment (Paige 1989:108). Although Somoza Garcia "paid" for all the land he acquired, such compensation usually amounted to only one-half its real value (Millett 1977:197). Even as late as 1978, Somoza obliged all government employees to contribute 5 percent of their salaries to his ruling Liberal Party (*La Prensa*, February 19, 1978).

As a result of exclusive rule, the Nicaraguan upper class could not function as a "ruling class" (Midlarsky and Roberts 1985:183; Sequeira 1984:99). Elite political organizations and the opposition were weakened and fractured by a combination of increased government resources, the repressive power of the National Guard, and US support for the Somozas. These resources rendered the moderate opposition and the upper class increasingly dependent on the government, and made the Somozas attractive partners for business ventures. Thus opposition factions were forced to compromise with the Somozas during most of the decades of their rule. In the 1930s, for example, some wealthy businessmen supported Somoza Garcia, believing that he might control labor unrest. But by 1944, many of these businessmen had come to oppose him and played important roles in the anti-government mobilization and protests over the next four years. Escalating government repression soon forced this elite opposition to change tactics and seek compromise. Conservative Party leaders Carlos Cuadra Pasos (1948) and General Emiliano Chamorro (1950) agreed to cooperate with the Somoza regime in exchange for one-third of the government's congressional seats and judicial appointments. This "pact of generals" became the basis for subsequent cooperation between the Conservatives and Somoza's Liberal Party. In reaction to this collaboration, many younger Conservative

---

[1] This estimate of casualties is from Close (1988:27). Cruz (1989:52) notes that dozens of people were killed.

Party members broke away and formed alternative political organizations (Booth 1982:99). Elite opposition was fragmented once again in 1971, when Conservative Party leader Fernando Agüero Rocha agreed to join a three-person junta to rule the country until a new constitution could be written that would allow Somoza Debayle to be reelected in 1974. The Conservative Party split once again over whether to accept this pact, which would give 40 percent of all public offices to the Conservatives (Booth 1982:90, 100; Diederich 1981:89).

The rule of Anastasio Somoza Debayle, the last Somoza, was particularly tumultuous. As mentioned above, his election in 1967 became very violent and bloody. The opposition began their campaign with rallies and slogans of "Basta Ya!" (enough already) and "Happy New Year Without Somoza" (*La Prensa*, January 3 and 4, 1967). While opposition rallies attracted large number of crowds throughout the country, the Somozas had to offer cash and alcohol to encourage people to participate in their rallies (*La Prensa*, January 1 and 12, 1967). At times the Somozas even threatened public employees that they should attend pro-Somoza rallies or risk losing their jobs (*La Prensa*, January 8, 1967). Although Article 25 of the Nicaraguan Constitution stated that the popular vote was direct and secret, Luis Somoza, the then president and the older brother of Anastasio, announced on the radio that he planned to vote publicly and encouraged all Liberals to do the same. He even stated that anyone who voted secretly would be considered an enemy of the government (*La Prensa*, January 7, 1967). On January 22, as leaders of the opposition pleaded for a fair and nonviolent election, the National Guard attacked an opposition march and killed hundreds of participants. Pedro Chamorro was arrested once again – the seventh time in thirteen years. He was even tortured while in jail (*La Prensa*, February 4, 1967). Although there were numerous reports of electoral fraud (*La Prensa*, February 6, 1967), Anastasio Somoza Debayle won the elections.

Exclusive rule and centralization of power expanded even more following the December 1972 earthquake that rocked Managua, killing more than 10,000 people and leveling 600 square blocks in the heart of the capital. According to one analyst, Somoza Debayle at this point represented the purest form of sultanic rule (Booth 1982:133). Somoza Debayle, who already occupied the two most powerful positions in the country, president and Chief Director of the National Guard, seized this opportunity to enhance his personal power and influence. Immediately following the earthquake, he imposed martial law, which would last eighteen months. During this period when civilian government was suspended, much of the country's significant financial and legislative transactions were conducted by decrees from the National Emergency Committee, headed by the president. Among the extraordinary fiscal powers assumed by this committee were the ability to levy taxes, to suspend prior laws granting tax exemptions, to contract foreign loans, and to exercise exclusive control over the budgetary process and direction of the public treasury. A permanent military tribunal was established, which heard more than 600 criminal cases in the next two-and-a-half months alone (*La Prensa*, March 2 and 3, 1973; April 4, 1973; June 9, 1973; November 20, 1973). In 1974, Somoza passed another law requiring every businessman appointed to the board of any state-run enterprise to belong to the political party that received the most votes in the last election (*La Prensa*, December 15, 1974). These policies insured a somocista monopoly at all levels of the state.

Thus, by the 1970s, the Somoza regime had evolved into a highly centralized entity that excluded the vast majority of the population from the polity. Somoza Debayle, the last Somoza to rule Nicaragua, not only ensconced himself in the two most powerful positions in the country, as president and Chief Director of the National Guard, he also received government salaries for being the country's only Division General as well as a retired senator. His combined income from these four salaries amounted to 28,879 córdobas, which was higher than any other leader in Central America (*La Prensa*, June 5, 1978). Somoza Debayle also placed relatives in important government positions (*La Prensa*, February 19, 1978), including his wife, Hope Portocarrero de Somoza, who headed JNAPS, the body that administered the country's hospitals. Clearly, Somoza and his associates controlled the state and were the providers of power and privilege in Nicaragua.

Growing political centralization and rising repression, in combination with government corruption in handling earthquake relief funds, generated much popular discontent. In late 1973 a public opinion survey of 982 people conducted by the Institute for Human Advancement in the cities of Managua, León, Jinotepe, and Matagalpa indicated prevailing popular discontentment with existing conditions. More than 90 percent of the respondents were dissatisfied with the economic situation and more than 78 percent expressed dissatisfaction with political conditions. Seventy percent condemned the penal code's restrictions on the liberty of the press. Seventy-eight percent believed that the situation in the country should change, while 57.8 percent favored a total change in both the system and its structures (*La Prensa*, February 13 and 15, 1974).

In this context, moderate/reformist opposition and political organizations once again mobilized against the Somoza regime. Their mobilization intensified particularly during the presidential election of 1974, in which Somoza Debayle was the leading candidate. As early as January of that year a group known as National Mobilization, composed of prominent representatives from diverse segments of the population, signed a statement condemning the Somoza regime for political repression and the lack of freedom and justice. The statement ended with the cry: "We want a new government! We seek fundamental change! We struggle for a more just system!" (*La Prensa*, January 2, 1974). Soon a relatively broad coalition began to emerge to confront the Somoza regime more effectively. The coalition consisted of seven political organizations – the Independent Liberal Party, the Nicaraguan Social Christian Party, the Nicaraguan Socialist Party, National Conservative Action, the Liberal Constitutional Movement, National Mobilization, and the Movement for National Salvation – plus the two largest labor organizations, the General Confederation of Workers (CGT-I) and Workers' Federation of Nicaragua (CTN).

In March, this group issued a statement, which was delivered to the Secretary of the Organization of American States (OAS). The statement declared that "There is no liberty of political or labor organization, no freedom of expression, no free elections . . . There exists an intolerable centralization of economic activities, with monopolies and embezzlement" (*La Prensa*, April 5, 1974). In June, this coalition had considerable impact when it called for a boycott of the presidential election slated for September. Three representatives from each member organization, twenty-seven persons in all, signed a document asserting, "there is no one to vote for." Their statement denounced the absence of freedom of expression, information, religion, and union organizations. They condemned both the subversion of the army into a repressive force in the service of particular interests, and the conversion of electoral rights into personal rule. The signatories criticized rising inflation in items of basic necessity, from which unscrupulous middlemen benefited, and singled out corruption in the distribution of earthquake relief, which had enriched a few at the expense of others. Finally, they concluded by affirming that they were "compelled to abstain from voting because there is no one to vote for and that such a vote does not fulfill its democratic function but is rather a joke on the part of those who believe themselves to be the owners of Nicaragua and its destiny; the government that arises from such a comedy cannot be recognized as legitimate by the Nicaraguan people" (*La Prensa*, June 26, 1974). Less than half the eligible voters actually voted in the September elections in which Somoza Debayle was declared the winner. Though martial law was lifted after the inauguration, government harassment of opposition activities continued.

Two factors led to the failure of the challengers of the early 1970s. First, the Nicaraguan capitalists, organized in various chambers and associations, never joined the coalition against Somoza. The coalition that signed the statement was predominately composed of professionals and labor leaders. Second, government repression put an end to political mobilization and protests. In addition to press censorship, the government passed the Libel Law to prevent criticism of the state, initiated punitive actions against the Church, and jailed a number of activists and opposition organizers. The government also took a few mild repressive measures against the twenty-seven signatories of the coalition statement and convicted them of violating a law requiring all citizens to vote. All were stripped of their citizenship rights for six months, meaning they could not participate in politics, vote, make political declarations, meet to sign petitions or grievances, or attend other public functions (*La Prensa*, August 13 and 15, 1974).

Government repression escalated at the end of 1974, following a Sandinista attack on a reception for US ambassador Shelton at the mansion of the Minister of Agriculture, José Maria "Chema" Castillo Quant, who had formerly been linked with Somoza Debayle's office of security. Although the US ambassador had just departed, a number of influential people, including government ministers, the Chilean ambassador, and close friends of the Somoza family had remained and were held hostage, forcing Somoza Debayle to accede to the invading guerrilla force's demands. As a result, the FSLN netted $2 million in ransom, a number of Sandinista prisoners including Daniel Ortega Saavedra were released from prison, and guerrilla communiqués during the invasion were disseminated by the country's newspapers, two television channels, and six radio stations. But the stunning attack brought down swift, relentless government repression. Immediately after the raid, Somoza Debayle declared a state of siege and martial law throughout Nicaragua that lasted thirty-three months. The National Guard launched a massive hunt for guerrillas in the mountains, arrested peasants, and interned them in concentration camps.[2] Hundreds of guerrilla supporters and others were exterminated. The far-reaching violence of these repressive measures, combined with total media censorship, increased government arbitrariness in dealing with not just the opposition, but the general populace.

In sum, the Somozas built a dynasty and a state that excluded the vast majority of the Nicaraguan population from the polity. Their exclusive control of the National Guard, along with external support, produced a remarkable political continuity. Although in the short run the Somozas succeeded in checking the opposition, in the long run the effect of

---

[2] According to a report of the Interamerican Commission of Human Rights, 338 peasants were arrested by the National Guard from 1975 to 1977. Only 17 were set free after being imprisoned for eighteen months without a trial (*La Prensa*, November 25, 1978).

exclusive rule was to reduce social support for the rulers and render them vulnerable to attack and challenge.

Martial law and centralization of power in the Philippines

Unlike Iran and Nicaragua, the Philippines possessed formal, democratic institutions, which affected the nature and outcome of social and political conflicts. These democratic institutions were formed while the country was a colony of the United States (Lande 1965:28; 1987:8–9). When the Philippines became independent in 1946, a competitive, two-party political system emerged that lasted until 1972, although no substantive differences existed between the Liberal Party and the Nacionalista Party (Rush 1986a:3). But an economic decline and elite divisions, combined with rising nationalism, generated social conflicts in the early 1970s and resulted in the elimination of democratic institutions. Although the movements were highly fragmented, Marcos responded harshly by restricting civil liberties and eventually declaring martial law in September 1972. During martial law, he centralized power in his own hands and those of a small group of cronies, and established exclusive rule. Supported by both an expanded military and the United States, Marcos was able to exclude the vast majority of the population from the polity.

Although formally democratic, the Philippines' political institutions soon came under the influence of wealthy segments of the population. Both parties selected persons of considerable wealth as their leaders (Lande 1965:40). Even though the Philippine Congress was not a parliament of landlords, the legislature became increasingly dominated by the wealthy (Stauffer 1975:26; Wurfel 1988:83). Only the wealthy could afford to run for office because of the custom of vote buying. Filipinos complained that elections were dominated by "guns, goons, and gold." A vote could normally be had for between 5 and 10 pesos (Landé 1964:115–117). An estimated quarter of the electorate sold its vote, making Philippine election campaigns among the most expensive in the world (Thompson 1995:22–23). Similarly, a report by the CIA indicates that as many as one-third of all votes cast in an average election were bought (Schirmer and Shalom 1987:131). By the 1960s, this practice virtually insured that wealth would predominate in congressional elections.[3]

Eventually, the political institutions began to exhibit strains as a result of economic decline, elite factionalism, and rising nationalism in the late

---

[3] In the 1969 election, candidates were required to report their incomes. Those elected to the House reported an average annual income of 70,000 pesos. Despite underreporting, this figure placed them in the wealthiest 0.5 percent of the population (Wurfel 1988:82).

1960s. The government's economic policies were at least partly responsible for the decline. Its high spending levels in the 1969 election increased the country's debt. Marcos and the Nacionalista Party spent approximately $200 million on that election, with roughly half of it coming from government sources (Timberman 1991:63). As a result, at the end of 1969, the country's first debt crisis boiled over. The Central Bank was obliged to assume the Philippine National Bank's interest burden on foreign credit lines (Baldwin 1975:74). To meet medium- and long-term debt service payments alone, the Philippines paid out nearly one-third of its merchandise export earnings and almost one-quarter of its total foreign exchange receipts (International Labour Office 1974:280).

To stabilize the financial situation, Marcos sought assistance from the International Monetary Fund (IMF) and asked foreign banks to extend their repayment terms. The IMF granted a stabilization loan of some $37 million, demanding in return devaluation of the peso and stringent monetary and credit measures (Lichauco 1973:39). The government immediately reduced expenditures, cut back services, laid off employees, and tightened credit and exchange restrictions. The exchange rate dropped from 2 pesos per dollar in 1960 to 5.75 in February 1970, contributing to economic difficulties and unemployment. In response, the stock market began a steady descent, while prices of imported goods, particularly fuel and spare parts, shot up (Noble 1986:80). As consumers' purchasing power dwindled, industrial production slowed (Tiglao 1988:30). Inflation, which had been rising at an average annual rate of 4.5 percent in the 1960s, jumped to 14 percent in 1970, and continued at the rate of 16.9 percent until 1974 (Doronila 1992:155). This rise caused economic hardship for the population. A survey that year by the Asia Research Organization, Inc. revealed that inflation forced families to cut back by as much as 71 percent on food and 59 percent on clothing. Eighty-three percent of the respondents identified unemployment as the country's most pressing problem (*Manila Times*, July 25, 1970).

At the same time, one segment of the Philippine elite became very nationalistic and opposed foreign investment and influence in the country. The roots of this elite nationalism can be traced back to 1962, when President Macapagal obtained a $300 million loan from the IMF in exchange for abolishing government controls and welcoming foreign investment in the Philippines. These policies had an adverse impact on some entrepreneurs who had hitherto been protected from competition. When Marcos took office in 1966 he acknowledged the problem by asserting that nearly 1,500 corporations were in a state of bankruptcy (Lichauco 1973:35). Nevertheless, he supported the 1967 Investment Incentives Bill, which generated intense opposition from pro-nationalist sectors because it invited foreign investment in "pioneer" areas. Marcos' decision to send 2,000 non-combat personnel to Vietnam further spurred both the nationalist and leftist movements, impelling nationalist entrepreneurs and intellectuals to condemn the high profit levels reaped by foreign corporations operating in the Philippines (ibid.:33). In 1971, the nationalist elite introduced seventeen bills in the National Assembly that would have nationalized various industries. They argued that foreign investors had taken over some industries and turned people into "mere workers and laborers, agents, and errand boys for alien capitalists . . . from their former position as proprietors and entrepreneurs' (*Manila Times*, February 14, 1971). One nationalist representative criticized the government for surrendering the country's economy to the United States, the IMF, and the World Bank (*Manila Times*, February 27, 1971).

Elite conflicts found expression in the 1969 elections, when violence intensified alarmingly. Election-related killings reached an all-time high of 243 in battles between local or provincial political warlords (Daroy 1988:9). The two presidential candidates, Senator Sergio Osmeña and President Marcos, were both well-known public figures, each of whom had been charged with massive corruption. The incumbent emerged victorious and thereby became the first president in Philippine history to be reelected, thanks in part to his money and threats of violence (Wurfel 1988:17).

Soon, elite divisions stimulated direct attacks against Marcos himself. In March 1971, Senator Benigno Aquino, Jr., the Liberal Party's secretary-general and campaign manager, accused Marcos of having channeled 26 million pesos earmarked for essential public services to his "favored congressmen" (Canoy 1984:2). Representative John Osmeña accused Marcos of squandering the country's money and resources by gross mismanagement of government affairs (*Manila Times*, September 17, 1971). When the Liberal Party's televised rally at Plaza Miranda was bombed, killing nine persons and injuring seventy-two, factionalism heightened within the elite. Aquino demanded that the president assume responsibility for the bombing and restore civil liberties.

During these conflicts, Marcos antagonized prominent members of his own Nacionalista Party. He failed to pass around state patronage, as incumbent presidents usually did, but instead concentrated it in the hands of his family and friends. Moreover, Marcos threatened to propose his wife, Imelda, as the Nacionalista presidential candidate in 1973. This nettled presidential aspirants Senator Salvador Laurel and Vice President Fernando Lopez. The result was the defection of important members of Marcos' party, including Lopez, Speaker of the House Jose Laurel, Jr., head of the Nacionalista Party and Senate President Gil

Puyat, and senators Salvador Laurel, Eva Estrada Kalaw, and Jose Diokno.

In the meantime, the economy continued its downward spiral, and the public was becoming more critical of the government and of Marcos. A survey in Greater Manila fifteen months after Marcos' reelection found that two-thirds of those polled disapproved of the way he ran the government. Eighty percent rejected a proposal that would rewrite the constitution either to permit Marcos to run for a third term or to allow the First Lady to become a presidential candidate (*Manila Times*, February 21, 1971).

These conditions, together with rising social and economic inequalities, fueled protests by students, their allies (workers and farmers) and segments of the middle class. The Philippines' formal democratic institutions combined with an economic decline led to the mobilization of a number of social groups in the early 1970s, but the struggles failed for a number of reasons. First, the movements of this period were very diverse in terms of organization, issues, and targets of attack. Second and more importantly, the protesters failed to forge a broad coalition of major social classes and groups to bring about change, although the conflicts resulted in the imposition of martial law and dissolution of democratic institutions. Of a total of 259 demonstrations in 1970, for example, only one appeared to have been organized by an overall coalition of students, workers, and civic and religious organizations. Although these protests were unable to effect major social change, the mobilization and collective actions of students and their allies, together with economic decline and popular discontent, did bring about congressional passage of the Constitutional Convention Act. Significantly, the Act denied Congress any role in revising the constitution (Doronila 1992:169).

The conflicts of this period were brought to an end abruptly by a Supreme Court ruling in August 1972, which invalidated titles to land held by US citizens who had purchased privately owned property after the Philippines gained independence in 1946. The judgment required these owners, along with any other Americans who had legally acquired public land since then, to dispose of their property by July 1, 1974. The Supreme Court's decision prompted the US ambassador to call upon Marcos, which, in turn, may have hastened his decision to introduce martial law.

The events immediately preceding the declaration of martial law in 1972 unfolded swiftly and concisely. On September 8, Defense Secretary Enrile warned of impending communist rebellion, despite the fact that at that time fewer than 800 communist guerrillas were actually operating in only four regions of the country. Following Enrile's statement, a rash of bombings occurred. Although the bombings evidently had been designed only to frighten, one person was killed (Canoy 1984:3). Later, a defecting Marcos aide would attribute many of the bombings to military crews (Chapman 1987:95), while another source suggested that a sergeant from the Firearms and Explosives unit of the Philippine Constabulary had set off the explosions (Overholt 1986:1140). On September 20, Marcos conferred with the commanders of his armed forces and discussed the idea of martial law, which all but the vice chief of staff endorsed. Then on the night of September 22, Enrile's car was allegedly ambushed – an attack that later the defense secretary admitted had been staged (Wurfel 1988:20). Marcos declared martial law the following day.

Quickly, the country's political sphere, which had opened up during the 1960s, now contracted with exclusionary policies (Hawes 1987:40). Marcos repressed all opposition and in rapid succession expanded the amount of foreign loans, foreign aid, and new investment from abroad in order to finance martial law (Lande 1986:116; Overholt 1986:1142). Marcos dismissed Congress, a bastion of support for agricultural exporters, and announced a limited program of land reform in rice and corn lands (Hawes 1987:39–40). He also shuttered pro-opposition newspapers, radio stations and television stations, and banned demonstrations. Within a short time, hundreds of the president's "enemies" and suspected opponents were arrested. More than a dozen Constitutional Convention (ConCon) delegates were detained, while others went underground or fled the country (Wurfel 1988:115). By 1977, some 70,000 Filipinos had been imprisoned at one time or another for their political actions and beliefs (ibid.:124).

With martial law fully in effect, Marcos was able to gain control over the main sources of power and wealth in the country for himself, his family, and their associates. Marcos achieved control by centralizing governmental institutions, introducing numerous administrative changes, and establishing new organizations, all under the excuse of greater efficiency (Timberman 1991:82–83). He revised the Philippine constitution nine separate times to ensure control and pursue his policies. His threats, bribes, and intimidation of ConCon delegates enabled him to alter the new constitution in his favor. The executive branch, in particular, achieved a great deal of autonomy *vis-à-vis* the other branches of government. Presidential decrees were issued restricting or even contradicting nationalistic rulings by the Supreme Court. Marcos also strengthened his hand against the landholding elite who dominated provincial politics by disbanding the private armies of regional politicians and confiscating their arms. The First Lady, Imelda, headed twenty-seven government offices, in addition to serving as Minister of Human Settlement and governor of Metro Manila (Canoy 1984:221). By 1981, Imelda

Marcos controlled public and private funds totaling 50 percent of the entire government budget (Overholt 1986:1148).

Marcos also continuously assailed elite privileges and preexisting disparities as a means of justifying his authoritarian rule after imposing martial law. The previous economic and political institutions, he argued, had been largely irrelevant to the basic needs of most Filipinos and merely favored and enhanced the power of those who were already well placed within the system. Successive changes in political leadership, he charged, had brought no improvement to the lives of ordinary people, but had only benefited the economic and political intellectual elite. The poor, he said, look upon periodic elections only as opportunities to gain small favors, or a few pesos, from politicians. Because political change was immaterial to the poor, martial law would not trouble them. The only opposition to it, asserted Marcos, was from the Filipino oligarchy (Marcos 1980:17–18). Representative democracy, he declared, had been dying in the Philippines long before the political crisis of 1972. It simply could not survive in the context of "a rapacious oligarchy and an electorate, enfeebled by poverty, [and] open to corruption" (ibid.:39).

Marcos relied heavily on the armed forces, as did the Shah and Somoza, to maintain his power and carry out his policies. The "defense" budget in current pesos grew nearly tenfold, from 608 million pesos in fiscal year 1972 to 5,381 million pesos in fiscal year 1977. In constant dollars, the budget increased more than threefold, a much more rapid pace than elsewhere in Southeast Asia. Over the same period, military expenditure as a percentage of the total budget nearly doubled to 22.6 percent in 1977. During the 1960s, Philippine force levels, including army, navy, air force, and constabulary, were around 35,000. In 1971 the regular armed forces totaled 58,100, with another 400 comprising the Civilian Home Defense Force (CHDF). By 1982, the regular forces had nearly tripled to 158,300, while the CHDF ballooned exponentially to 65,000. Philippine defense expenditures also skyrocketed from $136 million in 1972 to $910 million in 1982 (Youngblood 1990:44–45). Immediately after the declaration of martial law, all officers were promoted one grade, their salaries and benefits were increased, and a company was set up to help invest their new wealth (Thompson 1995:54–55). During the first three-and-a-half years of martial law, the base pay for officers more than doubled (Wurfel 1988:148).

Furthermore, Marcos undertook the largest reorganization of the armed forces in Philippine history, promoting his relatives and loyalists to top positions. He began to politicize the military during his first term to circumvent congressional scrutiny. To assure the future support of the military leaders he built a faction of loyal young officers headed by his cousin and former chauffeur, Major Fabian Ver (Thompson 1995:54). During Marcos' first term in office several special forces were also established; they were slated to be used against communists, but were also deployed against traditional opponents (ibid.:35–36).

Again like the Shah and Somoza, Marcos maintained a friendly relationship with the United States. Half a century of colonial experience had produced within the Philippines a high level of political dependence on the United States. After formal independence in 1946, the USA remained a major trading partner and market for Philippine goods, most particularly sugar, which was sold duty-free until 1974. At the same time, parity rights endowed American corporations with investment rights comparable to those of Filipinos. Moreover, the Vietnam War conferred key strategic significance upon the Philippines, home of Clark Air Force Base and Subic Naval Base, which were essential to the US conduct of the war between 1965 and 1972 (Sullivan 1987:542).

After the declaration of martial law, the Philippines received substantial financial resources from the United States. In 1973, $85.7 million was received from the US Agency for International Development, up dramatically from $30.5 million in the previous year. Total US Agency for International Development (AID) loans and grants in the four years prior to martial law totaled $56.2 million; in contrast, total loans and grants over the next four years shot up to $240.5 million. Marcos obtained augmented financial support from other United States government sources as well. Concessional loans from the Export/Import Bank, overseas private investment corporations, and the Commodity Credit Corporation rose from $509.3 million in fiscal years 1969–1972 to $1,097.1 million in fiscal years 1973–1975 (Wurfel 1988:191).

At the same time, because the United States depended on its Philippine military, the Philippines could also gain leverage in resisting certain adverse US policies. As a result, President Carter's human rights policies, which succeeded in bringing about local elections, were ineffective in reducing violations of human rights. Between 1978 and 1980, the number of kidnappings and "salvagings" of Filipino citizens reached the staggering figure of over 8,000, and more than 50,000 persons were arrested on charges of subversion (De Dios 1988:78). Even rulings by the Supreme Court demanding accountability from the presidency for such actions were ignored. Despite growing human rights violations, Carter resumed support for Marcos and, in May 1978, even sent Vice-President Mondale to Manila in a gesture of friendship (Hawes 1987:145). After a new bases agreement was signed in 1979, Carter was less inclined to advise Marcos on human rights. The United States' economic support had declined in real terms, with a corresponding reduction in American influence (Wurfel 1988:235). Eventually, in October 1978, the US Congress offered only a token response to human rights violations by voting for a slight reduction of 8 percent in the Carter-sponsored $40 million aid package, which scarcely amounted to a slap on the wrist for Marcos (De Dios 1988:77).

The election of Ronald Reagan strengthened the position of the Marcos family for several years. As governor of California, Reagan had been the personal guest of Mrs. Marcos at the inauguration of the Cultural Center and the Marcos family regarded Reagan as "an old friend from way back" (Canoy 1984:251). Five months after taking office in 1981, Reagan, who had no human rights policy and was determined to promote American friends everywhere, sent Secretary of State Haig to Manila. Haig delivered a letter to Marcos offering to help the Philippines fight terrorism by possibly prosecuting Filipino rebels based in the United States. Immediately thereafter, FBI agents did indeed visit all moderate Filipino opposition leaders in the USA (Poole and Vanzi 1984:61–62). Less than two weeks after Haig's visit, Vice-President Bush represented the United States at the inauguration in Manila of Marcos, who had been reelected for the third time against only token opposition. Bush declared: "We stand with the Philippines. We stand with you, sir. We love your adherence to democratic principles and to the democratic processes, and we will not leave you in isolation" (ibid.:63). As a gesture of good relations, in early 1983, the United States negotiated a new five-year lease of the Philippine military bases with a compensation of $900 million, nearly double the $500 million paid for the previous lease signed four years earlier (Silliman 1984:151).

Secure in his position and the support of the United States, Marcos responded to international criticisms and the Pope's visit to the Philippines by lifting martial law in January 1981. Although Marcos permitted some liberalization, including limited freedom of the press, he retained most of the martial law apparatus including all his emergency powers, which permitted him to declare martial law at any time (*New York Times*, January 17, 1981). The "Transitory Provision" which he had introduced into the constitution gave Marcos dictatorial power (Ambassador Sedfrey Ordonez, interview, May 1999). Even though the opposition boycotted the 1981 presidential election, the government stated that failure to vote would be treated as a serious crime (De Dios 1988:79). Marcos applied intimidation and repression to force the public to participate. Numerous protestors were arrested throughout the country and several people were killed and many injured in protest against the presidential election (Wurfel 1988:252). Although large segments of the registered voters actually boycotted the election, it was declared that 88 percent of the electorate voted and Marcos received 88 percent of the votes. Thus, Marcos installed himself as president of the Philippines once again.

In sum, although the Philippines' polity prior to the declaration of martial law differed from those in Iran and Nicaragua, by the early 1970s it also became centralized and assumed an exclusive character. In the context of an economic decline and rising social conflicts, Marcos succeeded in abolishing formal democratic institutions that had existed in the Philippines for decades. He repressed and eliminated challengers and opponents, and concentrated all power in his own hands. Unlike the Shah and the Somozas, Marcos' rule was not dynastic, yet, for all practical purposes, Marcos retained power long after his first two legitimate terms of office expired. Like Iran and Nicaragua, the Philippine state received the economic, political, and military support of the United States, which enhanced its capacity to exclude the vast majority of the population from the polity and political processes. With centralization of power and the decline of his support base, Marcos, like the Shah and the Somozas, relied increasingly on the military. In the end, these developments also rendered the state and Marcos' rule vulnerable to challenge and attack.

Conclusion

As we have seen, all three states came under exclusive control of the rulers and became increasingly centralized in response to earlier rounds of conflicts, which had strong nationalistic components. During these conflicts, powerholders in all three countries succeeded in weakening or eliminating alternative challengers. Characterized by exclusive rule and highly personalistic features, rulers also rendered political parties and popular participation in politics largely meaningless, as they themselves made all the most important political decisions. As a result, these regimes could rely on only a narrow base of support among the public and consequently remained vulnerable in times of challenge and attack. To maintain power, the states in all three countries relied heavily on external support and the armed forces. Although political dependence on the United States provided substantial financial and military resources to these states, in the end political dependence also undermined them and increased their vulnerabilities. Repression in each case severely restricted the capacity of various groups and classes to engage in collective action, and limited the mobilization options in subsequent rounds of conflict, but in the end repressive measures failed to keep these regimes in power.

To be sure, the three regimes varied in the extent of repression and demobilization of opponents and the existence of autonomous organizations in the civil society, which affected mobilization options in future conflicts. Iran's regime achieved the greatest degree of demobilization and repression of the opposition and their organizations. The Shah, supported by a powerful military, the secret police and the United States, was able to eliminate all his secular opponents and weaken the religious clergy. He fully succeeded in preventing the emergence of autonomous groups and classes. In this sense, he was the ultimate "sultan." Marcos in the Philippines was at the other extreme. Unlike the Shah, he did not represent a dynasty, but he refused to relinquish power long after his two terms had ended. Marcos used coercive powers to reduce the autonomy of the upper class and the opposition. Although successful in the short run, his strategy failed in the end in part because he did not totally dismantle all political organizations and associations. Elite organizations and business associations survived and played some role in the political conflicts of the 1980s. In 1984, Marcos even staged an election for the National Assembly, in which the opposition won fifteen of the twenty-one seats in Metro Manila. Although Marcos had managed to control the Supreme Court during most of the martial law years, once social conflicts erupted, he could no longer completely silence the Court. On a few occasions the Philippine Supreme Court demanded government accountability for the disappearance of labor leaders. Furthermore, because Marcos had to create his own cronies in the military, his control of the armed forces was never complete. He engendered divisions in the armed forces, which he could not contain. Lastly, the Somoza rulers of Nicaragua lay in between these two extremes. Like the Pahlavis in Iran, the Somozas had, for all practical purposes, established a dynasty that exerted complete domination over the state and the National Guard, which operated as their family tool. Unlike the Shah, however, the Somozas allowed the formation and operation of moderate opposition organizations. Also unlike the Shah, they permitted the formation of associations by business and occupational groups. Under ordinary conditions these organizations and associations were rendered largely ineffective. In times of conflict, however, they could play a role in the mobilization process.

Once power was secured, these regimes increased their intervention in the economy and attempted to promote economic development. The next chapter will analyze this topic.

3   State intervention and contradictions

Exclusive rule and greater centralization, combined with increasing resources, enabled the three states to intervene extensively in the economy and promote development. To varying degrees, state intervention turned each government into a key economic actor and the center of capital allocation or accumulation. These governments controlled major banks, enterprises and sources of revenue in their countries. They actively affected capital allocation through their control of the banking system by means of their own revenues, foreign aid, or extensive borrowing. These states also expanded their regulation of the economy, thus affecting many aspects of the market. All three governments also deliberately pursued development strategies that favored private sector capital accumulation. These efforts often paid off as state intervention produced impressive results, most notably growth in the initial stages.

Despite impressive growth rates, the development strategies employed by the three governments laid the foundation for contradictions and conflicts. Although these states achieved a high level of autonomy from the privileged groups and classes, state intervention largely served particular, rather than general, societal interests. In the first place, it enriched state rulers, their associates and allies who accumulated massive wealth often in a short period of time. Furthermore, government development strategies, whether in the form of import-substitution or export-led industrialization, served the interests of modern, capital-intensive sectors of the economy while working against the small, traditional sectors. In addition, state allocation and accumulation policies often favored large capitalists, protecting them against competition while providing them with favorable conditions and resources. At the same time, these policies excluded small and medium-sized enterprises, exposing them to the vagaries of the market system. State intervention also served the interests of capital against the working classes. In the end, state intervention and state development strategies increased social inequalities and narrowed the social basis of support for the state.

State development strategy in all three countries also increased

55

economic integration into the world market, leading to increased dependence on the world economy. While such integration provided significant opportunities for these economies, in the long run dependence also rendered these countries vulnerable to adverse international economic conditions. In time, all three countries, to varying degrees, confronted adverse international conditions that were beyond their control.

Eventually, external economic changes, combined with internal economic downturns and contradictions, set the stage for social and political conflicts. In each case, increased state intervention had undermined the market mechanism and politicized the process of capital allocation and accumulation. As a result, the states, rather than market forces, were identified as responsible for rising inequalities and economic decline or crisis. Thus, state intervention increased each state's likelihood of becoming vulnerable to attack and challenge during crises and conflicts. The social and political conflicts, in turn, worsened economic conditions and further contributed to the difficulties of these regimes.

State intervention and economic development in Iran

In comparative terms, the Iranian government was the most interventionist of the three cases, becoming the nation's single largest banker, industrialist, employer, and landlord by the end of the Pahlavi regime. Increased state resources, including support from the United States, along with weaknesses in industrial capital and the private sector, combined with reduced social support to produce favorable conditions for the expansion of state intervention in the Iranian economy.

Of course, rising oil revenues provided the critical resource needed for the expansion of state intervention. The state-owned National Iranian Oil, at its height in 1977 before operations were disrupted by strikes, was the second largest industrial corporation outside the United States and the seventh largest in the world (*Fortune*, August 13, 1979). This was made possible by the nationalization of oil in the early 1950s, which dramatically increased the significance of oil for the state and the country's economy. Oil revenues shot up from 2,500 billion rials in 1954 to 37,177 billion rials in 1963, an almost fourteenfold increase. By 1973, revenues had swollen to 178,196 billion rials. The share of oil in the state's total revenues climbed from 45 percent in 1963 to 56 percent in 1971. In 1977, despite a downturn during the mid-1970s, oil's share expanded to 77 percent. Oil's share in the GDP jumped from 21.28 percent in 1963–1964 to 51.9 percent in 1972–1973 (BMI 1978:94–95). Despite some decline later on, oil revenues from 1977 to 1978 accounted for more than 35 percent of the country's GDP.

Table 3 *Public share of fixed capital formation in Iran, 1963–1977*

Year	Percentage
1963	35.38
1970	49.00
1977	55.10

Source: Bank Markazi Iran, *Annual Report and Balance Sheet.*

These expanding oil revenues enabled the state to intensify its intervention in capital formation. As table 3 shows, the public share of fixed capital formation rose from 35 percent to 55 percent between 1963 and 1977.

By investing in a variety of capital-intensive industries, the state became the largest industrialist in the country. Sixty percent of all industrial investment in 1975 was made by the state (Halliday 1979:149). In 1976, the state itself owned 130 large factories and workshops and had entered into an additional 55 joint ventures with domestic and foreign corporations (SCI 1981a:30). Among the state's holdings were all petroleum plants and four large petrochemical plants, as well as all oil refineries. The state also invested in machine-tool plants, steel, aluminum, copper, cement, textile, sugar mills, tobacco, and cigarettes, and owned the Iranian Carpet Company.

Furthermore, state economic activities extended far beyond the manufacturing sector. Nearly 69 percent of all financial capital was held by the state (SCI 1976b:1, 8). It owned the entire railway and air transportation systems, the main sea transport, National Arya shipping, and all communication facilities. Many utilities, all major dams, and a sizable number of insurance companies and agrobusinesses were also owned by the state. Moreover, the state was the largest landowner in urban areas, owning 33.8 billion square meters of land near large cities, including more than 15 billion square meters near Tehran (*Ettelaat*, May 11, 1977). Approximately one-third of the government-owned land was located within large cities where land prices were highest. It also ventured into the distribution sector, directly and indirectly, distributing a number of essential goods throughout the country. In all, the state became the largest industrialist, banker, landlord, and trader in Iran.

State-sponsored development brought impressive results in economic growth and increased national income. The GNP, which had risen by 8 percent per year in the 1960s, rose by 14.2 percent in 1972–1973, 30.3 percent in 1973–1974, and 42 percent in 1974–1975. GNP per capita rose from $450 in 1972 to more than $2,400 in 1978 (Halliday 1979:138). The non-oil GDP also grew at an impressive rate of 15 percent a year from 1973 to 1977 (Amuzegar 1991:58). Industrial growth for the decade of 1965–1975 was 15.2 percent per annum, almost twice as high as the average growth of this sector in other developing countries. In 1968, the country manufactured 20,222 automobiles and jeeps, 1,879 trucks and vans, and 141,000 refrigerators. By 1976, production had increased to 102,000 automobiles and jeeps, 55,322 trucks and vans, and 513,000 refrigerators. Most manufacturing industries experienced similar high rates of growth (BMI 1971:147; BMI 1976:140–141). For a time it appeared that Iran would become a regional industrial power in the Middle East.

To develop the private sector, the Iranian government encouraged import-substitution industrialization and pursued regulative policies that were significant features of Iran's economic development. The import-substitution industrialization strategy was to limit licensing to certain entrepreneurs and protect them through high tariffs. The effect of the strategy was to encourage the rise of monopolies and increased inequality (Mohtadi 1987:54). Tariff protection for many goods reached as high as 200 to 300 percent. The state's financial policies also granted cheap credit to a small class of capitalists engaged in the modern industrial sector. These credit subsidies alone transferred an estimated $730 million to such enterprises in 1975/1976 and $1.27 billion in 1977/1978. The latter transfer was estimated to be approximately two-thirds of all private profits in the manufacturing sector (Salehi-Isfahani 1989:367). Between 1971 and 1975, loans to the private sector increased by 289 percent (Bashiriyeh 1984:87). The results were impressive. From 1972 to 1973, the number of registered companies in large cities rose from 1,517 to 2,208, an increase of 46 percent. Their capital grew more than threefold, from 14.2 to 52.8 billion rials. Between 1962 and 1978, investment in the private sector rose dramatically by 250 percent. The government also provided tax holidays to the large modern enterprises and kept wages down for most of the period under consideration.

State intervention and economic development in Nicaragua

As in Iran, a combination of rising economic resources, weaknesses in the private sector, and economic and political support from the United States provided favorable conditions for state intervention in Nicaragua. Weakness in the Nicaraguan entrepreneurial class had become particularly noticeable in the early 1950s, necessitating state intervention. At that time, a World Bank study concluded:

Up to the present time, domestic private enterprise has, with few exceptions, done relatively little to develop the country's productive capacity. This has remained the case even in the last three and a half years when there has been a sharp rise in national income . . . Private enterprise, on the other hand, has often been unimaginative and unduly cautious. (International Bank for Reconstruction and Development 1953:100)

The Nicaraguan government began active intervention in the economy to promote economic development following World War II. The state expanded the nation's infrastructure by building highways, roads, and rail systems;[1] extending electric power; and, most importantly, allocating capital for economic investment. In the 1960s, the National Economic Council drew up plans to reduce Nicaragua's vulnerability to fluctuations in the world market. The Planning Office encouraged agricultural diversification and promoted industrial development within the framework of the Central American Common Market. The state also established and enhanced the resources of a number of autonomous enterprises to speed up economic development. These entities included the Central Bank of Nicaragua, the National Bank of Nicaragua, the Mortgage Bank of Nicaragua, the Bank of Popular Credit, the National Development Institute (INFONAC), the National Assembly of Assistance and Social Foresight (JNAPS), the Irrigation Company of Rivas, the Agrarian Institute of Nicaragua (IAN), the National Company of Light and Power (ENALUF), the National Institute of Electrical Energy, and the Port Authority of Corinto.

Although the Nicaraguan government was not itself a major actor in the industrial sector, as the country's largest banker it dominated the financial arena and played the most significant role in capital allocation. Throughout the 1960s and 1970s, the government received substantial aid in the form of grants and low-interest loans from the United States and multilateral institutions. As table 4 indicates, between 1969 and 1978 Nicaragua received the most aid per capita in Latin America. After the Managua earthquake, state influence in society and the economy expanded dramatically following the massive influx of aid from thirty-five countries and the huge amounts of capital loaned by foreign banks, all of which were directly administered by the National Emergency Committee. The government also resorted to heavy borrowing from domestic sources. This abrupt surge in resources only intensified the government's

---

[1] The construction of roads completed physical integration of the country, which, even in the Pacific Region, had been lacking at the beginning of the 1950s.

Table 4   *Official development assistance per capita for Nicaragua and other countries, 1969–1978 in dollars*

Country	Average per capita
Nicaragua	14.35
Costa Rica	11.39
Honduras	10.77
El Salvador	6.23
Guatemala	5.66
Latin America	4.36
Africa, Asia, Latin America	5.60

Source: UN *Statistical Yearbook.*

pivotal role in allocating capital. As a result, Nicaragua's external public debt increased from $155 million in 1970, accounting for 20.6 percent of the GNP, to $964 million in 1978, representing 45.8 percent of the GNP. At the same time, the government's domestic borrowing rose from 17.5 million córdobas in 1971, to a peak of 772.5 million córdobas in 1978 (IMF 1982:510). In terms of the proportion of the GNP absorbed by the public debt, only Panama and Peru exceeded Nicaragua in 1978 (World Bank 1980:138).

The vast resources also enabled the state to expand its share of capital expenditure in total gross fixed capital formation. As shown in table 5, the central government's share of fixed capital expenditure increased from 20.48 percent in 1970 to 33 percent in 1977. Total government fixed investment rose from 25.23 percent in 1970 to 50.2 percent in 1977 and 54.9 percent in 1978.

In the agricultural sector, the state played a central role in achieving diversification and development. Historically, Nicaragua's economy had been based almost solely on coffee and bananas. In the 1950s, the state encouraged cotton production by building appropriate infrastructures and providing favorable exchange rates, tariffs, and pricing policies, all of which stimulated investment in labor-saving machinery. Although Nicaragua probably had fewer than 500 tractors in 1950, five years later there were 2,500 (Biderman 1983:16).

With state subsidies, irrigation and research projects were initiated, as was the construction of storage, processing, and marketing facilities. More important was the state's policy of providing subsidized credit for these projects through the National Bank and INFONAC. Cheap loans and technical assistance to promote production went to industries such as tobacco, beef, shrimp, bananas, and irrigated rice, many of which

Table 5   *Government share of capital expenditure in Nicaragua, 1970–1978*

	1970	1977	1978
Central government	20.48	33.00	29.17
All government levels	25.23	50.20	54.90

Sources: IMF, UN *Statistical Yearbook*, UN *Economic Survey of Latin America.*

were industries in which the Somoza family had significant business interests.[2]

A few commodities received special attention and expanded rapidly. As noted above, cotton was one example. By the mid-1950s, cotton growers were receiving two-thirds of all bank credit (Biderman 1983:14; Spalding 1994:36). In the 1960s, the National Bank provided 85 percent of the financing for cotton, which represented the highest state support for cotton anywhere in Central America (Williams 1986:26). The National Bank also extended credit based on cotton yield, which further encouraged rationalized production (Brooks 1967:194). Similar attention to the expansion of beef for export in the 1960s led to even greater diversification of agroexports. Land allocated to cattle-raising doubled between 1960 and 1975, and the share of beef in total exports tripled between 1960 and 1970. This state policy paid off by 1973 when Nicaragua became the fourth largest exporter of beef to the United States (*La Prensa*, December 22, 1973).

Industrial development was promoted through a policy of import substitution. With the Alliance for Progress, US economic assistance more than doubled and military aid rose sevenfold. These resources enabled the state to take crucial steps toward industrialization in the early 1960s. In addition to building infrastructure, the state extended favorable exchange rates, tax holidays, and subsidized credit. Through limited licensing, the state eliminated business competition, thereby providing entreprenuers with secure markets. Equally important was state repression, which kept wages low and prevented strikes to promote accumulation of capital.

These economic policies generated rapid economic growth in the decades following World War II, a period which can be characterized as the most dynamic in Nicaragua's economic history. Although the economy experienced sharp cyclical downswings in the late 1950s and late 1960s, the GDP grew at a real average rate of 5.2 percent in the 1950s,

[2] Equally significant, throughout this era the state prevented most rural workers from organizing unions; as a result, wages were kept low, and capital accumulation was rapid.

7 percent in the 1960s (Heriot 1982:115), and 5.6 percent between 1970 and 1978 (Spalding 1994:39; Weeks 1985:50). Per capita income in Nicaragua increased from $155 in 1951 to $424 in 1971 and to $830 in 1977.[3] Between 1950 and 1977, Nicaragua's agricultural sector grew at an average annual rate of 4.7 percent, a rate surpassed in Latin America only by Venezuela. The productivity of agricultural labor rose by 4.6 percent per year during the same period, the highest in Latin America (Baumeister 1985:15–16; Paige 1985:92). Nicaraguan cotton production obtained the highest yields in the world for nonirrigated land (Brooks 1967:208). Land planted with cotton increased fivefold from 1950 to 1970, and cotton production rose from 3,300 tons in 1950 to 125,000 in 1965. By 1967, Nicaragua was the largest cotton producer in Central America and the eleventh in the world, supplying 2.4 percent of the world's total cotton exports (Paige 1985:92). The cattle industry also expanded to the extent that, by 1973, Nicaragua accounted for one-third of Central America's entire beef exports (Williams 1986:166).

In the same period after World War II, the state's policies, augmented by ever more economic aid from the United States and the Central American Common Market, generated growth in the industrial sector as well. Industrial production rose from 15.7 percent to 29 percent of the GDP between 1950 and 1970. The basis of this growth was manufacturing, which increased its share of the GDP from 11.5 percent in 1950 to 23.7 in 1977. From 1960 to 1970, manufacturing grew at 11.1 percent annually, a rate second only to Brazil in Latin America (Heriot 1982:132). By 1979, manufacturing's share of value added in the GDP was 25.4 percent, by far the highest in Central America (Weeks 1985:135).

State intervention in the market economy in the Philippines

Unlike Iran and Nicaragua, the Philippine state was regulative, not hyperactive, after independence in 1946. A free market economy was the Philippines' legacy from American colonialism in the first half of the twentieth century. The main exceptions were a number of public enterprises created by the government, beginning in 1935, to produce steel, cement, textiles, and electric power, and to operate railroads. In 1954, the government reversed its policy and began to sell off these enterprises to the private sector (Golay 1961:242–243). The result was that, despite some continued state interests in railroads, hydroelectric power, water distribution, and commercial banking, by 1972 the Philippine economy was in the

---

[3] The figure for 1951 is from the International Bank for Reconstruction and Development (1953), p. 75, and the figure for 1977 is from World Bank (1979), p. 126.

hands of the private sector (Power, et al. 1971:70–71). As reported in a World Bank study, "Until the early 1970s the Philippines economy was controlled and dominated by the private sector. The public sector was small and played only a relatively minor role in economic development. By international standards, the Philippines had low levels of government revenues and expenditures" (Cheetham and Hawkins 1976:387).

In general, the low level of state intervention in Philippine capital formation shifted the burden of capital allocation and accumulation to the private sector and market forces. Private sector savings financed the largest portion of investment in manufacturing, while government resources represented a mere 5 percent of the capital (Sicat 1972:24). Consistent with low state intervention, the average share of state capital expenditure in total fixed capital formation during 1965 to 1969 remained barely above 18 percent, one of the lowest among developing countries.

The state did intervene in the economy in the form of regulation, particularly during economic downturns or when it attempted to promote specific areas of the economy. These interventions often took the form of tax exemptions, import and exchange controls, and tariffs. State intervention widened during a time of economic difficulties and bottlenecks occurring at the end of the 1940s, when declining prices for agricultural exports and growing imports of consumer goods were generating ever-greater balance of payments deficits. Import controls were imposed in 1949, and exchange controls in 1950 (Valdepenas and Bautista 1977:169). In 1953, the government passed another tax exemption law to encourage new industries, which remained in effect until 1962 (Baldwin 1975:42), and in 1957, a high tariff was initiated to protect domestic producers. Together, these policies comprised a program of import-substitution industrialization, which endured for more than a decade. Eventually, the slow pace of economic development led to the passage of the Investment Incentive Act in 1967, which granted special tax privileges to key domestic industries.

The imposition of martial law in 1972 enhanced state resources and expanded state intervention in the economy. State intervention increased as the government stimulated its economic assets by borrowing and otherwise obtaining massive amounts of capital from international agencies and the United States government. These resources enabled the state to become a relatively more prominent economic actor. As noted in chapter 2, in fiscal year 1973, the Philippines received $85.7 million from the US Agency for International Development (AID), a dramatic increase over the $30.5 million received in 1972. In contrast to such loans and grants in the four years prior to martial law, which totaled $56.2 million, the total amount received during the next four years skyrocketed to $240.5 million. Marcos also obtained concessional loans from the Export/Import Bank, overseas private investment corporations, and the Commodity Credit Corporation, rising from $509.3 million in 1969–1972 to $1,097.1 million in 1973–1975 (Wurfel 1988:191). From post-World War II independence until 1973, the Philippines also received $301 million in loans from the World Bank and its counterpart, the International Development Association. From 1974 through 1978, the amount shot up to $1.34 billion (ibid.:194).

The state also borrowed heavily from private banks and institutions in the Philippines and abroad. Increased borrowing inflated the external public debt from $1.1 billion in 1970 to nearly $21.8 billion in 1986 (Boyce 1993:262). As a result, the state and economy became ever more dependent on the world market and external agencies.

With increased resources, the state redoubled its intervention in the economy and in capital formation (as shown in table 6) and further restricted the operation of the market mechanism. State regulation, ownership, investment, finance, and expropriation expanded to an unprecedented extent. The state took ownership of Philippine Airlines and created the National Steel Corporation by taking over several steel mills. Several multinational oil corporations sold all or part of their interests to the state-owned Philippine National Oil Company.

An additional factor contributing to state intervention was economic failure. State financial institutions – mainly the Philippine National Bank and the Development Bank of the Philippines – funneled large sums of money into corporations that had been negatively affected by the world market and rising interest rates. State managers thereby became more prominent in private companies (Hawes 1987:138). Another pattern evolved with the collapse of crony-run enterprises in which the state had made large investments. In such cases, the state had little choice but to take over these failed corporations. By the time of Marcos' ouster, the government owned numerous banks, finance corporations, hotels, mines, several mills for the production of paper, textiles, and sugar, as well as construction companies, shipping lines, and steel mills (ibid.:138). By 1983, 208 state corporations existed, most of which were established after martial law (Villegas 1983:120). The government also became the largest landowner in the country as a result of defaults by peasants on land payments (Bello, et al. 1982:74). The government's National Food Authority took over wheat trading at the wholesale and at the retail levels, replacing family-run enterprises.[4]

[4] According to some analysts, although wheat could have been subsidized and therefore made cheaper, in actuality it became more expensive because the difference in price was made up by taxes (Villegas 1986b:168).

Table 6 *Public share of fixed capital formation in the Philippines*

Years	Percentage
1969–1971	19.20
1978–1980	28.60
1983–1985	21.26

Source: World Bank (1991).

State intervention produced some positive results. The government racked up impressive growth rates by increasing expenditures on infrastructure programs and providing credit subsidies. In the agricultural sector, government land reform initiated in 1972 redistributed land to more than 111,000 tenants, more than during the previous twenty-five years of democratic rule. Known as the Masagna-99 program, the reforms declared all tenants to be owners of the rice and corn lands they worked, with certain proscribed limits. Although the reforms affected only 11 percent of tenants, they generated impressive results in rice production. The government also introduced new, high-yielding varieties to boost the production of rice, resulting in self-sufficiency in the basic food staple for the first time in seventy-five years (Steinberg 1990:128).

In manufacturing, the government's economic policies promoted domestic manufacturing for export. Between 1971 and 1980, exports of electrical and electronic equipment and components jumped from $280,000 to $671 million. Garment exports rose from $36 million to $500 million, while handicraft exports multiplied in value from $9 million to $154 million. Exports of food products and beverages, chemicals, furniture, footwear, toys, and sporting goods all increased (Hawes 1987:141). In large measure, these exports rose as a result of significant new government investment in the manufacturing sector during the 1970s. The country's GNP per capita rose by about 38 percent from 9,558 (in constant pesos) in 1972 to 13,146 in 1981 (Boyce 1993:15). Although less than Iran and Nicaragua, state intervention did produce impressive economic growth in the Philippines.

Results of state economic intervention: rising inequality in Iran

Despite impressive growth and development, the state's development strategy in Iran led to a number of contradictions that set the stage for rising conflicts in the late 1970s. In particular, the state's policies played a central role in bringing about rising economic inequalities.

Small, traditional manufacturing establishments, which in 1976 accounted for approximately 98 percent of the manufacturing sector and employed more than two-thirds of the urban labor force, did not benefit from the grants, subsidies, and interest-free loans extended to the modern sector. In 1973, traditional handicrafts received only 0.2 percent of all state payments allocated for industrial development. By 1976, the amount had increased to 5.2 percent, which was still very low given this sector's predominance (BMI 1976:144). Traditional industries such as rug-making, which employed nearly one-half of the country's manufacturing labor force, and shoe-making were not protected, and both were forced to compete with machine-made imports.

While promoting capital accumulation, the state pursued policies that demobilized the labor movement. After the *coup d'état* of 1953, the government repressed independent labor unions. Later, in 1959, a new labor law passed by the government required every labor union to be approved by the Ministry of Labor. When union leaders were elected, the SAVAK insured that unions remained under government control by electing either SAVAK agents or employees who could be controlled. In addition, unions were confined to individual factories, and no industrywide unions were allowed to emerge. The result was the fragmention of labor power. More importantly, the government banned strikes and thus reduced workers' capacity for collective action and bargaining against employers, and affected their income.

The state provided the pastoral nomadic sector with little support (Garthwaite 1983:141). This failure, in conjunction with uneven capital allocation policies, led to an intensification of regional inequalities and other adverse effects in regions such as Sistan, Kerman, and Kurdestan (Amirahmadi 1990:203–205; Jabbari and Olson 1981:179).

The state's taxation policies aggravated existing inequalities. The poorest 10 percent of the population paid 11 percent of their income in taxes, whereas the richest 10 percent paid only 8 percent in taxes (*Kayhan*, October 23, 1978). Many of the wealthy did not even bother to pay taxes.

State development strategy increased rural–urban income disparities. Interested in rapid industrialization, the state largely neglected the agricultural sector. Despite substantial international pressure, the government took more than a decade to initiate a land reform program (Najmabadi 1987:86). Even then, the government's land reform excluded one-half of all village families from receiving land because they lacked formal sharecropping agreements with landowners. Of those peasants who were able to obtain land, more than 72 percent acquired less than six hectares; in all, approximately three-quarters of the peasantry received less than the seven hectares necessary for subsistence (Hooglund 1982:90). Thus, as was the case in Nicaragua and the Philippines, Iranian agrarian reform failed to solve the issue of land tenure, the fundamental problem plaguing the agrarian population.

Following the land reform, the state continued to neglect the agricultural sector. The result was that, although the agrarian sector employed more than 50 percent of the labor force, the share of agricultural output in the GNP was only 9.4 percent in 1977–1978 (BMI 1978:95). This imbalance emerged, in part, from the government's capital-allocation strategy, which largely ignored the technical needs of the agricultural sector. Only a minority of owners whose holdings averaged 250 acres or more practiced capitalist agriculture, using wage laborers, machinery, and production inputs such as fertilizers. In 1975, the entire agrarian sector contained approximately 41,000 tractors and 2,633 combines, which were unequally distributed with one-fourth of all tractors and nearly 28 percent of all combines located in the two provinces of Mazanderan and Khorasan.

A combination of 3 percent population growth, increased urbanization, and rising income meant that the demand for food increased. Inadequate supplies forced the state to import and subsidize foodstuffs, which further reduced agricultural growth. In 1972, imports of food and live animals amounted to $206 million. By 1977, imports had increased more than 621 percent, to $1,485 million (BMI 1977:154). These conditions forced producers in parts of the country to abandon their cultivable land, which led to increased peasant migration to urban areas. In Dezful, for example, where some of the best rice in the country was produced, the amount of land formerly allocated for cultivation had been 130,000 hectares, which fed the entire population of the province of Khuzestan. By 1978, only 6,000 hectares of land were allocated to rice production in Dezful. The resulting migration of thousands of farmers and peasants to cities in search of other jobs exacerbated urban problems such as housing, employment, and services. This intensified pressures on urban resources and further widened social inequalities (*Kayhan*, January 10, 1978).

Housing shortages were particularly acute. Rents in some parts of Tehran skyrocketed by an estimated 1,000 percent, according to an official newspaper of the Shah's own party (*Rastakhiz*, September 16, 1977). By the mid-1970s, rents had risen to the point where urban workers had to spend more than one-half of their income on rent (*Ettelaat*, June 11, 1977), a situation that even the Shah himself condemned (*Ettelaat*, April 14, June 1, 1977; and *Kayhan*, February 15, 1977). As a result, shantytowns sprang up on the outskirts of urban areas. In Tehran, at least twenty-four large shantytowns containing thousands of families had risen on the edge of the city (*Ettelaat*, August 6, 1997). For Tehran, estimates ran from 500,000 to more than one million people (Kazemi 1980:3). Most shantytown dwellers were unskilled workers, along with some recent migrants from rural areas, peddlers, artisans, and even some white-collar employees (Parsa 1989:78).

Adverse economic conditions inevitably affected the distribution of income in the country. In a study of income distribution, the International Labor Office concluded that in 1969–1970 the Gini coefficient, a measure of income inequality, was higher in Iran than in any country in the Middle East, Southeast Asia, or Western Europe, and was as high as or higher than in Latin American countries for which data were available. Another study noted that the Gini coefficient in the distribution of consumption expenditures increased during 1972–1979 (Amirahmadi 1990:199). Between 1959 and 1974, the share of household expenditures of the top 20 percent of urban households rose from 52 to 56 percent, while that of the bottom 40 percent declined from 14 percent to 11 percent (Walton 1980:283). The share of expenditures of the bottom 10 percent of households decreased from 1.77 percent in 1959–1960 to 1.34 percent in 1971–1972, a trend that reversed itself fractionally by increasing over the next two years to 1.37 percent. In contrast, the share of the top 10 percent of households rose from 35.4 in 1959–1960 to a peak of 39.5 percent in 1972–1973, and then dropped slightly to 37.99 in 1973–1974 (Pesaran 1976:268).

Political power was used effectively to promote accumulation of wealth in the hands of a small number of people. The Pahlavi Foundation, supposedly a charitable organization, was the Shah's main instrument for vast financial operations. The Foundation received an annual subsidy of over $40 million (Abrahamian 1982:437–438). It became the most powerful economic entity in the country after the government (Zonis 1971:49). Other members of the royal family also used their political power to enrich themselves. A CIA report of 1976 stated that Princess Ashraf, the Shah's twin sister, had a "near legendary reputation for financial corruption" (Katouzian 1998:199). In addition to participating in the most lucrative enterprises, the royal family also benefited enormously from access to oil revenues through corrupt practices. In the last few years of the monarchy, substantial sums of money from state oil revenues – perhaps as much as $12 billion – were reportedly transferred to the royal family's bank accounts held in foreign countries (*Washington Post*, January 17, 1979). Not surprisingly, the royal family, consisting of sixty-three princes and princesses, was itself the wealthiest family in the country, owning 137 of the 527 largest corporations and financial institutions (Ravasani 1978:109–117).

The royal family also used its political power to reward and enrich its allies and supporters. As a result, by the monarchy's end, wealth was extremely concentrated in Iranian society. In 1974, forty-seven wealthy families controlled 85 percent of all firms with turnovers of more than 10 million rials (Halliday 1979:151). The upper echelon of the country's wealthholders remained exceedingly small, being composed of roughly 150 families who owned 67 percent of all industries and financial institutions in the country (Bashiriyeh 1984:40).

Economic inequality in Nicaragua

As in Iran, the Nicaraguan government's development strategy in the form of import-substitution industrialization had important social and economic consequences. Like Iran, Nicaraguan government policies were not neutral despite exclusive rule and state autonomy from the upper class. Instead, government policies served the interests of high government officials, large landlords, and big industrial, financial, and commercial capital. Government policies consistently and systematically excluded small and medium-sized capital. The state also repressed the working classes in order to facilitate the process of capital accumulation. In combination, these policies resulted in massive accumulation of wealth and rising inequalities. Increased state resources and state intervention after the Managua earthquake of 1972 also expanded government corruption, adversely affected the poorer segments of the population and inevitably increased social and economic inequalities.

Various government development policies directly contributed to rising inequalities. The government's policy of stimulating industry provided generous incentives for large producers, including tax and duty exemptions, low-interest loans, and other benefits, which were not extended to small and traditional producers. These government policies generated monopolies and oligopolies, which were protected from competition, although occasionally the government authorities denied such allegations (*La Prensa*, November 28, 1974). The government consistently favored industrialists over workers by preventing labor mobilization and collective action. Government taxation policy also furthered inequality by demanding markedly less from large producers and the wealthy. Small businesses complained that the same tax rate was applied both to capital income and income received from labor, a policy that worked to the detriment of small investors (*La Prensa*, December 14, 1974). Still worse, the Constitutional Assembly approved a new tax package that raised taxes on various segments of the middle classes and skilled labor in 1974 (*La Prensa*, November 6 and 9, 1974). Finally, repression of working-class organizations demobilized large segments of this class and enhanced the process of capital accumulation for big capital, thereby increasing social inequalities.

Government capital allocation policies overwhelmingly favored the export sector and virtually ignored basic grain production for domestic consumption. Infrastructure investments, credit, and subsidized inputs were primarily directed toward large producers of exports. Throughout the 1960s, for example, between 80 and 90 percent of all bank loans for agriculture went to export crops, even though less than 50 percent of the agricultural land was devoted to their production (Dorner and Quiros 1973:224; Enriquez and Spalding 1987:107–109). In 1976, the large producers of cotton, coffee, and sugar exports received 90 percent of the capital allocated to the agricultural sector (Deere and Marchetti 1981:45). Although the government launched the Rural Credit Program in 1959 to help small producers obtain financial credit, the impact of the program was limited. By 1978, the project had extended credit to only 28,000 small producers (Enriquez and Spalding 1987:111). Most small producers had no access to government credit and were dependent on financing through wholesalers or agroindustrial capital. The result was that they remained forever indebted and forced to sell their harvest in advance with no hope of controlling prices.

Consequently, these policies gave rise to inequality in the distribution of wealth and income. Although longitudinal data are not available for this period, all experts agree that the inequalities worsened. In 1977, the lower one-half of income earners garnered only 15 percent of the national income, while the top 5 percent received 28 percent. This was the highest degree of income polarization in Central America (Gibson 1987:31; Vilas 1986:56; 1995:21). Working-class income, which had been rising in the 1960s, declined during the following decade, owing to a combination of inflation, unemployment, and reduced employee compensation. By 1979, the working class's real wages had fallen by one-third from their 1967 level (Booth and Walker 1989:55–56).

The agrarian sector had a highly unequal land tenure system. Agrarian land was disproportionately distributed to an extreme,[5] with 5 percent of the population owning 85 percent of the agrarian land, while nearly 40 percent of the populace owned no land at all (Gibson 1987:20; Gilbert 1990:3). An AID-sponsored inquiry undertaken in 1972 concluded that,

---

[5] A study carried out by the Instituto Historico Centroamericano (IHCA) and published in 1975 found that 50.9 percent of the landowners owned from one to seven hectares, which comprised but 3.5 percent of the land in Nicaragua; in contrast, 4.9 percent of the landowners held more than 500 hectares, which amounted to 58.8 percent of the land. These data were cited in *La Prensa*, April 1, 1979.

if ignored, such differences between haves and have-nots could lead to social upheavals (Biderman 1983:23). The Agrarian Institute of Nicaragua aggravated the situation by distributing sizable land holdings to more than twenty government officials and their families. Somoza Debayle, himself the largest landholder in the country, received substantial amounts of land (*La Prensa*, December 30, 1977). In another instance, the Institute drew up plans to distribute state lands in the province of Zelaya to thirty-four active and retired members of the National Guard and nineteen civilians who had no agrarian experience, including Somoza Debayle's private secretary (*La Prensa*, April 14, 1978). As a result, by the conclusion of Somoza rule, the landless rural labor force in some areas of the country had risen by more than 1,000 percent since the 1950s (LaFeber 1984:227).

The principal beneficiaries of state-sponsored economic development were the three segments of the Nicaraguan business sector, which included the Nicaraguan Bank, or BANIC, the Bank of America, or BANAMERICA, and the Somoza family and its closest collaborators, who also invested substantially in modern agriculture, industry, and commerce (Strachan 1976:50). Although these three factions converged through various joint ventures in the 1960s and early 1970s, the Somoza group always held the upper hand.

Even more than in Iran, economic success in Nicaragua was closely linked to political connections and control over state power. The Somozas were particularly adept at using public power for familial aggrandizement. Extracting funds from the state and its autonomous entities, the National Bank, National Light and Power Company, National Lottery, and the National Social Security Institute, as well as from US economic and military aid, among others, the Somoza faction enjoyed a competitive advantage over its two rival groups. The Somozas used creative mechanisms to take advantage of the opportunities provided by the Central American Common Market's reduction of trade barriers and by US aid, to accumulate capital. These included using state power to classify family-owned enterprises as tax exempt, granting legal monopolies to Somoza companies, obtaining loans at highly favorable rates, and receiving government contracts without public bidding. Numerous Somoza-owned businesses were repeatedly reclassified as belonging to Category A, which received exemptions from various taxes (*La Prensa*, December 9, 1977). Even where exemptions were not granted, Somoza companies sometimes flouted regulations imposed on competitors. The Somoza-owned cement company, for example, operated a fleet of twenty-five cement trucks, ten tractor-trailers, and ten dump trucks in Masaya for at least one-and-a-half years without license plates (*La Prensa*, November 21, 1977).

The earthquake in Managua on December 22, 1972 provided the Somozas with still another opportunity to expand their wealth. With the expansion of state intervention and resources, government corruption proliferated (Millett 1982:39). After the earthquake, when large segments of Nicaraguans faced severe economic hardships, various reports demonstrated that the family's economic activity was expanding at an accelerated rate through investments in at least eight new enterprises, including oil, fertilizer, cigars, tuna, and geothermal ventures. In the two years after the quake, government corruption reached heights that sometimes attracted international headlines. Between March and December 1973, *La Prensa* reported at least twenty-five major cases of corruption at the national level. These incidents included numerous reports of the disappearance of donated food and clothing or their resale by government functionaries, and lucrative government contracts awarded to businesses owned by high-ranking officials without public bidding or through other questionable procedures. The Nicaraguan treasury, for example, acknowledged receiving only one-half of the $32 million in relief aid extended by the US government (Diederich 1981:100). In one highly publicized case, the president of the Chamber of Deputies bought a piece of property for 120,000 córdobas and resold it two days later for 8 million córdobas to the state-owned Mortgage Bank as a site upon which to construct new housing (*La Prensa*, June 11, 1973). Another scandal centered around a donation by the Colombian government of 100 houses in Managua. Although the houses were slated to be distributed by lottery, the first fifty were given to employees of Lanica, the Somoza-owned airlines, and to public employees of the Census Bureau, the Mortgage Bank, and other state institutions. Several recipients were drivers for high-ranking National Guard officers, all of whom owned at least one other house (*La Prensa*, September 11, 1973). The remaining houses were given to fifty families who were assessed payments of 150 córdobas per month for fifteen years by the Mortgage Bank, causing discontent among those who were supposed to have received the houses free of charge (*La Prensa*, October 29, 1973).

After the earthquake, Somoza continued to use his power for private gain. After suffering a heart attack in 1977, he used government money to construct an airport at Montelimar, his private estate, at a cost to the national treasury of more than 25 million córdobas. He also caused the Nicaraguan Pacific Railroad to be extended to the Somoza family's privately owned port, Puerto Somoza, funding this with 18 million córdobas borrowed from the Inter-American Development Bank (*La Prensa*, December 27, 1974). Two million dollars donated by the government of Brazil for the reconstruction of Managua after the earthquake was spent on buying Mercedes Benz trucks. Somoza Debayle defended the purchase, declaring that they were the only type of trucks suitable for Managua streets, but neglecting to mention that he himself owned the Mercedes Benz franchise in Nicaragua (*La Prensa*, August 29, 1973). The Law of Reserved Cargo gave a monopoly of shipping on the Atlantic coast to the Nicaraguan Merchant Marine Lines, also known as Mamenic, a shipping company owned by the Somoza family, which reaped enormous economic profits for its owner (*La Prensa*, July 9, 1973). But commercial users suffered huge losses when imports were delayed up to three months because the Mamenic firm could not handle the increased volume of shipping coming in following the earthquake (*La Prensa*, June 16, 1973). In 1974 and 1975, twenty Somoza enterprises received more than $17 million in loans from INFONAC (the National Development Institute), in violation of its own bylaws.[6] Another eight unknown firms, presumably phantom companies, were beneficiaries of INFONAC loans totaling 28 million córdobas (*La Prensa* August 3, 1978).

Whenever opportunities arose, Somoza arranged lucrative deals with the government for companies he owned. For example, he hired his own company, Energetics, to drill wells in a search for geothermal energy at a cost to the state of $7,000. In this particular case, Somoza's firm won the government contract despite exceeding by $5,000 bids from two French companies, whose success rates were 75 percent, in contrast to Energetics' success rate of only 40 percent. Twenty of the wells drilled at government expense were entirely on Somoza Debayle's own land. He received a profit of 848,203 córdobas by selling eight manzanas of land to the state to construct a portion of the southern highway circumventing Managua (*La Prensa*, January 8, 1974). After the earthquake, the cement company owned by his family received lucrative government contracts to pave highways with bricks, despite their unsuitability and greater expense compared with asphalt. By the end of 1974, eighteen highways had been paved with Somoza bricks (*La Prensa*, December 22, 1974).

These mechanisms proved extremely beneficial as the Somoza family expanded into interregional commerce, fishing and fish canning, meat packing, tobacco products, shoe manufacturing, and rice growing and processing. Somoza capital dominated a number of sectors. Sugar production, for example, was centered around six sugar mills, four of which belonged to the Somoza family. The Somozas also controlled 73 percent of rice production and 100 percent of cigar tobacco (Baumeister 1985:16). Somoza was the single largest exporter of beef to the United

[6] INFONAC's bylaws did not permit extending loans to individuals who had savings accounts in INFONAC larger than 25,000 córdobas.

States, accounting for 50 percent of all meat exported from firms in Nicaragua (*La Prensa*, June 3, 1978). The Somoza family owned 168 factories, including the country's only cement factory, the only shipping line, and the only firm constructing roofs. The family-owned Puerto Somoza was valuable as one of only a few ports in the country. Within the city of Managua, the Somoza family was far and away the largest possessor of private property, with holdings valued by the census at 23,701,825 córdobas (*La Prensa*, March 16, 1978). They owned even more land than the Catholic Church (*La Prensa*, June 12, 1974). In 1978, a Nicaraguan congressional deputy pointed out that the Somoza family fortune[7] was estimated to exceed the entire annual budget of Nicaragua for 1977 (*La Prensa*, February 23, 1978).

In sum, state allocation of capital in Nicaragua was highly uneven: large, modern enterprises were favored over small, traditional firms, which constituted the majority of the producers. Under their dominion, the vast majority of the population was excluded from critical economic resources and political processes. The Somozas effectively used state power for capital accumulation. The state's policies toward urban and rural workers were repressive and designed to produce rapid capital accumulation. The immediate consequences of these policies were social inequality and economic polarization.

Rising inequality in the Philippines

Although market-based, Philippine economic development was also accompanied by a rising level of income inequality prior to the imposition of martial law in 1972. According to the ILO, the distribution of income, which remained virtually unchanged between 1956 and 1971, was one of the most unequal in the world (ILO 1974:10, 365). The Philippine Congressional Economic Planning Office also admitted the existence of inequality in a statement issued in 1969: "There is too wide a gap between rich and poor to permit anything else but make the rich richer and the poor degraded and miserable" (cited in Sicat 1972:283). In 1965, 11.6 percent of all families (approximately 600,000) in the country received a mere 1.4 percent of the total family income (Bureau of Census and Statistics, April 1968). In contrast, 2.6 percent of the families earning 10,000 pesos and above received 20.8 percent of the total family income.

---

[7] Somoza Debayle had unquestionably enriched himself. Upon arriving in Miami, he told reporters that he was worth only $100 million, but US government sources placed the figure closer to $900 million (Black 1981:34). Property expropriated after the revolution revealed that the Somoza family and close allies owned approximately 20 percent of the total land area under cultivation, 40 percent of the processing industries, and the entire banking system (Baumeister 1985:15).

Seven out of every ten families belonged to the low-income stratum, two were of middle income, and only one belonged to the high income group (Daroy 1988:12).

Rising economic inequalities attracted the attention of government officials. In the early 1970s, some high-ranking government officials, including the Secretary of Finance, expressed sympathy with student demands for social justice and acknowledged the need to eradicate poverty (*Manila Times*, February 8, 1970). Even President Marcos declared one goal of his reforms to be to narrow the gap between rich and poor (*Manila Times*, May 3, 1970).

Philippine development experience was also characterized by unevenness from one region to another. A widening gap arose among the various regions, with Manila and Rizal developing much faster than the others (Sicat 1972:347–378). Industrial growth, in particular, was highly uneven, with more than one-half of all manufacturing jobs being located in the Manila area. Manila, with 10 percent of the islands' 50 million inhabitants, dominated the entire country in manufacturing growth and consumed 90 percent of the nation's electrical energy. By 1971, the mean family income in urban areas was twice as high as that of the mean family income in rural areas (Wurfel 1988:53) and approximately three times as high as in the three regions with the lowest average income (ILO 1974:378).

Shifts in state policies in the 1960s affected the distribution of income and played an important role in the subsequent conflicts. As noted previously, in 1962, President Macapagal obtained a $300 million loan from the IMF in exchange for abolishing government controls and welcoming foreign investment in the Philippines. These policies had an adverse impact on some entrepreneurs who had hitherto been protected from competition. When Marcos took office in 1966, he asserted that nearly 1,500 corporations were in a state of bankruptcy (Lichauco 1973:35). Nevertheless, his Investment Incentives Bill of 1967 generated intense opposition from pro-nationalist sectors because it invited foreign investment in "pioneer" areas. This Bill was the beginning of the state's shift away from import-substitution industrialization and toward export-led industrialization, which was pursued later in the 1970s. As in Iran and Nicaragua, during martial law repression of labor organizations prevented their mobilization and enhanced capital accumulation.

Income inequalities in both rural and urban areas throughout the country remained very high (Jackson 1989:17). Although the state had attained a high degree of autonomy, the government's development strategy was not neutral, but rather served particular interests. In 1971, the bottom 40 percent of the population received 11.9 percent of the country's total income. By 1981, in the context of the economic crises beginning in the early 1980s, their share had dropped to 9.3 percent. In 1971 the top 20 and 10 percent of the population had netted 52.6 and 37.1 percent, respectively, of the total income. By 1981, their shares had increased to 58.6 and 42.0 percent, respectively (Schirmer and Shalom 1987:177). Similarly, the Center for Research and Communication, a business- and church-supported study group, reported that, in the midst of extreme poverty, the wealthiest 10 percent of all families earned 45 percent of the national income in 1981, up from less than 30 percent in 1971. The poorest 70 percent of families, on the other hand, earned just 31 percent of the national income in 1981, compared with 48 percent a decade earlier (Hawes 1987:133).

The agrarian sector was characterized by a high level of inequality. As in Iran and Nicaragua, the land reform introduced into the Philippines was not comprehensive. Reform was limited to rice and corn land and thus applied to only 40 percent of the peasantry. Even then, land reform fell short of its promise. As of June 1984, twelve years after its inauguration, less than 17 percent of the 752,927 hectares slated for redistribution had actually been transferred. Only between 2.27 and 5 percent of the targeted population were estimated to have become the real owners of the land (Koppel 1987:161; Tiglao 1988:37–38). The long-term outcome of the land reform program was likewise problematic because only 10 percent of tenants actually made payments on the government loans they received to purchase land. Eventually, some peasants even sold their land illegally to landlords (Overholt 1986:1143). As a result, landlessness in the countryside actually increased following land reform (Hawes 1990:273). Shortly after Marcos fled the country, the new government declared the land reform program to be an unqualified disaster.

Government policies encouraged land grabbing and the expulsion of rural producers from their land. The National Development Company, an administrative organization of the state, was responsible for dispossessing small settlers and landowners occupying areas that had been slated by transnational agribusiness corporations for the production of pineapples, bananas, palm oil, rubber, and a number of lesser crops. Thus the coercive power of the state was called into play to intimidate or forcibly evict smallholders who stood in the way of agribusiness (Hawes 1987:131). As many as 20,000 hectares originally held by tenants and smallholders ended up in the hands of agribusiness (Wurfel 1988:173). Consequently, the class of landless farm laborers multiplied rapidly. Land conflicts intensified due to growing population and diminishing land frontiers, while the average size of farms shrank from 3.61 hectares in 1971 to 2.63 hectares in 1980 (Hawes 1990:272–273). Another result of these conditions was the rapid rise of shantytowns in Manila where rural migrants and urban poor could live. By the early 1980s, approximately one-third of the population of Metro Manila lived in such shantytowns.

Farmers' conditions in the 1980s deteriorated because they could not obtain credit to buy farm implements and expensive fertilizer. Although agricultural productivity had increased between 1970 and 1980, and for some of these years the country was self-sufficient in rice, the peasantry did not benefit from economic development. In 1985, 63 percent of the entire rural population lived below the poverty line (Kessler 1989:17). In rice-producing regions such as Central Luzon and Southern Mindanao, that figure rose to more than 80 percent (Tiglao 1988:37).

The disparities in development between regions adversely affected regional minorities. Government funds were heavily expended in Mindanao to combat regional guerrilla groups that opposed the government. In that region the Muslim community, plagued by economic backwardness and lacking government resources and capital, instigated a rebellion against the government (Steinberg 1990:120). Although old hostilities between Muslims and Catholics featured in the conflicts, the root of the problem lay in land grabs and disputes over timber rights and logging operations.

Land grabbing began in response to rising sugar prices (*Manila Times*, February 23, 1970). Sugar industry leaders and even government officials applied for titles to land and, upon receipt, used either persuasion or force to drive any previous settlers away (*Manila Times*, February 23, 1970). In 1966, President Marcos nullified a proclamation by President Macapagal, which had set aside land for the Mindanao Muslims (*Manila Times*, February 23, 1970). The consequence was a massive land grab by Christians in the region. In the 1960s, as many as 3,200 land-hungry northerners entered Mindanao per week (George 1980:115). All unregistered land was legally considered public land and thus could be parceled and settled by anyone filing the necessary papers in Manila. In this way, a Mindanao family could quickly be displaced from land it had occupied for generations (ibid.:115) Land disputes multiplied by the thousand. During one month alone in 1962, disputes broke out over 20,000 hectares valued at 20 million pesos (ibid.:121). Eventually, this practice was condemned by the Catholic Bishops Conference of the Philippines (*Manila Times*, July 10, 1970).

State power was increasingly used to accumulate wealth. Corruption became a principal means of capital accumulation. Under martial law a few powerful families, including the Lopezes and the Jacintos, lost their holdings (Goodno 1991:106; Timberman 1991:83). The family of Aquino's wife, the Cojuangcos, had to sell some of their holdings to

Eduardo Cojuangco, Corazon Aquino's estranged cousin, a Marcos supporter. Large land holdings were broken up by Marcos' land reform of rice and corn lands, while old wealth was adversely affected by government intervention in sugar and coconut exports.

Despite a period of decline prior to martial law, corruption rapidly expanded once civilian rule was suspended. Whereas corrupt deals involving more than one million pesos were formerly condemned, under martial law scandals that profited the ruling group by ten to twenty times as much scarcely drew attention. Corrupt economic activities were harmful to the economic elite, either by leading to outright property losses or by denying them business opportunities (Wurfel 1988:243). Marcos came to be known as "Mr. Ten Percent" because of the commission he exacted from every contract with the government (Tiglao 1988:41). The green revolution project alone, under the direction of Imelda Marcos, was unable to account for more than 15 million pesos of the money allocated to it between 1969 and 1985 (Malaya, November 22, 1985).

The First Family, in particular, accumulated enormous wealth during martial law through a network of proxies reinforced by political power (Wurfel 1988:237). Throughout the 1970s, the president's annual salary was approximately $13,000. Nevertheless, by the time he left office Marcos had amassed $10 billion, according to one estimate (Steinberg 1990:128). Evidence from the Office of Budget and Management of the Philippines suggests that from 1966 to 1985, the total base salary earned by both Marcoses was 2,288,750 pesos (Javate-de Dios, et al. 1988:356), or slightly more than $127,000. But the Marcos family's "hidden wealth," or real estate, amounted to over $510 million, according to the Philippine opposition. Their total wealth amassed during the two decades is estimated at between $5 billion and $15 billion (Thompson 1995:52).

In the economic climate prevailing under martial law, friends and relatives of the First Family had easy access to government credit, contracts, and permits required of foreign investors, and often became partners in joint ventures (Schirmer and Shalom 1987:170–174). By 1975, thirty-one of the thirty-five most economically and politically influential people in the country were closely connected to the First Family (Thompson 1995:54). A study undertaken by a group of concerned businessmen and professional managers in 1979 revealed the assets of the cronies to be as follows: the Benedicto Group, 11 companies; Eduardo Cojuangco, 9; Rodolfo Cuenca, 17; the Herdis Group, 37; the Elizaldes, 12; Juan Ponce Enrile, 10; General Romeo Espino, 11; Antonio Floirendo, 5; the Marcos Group, 48; Romualdez, 60; Silverio, 21; Geronimo Velasco and Luis Villafuerte, 9 each (Canoy 1984:105–120; Javate-de Dios, et al. 1988:399–406).

Some of the cronies were from modest backgrounds but parlayed their friendship with Marcos into great wealth. Herminio Disini was a mediocre small businessman who played golf with the president. His cigarette filter business received a tremendous boost in 1975 when Marcos imposed a 100 percent duty on imported filters, while exempting Disini by allowing him to pay a paltry 10 percent tax. By the end of Marcos' rule, Disini's conglomerate had an estimated worth of $1 billion (Goodno 1991:106).

Cronies also made use of their government connections to obtain government-guaranteed loans. During martial law, crony enterprises defaulted on foreign debts of $4 billion, which, because they had been guaranteed by the state, accounted for roughly 20 percent of the Philippine government's total foreign debt (*Malaya*, April 23, 1985). Nor did cronies pay their fair share of taxes; their tax debt reached 1 billion pesos by 1985 (*Malaya*, March 7, 1985). Estimates of "ill-gotten wealth," illegally acquired funds that were transferred abroad, ranged as high as $10 billion (Hawes 1990:275).

Economic pressures and declining resources

Iran

The Iranian state's development strategy bound the economy ever more tightly to oil and the world market, over which the state had no control in the years prior to the revolution. Such a high level of dependence on oil had important consequences for the economy. First, the increasing economic significance of oil meant that by 1976, non-oil products totaled only approximately 3 percent of all exports (BMI 1976:57). Second, increased oil revenues enabled the government to ignore the agricultural sector, which contributed to its deterioration.

Third, increased oil income in the first half of the 1970s created a problem of revenue absorption because the oil industry's rapid growth was not matched by expansion in other economic sectors. The result was consumer price inflation. To curb inflation, the state pursued two policies. Tariffs were lifted to encourage imports, and a policy of price controls was implemented along with an "antiprofiteering" campaign. In August 1975, prices of 16,000 items were rolled back to their levels of January 1974, a move that had an adverse effect primarily on retail markets. By 1977, these measures had failed to control inflation. To remedy the problems, the government brought on an economic recession. In 1977, under a new prime minister, state expenditures were reduced, and a number of ambitious state projects were abandoned before they had begun. To control inflation, the state also restricted access to bank credits (*Ettelaat*, August 23 and 29, 1977) while continuing the antiprofiteering campaign. In addition, it imposed controls on urban land dealings and speculation, which had flourished during the previous several years.

Fourth, although the state and economy had become highly dependent on oil revenues, these did not expand as anticipated. Continued worldwide recession, a mild European winter in 1975, and a relatively modest increase in the OPEC price of oil soon diminished Iranian oil production and revenues. By December 1975, oil production was running 20 percent below that of the previous year. To carry out its projects and meet its financial needs, the state raised taxes on public corporations and the self-employed (*Kayhan*, February 1 and 23, 1977), and began borrowing funds from abroad. As income continued to decline, state expenditures exceeded revenues. The deficit for 1976 was 37.6 billion rials. The following year it increased sharply to 388.5 billion rials (BMI 1977:139), and in 1978, reached 550.2 billion rials (IMF 1981:429).

Finally, the decline in oil revenues affected the entire economy and society. Although macroeconomic data do not indicate a major crisis, they clearly show an economic decline. While the GDP had grown by 17.2 percent in 1976, its growth suddenly fell to -1.3 in 1977 and then dropped sharply to -11.9 in 1978. As the new economic policies curtailed all economic activities, the drop in revenues was felt throughout the economy. The production of large manufacturing firms declined, as did the value of industrial and non-oil exports (BMI 1977:111, 152). Carpet exports, the largest non-oil export, declined by 13 percent in both value and volume in 1977. The largest cotton textile mills had difficulty maintaining operation (Moaddel 1993:120). Shortages of funds and electricity along with slowed industrial production also provoked worker layoffs. In Tehran alone, tens of thousands of private housing projects were halted by lack of capital and construction materials (*Ettelaat*, November 16, 1977). Although the state and the oil sector continued to generate declining though still significant revenues, these resources did not trickle into the private sector during the recession. Combined with mounting economic inequalities, the recession adversely affected the interests of broad segments of the population and contributed to setting the stage for the emergence of social conflicts.

Nicaragua

As in Iran, Nicaraguan state policies were largely responsible for the economic development of the country. Despite some success, these development strategies failed to construct a strong, independent economic structure.

Although the formation of the Central American Common Market in the 1960s generated some industrial development in Nicaragua, it failed to produce genuine import substitution. In fact, industrial development only increased the country's external dependence. By 1974, Nicaragua imported 96 percent of the components used in the manufacture of rubber products, 95 percent of those used in electrical appliances, 88 percent in printing and publishing, 85 percent in metal products and 65 percent of the components of chemical products (Harris 1985:39).

Nicaraguan development was highly dependent on agroexports and the world market and, in consequence, was extremely vulnerable to fluctuations in the world economy.[8] Although the government succeeded in introducing some measure of diversification, the largest share of the country's exports was composed of only two commodities, coffee and cotton. Their portion of the total exports climbed from 37.1 percent in 1970 to 54.9 percent in 1977 (UN 1978:357). But after the 1973 oil shock, cotton producers, in particular, were adversely affected by the skyrocketing cost of petrochemicals, pesticides, and fertilizers. Between 1972 and 1977, prices of these commodities jumped by 408 percent, 117 percent, and 150 percent respectively. In contrast, the price that growers could get for their cotton increased by only 97 percent. Thus the cost of producing cotton, much of which was due to pesticides, exceeded the earnings of cotton exports by 1977–1978 (Paige 1985:101). Table 7 shows the changing prices for other commodities.

High oil prices in 1973–1975 and again from 1977 to 1981, combined with worldwide recession and rising international interest rates, produced negative reverberations throughout the Nicaraguan economy (Williams 1986:162). Shifting international prices led to declining terms of trade and an unfavorable balance of payments, as the prices of Nicaragua's agroexports deteriorated and the cost of imported manufactured goods rose (Harris 1985:37). Between 1960 and 1964, Nicaragua had enjoyed a surplus in the balance of payments of more than $132 million. By the mid-1960s, however, trade imbalances began to appear. Between 1965 and 1978, Nicaragua accumulated a negative trade balance of more than $8.2 billion (Vilas 1986:58).

[8] Other structural changes in the world market economy also complicated Nicaragua's crisis. The devaluation of the dollar, to which the córdoba was pegged, boosted the prices of Nicaraguan imports from countries other than the United States. Because 70 percent of Nicaragua's electric power was generated by oil, higher oil prices contributed to the country's inflation rate and reduced foreign exchange. Finally, despite rising coffee prices on the international market, Nicaragua's foreign exchange declined in response to the decreasing value of cotton, sugar, and meat exports.

Table 7   *Price increases of key commodities affecting Nicaraguan agriculture (percent)*

Commodity	1972–1977	1972–1978
Coffee	488	298
Oil	408	376
Fertilizer	150	160
Pesticide	117	117
Cotton	97	100
Beef	37	73

Source: Calculated from Williams (1986:207).

Rapidly accumulating foreign debt was exacerbated by continued government borrowing. By 1977, Nicaragua's foreign debt had reached $1 billion, a fourfold rise in six years and the highest debt in Central America. To finance earthquake reconstruction, the state contracted an uninterrupted string of loans from international sources, often on very unfavorable terms (*La Prensa*, July 2, 1978). The external public debt alone increased by 3,864 percent between 1970 and 1976 (*La Prensa*, January 8, 1978). By 1979, Nicaragua had amassed an external debt of $1.65 billion, mostly in the form of short-term credits with US commercial banks. This amount was equivalent to roughly $4,000 per family and was greater than Nicaragua's entire national income (Harris 1985:40). In 1978, foreign debt payments absorbed 23.6 percent of the country's export earnings. Elsewhere in Central America, in contrast, the figures were only 2.9 percent in Guatemala, 6.2 percent in El Salvador, 9.4 percent in Honduras, and 15.8 percent in Costa Rica (Baumeister 1985:16). By that time, the Nicaraguan government faced grave difficulties in meeting its international financial obligations.

External pressures and internal developments had adverse effects on the Nicaraguan economy, which in part set the stage for the political conflicts in the latter part of the 1970s. The Nicaraguan GDP, which had grown at an average annual rate of 6.4 percent during 1971–1974, dropped to 0.3 percent between 1975 and 1978. While the growth rate was a mere 0.9 in 1977, it fell to −6.9 in 1978. The consumer price index rose during 1972–1979, but in 1977 the average monthly salary declined for all sectors of the economy, except agriculture (Vilas 1986:92–97). These changes adversely affected the poorer segments of the population.

The Philippines

As in Iran and Nicaragua, government attempts to industrialize and diversify the Philippine economy did not succeed. By the mid-1980s, the economy was heavily dependent on a few agricultural crops whose earnings had been declining. The Philippines' most important exports were coconut and coconut products, the prices of which fell in the world market by 30 percent in 1980. Earlier, the new National Coconut Authority, confident that the Philippines controlled more than 60 percent of the world coconut oil market, raised prices drastically even though world market commodity prices were weak. When palm oil investments matured at the same time, however, consumers easily switched, and the coconut oil market collapsed, affecting 16 million Filipinos, or roughly one-third of the country (Overholt 1986:1150). By late 1982, the world price for sugar, the country's second most important export, hit a ten-year low. Dismal commodity prices for coconuts, sugar, and copper resulted in a 42 percent deterioration in the financial returns of trade for the Philippines (ibid.:1149). These problems were exacerbated by the dramatic increase in the price of oil that began in the latter part of the 1970s. For example, in 1980, more than 43 percent of the country's export proceeds went to purchase oil imports.

A major consequence of declining export earnings was increasing difficulty in meeting international financial obligations. By the end of 1982, the country was in the midst of its worst balance of payments crisis (Villegas 1986b:145). That autumn, the Philippine Central Bank was warned by at least one major US bank that immediate rescheduling was required to avoid an economic tragedy. By January 1983, the Philippines' external debt had reached an estimated $16.6 billion, while the debt service payment for that year was $7 billion, which accounted for 79 percent of the country's exports (*Time*, January 10, 1983; IBON, January 31, 1983).[9] Government officials met with the Japanese prime minister and informed him that the Philippine financial situation was desperate unless the Japanese bailed out the country (Overholt 1986:1154). Aware of the approaching crisis, the Central Bank began to falsify its reserves and current account statistics.

Official reserves continued to decline by $1.4 billion between December 1982 and July 1983, even before the political crisis ignited by Aquino's assassination, and they dropped by another $0.2 billion in August and September (Overholt 1986:1153). During the entire year of 1984, the country had barely enough foreign exchange to import oil and

[9] The source of *Time*'s report was Morgan Guaranty Trust Company.

food. Marcos blamed the financial crisis on the country's increased dependency on world market forces. Critics charged, however, that the debt trap was the consequence of his own policies (Wurfel 1988:337).

Rising international debt and declining earnings repeatedly forced the government to borrow more money from international banks and financial institutions to meet its obligations. During martial law, the state borrowed on an unprecedented scale from more than 480 international creditors to finance its development projects. Yet, as economic conditions continued to deteriorate and the country could not meet its financial obligations, the government had to resort to additional borrowing. Every time the government borrowed money, the IMF imposed certain conditions on the Philippines, resulting in further adverse conditions. The IMF conditions often included devaluation, reduction of state intervention and regulation of the economy, elimination of price controls, tightening of credit, and reduction of tariffs, which often caused bankruptcies and a rise in unemployment. Currency devaluation was among the most severe consequences of these economic problems. Between 1965 and 1985, the value of the Philippines peso dropped by 80 percent *vis-à-vis* the US dollar.

Another difficulty resulting from the country's economic dependence and decline involved foreign investment and capital flight, which became a feature of the Philippine economy. In 1980, foreign investors withdrew more than $100 million in equity capital, by far the largest annual amount on record. In the first six months of that year, 137,000 factory jobs evaporated. By 1983, major automobile assemblers stopped operation. When Ford Philippines closed down, 10,000 workers were dismissed (Hackenberg and Hackenberg 1987:224). Between 1972 and 1986, Filipino entrepreneurs divested more than $12 billion out of the Philippines (Boyce 1993:295), an amount constituting more than 44 percent of the national debt.

Economic deterioration and capital flight in the latter part of Marcos' rule resulted in the collapse of a large number of enterprises, which intensified the government's problems. The financial upheavals led to crisis in most of the manufacturing firms owned by Marcos' cronies, most notably the Construction and Development Corporation of the Philippines, the Herdis Group, the Disini Group, and the Silverio Group. The collapse of large firms backed by government guarantees quickly made the state owner of some 230 ailing firms (Overholt 1986:1150). From 1978 to 1982, state loans to government corporations to rescue these firms jumped nearly tenfold, from 2.6 billion pesos to 22 billion, which represented an increase from 9.9 percent to 22 percent of total government expenditures (Javate-de Dios, et al. 1988:89). In 1985 Marcos announced that the deficit of fifteen of the largest government corporations alone amounted to approximately 10.2 billion pesos in just one year (*Malaya*, April 9, 1985).

The economic decline of the early 1980s also affected the financial sector and generated instability in the banking system. The Banco Filipino failed in 1984, forcing the government to step in and rescue it in order to keep the entire banking system operational (*Malaya*, August 6, 1984). Following Banco Filipino's "bank holiday," most of the country's commercial banks froze lending activities in an attempt to conserve liquidity (*Malaya*, April 10, 1984). This condition further contributed to the economic downturn.

Finally, declining international earnings and internal difficulties affected macro-economic indicators. Although the government's economic policies had initially generated impressive growth, by the end of Marcos' rule macro-economic indicators showed a major downturn. While the GDP growth rate during the first seven years of martial law had averaged better than 6 percent, the growth rate dropped to −3.6 percent between 1981 and 1985. After the assassination of Aquino in 1983, the crisis intensified. In both 1984 and 1985, GDP growth rate declined by 7.3 percent. In 1984, inflation was averaging 50 percent for the year,[10] and a drop in industrial production had led to layoffs of more than 400,000 workers (Villegas 1986b:145). The economic slide had a severe effect on per capita income, which declined some 14 percent between 1983 and 1985 (Villegas 1986a:135). The economic downturn contributed to setting the stage for social and political conflicts.

Conclusion

These states attempted to develop these countries through greater intervention in the economy during the period under investigation. In comparative terms Iran, which possessed greater resources, was the most interventionist. The Philippines, the poorest of the three, was the least interventionist. Nicaragua, whose intervention expanded particularly after the 1972 earthquake, was between the two extremes.

As evidence presented above indicates, intervention in all cases had positive results on economic growth in the initial stages. Yet state intervention also generated the seeds of contradictions and conflicts. Despite state autonomy from the upper classes, government development strategies served particular rather than general interests. Beyond serving the

---

[10] The inflation rate in Metro Manila reached 40 percent in February 1984, the highest since World War II (*Malaya*, May 4, 1984). In August, the rate climbed to 60 percent (*Malaya*, August 16, 1984).

interests of state rulers and their allies, state policies enriched only fractions of the capitalist class. Invariably, these policies excluded broad segments of the population, particularly the working classes. In the end, state policies, combined with rapid economic development, increased social and economic inequalities.

These developments were accompanied by the growing integration of these economies into the world market, which was beyond their control. State development strategies in all three countries made their economies vulnerable to international economic change because of increased economic dependence on the world market and international financial institutions. The economies of these countries were particularly vulnerable to fluctuations in the world market because these economies had become dependent on a single or a few commodities, which they could produce for sale in the world economy. Even Iran, which benefited enormously from increased oil revenues, was negatively affected by a decline in the world demand for oil in 1975. In response, the state was forced to cut domestic credit, raise interest rates and taxes, and scrap a number of ambitious projects, all of which had a deleterious effect on the economy and society. Similarly, dependence on international financial institutions generated economic difficulties for the population in the Philippines. High foreign debts and a balance of payments problem that necessitated repeated currency devaluation had a negative economic impact, invoking rising inflation and a sudden drop in the standard of living of large segments of the population. This, in turn, generated nationalist tendencies directed against the United States, multilateral agencies, and the state itself.

Eventually, internal changes and external pressures generated economic downturns that set the stage for conflicts. Because of increased intervention in the economy, the three states rendered themselves vulnerable to challenge and attack. Had the crises or the downturns and rising inequalities been generated through the market mechanism alone, these states might have escaped major political crises. But increased state intervention in the economy precluded that outcome, and once social conflicts erupted, these states became targets of attack.

Part II

Mobilization and collective action

Prelude

Under highly repressive regimes, social movement actors may mobilize and engage in collective action when opportunities become available. Favorable opportunities for collective action emerge when repression declines or the state becomes vulnerable to challenge and attack. Repressive regimes that are highly dependent on external powers may have to introduce changes and reforms that are recommended or demanded by their more powerful outside supporters. In the context of weak social bases of support, external pressures to liberalize or open up the polity may generate conditions for large-scale insurgency. Furthermore, reduction of external support may render dependent regimes vulnerable to challenge and attack, which may also be a result of economic and political crises among states generally. In times of national polarization, regimes that have weak bases of support may become vulnerable if they resort to repressive measures to intimidate the opposition. Repressive measures against public figures and well-known challengers may render the state vulnerable by generating a coalition among opposition organizations and major segments of the population.

Opportunities, vulnerabilities, and collective action

Given that the Shah's regime was so dependent on outside support, external pressures played an important role in leading the Iranian government to undertake minimal gestures that provided an opportunity for opposition to mobilize. Amnesty International, the International Commission of Jurists, and the UN-affiliated International League for Human Rights began to expose the Iranian government's violations of human rights in the mid-1970s. Amnesty International accused Iran of being one of the world's "worst violators of human rights." In the 1976 US presidential campaign, Jimmy Carter singled out Iran as a country where human rights had been violated (Abrahamian 1982:498–500). Members of the American Congress began to question the wisdom of selling so much weaponry to a regime in which power resided solely in one man.

After hearing evidence presented by two of the aforementioned organizations, the chairman of the House of Representatives' Subcommittee on International Organization declared that the Iranian regime could not be considered stable unless it permitted "popular input," created democratic structures, and allowed democratic freedoms (ibid.:499–500).

Although the Carter administration did not really press the Shah to introduce major political changes (Sullivan 1981:19–20), the Shah, having been dependent on the United States for so long, decided it was necessary to introduce minor changes to improve his record on human rights. Thus the Iranian government initiated small policy changes in its treatment of political opponents. In March 1977, the government released 256 political prisoners and in May permitted the International Red Cross to visit others. It also introduced legal changes, which provided civilian trials for political opponents who criticized the government.

The introduction of an element of vulnerability into the Shah's regime prompted the opposition to quickly seize upon the opportunity. As a result of these changes, secular, leftist, and moderate political groups began mobilizing for collective action. Defunct organizations such as the National Front and the Writers' Association were revived by early June 1977 and began publishing statements demanding political freedom and reform. By the fall, students throughout the country were undertaking collective action against the regime. In 1978, student protests were expanded and followed by forty-day cycles of mourning and closures of the bazaars. These protests in turn forced the regime to proclaim greater reforms and liberalization at the end of the summer of 1978. The proclamations then led to the expansion of the mobilization by the industrial working class and the population of smaller cities in the fall of 1978. The result was an upsurge of mobilization and collective action. Prior to the proclamation of liberalization, approximately seventy cities had experienced some form of collective action. After a military government stepped in some ten weeks later, roughly a hundred additional cities were rocked by anti-government collective action.

The Somozas in Nicaragua too were politically dependent on the United States for decades. This friendly relationship underwent a change with the election of President Carter, who pressed Somoza to respect human rights. US policy shifted following reports by American military attachés which declared that, after they had worked with the Nicaraguan National Guard in rural "counter-insurgency" operations for two years, the guerrilla threat had been eliminated. On the basis of this information, the Carter administration urged Somoza to rescind martial law (Walker 1985a:20). Extreme political dependence on the United States now prevented the Nicaraguan leader from pursuing an autonomous domestic policy. Hence Somoza, who also believed that the FSLN had been eliminated, repealed the state of siege on September 19, 1977. The subsequent reduction of repression provided a critical opportunity for mobilization, and the opposition responded with alacrity.

In the months that followed, the Carter administration pursued policies that often adversely affected the Somoza regime and advanced the opposition's ability to mobilize and act collectively, even though for much of this time the United States had no declared policy of replacing Somoza's rule. Early on, Carter administration officials attempted to make US aid contingent on human rights improvements. Low interest AID loans were reportedly suspended because of administrative inefficiency and personal gains by Nicaraguan officials from land purchased at inflated prices for housing construction with AID funds (*La Prensa*, October 5, 1977).

The lifting of the state of siege rapidly expanded political mobilization by segments of the Nicaraguan population against the regime. The assassination of Pedro Chamorro in January 1978 intensified popular mobilization and led the capitalist class to join the opposition.

As popular collective action exploded in the wake of Chamorro's assassination, the US ambassador went so far as to suggest that Somoza announce his retirement from politics and the army when his term expired in 1981, and on February 28, 1978 the Nicaraguan president complied and announced this intention (Somoza 1980:107). On June 30, President Carter wrote a letter to Somoza Debayle expressing encouragement of his steps to improve human rights, but three weeks later, the US administration warned Somoza that if he re-imposed martial law or repressed the opposition, the USA might break relations with Nicaragua (ibid.:144–145). The US government also withheld arms sales to Nicaragua and blocked an IMF loan in November. Somoza rejected the OAS election guidelines issued on December 20, and on February 8, 1979, the United States announced a number of measures designed to force his resignation, according to Somoza (ibid.: 416).

Equally significantly, the USA intervened directly to prevent Somoza from repressing the opposition. When the Nicaraguan government filed charges against Los Doce, twelve opposition leaders, for allegedly conducting "subversive activities" in Costa Rica, the US embassy in Managua objected and compelled Somoza to withdraw them (Somoza 1980:105). Upon their return, Los Doce traveled to most of the country's major cities, mobilizing the opposition and calling for the regime's overthrow with virtual impunity. Somoza complained, "My cabinet and I knew that if we touched one of them, the US Embassy would come down on us with full force" (ibid.:106).

At each step, the policy decisions made by the Carter administration had a decisive effect on the opposition's ability to mobilize against Somoza. In particular, US pressure on the Nicaraguan leader to announce his retirement, and his subsequent compliance, spurred activity by the opposition. The threat of ruptured relations with the USA restrained the Nicaraguan leader from shutting down the anti-government press and jailing opposition leaders.

Unlike in Nicaragua, the United States did not play an aggressive role in the opening stage of the conflicts in the Philippines. In the context of growing popular mobilization in response to Aquino's assassination and the rising threat of communism, the United States gradually shifted its policies towards Marcos and pressured him to introduce reforms. Yet, due to conservative ascendancy and political divisions, it took the United States a long time to fully break with Marcos, which enabled him to avoid serious changes and remain in power.

After the murder of Aquino, US ambassadors Armacost and Bosworth created diplomatic distance between the USA and Marcos. The first sign of a policy shift came when Ambassador Armacost attended a funeral mass for Aquino (*Malaya*, September 9, 1984). Later, Ambassador Bosworth stated that: "We seek leaders who are accountable through democratic procedures, economic decisions that can stand the test of competition in the marketplace, and ideas that are subjected to free debate" (Diokno 1988:167).

But Washington's position did not change drastically until the summer of 1985 once it became clear that Marcos would rather see a communist Philippines than relinquish personal advantages. Reagan sent Senator Laxalt to Manila to press for presidential elections, but Washington did not reduce military and economic support (Overholt 1986:1161). Finally, the US government held up wheat and rice sales for several months to force the Marcos regime into making economic reforms (*Malaya*, July 17, 1985). The US House of Representatives slashed $75 million in military aid from the Philippines' assistance package (*Malaya*, July 17, 1985). The USA wanted a stable succession because Marcos' health was seriously deteriorating.

Eventually, these pressures were successful in forcing Marcos to hold an early presidential election. Although his term was set until 1987, he announced a snap election the first week of November 1985, and then secretly attempted to manipulate the Supreme Court to invalidate the election result (Chapman 1987:236). The Supreme Court rejected Marcos' plan. US pressure and popular mobilization combined to make the Supreme Court, long controlled by Marcos, more autonomous. Marcos' coalition was clearly weakening, and his forces became so disorganized that they were unable to undertake what was necessary to insure his election victory as smoothly as they had done on previous occasions. In the end, the USA succeeded in affecting the final outcome of the Filipino conflicts.

In sum, the USA played a part in the conflicts of all three countries, but clearly could not determine their outcomes. A very mild US pressure in Iran resulted in the reduction of repression and provided favorable opportunity for the opposition to mobilize. Although the United States favored the removal of the Shah, it could not control the ultimate outcome, namely, the elimination of liberals and formation of a theocratic state. US policy was more consistent and more resolute towards Somoza in Nicaragua. US pressures were crucial in providing opportunities for mobilization in the opening stages of the Nicaraguan conflicts. As occurred in Iran, the USA favored the ouster of Somoza but could not prevent the FSLN from assuming complete power and excluding the moderate elements in the revolutionary government. In contrast to Iran and Nicaragua, the United States did not play a major role in the initial stages of the conflicts in the Philippines. But it eventually did pressure Marcos to hold elections, which enabled the moderate forces to affect the outcome of the conflicts.

The next four chapters will analyze collective actions and interactions of students, clergy, workers, and capitalists. The analysis will focus on objective and articulated interest, organization, opportunity structures, demands and ideologies of these actors to present a comprehensive picture of the causes and the processes of revolutions in the three countries.

4   Students: relentless revolutionaries

Social theorists have often maintained that social revolutions generally do not begin with revolutionary intentions and that the causes and the processes of revolutions cannot be understood in ideological terms (Skocpol 1979:17). Analysts of large-scale social conflicts have argued that the collective actions of ordinary people and working classes are, by and large, conservative in nature and involve attempts to defend and preserve established rights (Calhoun 1983; Goldstone 1991b: 419–420; Hobsbawm 1973:12; Migdal 1974:248; Moore 1978:351–352; Scott 1979:129). These analyses, which originated largely from the European historical experience, cannot be applied to students in contemporary revolutions in developing countries. Students in developing countries have been at the forefront of revolutionary struggles and have revealed a very intense interest in fundamentally transforming the social structures. They have enjoyed immense prestige and have often played a very significant role in the revolutionary process. But even scholars of revolutions in contemporary developing countries have failed to examine the significant role of students in revolutions.

As relentless revolutionaries, students have leapt to the forefront of the insurgencies in both timing and frequency of collective action in contemporary social revolutions in developing countries. Highly concentrated in colleges and universities, students possess extensive communication networks, which facilitate their collective action. Students in higher education often benefit from universities' relative autonomy – where it exists – and academic freedom, which provide them, at least theoretically, with immunity and insulation from state repression. A certain amount of such immunity also derives from the fact that, historically, students have been drawn from relatively privileged social backgrounds and often occupy relatively high-ranking positions after graduation. Together these factors enable students to mobilize rapidly during periods of insurgency. High levels of mobilization, conflict, or repression on one campus can potentially lead to conflicts on campuses elsewhere. Given the considerable prestige and respect that students and universities usually enjoy in society, student mobilization has the potential to escalate conflicts in the rest of the country, even though students may be concentrated in only a few major cities. In combination, these factors help explain the leading role played by students in political insurgency.

Students have also been in the vanguard of ideological struggles as well, exhibiting a decided propensity to break with the past and oriented toward reconstructing the entire social order. They have consistently opposed exclusive rule and centralization of state power, highly authoritarian and repressive regimes, and rising social inequality produced by state development strategies. Lacking direct involvement in the mode of production, students do not generally present economic claims, except when defending the interests of the working classes. Instead, students develop greater interest in theoretical and ideological issues, especially because they are immersed in the production and reproduction of knowledge and ideas. The relative autonomy of universities and immunity of students from repression inevitably provide them with much greater social space than other groups in which to engage in ideological debate over the shape of the social structure and the allocation of power and privilege. Ideological debates perhaps were further stimulated when higher education expanded, and universities admitted students from diverse backgrounds. Universities and colleges have commonly been the main centers for revolutionary and leftist political organizations. In addition, students have tended to form radical coalitions with workers against the state and the upper class. Thus, students, along with dissident intellectuals, are often the avant-garde of revolutionary movements. Because of their political and ideological struggles, students, despite theoretical immunity, have often been the principal targets of government repression.

For several reasons, students in many developing countries were attracted to some form of socialist movement in the latter part of the twentieth century. First, students often opposed those governments and ruling classes that were supported by the United States. Students shifted toward socialism to oppose the alliance by their rulers with the USA, the principal defender of international capitalism. Second, students were attracted to socialism because of revolutions in China, Cuba, and Vietnam, and perhaps to some extent because of the rise of the New Left student movement in Europe and the United States. Third, students in many developing countries were led to advocate the building of egalitarian, alternative social orders by rising inequalities generated by state-sponsored capitalist development strategies, which adversely affected broad segments of the population. Fourth, student politics were tilted to the left and to socialism with the expansion of higher education and the entry of students from middle- and working-class backgrounds. Consequently, students in developing countries often embraced revolutionary movements, which advocated egalitarian and radical social transformations.

Although a small minority of the population, students in all three countries remained in the forefront of political insurgency in the years prior to the overthrow of these regimes. During the major political conflicts, students were often the first social group to engage in collective action, and they did so more frequently than other groups and classes. They were also more ideological and revolutionary than other groups and often favored the complete alteration of the state and the social structure. Student opposition to state power was a response to exclusive rule and increased social inequalities. As privilege became increasingly coupled with access to the state in all three cases, students developed a unique interest in restructuring the state and the social order. As a result, students together with dissident intellectuals in all three countries formed radical organizations, which advocated armed struggles. They were indeed relentless revolutionaries. The dominant ideological trend in all three countries was some variation of socialism or Marxism, except in Iran where leftist students competed with an Islamic minority.

In comparative terms, the three cases exhibit variations in students' organization and capacity for collective action. In Iran and the Philippines many students lived in campus dormitories, which facilitated their mobilization. But Iranian students were the most repressed and least organized, while Nicaraguan and Filipino students enjoyed relatively high levels of organization. Intense repression and the lack of university-wide organizations in Iran meant that their collective actions in the early revolutionary struggles were often short-lived. In contrast, students in Nicaragua and the Philippines were able to organize prior to the insurgencies and launch relatively sustained collective actions.

The students' role in affecting the outcome of the conflicts was contradictory. On the one hand, frequent student mobilization and insurgency were important components of the challenges to the regime and encouraged other social groups to mobilize. On the other hand, students' intense ideological orientation sometimes targeted both the state and the capitalist class, intensified social conflicts, and prevented the formation of broad coalitions. The absence of such coalitions often reduced the likelihood of revolutions. Students' political and ideological orientation in Nicaragua and the Philippines in the early 1970s contributed to the intensification of class conflict and thus prevented the formation of broad coalitions. Filipino students' politics after the assassination of Aquino until the final stages of the conflicts played a similar role and contributed to the absence of a broad coalition in the Philippines. In Iran and Nicaragua, however, students joined the coalitions that opposed the Shah and Somoza and contributed to the overthrow of both regimes in 1979.

Iranian students and the revolutionary struggles

Although neglected by analysts of the Iranian revolution, particularly those who base their explanations on ideology, students were always in the forefront of Iran's political conflicts and became the principal targets of violent repression. In the decades prior to the revolution, the Iranian student movement produced important political leaders and organizations. Student activists in the 1950s and 1960s later became the leaders of moderate political and professional organizations, which challenged the regime in the initial stages of the revolution. The student movement also produced the leading guerrilla organizations, the Iranian People's Fedayee Guerrillas (Feda'iyan) and the Iranian People's Mojahedeen Organization (Mojahedeen), which launched daring attacks against the regime in the 1970s. Students were the principal supporters of these organizations in the 1960s and much of the 1970s, and stood alone as the only voice of opposition against the government during years of political repression and demobilization.

Students' intense and significant struggles during the revolutionary conflicts attracted the attention and admiration of Islamic leaders. Ayatollah Khomeini and his clerical supporters repeatedly praised students and called the universities bastions of struggle against the Shah's dictatorship and imperialism. Khomeini specifically urged an alliance between university people and the clergy. He asked intellectuals and university students at the end of 1977 not to reject the clergy because they lacked political education. He even suggested that if the clergy were not politically educated, intellectuals should educate them (Khomeini 1983, vol. I:434–437).

Tehran University, the country's oldest institution of higher education, enjoyed great prestige and, in 1978, was referred to as the "bastion of freedom." The contributions of students were recognized during important religious occasions when marchers stood in front of Tehran University and hailed them (*Kayhan*, September 4, 1978). Shortly before the monarch's ouster, Tehran University became the favorite venue for opposition leaders because of the prestige and publicity it afforded. A group of Khomeini's clerical supporters took refuge there and demanded his return from France in early February 1979, when the government had initially blocked it. Mehdi Bazargan, the first prime minister of the Islamic Republic, announced some of his major proposals at the university on February 9, just two days before the Shah fled, and the new regime chose it as the site of their Friday prayers, in part because of the relentless struggles of students and the prestige of the university.

In broad outline, student opposition to the monarchy was a response to exclusive rule, greater state intervention in the economy, political central-ization, repression, and rising social inequalities. Students opposed the removal of Dr. Mosaddegh from power and the subsequent repression of moderate political organizations that led to the establishment of an ex-clusive rule in Iran. Increased state intervention also affected the careers of students after graduation. Because economic power resided in the state, those who sought material reward and privilege required access to political power as well. Hence, large, though declining, proportions of college graduates inevitably ended up working for the government after graduation. To obtain the best positions, proper connections were necessary. Students who lacked such connections had a compelling rea-son to oppose the government, especially as power and resources became increasingly centralized. Students' conflicts with the government during the final years of the monarchy were exacerbated by the government's policy of granting free tuition in exchange for working for the state after graduation (Menashri 1992:249–253).

In the decade preceding the revolution, several factors radicalized students' politics and led to their ideological shift, radicalization, and support for noninstitutional means of struggle. First, the removal of Dr. Mosaddegh from power and the formation of exclusive rule in 1963 had a powerful impact on the student movement. Specifically, government repression in 1963 eliminated all institutional options for political mobil-ization and led some students to favor alternative options for struggle. Second, the conservatism and eventual demobilization of the National Front's leaders impelled students to break away from the Front, never to follow its lead thereafter (Parsa 1989:170). Third, the student movement was also influenced by the nature of the alliance between the monarchy and the United States. Students opposed American support for the repressive rule and their movements revealed an anti-American charac-ter. Fourth, the rise of the Marxist Feda'iyan and the Mojahedeen, which advocated a classless Islamic society, actively challenged the regime throughout the 1970s.[1] Finally, the expansion of higher education in-creasingly brought in students from less well-off families, some of whom had difficulties obtaining the basic necessities. These students were only too aware of their own and the country's socio-economic problems and generally favored radical transformation of the social structure (*Kayhan International*, October 9, 1978).

[1] On the rise and struggles of the Mojahedeen, see Abrahamian (1989).

Over the past several decades, Iranian students have embraced nationalism, socialism, Marxism, and some variations of Islam. The rise of
political organizations often played an important role in inspiring students and their ideologies. In the 1940s and early 1950s, the Iranian
student movement was strongly influenced by the socialist and nationalist
movements present on the national scene, which divided the activist
students into two camps. The influence of the communists, the Tudeh
Party, was effectively eliminated from universities by the repression that
followed the *coup d'état* of 1953. Instead, student activists until the early
1960s, including socialists and Marxists, joined the second National
Front. The secular nature of the student movement was evident in June
1963 when, with individual exceptions, university students did not join
the uprising sparked by Khomeini's arrest (Parsa 1994). Students at
Tehran University remained on campus, shouted slogans against dictatorship and in favor of Mosaddegh, and prominently displayed a banner
proclaiming, "The murderous and bloodthirsty Shah spills the blood of
the people" (Jazani 1979:130–131).

The political repression of 1963 led some students and intellectuals to
adopt an Islamic ideology. In the following years, a sizable minority of
students supported some form of an Islamic society. A handful backed
Ayatollah Khomeini and his politics. A larger segment of activists who
advocated Islamic socialism often supported the Islamic Mojahedeen.
Mojahedeen supporters actually accepted the Marxist materialist interpretation of history and proclaimed their goal of establishing a classless
Islamic society. The Mojahedeen grew in part as a result of the writings
and speeches of Ali Shariati, an advocate of Islamic socialism.

Despite some successes, Islamic socialists in the universities soon experienced a decline. The Mojahedeen were subjected to a massive repression in which more than a hundred members and leaders of the organization were arrested and imprisoned (Abrahamian 1989:128). In 1972
government repression also closed down the Hoseinieh Ershad Islamic
center where Ali Shariati had criticized both traditional Islamic clergy and
Marxism for three years. Shariati was arrested once the government
realized that he was an Islamic socialist who promoted the cause of a
classless Islamic society. The Mojahedeen experienced another setback
in 1975 when a segment of the organization adopted Marxism-Leninism
and discarded Islamic ideology. In all, government repression and internal divisions brought about the disorganization and demobilization of the
Mojahedeen.

Thus, the student movement and ideology during the 1970s remained
largely within the secular, socialist camp, although a sizable minority still
advocated some sort of an Islamic society even as they cooperated with

the secular socialists. Most politicized, activist students adhered to secular socialist ideology, illustrated by the fact that every year university students throughout the country observed the Shanzdah-e Azar. On that day, students commemorated the slaying of three students by the government in 1953 during the visit of then-vice-president Richard Nixon. Shanzdah-e Azar became the unofficial student day and was always marked by rallies and protests. In sharp contrast, students never held any observances on June 5, the date of a rebellion sparked in part by the arrest of Ayatollah Khomeini in 1963. Nor did students ever commemorate the date Khomeini was exiled from Iran.[2] Most activist students supported the Feda'iyan which, during years of repression and silence on the part of the general populace, initiated armed struggle against the government. The government was fully aware of students' support for the Feda'iyan and often repressed the socialists. For example, fearing student insurgency after the Feda'iyan began fighting in Siahkal in 1971, the government decreed a week-long, unscheduled vacation in Tehran's universities (Abrahamian 1982:488). Nevertheless, students commemorated the Feda'iyan slain in Siahkal in March and persisted in mourning martyred Feda'iyan in the years that followed. On one occasion in 1976, student demonstrations for the Feda'iyan martyrs were so intense that the Shah ordered two major universities to close, though he quickly reversed his decision for fear of sparking an even greater uproar (Alam 1991:488). Aware of students' strong support for the Feda'iyan, the Shah once remarked, "the dangerous young communists had made universities their primary bastions" (Kian 1993:465).

Students' capacity for collective action was affected by government policies in contradictory ways. On the one hand, their ability to mobilize and act collectively was unintentionally heightened by state policies designed to expand higher education and increase the numbers of students in post-secondary institutions. The number of students rose to 160,000 in 1978–1979 from 22,882 in 1961–1962. Tehran alone had more than 81,000 students in institutions of higher education in 1978. This concentration in schools and dormitories provided students with a ready-made communication network and enhanced their ability to mobilize in times of social conflict. In addition, greater numbers of students of a lower socio-economic status were drawn from provincial cities and towns; some of them were attracted to leftist or religious ideologies.

On the other hand, students' capacity for mobilization was adversely affected by government policies and repression. University autonomy, immunity, and academic freedom were regularly violated by the state's

[2] The only exception was just a few months before the revolution, on November 4, 1978, when some students were aware of the anniversary of Khomeini's exile.

direct intervention in institutions of higher education. Students were forbidden to organize or engage in political activities on campus. The government maintained a campus guard and office of "Student Affairs," which was allegedly tied to SAVAK and represented a source of conflict. As a result, students had great difficulty building organizations and holding open political and ideological discussions and debates. Faced with these obstacles, students employed two main strategies to carry their ideological activities. The first was mountain climbing – a favorite activity of leftists – away from cities and the authorities. When discovered by the government, large numbers of students were often arrested and injured during these excursions (*Ettelaat*, April 22, 1978). A second option for organizing and ideological discussions was the maintenance of dissident political and religious books in unofficial student libraries. In the fall of 1977, just as political conflicts were intensifying, the government systematically attacked these libraries and confiscated their books.

In spite of these difficulties, in the final decade of the monarchy, students were the only major collectivity to oppose the government. During the revolutionary struggles, students initiated some of the most important collective actions that marked the beginning of the insurgencies that eventually culminated in the revolution. Students began sustained activism against the Shah in the fall of 1977, when the government's limited reforms provided an opportunity for the secular intelligentsia to mobilize against the regime and demand political change. In early 1977, an opening was created by a law declaring that all political detainees had to be charged or released within twenty-four hours and that trials for political opponents were to be held in civilian, rather than military, courts. In response to this legal reform, students' usual preoccupation with educative matters dwindled as they converted colleges into centers for political opposition and information. Between the fall of 1977 and that of 1978, students organized more actions than any other collectivity. In the ten largest cities of the country, students organized 128 demonstrations. These early actions often consisted of short-lived events, such as shouting anti-government slogans in the streets or on university campuses. In Tehran students organized eighty-four demonstrations and rallies, thirty-nine of which were short-lived rallies manifesting opposition to university authorities and the government. In addition, students boycotted class forty-eight times to protest against political repression.[3]

---

[3] The data presented were in large part collected from various sources that included *Ettelaat*, *Kayhan*, *Rastakhiz*, *Payam-e Mojahed*, *Zamimeh-e Khabar Nameh*, *Payman*, *Shanzdah-e Azar*, and occasional pamphlets published by various opposition organizations. Interviews with a large number of people who were students at the time of the revolution constituted another major source of information.

Student protests occurred independently of actions by the clergy, as convincingly evidenced by the timing of such protests. During the first three-and-a-half months of the 1977–1978 academic year, students held at least twenty rallies and demonstrations and twenty-one class boycotts, even before segments of the clergy were mobilized by the massacre of Qom clerical students in January 1978.[4] These student events were organized primarily by leftists, not religious groups, and took place before the clergy mobilized. In fact, mobilization and collective action by students were factors in the clergy's own mobilization, which emerged later. It was also in the fall of 1977 that students took the lead and shouted the slogan of "Death to the Shah." Even when clerics finally mobilized and opposed the monarchy, university students never invited any clergy to participate or speak at the various campus events held during the last eighteen months of the monarchy.

Secular, leftist students were in the forefront of the revolutionary struggles. These students came in large numbers to fourteen nights of poetry reading organized by intellectuals to criticize the regime. Participation by leftist students was especially large because, of sixty-four poets and writers invited to participate, some 66 percent were leftist, 28 percent were liberal-nationalist, and only 6.3 percent followed some sort of Islamic ideology. The growing popularity of these events as occasions for student mobilization led to government repression, which eventually put an end to the poetry nights. At what turned out to be the final such event Saeed Sultanpour, a Marxist poet and playwright, was scheduled to speak about art and its influence on society when conflict erupted outside the hall and some fifty students were arrested. Instead of his prepared speech, Sultanpour reacted by reading his revolutionary poetry. The audience decided to stay in the building as a spontaneous overnight protest against the students' arrests (Parsa 1989:178). The next day as students left the building, anti-government demonstrations broke out, and students shouted radical, leftist slogans, such as "Solidarity! Struggle! Victory!", "Workers' Government," and "Death to the Shah." The left's momentum was checked when government repression put an end to subsequent poetry nights. In contrast to the popular secular poetry nights, student attendance at religious activities and protests during the fall of 1977 was much smaller and less enthusiastic.[5] In a series of lectures held in Ghoba Mosque the speakers, including Mehdi Bazargan, who later became the

---

[4] Students' activities were so intense that by the end of the fall term, many colleges were almost completely closed down. The situation led the government to organize a rally of 5,000 in Tehran University on its own behalf, condemning the students (*Payam-e Mojahed* 1978, No. 53).

[5] My source is Assef Bayat (interview, April 1998) who participated in both sets of events.

first prime minister of the Islamic Republic, Dr. Payman, and other modernist Islamic intellectuals, attacked rival secular, materialist, and Marxist ideologies (Bayat 1998:150).

Leftist student supporters of the Marxist Feda'iyan organized the largest student demonstration of the year – tens of thousands of people – at Tehran University in December 1977 to commemorate Shanzdah-e Azar. In Rezaieh, university students even shouted pro-Feda'iyan slogans. A few weeks later, on December 25, Marxist students at Tehran University organized an even larger rally against the government.[6] As conflicts escalated, students attacked university guards and officials whom they identified as agents of repression. In a few instances, students even assaulted statues of the Shah, and at the National University and Tabriz University, they succeeded in pulling down the Shah's statue. Even students on traditionally nonpolitical campuses, such as the all-female Farah University, demonstrated and shouted slogans demanding freedom for political prisoners and "Solidarity! Struggle! Victory!" Their actions resulted in a number of arrests and surprised Islamic observers (*Payam-e Mojahed*, No. 53:7). Student protests were so intense during the fall of 1977 that they resulted in the virtual closure of the campuses before the end of the term.

The government quickly responded to student mobilization and growing politicization with threats and repression. Universities throughout the country, but especially in Tehran, were repeatedly attacked by government forces. Students' libraries were ransacked in the fall of 1977 and their books confiscated. A large number of students were expelled from colleges and universities, while many others were imprisoned. University officials in Tehran announced in December 1977 that the universities would close unless classes filled up (*Kayhan International*, December 6, 1977). At Tehran University, all classes in the economics department, with the exception of those for first-year students, were suspended that fall. To counter student strikes, the government organized a rally of some 5,000 persons at Tehran University the day following the large Shanzdah-e Azar demonstration. The rally organizers issued a statement expressing resentment and anxiety over the violent events at the university and demanding that classes resume (*Kayhan International*, December 8, 1977). The government-controlled media reported that the participants were concerned parents of university students, but opponents charged that the participants were largely government employees. Occasionally, government forces used extreme measures to repress students. For example, in May the following year, a student dormitory in Tehran (Amir

---

[6] One source, a film titled *Iran: A Revolution Betrayed*, shows glimpses of this event and estimates that 100,000 people participated in the event.

Abad-e Shomali) was attacked by government forces (*Ettelaat*, May 31, 1978), who fought with students for several hours; several students were killed, and many were injured.

The promise of political reforms and reduction of repression in the fall of 1978 deepened political divisions among students. Pro-Khomeini students, a decided minority in most universities when the insurgency began, gradually gained new adherents by the fall when new political opportunities emerged. The promise of political liberalization by Prime Minister Sharif-Emami and a temporary reduction in repression generated mobilization among religious students who had been inactive in the initial stage of the insurgency. The politicization of these students expanded support for the pro-Khomeini camp. Many of these students had been nonpolitical individuals who came from smaller cities and towns and lacked preexisting connections to the other students at the universities. They had not previously been exposed to secular, radical university politics. The pro-Khomeini student faction also attracted some additional support from backers of the leftist Islamic Mojahedeen. They also gained some right-wing allies among non-student supporters of Khomeini who infiltrated the university in order to disrupt mobilization by secular leftists. The right-wing faction of Islamic students and their external allies soon became hostile toward the secular socialists and even occasionally came close to clashing with them (*Kayhan International*, October 26, 1978). There were actual instances when the right-wing faction of the Islamic forces violently attacked secular, leftist students on university campuses causing injuries (Homa Nategh, interview, June 1999).

Despite the expansion of the pro-Khomeini faction, the bulk of university students remained in the secular, socialist camp. In the fall of 1978, they boycotted classes. As a result, although the Shah and the Queen took part in the opening ceremonies at Tehran University, the universities did not reopen until three weeks later than usual. Leftists held rallies that attracted large crowds, and their slogans dominated the universities: "Augment and expand the movement of Iranian laborers," and "March toward the formation and expansion of the masses of workers, farmers, and university students of Iran" (*Kayhan International*, October 22, 1978). Everywhere they demonstrated and demanded political freedom and the release of all political prisoners.

In the fall of 1978, the student protest was spurred by a group of faculty who had formed the National Organization of University Professors and held a "solidarity week" on campuses throughout the country, in October. Organizers of the solidarity week issued a number of demands: eliminate the military government imposed by the new prime minister in twelve cities; identify and punish those responsible for recent killings; remove university guards and dissolve the university security office; reinstate all students and faculty expelled during the past several years; and, most importantly, grant autonomy to universities and colleges. Students invited leftist and Marxist speakers, such as Hezar Khani, to speak at their events (*Ettelaat*, October 29, 1978). Throughout the country, students organized massive rallies, sit-ins, and even hunger strikes to protest against repression and demand the release of political prisoners. The scale of the mobilization and protests, within the context of other conflicts, forced the government to grant autonomy and political freedom to all universities and colleges (*Ettelaat*, October 23, 1978).

In response, student protests assumed a truly revolutionary character. On November 4, thousands of high school students participated in rallies at Tehran University. Leftist students sang the "Ay Rafighan" ("Oh, Comrades") song and invited a worker to speak about Samad Behrangi's fable, *The Little Black Fish*.[7] When a soldier deserted ranks and joined the protesting students, troops opened fire and killed a number of student protesters (some sources claimed sixty-five). Youths who had watched the event on television took to the streets the next day, destroying and burning government buildings, offices, and property. At this time, the Shah decided to remove Prime Minister Sharif-Emami's civilian cabinet and replace it with a military government, which quickly closed down the universities and thus curtailed students' ability to act collectively. The universities remained closed from November 1978 until January 1979.

Reopened on January 13, 1979, universities once again became centers of political opposition against, first, the monarchy and, eventually, the Islamic Republic. The new political opportunities created by the Shah's removal and the release from prison of Mojahedeen and Feda'iyan leaders made possible the continued hegemony of the left on campuses. At this point, students also mobilized to promote the interests of workers. As employers began expelling striking workers from factories, students rushed to factories in support of workers. In the final days of the monarchy, factories were often the sites of slogans that celebrated the unity of students and workers: "Students, workers, may your alliance be blessed."

After the overthrow of the monarchy, leftist students remained in the forefront of political and ideological struggles. Although many religious students initially fell in with the pro-Khomeini faction, most soon proved to be unreliable as supporters of Khomeini, and they joined various leftist organizations to oppose the Islamic Republic. Grouped into various leftist organizations, including the Mojahedeen, students soon clashed

---

[7] Behrangi was a Marxist teacher and writer killed, allegedly, by the SAVAK.

with both the liberals and the clergy in the government. Students declared their support for opposition demands, including democratic freedoms, workers' councils, land reform, women's rights, and autonomy for ethnic minorities.

The new government's reaction to student mobilization and collective action was swift. Khomeini had evidently long regarded university students and faculty as some of his principal enemies. His clerical supporters had scheduled a visit to Tehran University for him to make a public statement upon his return to Iran. But when he arrived, Khomeini refused to go to the university and instead visited the cemetery to pay tribute to the martyrs of the revolution. Government officials soon complained that the Feda'iyan and Mojahedeen were using university resources to attack Islam and the Islamic Republic. According to top clerical officials in the government, the forces of Islam in the universities had been weakened by the activities of these groups (*Jumhuri Eslami*, December 23, 1982). Khomeini, who had earlier lauded university students for their struggle against the monarchy, dictatorship, and imperialism, now declared, "Universities were bastions of communists, and they were war rooms for communists" (*Christian Science Monitor*, December 19, 1980).

In April 1980 militant clerics, with the support of the liberal faction of the government, unleashed a "cultural revolution" to Islamicize the universities. Government forces enlisted the help of club-wielders to attack students throughout the country, killing approximately a hundred students. The government, in an unprecedented move, closed all universities and colleges for at least two years, and many remained closed for several years. Thousands of students who were considered leftist or anti-government were expelled from the universities. Political and religious standards were then applied to all incoming university students, and Khomeini announced that only those without affiliations to either eastern or western ideologies would be permitted entrance (*Ettelaat*, August 28, 1982). As during the revolutionary struggles, students and youth became the principal targets of repression and violence. Between 1981 and 1985 nearly 4,000 students involved in political opposition activities were either executed or killed in armed struggle (*Mojahed*, Appendix to No. 261, September 6, 1985).

To summarize, despite severe repression, ideological divisions, and the lack of formal organizations, Iranian students were in the forefront of the revolutionary struggles and played an important role in the insurgency that overthrew the monarchy. Students opposed exclusive rule, political repression, and rising inequalities. Iranian students overwhelmingly favored some form of socialism. Compared with other social groups and classes, they launched the largest number of events of collective action. Although students' capacity to act collectively was, at times, restricted by the government's closure of colleges and universities, and by their own boycotts, students' opposition to the monarchy and their support for the revolution were significant. As a result, students and youth were the main victims of repressive violence. Statistics made public by the government in March 1998 indicate that 72 percent of those killed in the revolution were between the ages of 14 and 24. Yet it is important to underscore the fact that student support for the leadership of the Iranian revolution was based on tactical coalition and political opportunity, rather than ideological consensus. As this analysis has demonstrated, the secular socialist movement clearly had the hegemony of the anti-Shah movement in the colleges and universities throughout the country.

Students and the state in Nicaragua

As in Iran, students in Nicaragua were highly political and among the foremost opponents of the Somozas. As early as 1939, three years after Somoza Garcia assumed power, university students organized political demonstrations and clashed violently with the National Guard. Generations of student leaders gained experience in universities during the nationwide conflicts of 1944–1948, 1959–1961, and 1970–1979 (Booth 1982:108). The student movement during these years trained a number of political activists who later were influential in national politics, including Pedro Joaquin Chamorro, editor of *La Prensa* and leader of UDEL (Democratic Liberation Union), Rigoberto Lopez Perez, who assassinated Somoza Garcia, Dr. Rafael Córdova Rivas, Dr. Leonte Pallias Tifer, Dr. Virgilio Argüello, and Tomás Borge Martinez, Carlos Fonseca, and Silvio Mayorga, the last three the founders of the Sandinista National Liberation Front, or FSLN (*La Prensa*, June 6, 1974; Foroohar 1989: 113–114). Most of the members of the FSLN were either university students, graduates, or drop-outs.

The nature of the Nicaraguan state, like that in Iran, influenced students to move toward ever greater political opposition and an ideological shift toward advocating a radical transformation of the state and society. Exclusive rule and centralization of power drastically limited the capacity of the moderate political organizations and thus encouraged radicalism among students. Government reliance on the National Guard and repression of the moderate opposition in 1967 strengthened the position of those who advocated armed struggle. State development strategy generated increasing inequalities and encouraged students to advocate socialist transformation, especially as the expansion of the educational institutions absorbed a growing number of students from less well-off backgrounds. Increased state resources and government intervention in the economy made the securing of privilege increasingly contingent on access to the state, which was not readily obtainable. The Somozas' heavy political and economic dependence on the United States also contributed to the student shift in favor of nationalist and socialist ideologies. Finally, the rise of the Sandinistas provided leadership for the Nicaraguan students and encouraged them to adopt an ideological stance against Somoza and the United States.

Given the nature of the Nicaraguan polity, the expansion of higher education and admission of students from middle- and even working-class backgrounds into the universities fueled support for radical ideologies. But in the Nicaraguan context even many students from upper-class backgrounds came to support Marxist or socialist ideologies and organizations. Students' support for the FSLN began in 1962 when a group of sympathizers organized the Revolutionary Student Front, or FER. Although student activism declined somewhat during the next few years due to repression and economic prosperity, this organization rapidly gained hegemony within the student opposition as a whole. Four years after its formation, FER's candidate in the student elections at the UNAN in Managua lost by only seven votes. In 1966, FER carried out the first student-led strike to protest against the Liberal Party's convention held to nominate Somoza for president. FER controlled all the major student organizations in Nicaragua by 1970 (Ruchwarger 1987:16).

Even students who followed religious ideologies often opposed the government and supported the FSLN during important political conflicts. A notable example was the Christian Youth Movement, which emerged at UCA, the Jesuit-run Central American University, in the early 1970s. This movement challenged the university's curriculum and its tacit support for the government. When university officials refused to discuss their grievances, students occupied Managua's cathedral in October and November of 1970 and again in May 1971, to protest against human rights violations and the presence on campus of National Guard units. Five other churches across the country were likewise occupied by students in actions supported by twenty-two priests. Eventually, more than a hundred students were expelled from UCA and arrested (Berryman 1984:61; Dodson and O'Shaughnessy 1990:122). This group later founded the Revolutionary Christian Movement, which linked up with the FSLN after the earthquake and contributed resources to the Sandinistas in the late 1970s (Dodson and O'Shaughnessy 1990:125; Montgomery 1982/1983:212).

The Nicaraguan students' capacity to undertake collective action also was enhanced by the government's own educational policies. The expansion of higher education in Nicaragua was largely the result of the government's economic policies and industrial development. In the 1960s Nicaragua's participation in the Central American Common Market spurred rapid economic development, which necessitated the use of certain skills and increased the need for higher education. As a result, several new universities were established to provide the necessary training. By 1979, Nicaragua possessed nine universities and two technical schools. With this proliferation in universities, the number of students enrolled in higher education skyrocketed from 955 in 1958 to 9,385 in 1970, an increase of 882 percent. Between 1970 and 1975, enrollment figures nearly doubled, climbing to more than 18,000, and by 1978, there were nearly 24,000 students in the nation's colleges and universities (Close 1988:156–157). This student growth rate was the fifth highest in Latin America between 1965 and 1975 (Wickham-Crowley 1989:142). The number of secondary students rose even more rapidly from 5,667 in 1958 to approximately 100,000 in 1978. This rapid expansion and concentration of students provided a powerful communications network, which facilitated mobilization and collective action.

Unlike the Iranian government, the Nicaraguan government granted a measure of autonomy both to the press and to institutions of higher education, which permitted students to organize. Autonomy was granted to the universities, in part, because of the persistent struggles of faculty and students (Zwerling and Martin 1985:71). Autonomy prevented the National Guard from entering the universities, which meant that the government was forced to rely on spies for information about radicals' activities. When the government violated the principle of university autonomy, students launched massive collective actions to preserve it. University officials in higher education, particularly UNAN, the National Autonomous University of Nicaragua, tolerated student activism and thus facilitated student mobilization against the regime (Booth 1982:112).

Collective action by students in support of the FSLN began in the early 1970s and continued until the Somoza regime was ousted. Student supporters of the Sandinistas, organized in FER, held demonstrations every time the National Guard repressed the FSLN. FER worked closely with mothers of political prisoners in the early 1970s to organize hunger strikes on behalf of such prisoners, many of whom were members of the FSLN. Students also formed coalitions with activist workers and radical labor organizations that were independent of the FSLN. In one example, students and workers in Leon joined demonstrations against public transportation fare hikes in January 1971. Later, during the revolutionary conflicts, students demonstrated in large numbers, provided support for FSLN guerrillas, participated in ambushes against the National Guard, and worked with other segments of the population against the Somoza regime. Students were among the initial members of the FSLN's first umbrella organization, United People's Movement (MPU), formed in July 1978 with the explicit goal of overthrowing the Somoza regime. FER was one of the first organizations to join this initiative (*La Prensa*, July 21, 1978). Of the fourteen organizations that joined MPU at its inception, seven were student organizations.

Like students in Iran, Nicaraguan students were in the forefront of collective action against the government during the two main periods of conflicts, in 1973–1974 and 1977–1979. In the initial period, student mobilization reached a peak following the earthquake of 1972, which devastated Managua and caused extreme suffering among most of its population. As FER and the Christian Youth Movement joined with each other to carry out humanitarian work, they could not sidestep the country's political problems. Both organizations soon began actively mobilizing students to participate in anti-government protests. Between March 1973 and December 1974, university and secondary students carried out more demonstrations than any other social group. Of seventy-two demonstrations held during this time, students were responsible for twenty-eight events, or roughly 39 percent. Students were the main social group participating in popular demonstrations as well, which accounted for twenty additional events of collective action. Students also organized thirty-four class boycotts, twenty occupations of sixteen churches, and four hunger strikes. Students formed coalitions with working-class protesters, organizing three joint demonstrations with workers and one with peasants. Of twenty-eight student-initiated collective actions, twenty-one were in support of striking workers. Students regularly organized solidarity rallies and bonfires to back striking construction workers (*La Prensa*, April 4, 1973). Students also marched to protest against repression and arrests of peasants and on behalf of peasants involved in a land dispute with landowners (*La Prensa*, September 20, 1974).

Of those social groups that participated in protests, students were the most politicized, always evinced concern for broad social issues, and consistently confronted the state. Although in this early period they were not yet calling for the overthrow of the government, the political aspect of their mobilization is evidenced by the fact that eighteen of their actions were protests against the arrest and the mistreatment of political prisoners. Students occupied churches in several cities in December

1973 in solidarity with Sandinista political prisoners who declared a hunger strike (*La Prensa*, December 26, 1973 and January 2, 1974). Students also initiated four hunger strikes of their own to demand the release of political prisoners, and they collected money for mothers of political prisoners (*La Prensa*, January 2, 1974). Of forty-four student-initiated protests of various kinds, only five were directed against inflation, even though the cost of living had risen sharply due to the earthquake.

The student mobilizations of the early 1970s had two critical consequences. First, students' support for workers against employers intensified class conflict and social polarization. Heightened class conflict, in turn, reduced the likelihood of coalition formation. Second, students' high level of collective action and politicization, together with their alliance with workers against employers and the state, provoked government repression aimed at demobilizing the opposition. Hundreds of students were arrested for demonstrating against the treatment of political prisoners, on behalf of striking workers, and in opposition to urban bus fare increases.[8] This period of student mobilization and collective action came to an abrupt end with the declaration of martial law and the imposition of a state of siege at the end of 1974.

Student mobilization following Chamorro's assassination

Though sporadic demonstrations occurred over the subsequent three years, the student movement did not rebound until the fall of 1977 when a reduction in repression by the state provided greater opportunities for collective action. Student mobilization and politicization began as soon as opportunities arose and continued through the latter part of 1977. Once again, students were among the principal initiators of popular demonstrations, organizing four rallies, occupying nine churches and a school, and joining in one protest with workers. During this time, student mobilization became even more politicized. As the number of political prisoners swelled, students, in particular, galvanized support for them. Students expressed solidarity with political prisoners in thirteen events and protested against government repression in four demonstrations. One prominent slogan during this period was "Christmas '77 without political prisoners" (*La Prensa*, December 21, 1977).

Students' political activity was widespread. In the Regional University

---

[8] In one well-publicized case, Miriam Rubi, a 23-year-old student, was arrested by agents of the Office of Security for distributing leaflets in support of striking workers at Fabritex (*La Prensa*, August 2, 1973). She was sentenced to six months in jail but was released as a result of the widespread protests initiated on her behalf.

Center (CUR) in Carazo, for example, a group of university students initiated a campaign of marches against human rights violations and demanded amnesty for all political prisoners (*La Prensa*, January 13, 1978). Other CUR students held poetry recitals and marches on behalf of political prisoners (*La Prensa*, January 5 and 9, 1978). In Managua, students demanded freedom for political prisoners and protested against repression of the peasantry, which the government initiated in an effort to wipe out the FSLN. These students carried placards reading: "Where are our peasant brothers and sisters?" and "Freedom to political prisoners" (*La Prensa*, December 14, 1977). In Estelí, students occupied the cathedral and called for an end to the practice of keeping jailed political prisoners in solitary confinement (*La Prensa*, January 4, 1978). Students in all three University Centers of the National Autonomous University – in Managua, León, and Carazo – declared strikes and occupied university buildings to protest against the reelection of the university's rector, whom they denounced as unpopular among students and workers. The vice-rector, in particular, was excoriated as "a man of clear Somocista ties and positions, and [an] everlasting enemy of students" (*La Prensa*, January 9, 1978).

The assassination of Pedro Chamorro in January 1978 ignited intense, popular mobilization, which increased both the state's vulnerability and the FSLN's activity. Once again, students were by far the most active social group involved in protests against the government. Students led 182 demonstrations, occupied schools and churches on 224 occasions, organized 156 class boycotts, and engaged in 10 hunger strikes. In addition, students were among the principal actors in 374 popular demonstrations undertaken by various social groups and classes. Students' radicalism was again revealed by the fact that they organized 28 demonstrations alongside workers and 4 demonstrations with workers and peasants together.

The most striking aspect of students' protests at this time, unlike 1973–1974, was their ideological and political support for the FSLN. Students expressed solidarity with Sandinista political prisoners in 515, or 90 percent, of 572 demonstrations, occupations, class boycotts, and hunger strikes. In 349 of these events, or 61 percent, students protested against government repression. Students also demanded reforms in schools and colleges in 221 protests, which comprised 38.6 percent of the total; some of these demands were in response to restrictions introduced by the government. Students' radicalism and the ideological nature of their positions were evident in the fact that 67 events, or 11.7 percent, expressed solidarity with peasant struggles and peasant land invasions. Students also protested against the dictatorial nature of the regime in 53

events, or 9.3 percent of the total, and explicitly called for the establishment of a democratic system. In contrast, only 23 student protests, or 4
percent, mentioned Chamorro's slaying, indicating the radicalism and
anti-elite politics of students. Finally, in 6 events students commemorated the anniversary of the assassination of Augusto César Sandino,
whom they called the "General of Free Men."[9]

In 1978, collective action by students supporting political prisoners
became a major political issue nationwide. In April, striking students in
Chinandega marched with placards demanding, "Cease the isolation of
Marcio Jaen and Tomás Borge," "All against the dictatorship," "Students united will never be defeated," "We ask for justice in the assassination of Pedro Chamorro," "Your blood was not shed in vain" (*La
Prensa*, April 11, 1978). For three weeks, similar demonstrations and
strikes were held elsewhere in the country.[10] At the end of June, more than
30,000 students in Managua and other cities boycotted classes and
occupied schools in another protest against government repression. In
Matagalpa, Estelí, and other cities, students joined journalists and others
who had been on hunger strike to protest against the government's
closure of a radio station (*La Prensa*, June 29, 1978).

The nationwide mobilization of university students also activated high
school youth, who had not been very active prior to the imposition of
martial law. Protests by high school students followed the same pattern as
those of university students. The Association of Secondary Students
(AES) and the Secondary Student Movement (MES) initiated a series of
strikes, which became the largest and longest student strikes in
Nicaraguan history. Their first strike, begun on April 6, 1978, was organized to protest against the government's treatment of two FSLN political
prisoners, Tomás Borge and Marcio Jaen. Within two days, students had
seized control of some twenty schools and secondary institutes across the
country. In the end, this national strike embraced approximately 60,000
students out of a total of 100,000, and shut down universities and
secondary schools throughout most of the country.

In Managua, striking students occupied fifteen schools and four
churches in solidarity with Marcio Jaen's mother, who had embarked
upon a hunger strike that was to last thirty-three days, the longest in the
country's history (*La Prensa*, April 10 and 29, 1978). Representatives

---

[9] To protest against government repression, university students continued their mobilization and collective action. They initiated a number of demonstrations, burned buses and
Somoza's effigy, commemorated the assassination of the "General of Free Men," and
exploded bombs (*La Prensa*, January 26, 31, and February 24, 1978).

[10] Higher education students also continued their opposition to the government, organizing
strikes in response to government repression and demanding release of political prisoners
(*La Prensa*, May 28, 1978).

from twenty-eight secondary schools in Managua issued a statement containing a number of demands typical of the students' concerns: an end to the solitary confinement of FSLN prisoners, Borge and Jaen; solidarity with striking students, especially those in Masaya who were demanding the removal of two teachers; the reopening of the National School of Agriculture and Cattle-Raising and rehiring of fired professors; freedom of expression and organization for students; and the release of jailed students.

Continued student mobilization and government repression culminated in the declaration in July by the AES of yet another nationwide strike as evidence of their enhanced solidarity. Students in eleven cities stayed away from classes, demanding an end to repression, freedom for all political prisoners, land for peasants, and changes in the educational system (*La Prensa*, July 3, 1978). In August, a group of high school students peacefully occupied the OAS building in Managua. They carried signs calling for "An end to repression" and "Solidarity with striking hospital workers and peasants who demand land." The next day they issued a statement vowing to continue their occupation of the building indefinitely until their demands were heard. They demanded that the Supreme Court issue a declaration in favor of arrested students and workers; appealed to the Interamerican Commission of Human Rights to investigate the repression of the people of Monimbó and other cities; and called for an end to the repression of young workers and students (*La Prensa*, August 7 and 8, 1978).

By fall 1978, university and high school students coalesced and actively mobilized as a single unit against the government. As political conflicts intensified in August and September, students boycotted classes throughout the country to support a general strike that demanded the resignation of Somoza and creation of a democratic government (*La Prensa*, September 1, 1978). The boycott continued despite attempts by the Ministry of Public Education to end the strike. According to some estimates, more than 500,000 students of all ages stayed away from their schools, paralyzing the country's educational system (*La Prensa*, September 25, 1978). When students eventually returned to their classes, they continued to mobilize and act collectively against political repression and military occupation of their schools.

In the final months of the conflicts, politicization and mobilization by students, together with the government policies, severely disrupted educational institutions throughout the country. Students rallied against government repression of students, workers, journalists, and radio stations, and against the devaluation of the córdoba, the Nicaraguan currency. At times, students organized long marches to Managua to protest against the government (*La Prensa*, January 29, 1979). In one instance, a group of UNAN students and their professors occupied the Ecclesiastical Curia in Managua for forty-eight hours to protest against the deaths of five youths in a Leon church. They called upon the Catholic Church to excommunicate Somoza (*La Prensa*, February 20, 1978). Students once more went on strike nationwide on May 18 to commemorate Sandino's birth (*La Prensa*, November 9, 1978). In the final months of the struggles, students raised money for the FSLN, made bombs, collected arms, and fought along with the Sandinistas to overthrow the Somoza regime.

In addition to outright repression, government attempts to demobilize student protesters included reducing the budget for higher education, dismissing faculty, and closing down universities. The government with-held financial support from UNAN, bringing the university to the verge of collapse. This type of repression often actually boosted solidarity and escalated the conflict as students elsewhere disrupted their own schools while supporting the targeted students (*La Prensa*, November 9, 1978). As in Iran, students and youths in Nicaragua were among the principal victims of repressive violence. The figures for Nicaragua were much greater, despite its smaller population. The Inter-American Commission on Human Rights described the government's actions as "a general repression by the National Guard against male youth between 14 and 21" (Booth 1982:111). An analysis of the ages of the participants in the final insurrection shows that students comprised the largest group. Of all those slain in the insurrection, 71 percent were between the ages of 15 and 24. An examination of the occupational backgrounds of those who died reveals that students comprised the largest single category, 29 percent. Of these, 50 percent were born into families whose parents were self-employed artisans and small traders (Vilas 1986:108–115).

In sum, Nicaraguan students mobilized and opposed the Somoza regime throughout the decades prior to the revolution. Their ideology shifted gradually to favor the Sandinistas and socialism, beginning in the early 1960s when the FSLN was formed. By the early 1970s, supporters of the FSLN dominated the student movement. Nicaraguan students occupied the vanguard of the conflicts of the early 1970s, allied them-selves with radical labor, and often targeted both the state and capitalist employers in their protests. Mobilization and collective action by students may have been a factor contributing to the absence of a broad-based coalition against the Somoza regime. During the revolutionary conflicts, students carried out the largest number of collective actions. Unlike the early 1970s, these protests were primarily aimed at Somoza and the government. Students were the main social group to support the FSLN politically and ideologically. Finally, students along with youth were the principal targets of government repression and the victims of violence during the final insurrection.

Students' mobilization in the Philippines

Although a combination of formal, democratic institutions and a low level of state intervention in the economy had reduced the likelihood of a student movement in the Philippines, a number of changes in the 1960s prepared the ground for a dynamic student movement that lasted for about two decades. Economic decline and rising income inequalities along with rising intra-elite conflicts provided the context for the student movement. The Vietnam War and the American use of military bases in the Philippines also generated some nationalist reactions that fueled the student movement. Finally, students became politicized because increasingly they needed political connections to gain access to positions of power and privilege due to President Marcos' cronyism.

As a result of these changes, Filipino students launched a movement that became active throughout the presidency of Marcos and eventually contributed to his overthrow. As in Iran and Nicaragua, students stood at the forefront of political and ideological struggles. They engaged in the largest number of collective actions, or the "parliament of the street" as they were called in the Philippines. During the first phase of the conflicts in the late 1960s and early 1970s, the student movement trained a large number of activists who joined the underground opposition or the New People's Army after the imposition of martial law in 1972, aimed at removing Marcos from power. During the second phase of the conflicts, which began with Aquino's assassination in 1983, students mobilized on a massive scale and contributed to the state's vulnerability. Eventually, the initial phase of the movement was abruptly terminated by President Marcos' imposition of martial law in 1972, which closed down the democratic institutions that had permitted student mobilization. Repression during martial law eliminated all options for political activity, which in turn led to greater militancy and radicalism among students. As a result, the student movement shifted in favor of the radicals during martial law, and during the final phase of the conflicts that removed Marcos, the movement was completely dominated by the radical left. These students played a very important role in the conflicts of the 1980s that ultimately dislodged Marcos from power, although they did not favor the outcome of the conflicts.

The Filipino student movement began with a strong moderate ideology, which favored introducing some social reform to Philippine society rather than changing the entire social structure. Moderate students were organized and represented by the National Union of Students of the Philippines (NUSP), which dominated the student movement during the late 1960s. Even those who advocated socialism, like the Young Christian Socialists of the Philippines, remained within the moderate camp at this point. These students pressed for greater state intervention in the economy and society as a means of achieving their goals.

Although moderates initially dominated the student movement in 1970, the dynamics of the political conflicts enabled radicals to gain the upper hand. The inability of the moderates to bring about change and increasing government repression contributed to the students' political shift toward greater radicalism. As in Iran and Nicaragua, the expansion of higher education in the Philippines had increased the number of students from middle- and working-class backgrounds who favored alternative radical ideologies. The Vietnam War and the heavy American presence at Clark and Subic bases also contributed to nationalism and helped the cause of the radical students. As a result, some students found inspiration in Marxism (Lande 1986:126–128). These students were organized in the Marxist Patriotic Youth, or KM (Kabataang Makabyan), the Democratic Youth Organization, or SDK, and the Bertrand Russell Peace Foundation, among others.

While moderate students struggled to achieve social reforms through greater state intervention, student radicals targeted both the state and the class structure of the country. Moderates addressed educational issues, government corruption, higher wages for workers, and inflation, while radicals attacked the nature of the social structure, feudalism, "bureaucrat-capitalism," and imperialism.

The expansion of higher education and the nature of the state enhanced Filipino students' capacity for mobilization and collective action. As the number of institutions of higher education increased, so did the total number of students enrolled at colleges and universities. The number of students rose steadily from 271,791 in 1960 to 634,835 in 1969, and reached 1,973,182 in 1985 (UNESCO, *Statistical Yearbook*, various years). The concentration of these students at universities in major cities provided a ready-made communication network for mobilization and collective action. Unlike Iran, student mobilization in the Philippines was also enhanced by the existence of formal democratic institutions, which permitted students to organize and engage in ideological debate. Although students' capacity to mobilize was drastically curtailed by the imposition of martial law in 1972, they continued to engage in collective action whenever opportunities appeared.

The first phase of the student protests took place within the context of an economic decline, increasing unemployment and growing intra-elite conflict, which provided opportunities for mobilization and collective action. An ILO report stated that unemployment among college graduates was relatively high (ILO 1974:309), adversely affecting the future of Filipino students. Intra-elite conflicts also resulted in attempts by President Marcos to centralize power in his own hands. Although the Philippine state was much less interventionist and centralized than Iran or Nicaragua, President Marcos initiated policies during his first term in office that made privilege – in particular, future employment – contingent on access to the government. Increasingly, these conditions generated student interest in reshaping the structure of the state and of Philippine society.

Organized and concentrated in major cities, students were the most active group in the political arena and participated in a large number of collective actions during the conflicts of the early 1970s. In 1970–1971, students engaged in 214 demonstrations and 39 class boycotts, and issued 72 statements that were reported in the *Manila Times*. In addition, like Nicaraguan students, Filipino students formed coalitions with reformist and radical factions of the working classes and joined with workers and farmers in 76 demonstrations.

Because of sharp political and ideological divisions between moderates and radicals, the students' demands targeted different groups, thereby diffusing their impact. Students' main demands in 1970 revolved around educational issues (108 protests), followed by protests aimed at government repression and the rise of fascism (52 protests), and American imperialism and the presence of US military bases (17). Other political issues that concerned students were labor repression (6) and Marcos as puppet (4). Students also protested against rising inflation (14), the upcoming Constitutional Convention (15), low wages for workers (11), lack of land and price subsidies for farmers (3), and expulsion of students from colleges and universities (3). Finally, students protested the wealth and leadership of the Catholic Church (3), class inequality and injustice and corporate capitalism (3), and feudal agrarian structures (1).[11] Obviously, students protested against very different issues because of their ideological differences.

One demonstration on January 26, 1970 marks the beginning of heightened student mobilization and militancy, and the division between moderates and radicals. As the first nationwide demonstration of students in the Philippines, this protest was initiated by the moderate NUSP. According to the *Manila Times* (January 27, 1970) the event drew more than 60,000 students and labor participants, among them some 500

---

[11] Other protests were leveled against feudalism, bureaucratic capitalism, foreign loans, the state's nature as a reflection of class domination, and reactionary government.

students associated with the radical KM (Pimentel 1991:65). During the rally, according to police, these radicals violently attacked President Marcos and the First Lady as they were leaving the Congress (*Manila Times*, January 27, 1970). In the ensuing clash, forty-seven police officers and thirty-eight demonstrators were injured (Daroy 1988:6). The conflict soon led to new clashes and increased student militancy. Four days later during a demonstration in front of the presidential palace, radical students commandeered a fire truck, crashed into one of the gates, and entered the yard. Once inside, they stoned buildings and burned the fire truck and another car. The Battle of Mendiola, as this event has been called, lasted until the early hours of the next day. By the time it was over, the police had killed six students.

Government repression and growing conflict led to increased support for the radical KM, which grew to roughly 75,000 student members nationwide, while the moderate students declined in number (Pimentel 1991:83, 98). Seeking to broaden their movement, the radicals formed the Movement for a Democratic Philippines (MDP), a coalition of forty-six individual organizations representing students, labor, and peasant organizations active against the government. Despite their radicalism, the MDP initially sought dialogue with the government as a means of bringing about changes within the existing structure. In February 1970, MDP leaders met with President Marcos and presented a number of demands, including:

(1) a comprehensive review of US aid, particularly military, educational, and labor programs, and the elimination of those programs incompatible with nationalist aspirations;
(2) removal of three pro-US cabinet members;
(3) participation by the nationalist sector in all government and educational appointments;
(4) an end to surveillance, harassment, and lawsuits against participants in the previous month's demonstrations;
(5) an increase in minimum wages for industrial and agricultural workers;
(6) attention to hospitals and medical issues; and
(7) assistance to state universities (*Manila Times*, February 12, 1970).

These demands can be characterized as nationalist and reformist, rather than revolutionary, and the government agreed to most of them.

Political conflicts continued to escalate, however, and as the government's repression became harsher, MDP turned more radical, even militant. The following month, MDP organized a "People's March" through the main streets of Manila to denounce "American imperialism, fascism, and feudalism." The event drew 20,000 students, workers, peasants, and professionals, who shouted, "Long live the workers! Long live the peasants!" (*Manila Times*, March 4, 1970). Two weeks later, MDP organized the "Poor People's March against Imperialism, Feudalism, and Fascism," with some 6,000 students, workers, and peasants participating. A "People's Tribunal" accused Marcos of crimes against the Filipino people, including:

(1) raising prices because of puppetry to US imperialism;
(2) complicity in the exploitation of the working class by US imperialism, bureaucratic capitalists, and landlords;
(3) colossal graft and corruption;
(4) fascist acts of massacres to suppress the people's democratic rights; and
(5) fraud and terrorism in the most recent election (*Manila Times*, March 17 and 18, 1970).

Although overall student mobilization declined in 1971, student radicalism and militancy increased. By this time, students' protests were focused more narrowly on the nature of Marcos' regime and on government repression; attacks against the United States increased, while concerns with educational and economic issues declined substantially. A major clash occurred in January between the government and students who actively supported a jeepney strike, which had paralyzed transportation services in Manila. At the University of the Philippines, students staged a sympathy strike, which evolved into the so-called Diliman Commune. In protest against the killing of a student, university students erected barricades to cut off the campus from the rest of the city and fought with the police for twelve days. The university radio station was commandeered to broadcast antigovernment propaganda, and students used its press facilities to publish a paper called *Red Flag* (Daroy 1988:21–22).

MDP continued its mobilization in 1971, demanding radical changes in the social and political structures. In June, the organization formed the "Citizens' Committee to Oppose the 1971 Constitutional Convention as a US Imperialist-Feudal Conspiracy," which drew together forty-six groups affiliated with MDP. The committee demanded that the government:

(1) confiscate US imperialist, Japanese, and Kuomintang assets;
(2) redistribute large feudal land holdings;
(3) expel all US military personnel;
(4) scrap US–Philippine treaties and agreements;

(5) nationalize mines, transportation, power, steel, and other basic industries;

(6) institute free and universal education at all levels; and

(7) return all lands appropriated from national minorities (*Manila Times*, June 1, 1971).

Despite growing militancy among segments of the students, several factors caused the student movement as a whole to become increasingly ineffective. Following the Battle of Mendiola, divisions widened between student radicals and moderates to the point where they virtually ceased joint collaborative actions (*Manila Times*, January 22 and 25, May 28, 1970). One rare example of cooperation was a joint rally in August by militant and more moderate organizations, including the National Union of Students of the Philippines and the Young Christian Socialists of the Philippines, to protest against the "corrupt Marcos regime," which they accused of violating civil liberties and causing the growing militarization of the country (*Manila Times*, August 17 and 18, 1970). Although militant and leftist students gained greater support, were elected to campus positions at schools in Metro Manila, and organized the Student Alliance for National Democracy in seventy universities and colleges (*Manila Times*, November 10 and December 13, 1970), their expansion generated internal factionalism and the expulsion of certain elements within the MDP (Goodno 1991:60–61).

The student movement was also beset by growing government repression and, to some extent, harassment by campus authorities. Militant student groups accused government troops of carrying out fifteen massacres with impunity in addition to killing six students during the Battle of Mendiola (*Manila Times*, September 14, 1970). When the chairman of KM was arrested in June (Pimentel 1991:98), many radicals went into hiding. By the following January, forty students from the University of the Philippines at Baguio alone were in hiding from state forces seeking to "liquidate" them (*Manila Times*, January 29, 1971). By the end of 1971, the government had arrested numerous militants, including sixty-three from MDP, on charges of subversion, which carried the death penalty (*Manila Times*, December 11, 1971). By mid-1972, nearly two dozen people had been killed in clashes between demonstrators and police in Manila (Wurfel 1988:106). The state's repressive measures cut down on the frequency and size of demonstrations and reduced students' capacity to mobilize and act collectively.

Some universities and colleges, too, employed repressive tactics, expelling the most active and militant students. In Manila alone, 300 students were dismissed in 1970, while nationwide 800 students were barred from enrolling in institutions of higher learning (*Manila Times*, December 5 and 7, 1970). In June 1971, sharp increases in tuition at a number of colleges and universities diverted some students' attention away from broader social and political issues to more immediate educative concerns.

Despite heavy repression, Filipino students did not receive support from other social groups, which had the effect of demobilizing student activists. Unlike students in Nicaragua, Filipino students lacked the support of either the Church or much of the middle class. The absence of support was, in part, a result of protests by a segment of students who clamored for the resignation of Cardinal Santos, archbishop of Manila. Without social support, the end result was a gradual decline in the number of student-organized rallies and demonstrations. Although students on at least ten campuses boycotted classes, only 20,000 students took part in the August rally (*Manila Times*, August 17 and 18, 1970), in sharp contrast to the January 26 demonstration which, according to students' claims, had mobilized 80,000 college and high school students and 20,000 workers (*Manila Times*, January 26, 1970).[12] The following January, a "People's Congress" organized by MDP drew only 12,000 students and workers (*Manila Times*, January 26, 1971). In June 1971, both militants and moderates protested against the opening of the Constitutional Convention but at separate rallies, which drew a total of only 8,000 participants (*Manila Times*, June 2, 1971). Altogether the number of student demonstrations reported in the *Manila Times* declined from 145 in 1970 to 69 in 1971, while class boycotts fell from 35 to only 4.

In the end, although student mobilization and protests in the early 1970s failed to achieve their goal of bringing about social change, the movement had three important consequences. First, segments of both students and labor were politicized, thus creating a cadre of trained leaders for the next phase of the movement and, in particular, for armed resistance in the countryside. Second, student pressure was instrumental in passing the Constitutional Convention Act by Congress. As students had demanded, the Act denied Congress any role in revising the constitution.[13] The third, unintended, consequence of the movement was that rising student militancy prepared the way for the suspension of civilian rule. President Marcos called the growing radical-

[12] The *Manila Times* (January 27, 1970) reported that more than 60,000 people took part in the rally. The police estimate was approximately 30,000 students and 20,000 workers (*Manila Times*, January 26, 1970).

[13] Although the 1970 election of ConCon delegates was considered to be among the most peaceful, honest elections in Philippine history, it was nevertheless repudiated by militant and moderate students alike, in part because of the absence of workers and peasants among the delegates (*Manila Times*, June 1, 1971).

ization of students a threat to the country and used it to justify the imposition of martial law.

Student mobilization following the assassination of Aquino

Martial law had significant consequences for the student movement. In the first place, the student movement underwent a rapid decline as many students were arrested, disappeared, or went underground. Second, repression all but eliminated the moderate, reformist elements within the student movement who had been very active in the mobilizations of the early 1970s. Third, with their decline, the radical, militant factions quickly took center stage and became the main force within the student movement. Despite heavy repression, militant, leftist students organized the League of Filipino Students (LFS) in 1977 to address educational issues such as rising tuition and the lack of greater resources. The LFS soon became politicized and directed its attacks against the government, as exemplified in a student protest against the Presidential Commitment Order, which authorized the government to arrest and detain indefinitely individuals identified as a threat to national security (*Malaya*, June 18, 1983). By 1983, the LFS dominated campus politics and was the most powerful agent of student mobilization. It claimed thousands of members (*Malaya*, June 18 and August 6, 1984; September 8, 1985) and, according to a 1984 report, could quickly mobilize 100,000 people for mass action (*Malaya*, August 6, 1984). By the end of the Marcos rule, the organization had a nationwide network and was able to coordinate activities in hundreds of school campuses.

In the context of political polarization against Marcos, the assassination of Aquino in August 1983 rendered the regime vulnerable to challenge and attack and set off nationwide student mobilization. Students quickly revived the National Union of Students of the Philippines and formed other organizations, including the Student Leaders Forum, to mobilize for collective action. For the remainder of the year, students were among the principal protesters against the Marcos regime. Students were also among the primary participants in 103 popular collective actions involving different groups and classes acting together against the government. They joined in three demonstrations with workers and one with teachers. Student coalition with workers evidenced student radicalism. At the same time, students initiated fifteen independent demonstrations and took part in several class boycotts.

Students' demands and ideological stances clearly indicated that they had overwhelmingly shifted to the left. Unlike the early 1970s, when students targeted diverse issues, the principal target of student demonstrations during the conflicts of the 1980s was the government. Shortly after the assassination, thousands of students demonstrated against Marcos, hoisting banners which read "No reconciliation under a fascist regime" (*Malaya*, August 29, 1983). Manila students presented their analysis of the situation in their country in a public statement:

Senator Aquino is the latest in the long list of victims of political repression. We believe that his death aligns with the death and suffering of so many of our countrymen who have been unjustly deprived of their basic rights to life, to a decent livelihood, and to rightful dissent. We regret the attempts to stifle the truth that surrounds the death of Senator Aquino. We regret the moves of the Reagan Administration to prejudge, from 10,000 miles away, the killing of the former Senator and to absolve some parties even before the investigation has been finished. Like Senator Aquino, we firmly believe that national reconciliation can never be attained unless it is founded on justice, freedom, and democracy. (*Malaya*, September 5, 1983)

But soon students' slogans dealt more with general political and ideological issues than the specific issue of Aquino's death. Government political repression was the most frequently mentioned concern of students, appearing in nearly one-half of all demonstrations they initiated or helped to organize following the assassination. Students went farther than other protesters, calling for Marcos' resignation and protesting against imperialism and US military bases. The LFS played a leading role in the struggle against government repression and US policies toward the Philippines, and it attacked the deployment of army troops in Metro Manila to repress the people. In a public statement, the LFS stated: "The government's mood reflects its deep-seated fear of the growing people's resistance to the United States–Marcos dictatorship" (*Malaya*, November 24, 1983). In a number of events, students also staged bonfires and set fire to copies of major Manila newspapers in protest against lack of press freedom (*Malaya*, September 5, 19 and 26, 1983).

In the following two years, although mobilization by some social groups soon declined, students remained among the principal actors until Marcos was removed from power. In 1984–1985, they organized a total of 128 demonstrations and 274 class boycotts. They also organized an additional 32 joint demonstrations with workers and farmers as well as a few with teachers. Equally significant, students were also among the principal actors in the 261 popular demonstrations organized by various groups and collectivities during 1984 and 1985.

As in 1983, students' principal target of attack was the government and President Marcos. In seventy-three of their demonstrations, students condemned government repression, most especially President Marcos' order reactivating the secret marshals assigned to demobilize students through "salvaging" or summary executions (*Malaya*, June 25, 1984). Students also protested against what they called the "militarization" of the country and the schools (*Malaya*, March 1, 1984). In protest against government repression, students also undertook 116 class boycotts in memory of Aquino on the anniversary of his assassination. Furthermore, they undertook 94 class boycotts to protest against Marcos' National Service Law that required students to acquire training in civic, welfare, law enforcement, and military service. In one demonstration, when the First Lady's convoy passed by demonstrating students, protestors shouted, "Marcos, Hitler, Dictator, Tuta" (puppet) (*Malaya*, July 21, 1984). Students also defended the rights of the underprivileged classes. In a number of cases, students protested against the killing of workers and arrest of peasant leaders (*Malaya*, February 16, 1985; September 20, 1985).

Finally, students demonstrated their radical ideology and militancy in events where they protested against imperialist intervention. They undertook fifty-one demonstrations and class boycotts against the United States, the World Bank, and the IMF intervention in Filipino internal political and economic affairs. In fact, condemnation of the "US–Marcos dictatorship" remained a favorite slogan of militant students (*Malaya*, June 26, 1984). The League of Filipino Students (LFS) organized a number of rallies at the US embassy to denounce United States control over Philippine human and natural resources (*Malaya*, July 5, 1984). Thousands of students from thirty-five Manila colleges and universities boycotted classes and demanded that Marcos stop complying with the IMF and World Bank dictates which worsened the country's economic situation through devaluation (*Malaya*, July 6, 1984).

Throughout 1984–1985, the LFS continued in the forefront of the student movement and increased its capacity to act collectively. The LFS struggled for social justice and democracy. In various demonstrations, it condemned the government's "anti-people" policies that resulted in inflation and unemployment (*Malaya*, June 28, 1984). In 1984, the LFS called for a boycott of the National Assembly elections, which Marcos had promoted to channel the opposition into more controllable, institutional options (*Malaya*, April 2, 1984). The election boycott was picked up by other student organizations, including the NUSP, who followed the lead of the LFS (*Malaya*, April 16, 1984). Both groups demonstrated together repeatedly against government repression, Marcos, and his subservience to the United States. Several times while protesting against tuition hikes, LFS erected barricades that blocked access to campuses, which sometimes forced authorities to suspend classes indefinitely (*Malaya*, July 16, 1988). To commemorate the International Human

Rights Day, LFS organized a week-long "people's march" in Masbate province (*Malaya*, December 4, 1985). It also organized a metro-wide noise barrage in forty-eight colleges and universities in Metro Manila in protest against the acquittal of General Ver, the chief of staff of the armed forces allegedly involved in Aquino's assassination.

By 1985, the LFS was a national force, able to organize nationwide protest activities and general strikes. In November 1985, it organized demonstrations around military camps and headquarters to protest against the killings of students in October (*Malaya*, November 21, 1985). In Mindanao, LFS students in thirty-five universities and forty high schools joined with teachers to organize a general strike against the National Service Law (*Malaya*, May 3 and July 24, 1985). In Central Luzon, the LFS staged regional coordinated strikes against government repression and called for an end to US intervention in Philippine affairs (*Malaya*, September 20, 1985).

The government's reaction to such protests was to target LFS leaders and members for arrest, harassment, disappearance, and death. Police and military units placed the names of several student leaders on a "death list" in an attempt to stem growing student unrest on several Metro Manila campuses (*Malaya*, August 12, 1984). In state colleges and universities as well, authorities expelled or suspended LFS members and leaders (*Malaya*, August 21 and September 13, 1985). In reaction to repressive measures by school authorities, students in some campuses went on hunger strike (*Malaya*, October 3, 1985). The government also decided to enact tuition increases, in order to demobilize students by barring those who could not afford their school fees. The tuition hike did, in fact, cause enrollments to drop by about 45 percent in the more than 1,000 colleges and universities throughout the Philippines (*Malaya*, June 14, 1984).

In sum, Filipino students, like those in Iran and Nicaragua, were the most active social group during their country's political conflicts. They were in the forefront of political actions in both timing and frequency of collective action. The Filipino student movement differed from those in Iran and Nicaragua during the initial period of insurgency in the early 1970s because it was dominated by the moderate faction. Later, as a result of government repression, ineffectiveness of the moderates, and particularly the imposition of martial law, the Filipino student movement assumed a radical character similar to the student movements in Iran and Nicaragua. By the time of Aquino's assassination, the radical left led the Filipino student movement. These students rejected any compromise with Marcos, his backers in the Philippines, or the policies of the United States. Indeed, they struggled for fundamental transformation in the state and social structure of the Philippines.

Conclusion

The analysis of student politics clearly demonstrates the inadequacy of theories that claim that revolutionary struggles do not begin with revolutionary goals. The problem stems from the fact that virtually all analysts of revolution, including those who have sought to explain revolution in terms of ideological change, have neglected to study the role of students. Yet students were in the forefront of political and ideological struggles in each of the three countries. They were the first social group to mobilize, and they acted collectively with greater frequency than other social groups. A high level of concentration in universities and colleges (as well as dormitories in Iran and the Philippines) provided ready-made communication networks and facilitated student mobilization and collective action. In addition, students enjoyed immense prestige in all three countries and were privileged, at least theoretically, to benefit from the relative immunity of universities from state power. In combination, these factors enabled them to initiate the largest number of collective actions in these countries.

But, despite their greater capacity for collective action compared with other collectivities, students, like other groups, were able to intensify their collective action only when opportunities to do so arose. In Iran, students began mobilizing when the government proclaimed reforms and introduced a few mild measures that reduced repression and provided an opportunity for students to engage in collective action. In Nicaragua and the Philippines, although they had been active against the government, students intensified their mobilization following the assassination of leading challengers. In the context of growing polarization, the assassination of these challengers rendered the regimes vulnerable to challenge and fueled nationwide student mobilization.

The nature of students' mobilization and collective actions, the direction of their movement, and their alliances were strongly affected by the level of preexisting organization. Iranian students were especially hampered by the lack of organization and greater government repression, which continually violated university autonomy and immunity. An ideological split between secular and Islamic factions also generated organizational problems occasionally verging on hostilities. Compared with student protests in Nicaragua and the Philippines, Iranian student rallies, but not their class boycotts, were less organized, less coordinated, and more short-lived, particularly at the beginning of the insurgency. In contrast, students in Nicaragua and the Philippines possessed autonomous organizations and were less hampered by government violation of university autonomy. In the Philippines, students on some major campuses even had radio stations that disseminated news and encouraged student mobilization. As a result, student mobilization and collective actions in Nicaragua and the Philippines were more organized and better coordinated.

Students were also in the vanguard in ideological struggles, demanding a total break with the past and a restructuring of the social order. Students fought over issues related to the social structure and opposed centralization of power, exclusive rule, and rising inequalities promoted under state-sponsored development. In all three countries, students overwhelmingly opposed the USA's support for the existing repressive regimes. Although they occasionally complained about inflation or rising bus fares, students did not make strictly economic demands except when defending workers' rights. Instead, they demonstrated greater interest in the nature of the social structure. Preparing for future careers and positions, students favored altering the social structures toward greater equality, democratic freedoms, and expansion of the polity. Students' interest in the power structure derived, at least in part, from the fact that privilege was increasingly tied to access to the government in all three countries. Their interest in greater equality was in part due to the expansion of higher education and diversification of the student body. Thus, despite some divisions, major segments of the student movement in all three countries favored radical transformation of the social structure to serve the interests of the disadvantaged classes and collectivities. As a result, leading segments of the student movement in all three countries shifted toward socialism and forged alliances with Marxist challengers.

The Filipino student movement of the early 1970s was a major exception because it was dominated by moderates who only demanded specific social reforms. The existence of democratic institutions had of course contributed to the dominance of moderates in the student movement. Yet, even in the Philippines, the student movement was radicalized as a result of repression, centralization of power, state intervention (which made the government the principal dispenser of resources and privilege), and eventual economic and political crises. In Nicaragua and the Philippines, students formed alliances with radical segments of organized labor and, to a lesser extent, peasants and farmers. The Iranian student movement also embraced Marxism or some form of socialism, although it lacked ties to the working classes. This support for the working classes became public only in the final stages of the conflicts. Unlike students in Nicaragua and the Philippines, where students' ideologies converged, in Iran ideological divisions among students widened shortly before the Shah was overthrown.

To the detriment of humanity, in all three countries students, as relentless revolutionaries, were the principal targets and victims of violent repression. In all three countries, as conflicts escalated, governments violated university autonomy and immunity and resorted to violence to demobilize the students. The frequency of their collective action, their ideological orientation, and the fact that they – often together with dissident intellectuals – led the way in the revolutionary struggles, made the students the target of violent repression. Everywhere, students and youth constituted the majority of those arrested, imprisoned, tortured, killed, or disappeared.

Although students in all three countries mobilized more actively than other social groups, their politics did not always have the decisive impact on the eventual outcome of the insurgencies for several reasons. First, students constituted a small minority of the population in all three countries and were concentrated in a few major cities, notably the capital; hence, their collective actions did not have sufficient influence on the rest of the country except under conditions of crisis or widespread popular mobilization. Second, students controlled neither the production nor distribution of goods and services, and consequently their actions did little to disrupt these central social processes. Finally, students' ideologies and intellectual orientation were supported by only segments of the working classes; such support was especially strong where both groups possessed preexisting organizations. As a result, where students' collective action heightened social divisions and class conflict, their mobilization actually prevented coalition formation and thus reduced the likelihood of revolution. This situation prevailed in Nicaragua and the Philippines in the early 1970s when broad coalitions were not formed. Student radicalism and militancy in the Philippines in the final stages of the conflicts intensified social divisions, prevented the formation of such coalitions and consequently affected the outcome of the conflicts in that country.

In sum, student mobilization and collective actions succeeded only when their insurgency coincided with the struggles of other major social groups and collectivities. Whenever other classes and groups joined with students to form broad coalitions, they were able to bring about serious political crises. Of the three cases studied, only in Nicaragua did students succeed in helping their allies, the FSLN, to secure power. In Iran and the Philippines, they failed to be of much influence in the eventual outcome of the conflicts. Consequently, it is important to analyze the role of other collectivities in order to understand the outcome of social conflicts in these countries. Let us turn next to the religious sector and the leadership of the clergy.

5   Clergy: actors with relative impunity

From some sociological perspectives, religious institutions and their temporal representatives have often been identified with the forces of inertia and societal reproduction (O'Dea 1966:2–18). Nevertheless, segments of the clergy have become politicized and proactive in social change projects during the past several decades in many developing countries. The clergy's politicization has come about, in part, because of the formation of exclusive rule, centralization of power in the state, and increased state reliance on external sources of support. These developments have reduced the state's reliance on the clergy and religious institutions in social and political matters. The weakening or breakdown of the historical alliance between the clergy and the state has been a catalyst to the politicization of the clergy. In extreme cases, the result has been the expulsion of the clergy from the polity. Politicization of the clergy has also been caused by adverse government policies imposed against certain social groups that constituted the bases of the religious institutions, such as exclusion of segments of the elite from the polity, or intense economic and political exclusion of the poorest sectors of the population.

In addition to politicization, some clergy have also adopted ideological shifts. Although the majority of the clergy have followed existing, dominant ideologies, a segment, often in the lower ranks, has adopted alternative ideologies that favor social revolution and a radical transformation of the social order. This ideological shift by clergy is facilitated in part by the fact that, like students, clerics are directly involved not in the production of material goods, but rather in the production, dissemination, and continuity of the moral and ideological bases of the social order. This engagement with theoretical explanations, justifications, and standards of judgment for the social order may at times stimulate and facilitate the clergy's ideological shift. This ideological shift was also in part affected by ideological changes in Christian theology outside these countries. For example, the Second Vatican Council played an important role in the rise of liberation theology in Nicaragua and the Philippines. The clergy's shift away from an emphasis on social peace and harmony and toward favoring certain social groups is likewise instigated by rising social and economic inequalities and the state's repression of disadvantaged social groups. Finally, their ideological shift and radicalization may be stimulated and intensified where alternative, revolutionary, challengers rise and struggle to transform the social structure.

The clergy's politicization and participation in collective action against the government has the potential for significant consequences during social and political conflicts. When the clergy condemn the government and its repressive acts, it has the effect of isolating the rulers and reducing their social bases of support. The clergy's relative immunity and control of a social space safe from government interference enable them to play an important part in political mobilization. As a result, the clergy may become indispensable in political conflicts, particularly where they possess independent resources and the opposition is in need of the basic infrastructure for mobilization and collective action. Under such conditions, the politicization of the clergy can lead to the refocusing of religious networks, which may be activated for mobilization and political action.

In Iran, Nicaragua, and the Philippines, major segments of the clergy were politicized and became involved in political conflicts. In all three cases, the clergy had been adversely affected to varying degrees by exclusive rule, contraction of the polity and centralization of power. Iran's clergy were the most affected by the breakdown of the historical alliance between the state and religious clergy. Their political involvement also resulted from the government's attempts to institute social reforms that directly affected the interests of segments of the clergy. In Nicaragua, political disagreements arose between the Catholic Church and the government in the early 1970s, and these conflicts were intensified in the aftermath of the 1972 earthquake. Church intervention in political activities expanded dramatically during the massive political mobilization that followed the assassination of Pedro Chamorro. In the Philippines, increased government attacks and repression of certain members of the clergy resulted in political disagreements between the Catholic Church and the Marcos regime. The clergy's political involvement increased, as in Nicaragua, during the rise of political conflicts produced by the assassination of Benigno Aquino.

Ideologically, the majority of the clergy in all three countries pursued moderate or reformist, rather than revolutionary, politics. Despite some differences in their approaches, the leading clerics in Iran pursued a moderate political course. The only major difference between Iranian Shiite clergy and the Catholic Church in Nicaragua and the Philippines was that the former lacked a centralized hierarchy, which generated divisions and in the early stages of the conflicts hindered their capacity for mobilization. In all three cases, only a minority of the clergy pursued a radical or militant ideology. In this radical minority lies the main difference between Iranian clergy and those in Nicaragua and the Philippines. While the radical clerical minority in Nicaragua and the Philippines shifted to the left and advocated liberation theology, in Iran the radical clerical minority favored the formation of an Islamic government. In Latin America and the Philippines, the rise of a leftist movement may have contributed to the expansion of liberation theology, while in Iran, in contrast, the weaknesses of the religious left, the Islamic Mojahedeen, may have been a factor in an ideological shift among the militant clerical minority. In all three cases, broader political issues rather than ideological shifts affected the timing of the clergy's political mobilization.

In general, the clergy's participation in social and political conflicts had significant consequences. In all three countries, the majority, particularly the upper echelon of the ecclesiastical hierarchy, participated and played a role in the political mobilization and conflicts. Their historically privileged position and relative immunity from state power provided a great potential to affect social and political processes in these countries. The clergy's traditional immunity insulated them from government repression. Their independent resources provided the capacity to oppose and form alternative alliances against the existing political order in times of social conflicts. Furthermore, their control of safe, social spaces in churches and mosques allowed other social groups to mobilize through religious institutions and engage in collective action against the government. Finally, the clergy's politicization refocused and activated preexisting networks of religious institutions. As a result, their political stand helped to nationalize the protests, particularly where no other option existed for mobilization.

Of course, the clergy's contributions varied in the three countries. In Iran, the highest echelon of the clergy did not initiate the mobilization process. In fact, these preeminent clerics wanted to avoid political conflicts. They only responded to political pressures and opened the mosques for political mobilization. In the end, these clerics just followed the events rather than leading them. In Nicaragua, in contrast, the Catholic Church took a leading position in opposing the government. Although it played a significant role in the process, in the end it could not determine the outcome. Finally, in the Philippines, the upper echelon of the clergy was rather conservative in contrast to Nicaragua. Yet, they succeeded in playing a significant role in the last days of the struggles, which affected the outcome of the conflicts.

Shiite clergy and the state in Iran

In the fifteen years prior to the revolutionary conflicts, state policies adversely affected the social, economic, and political status of the clergy in Iran. The number of clerical students, mosque attendance, and donations to the mosques were all in decline. As a result, many clerics had become increasingly dependent upon various government agencies, including the SAVAK, for survival. In addition, the clergy's politics were not internally coherent enough to mobilize the population against the regime, although most of them were adversely affected by government policies.

The vast majority of the clergy were not revolutionaries by any stretch of the imagination. A small minority of clerics supported the monarchy, and of these more than one hundred were defrocked after the revolution (Parsa 1989:292). The vast majority of the clergy, including the highest echelons in the religious centers of Qom and Mashhad, were moderates and did not favor a revolution. Nevertheless, this echelon of the clergy played a significant role during the initial stages of the revolutionary conflicts. They had national recognition and could activate mosque networks for religious and mourning ceremonies, of which there were approximately a hundred each calendar year. In the absence of other mobilization options, moderate clerics played a significant role in popular mobilization in the initial phase of the insurgency. Furthermore, their mosque networks proved to be the safest places where people could mobilize and remain relatively secure from government repression.

Only a minority of the clergy supported Khomeini and favored the overthrow of the monarchy. Although these clerics were crucial in the final stages of the revolutionary conflicts, their claims of centrality are highly exaggerated. Some analysts, following statements made by those now in power, have maintained that the clerics who supported Khomeini carried out their organizational activities in secret. While there is an element of truth in this statement, in reality the number of these clerics was very small, and they did not begin to mobilize against the government until a number of other major groups and collectivities had already done so. The pro-Khomeini clergy were concentrated in a few cities, while the revolutionary struggles were carried out by the population throughout the country where these clerics had little or no presence. The following summary reviews some highlights of the clergy's contributions to the Iranian revolution, beginning with the government's policies that adversely affected the clerics.

The Shiite clergy's political opposition to the government dated back to the early 1960s, when government policies significantly affected the clergy. A decade earlier a small number of politicized clergy opposed the Shah in his confrontation with nationalists led by Prime Minister Mosaddegh, but the clerical majority remained nonpolitical. During these conflicts, the highest religious leader in the country, Ayatollah Burujerdi, supported the Shah against Mosaddegh and welcomed the monarch's return to power (Parsa 1989:191). Changes in the government's policies at the end of the 1950s, however, set the stage for conflict with the clergy (Akhavi 1980:101–103; Bakhash 1984:24). In May 1961, the Shah ordered a broad program of reforms, including land reform, and dissolved the landlord-dominated Majles. Most clergy were against the land reform measures, since they would have reduced considerably the holdings of both mosques and some individual clerics. Land reform and other measures such as women's franchise were later incorporated into a program the Shah called the "White Revolution."

The clergy were divided in their response to the White Revolution. Only a small minority with ties to the government actually supported the Shah outright (Akhavi 1980:103), while most clergy opposed both land reform and the vote for women. In some parts of the country, notably Azerbijan, Isfahan, and Kirman, land reform was their main concern because the clergy themselves, along with mosques and religious institutions, stood to lose under the proposed reforms. Some preeminent clerics, including Ayatollahs Shariat-Madari and Mohammad Reza Golpaygani, pronounced women's franchise unacceptable and specifically requested that the Shah withdraw this proposed reform. Still other clergy, notably Ayatollah Taleghani, adopted a radically different position, criticizing the Shah's dictatorship and the capitulation laws and advocating justice for the poor (ibid.:101).

Ruhullah Musavi Khomeini was among the preeminent clerics, although relatively young and obscure in the early 1960s. He soon became well known, however, for his vociferous opposition to the Shah. Khomeini condemned virtually all the features of the White Revolution and their broader implications for Iran's place in the world. Khomeini denounced the entire referendum organized by the Shah as contrary to the nation's interests. A central theme of many of Khomeini's attacks was the position of the clergy and of Islam, both of which he believed to be threatened by the reforms. He rejected women's suffrage and equality as heretical Baha'i principles (Khomeini 1983, vol. I:56). He opposed land reform, arguing that it would have negative economic consequences (ibid.:13). Khomeini fulminated against Iran's economic penetration by Israel and the United States, the loss of Iranian markets, and bankruptcies among farmers and bazaaris (ibid.:112).

Most important, and a point that has been ignored in other analyses of the period, Khomeini was the only political or religious leader at this time who actually called for the overthrow of the Shah's regime. In preparation for Persian New Year in March 1963, Khomeini called for a time of mourning rather than of celebration, "to awaken Moslems and the country to the dangers that are ahead" (ibid.:27). In his message, Khomeini demanded that the "despotic government," which had violated the constitution, be removed and replaced by a new government, which respected Islam and cared for the Iranian people. On the second day of the New Year, Khomeini vehemently denounced an attack by the army against Qom clerical students who had organized a ceremony commemorating the martyrdom of Imam Sadegh. In response to the deaths and wounding of a number of these students, Khomeini condemned the ruling apparatus and its "Ghengis Khan-like nature. With this crime, the tyrannical regime guaranteed its own failure and destruction" (ibid.:38). Over the next few months, Khomeini repeatedly castigated the Shah's regime and its reforms, its violation of Islam and the constitution, and its economic policies, which adversely affected bazaaris. His utter rejection of the government and unwillingness to compromise made him well known and respected within certain segments of Iranian society.

Anti-government opposition reached a peak during the Shiite mourning month of Muharram in May and June. On June 3, Ashoura processions took an anti-Shah turn, and two days later Khomeini was arrested along with a number of other clerics throughout the country. Within hours of Khomeini's seizure, popular protests erupted in Tehran, Qom, Mashhad, Isfahan, Shiraz, Tabriz, and Kashan. Repression prevailed, and in the end the Shah's power was solidified. The price, however, was the breakup of the loose alliance that had existed between the clergy and the monarch since the Shah had first come to power more than twenty years earlier.

During the years that followed, the clergy's position was successively undermined by the centralization of state power, increased state autonomy from the clergy, rapid economic development, secularization, and a number of specific state policies. Supported by the United States, increased oil revenues, and a strong military, the state no longer relied on internal sources of support, thus bypassing the clergy and reducing their role in political affairs. Later during the revolutionary struggles, Ayatollah Shariat-Madari was to complain that the Shah's regime violated the historically established position of the clergy as intermediary between the government and people.

The state's policies and projects undermined the status and influence of the clergy still further during the following years. As the economic position of the clergy deteriorated in the 1970s due to various government policies and a decline in religious donations, large segments of the clergy became dependent on the state for economic assistance. Even some of the highest-ranking clerics requested financial help from the royal court (Alam 1991:215–216). The SAVAK and the prime minister's office distributed millions of dollars among some 15,000 clerics (Bakhtiar 1982:136; *Iranshahr*, December 24, 1982). The economic circumstances of many clerics worsened in 1977 when the government of Amouzegar cut the $35 million previously spent by the prime minister's office on thousands of the Shiite clergy (Taheri 1986:214).

Specific government policies adversely affected the clergy's position. One example was the Sazman-e Oughaf, or the Endowments Organization, created by the government to take charge of land donated by individuals to religious institutions. The Endowments Organization at times illegally appropriated and sold religious properties. During a severe housing shortage in 1976, the Shah ordered that such land be used for housing projects for workers (*Kayhan*, February 1977). In another instance, a ruined Tehran mosque with no income was turned into a large office building (Fischer 1980:115). Such policies accelerated the decline of a number of mosques. According to official figures, 20,000 mosques existed in Iran in 1965. Ten years later, the Endowments Organization reported only 9,015 mosques. Between 1960 and 1975, Tehran lost nine out of a total of thirty-two theological schools (Akhavi 1980:129). The regime closed three of the country's most important clerical schools, imprisoned several clerics and prohibited the few opposing clergy from giving sermons. In the educational sphere, government policies combined with secularization progressively undermined the position of the clergy. Monthly stipends for clerical students and teachers at religious schools were abolished and replaced by significantly smaller funds dispersed by the Endowments Organization (ibid.:140). By the mid-1970s, senior clerical students who had studied for several years received less than $30 per month (Tahmaseb Pour, interview, February 1999). The government further threatened to undermine traditional clerical practices by creating a Religious Corps in 1971, modeled after the Literacy Corps, to teach peasants "true Islam." Such state policies, plus growing secularization, contributed to a gradual decline in religious education.

Besides pursuing secular, anti-clerical policies, the Shah made a point of glorifying Persian identity and history at the expense of Shiite symbols. He abolished the traditional Islamic calendar, replacing it with one dating back more than two millennia, and celebrated 2,500 years of Persian civilization. The shift from an Islamic calendar to a secular one harking back to the historic Persian Empire violated an established religious symbol and inevitably alienated the clergy. Meanwhile, the monarch claimed that, as a devout Moslem, he received special assistance from

God: "Without divine favor, my revolution would not have been possible. Without God's support, I would be a man like all the rest! And divine assistance will guarantee the continuation of our work!" (Hoveyda 1980:12). These claims further riled the monarch's clerical critics.

The clergy also came under attack by some Islamic writers and intellectuals. Sadeghi Tehrani, a former clergyman who left the profession, in a book vehemently criticized the clergy for corruption, selfish materialism, ignorance, and failure to involve in politics. He accused some of the religious leaders of lavish consumption of religious contributions for themselves and their families (Tehrani 1970:99). He further blamed the clergy for the fact that most people, especially the youth, did not attend mosques and moved away from religion (ibid.:81, 106). The rise of modernist interpretations of Islam, such as the writings of Ali Shariati, a sociologist with a leftist perspective, also challenged the Shiite clergy. Shariati charged that the Shiite clergy did not represent the true Islam. In fact, for centuries the clergy had betrayed the cause of Islam by legitimizing the power of the rulers and the wealthy upper classes (Abrahamian 1989:113). Shariati accused the clergy of obscurantism, ignorance and hypocrisy which caused the flight of young Iranians towards western ideologies and culture (Boroujerdi 1996:110–113). Shariati's criticism caused the youth and even some clerical students to refuse to follow the lead of the highest religious leaders in religious matters (Tahmaseb Pour, interview, February 1999).

Finally, the growing secularization of the population and expansion of the educational institutions also adversely affected the Shiite clergy in various ways. The expansion of secular education and rising economic opportunities reduced the interest of many Iranians in traditional religion. As a result, in the years prior to the revolution, the number of ceremonies held in mosques decreased, and mosque attendance and financial donations[1] dwindled (*Kayhan International*, October 21, 1978). Conditions deteriorated so much that "many religious students were attempting to complete secular high school at night, but many also merely drifted" away from clerical study (Fischer 1980:127). More importantly, as economic opportunities expanded in the public and private sector, a growing number of clerics left their practices. A cleric who voluntarily left the profession stated that in the few years prior to the revolution hundreds[2] of clerics and

---

[1] Although it is impossible to find accurate figures for financial donations, interviews with a large number of Iranians confirm that mosque attendence had reached an all-time low by 1977.

[2] In 1973, in Qom alone at least 500 clerics who had already graduated and some clerical students left their schools and practices for regular jobs and other professions (Tahmaseb Pour, interview, February 1999).

clerical students left the institution every year (Tahmaseb Pour, interview, February 1999).

The clergy were increasingly aware of the population's declining commitment to religion and at times criticized it. For example, during the revolutionary struggles, a prominent cleric in a special mourning ceremony held at the Azerbijani mosque in the Tehran bazaar stated: "It has been a while that we have been asleep. Materialistic concerns filled our beings so much, and worldly, oppressive appearances looked so God-like that we had forgotten about our mission, commitment, and all the messages. But sleep, how long?" (*Zamimeh* 1978, no. 14:24). In the fall of 1977, clerics and modernist Islamic intellectuals who gathered in the Ghoba Mosque criticized rival, secular, materialist, and Marxist ideologies in the country (Bayat 1998:150). Ayatollah Khomeini, too, repeatedly denounced the cultural transformations taking place in the country. He declared, both before and after the revolution, that under the Shah "there was nothing left of Islam; there was only the name" (*Jumhuri Eslami*, December 25, 1982). "Our culture had been imported from the West. This culture penetrated all aspects of Iranian life, detaching people from Islam" (*Ettelaat*, December 20, 1982). Acknowledging a decline in the clergy's prestige in the political arena, Khomeini strongly pleaded with intellectuals and university students not to reject the clergy. "If they do not have political education, you should embrace them and give them political education" (Khomeini 1983, vol. I:434).

Clergy's politics during the revolutionary struggles

Despite the negative impact of government policies, intellectual criticisms, and growing secularization, the clergy were far from eliminated. Most of the clergy adapted to the new conditions, remained or became depoliticized, and avoided political issues. As a result, the mosque retained its immunity from the government's power. In fact, it became the only place where people could safely gather, express their grievances, and mobilize for action during the revolutionary struggles. But the clergy were not in a position to lead the struggles. As a result, in the wake of limited liberalization in the fall of 1977, the clergy did not initially take steps to oppose the regime. Khomeini was surprised by clerical inaction. In a statement he encouraged them to mobilize, saying that others had already begun mobilizing and that the clergy, too, should write and protest (Khomeini 1983, vol. I:437).

It was popular pressure that prompted the top-ranking clergy, led by the three Qom Marja-e Taghlid, the "source of emulation, to take action against the government's repressive measures. But at first these clerics lacked cohesion and consensus. When the Qom clerics gathered to develop a strategy for responding to a further massacre of rebellious Qom clerical students in January, 1978, they failed to reach agreement" (*The Freedom Movement* [Abroad] 1978, vol. I:54). As protests mounted, the highest religious leaders issued limited calls for mourning ceremonies and exhortations to remain calm and avoid confrontation. Ayatollah Shariat-Madari, one of the three, rejected a popular request for a national strike, even though the Qom bazaar had struck independently. Ayatollah Khonsari, Tehran's Marja-e Taghlid, advised Tehran bazaaris not to strike (*The Freedom Movement* [Abroad] 1978, vol. I:54).

Politically, the highest echelons of the clergy pursued a moderate line and eschewed collective action, especially violence, and favored quiet diplomacy. In ideological terms, they advocated the correct implementation of the constitution to eliminate anti-Islamic laws and practices, rather than the formation of an Islamic government. A few short months before the revolution, Ayatollah Shariat-Madari declared that while an Islamic government was their long-term goal, the strict observance of the constitution would give people all that was necessary for the time being (*Kayhan*, November 2, 1978). Similarly, the clerical community in the important religious center of Qom issued a statement upon the appointment of Prime Minister Sharif-Emami that called for democratic reforms, but stopped short of demanding the abolition of the monarchy or the establishment of an Islamic government (*Kayhan*, August 30, 1978). The three leading grand ayatollahs in Qom never closed off their option to compromise with the regime. As late as the period of Azhari's military government, appointed in early November 1978, these clerics met with government representatives who asked them to exhort the public to cease their opposition to the regime. The Marja-e Taghlid responded that they were willing to do so, provided the government implemented the constitution and respected Islam. At the same time, they feared that any such exhortation would fall on deaf ears and go unheeded (Ladjevardian 1982, tape 2:2–3).

Nevertheless, this moderate faction of the clergy, under pressure from the public, played an important role in opening the mosques for the cycles of mourning ceremonies that continued until the fall of 1978. The influence of the moderate clerics can be seen by examining public statements issued by the clerical community, which show that most clergy did not call for the overthrow of the monarchy or the establishment of an Islamic state. Table 8 summarizes protest statements and declarations by the clerical community (defined as three or more clerics) during major political events or ceremonies in the period from autumn 1977 to autumn 1978. Each of the fifteen statements condemned political violence and

Table 8 *Protest statements by clergy (frequency and percent) in Iran,*
September 21, 1977 to September 21, 1978

Demand	Frequency	Percentage
Condemn violence and repression	15	100
Condemn despotism/demand its removal	7	47
Condemn imperialism/demand independence	5	33
Condemn lack of civil liberties	5	33
Demand abolition of anti-Islamic laws	4	27
Demand improved conditions for workers and peasants	2	13
Demand return to Islamic calendar	2	13
Demand clerical supervision of laws	2	13
Protest taxes	1	7
Demand formation of an Islamic government	1	7
Condemn imperialist pillage	1	7
Demand nationalization/redistribution of pillaged wealth	1	7
Protest against poverty	1	7

N = 15.
Source: author's compilation.

repression. Seven statements also denounced despotism, while five deplored imperialist influences in Iran and the lack of national independence. Five statements condemned the absence of civil liberties, and two
called for improved economic conditions for workers and peasants. Four
of the statements urged the abolition of anti-Islamic laws, while two
statements demanded clerical supervision of laws passed by the Majles,
which had been a feature of the 1906 constitution. Finally, several issues
were mentioned in one statement each: nationalization of pillaged wealth,
taxes, poverty, and foreign exploitation. Only one statement called for the
formation of an Islamic government.

Indeed, those who favored radical transformation of Iranian society
along fundamentalist Islamic lines constituted a small minority of the
clergy. As Ahmad Khomeini, son of Ayatollah Khomeini, stated (*Ettelaat*,
September 23, 1979), the clerics who opposed the regime were only a
small minority. Because of limited size and capacity for mobilization, this
faction of the clergy failed to take advantage of an opportunity to mobilize
against the regime in 1975 during a revolt of pro-Khomeini clerical
students. On June 5, in an event ignored by all scholars of the Iranian
revolution, more than a thousand clerical students took control of the
Madraseh-e Faizieh-e Qom, a school for training clergy. Clerical students
from the Madraseh-e Khan, an adjacent school, joined them. The protesters raised a red flag, symbol of Shiite martyrdom, high enough to be

seen throughout the city of Qom; they also raised a banner that read "We commemorate the anniversary of the great rebellion of Imam Khomeini." The students also broadcast tapes of Khomeini's fiery speeches against the Shah.

The timing and place of the revolt were well chosen. The date was the twelfth anniversary of Ayatollah Khomeini's 1963 arrest and the subsequent massacre of protesters. The Madraseh-e Faizieh-e Qom was located near the shrine of Fatima, a pilgrimage site for Shiite Moslems from all over the country. From exile in Iraq, Ayatollah Khomeini himself endorsed the clerical students' protests. In a message of condolence to the Iranian people, he congratulated them for the "dawn of freedom" and the elimination of imperialism and its "dirty agents." In his message, Khomeini stated that by the second day of the rebellion, forty-five students had been killed, and that the government had refused the injured admission to Qom hospitals (Khomeini 1983, vol. I:359).

The student insurrection lasted for three days and nights until it was finally put down by several units of army commandos dispatched from Tehran. Dozens of students were killed and injured and more than five hundred arrested.[3] More than a hundred were convicted and given prison sentences ranging from seven to fifteen years. Following the repression of the insurgents, the school was shut down by SAVAK and remained closed until the end of the Shah's rule.

This protest went completely unnoticed by most of the Iranian population, although it was reported in the national press. The response to the Qom revolt was very limited. Clerical students in Mashhad also demonstrated against the government, and two clerics and approximately thirty clerical students were arrested. In Tehran and Tabriz, students protested against the repression of Qom clerical students. But no mourning ceremonies were held by the clergy or the public, and no bazaar shutdowns occurred anywhere in the country. The failure of the rebellion confirms the weaknesses of the pro-Khomeini clergy and the lack of a powerful Islamic movement ready to mobilize.

Pro-Khomeini activists constituted a very small minority of the clergy and were not very active in the years prior to the revolution (Pakdaman 1995:157). This faction of the clergy began mobilizing in December 1977 after other groups, such as the Writers' Association, the National Front, and leftist university students, had already engaged in collective action. Khomeini, witnessing the silence of his supporters, encouraged them to mobilize. In a letter to Ayatollah Motahari in Tehran, Khomeini suggested that a committee be formed to lead the movement. In addition to

---

[3] These figures are taken from a written statement by students at the Madraseh-e Faizieh-e Qom, in the possession of the author.

Motahari himself, he put forward four names, including Ayatollahs Beheshti, Anvari, Golzadeh-Ghafouri, and Mowla'i (Taheri 1986:181). The weaknesses of this faction are illustrated by the fact that none of these clerics had a national recognition, nor did the group share a similar ideology, except that they all opposed the regime. Beheshti and Motahari agreed with Khomeini's vision of an Islamic government, but the others had different views. Ayatollah Golzadeh-Ghafouri had socialist leanings and advocated a democratic Islamic society; Anvari and Mowla'i opposed clerical involvement in the government. These ideological divisions were so marked that the latter three clerics withdrew from politics after the revolution.

That the pro-Khomeini clergy were few in number was illustrated by their first meeting, in which they put together a list of clerics who would strongly support Khomeini's leadership. They could come up with the names of no more than seventy-five clergy in the entire country (Taheri 1986:190). As political conflicts mounted, the number of clerics opposing government repression grew but remained relatively small. This can be seen by analyzing the political statements issued by clerics during important political and religious events. With the total number of clergy estimated to be 85,000, only a small number of clerics signed statements or called for mourning ceremonies to commemorate massacres during the early months of the conflicts. For example, some thirty clerics from Isfahan signed a statement condemning the deaths of Qom students (Abouzar 1978, vol. I, part 3:32). The Tabriz massacre was denounced in separate statements signed by forty-one Qom clergy (*Zamimeh* 1978, no. 14:3), fifty-six clerics in Tehran (*Zamimeh* 1978, no. 14:20), and forty clerics from Yazd (*Zamimeh* 1978, no. 16:8). Thirty-nine Qom clerics signed a statement decrying killings in Yazd during a mourning ceremony (*Zamimeh* 1978, no. 16:6), while in Tehran, 101 clergy called for mourning ceremonies (*Zamimeh* 1978, no. 16:19). When police attacked the Tabriz clerical school, wounding many clerical students, forty clerics issued a statement condemning the action (*Zamimeh* 1978, no. 18:40). As the mourning cycles continued, seventy-seven Tehran clerics called for yet another mourning ceremony on June 17 (*Zamimeh* 1978, no. 18:29). Even public statements by supporters of Khomeini indicated that the number of his best-known, most outspoken supporters was small, and many in fact were imprisoned or exiled by the summer of 1978 (Abouzar 1978, vol. I, part 3:67; *Zamimeh* 1978, no. 18:27).

In addition to being limited in number, the militant clergy were also geographically concentrated in a few religious centers and large cities. This geographic concentration is evidenced by the distribution of the arrests of clergy. Data on such arrests during the first nine months of their protests, the most repressive period, indicate that roughly 25 percent were from Qom, 13 percent from Tehran, 7 percent each from Mashhad and Hamedan, 5 percent each from Isfahan and Semnan, 4 percent from Shiraz, 4 percent from Rezaieh, and the rest from other cities. Fully one-quarter of all arrests took place in the religious center of Qom, while an additional 45 percent occurred in only seven other cities.[4]

The pro-Khomeini faction of the clergy gained great momentum when the Shah promised liberalization and appointed Sharif-Emami as prime minister. The proclamation of a government of national reconciliation granted some concessions to the clergy, reduced repression against non-communists, and thus provided a greater opportunity for pro-Khomeini clergy to mobilize. Nonpolitical clergy in Tehran, Qom, and Mashhad who had been inactive until now acted to secure the release of fourteen clerics from jail and the reinstatement of twenty-one others forbidden to give sermons (*Kayhan*, September 2, 1978). Soon, virtually all clergy who had been in jail were freed by Sharif-Emami, and thereafter, only a handful of clerics were arrested. Even though a number of violent events occurred in the following months, only one cleric was killed.[5] It was during the brief "liberalization" that two militant clerics, accompanying marchers participating in religious ceremonies, publicly called for the first time for the monarch's overthrow and the establishment of an Islamic government (*Kayhan*, September 5, 1978).

Yet none of the pro-Khomeini clerics could lead the struggles because of lack of national recognition. Thus, they had to rely on Ayatollah Taleghani who was the most important cleric released from prison. Unlike Khomeini, Taleghani had been among the few clerics who had supported Prime Minister Mosaddegh and his National Front. Taleghani had also defended the poor and the working classes and favored running the country through popular democracy and people's councils, not the clergy in a theocracy. He also advocated workers' councils to run the factories. In fact, he was known as the "Red Ayatollah." Consequently, Taleghani was respected even among the left. Upon release from jail, Khomeini asked Taleghani (and Ayatollah Montazeri) to lead the movement. Thus, it was Taleghani who called for a march on the religious day of Tasoua, held on December 10, 1978. People responded overwhelmingly throughout the country, and the event became the largest march ever in Iranian history.

---

[4] Arrests do not give a complete indication of the distribution of radical clergy, for many doubtless avoided arrest by moving underground. Living clandestinely, however, would have limited their ability to mobilize the opposition effectively.

[5] Ashouri was killed by the military on December 4, 1978. See M. J. [pseud.] (1979:82).

The Tasoua resolution, the most important document in the Iranian revolution, which has been ignored by virtually all scholars of the subject, was put forward by a coalition of liberal political groups and clergy. It recognized Khomeini as the leader of the people and called for social justice and freedom based on Islamic principles, which had been a part of the 1906 Iranian constitution. It condemned despotism and imperialism, and called for social justice for workers and peasants. The resolution also called for the "eradication of any form of discrimination, human exploitation, class coercion, and economic domination that may result in the accumulation of wealth on the one hand and deprivation on the other." Significantly, the resolution did not call for the establishment of an Islamic government based on clerical rule (*Zamimeh* 1978, no. 22:11–16).

Several important conclusions emerge from the analysis of the march and the resolution. First, pro-Khomeini clerics lacked sufficient strength and popular support to publicly declare their principal objective, that is, the formation of an Islamic government based on clerical rule. Second, even at this late stage in the uprising, with only two months until the overthrow of the monarchy, pro-Khomeini clerics were not in a position of sufficient authority to lead the movement. Thus, they had to rely on Ayatollah Taleghani's authority and popularity. Third, Ayatollah Taleghani clearly influenced the content of the resolution, particularly regarding issues of human exploitation, class coercion, and accumulation of wealth. It is important to note that Ayatollah Taleghani never advocated the formation of a theocratic state.

Obviously, the Iranian clergy did not share a single ideological perspective during the revolutionary struggles. Ideological and political divisions were responsible for the conflicts that followed the removal of the Shah. During these conflicts, a number of clerics were imprisoned, a few fled the country, some were killed or executed by the government, and others who had been a part of the ruling clergy were expelled from politics. As leftists were attacked and repressed by the government, Ayatollah Taleghani became one of the first victims of the Islamic Republic. He received the highest votes of any candidate in the 1979 elections for the Assembly of Experts and the Majles. With his political standing and popularity, he became Tehran's prayer leader. In his last sermon, Taleghani warned the people of autocracy under the cover of religion (*Ettelaat*, September 1, 1979). He died three days later under very mysterious circumstances.[6] As moderates were expelled from the government, Ayatollah Shariat-Madari, the highest religious leader in the country, was stripped of his title of Marja'a Taghlid, "source of emulation," in 1982 and placed under house arrest until his death in 1985. Finally, as infighting intensified, Khomeini

---

[6] Interview with Taleghani's chief aide, Mohammad Shanehchi, Paris, April 1998.

dissolved the Islamic Republican Party, the only remaining party, in 1987. Soon a number of clerics who had played an active role in the revolution were expelled from the ruling circle. The conflicts culminated in the removal of Ayatollah Montazeri as the designated successor to Khomeini in 1989. He was violently attacked and confined to his home the following year. He was formally placed under house arrest in 1997.

To sum up, state policies beginning in the early 1960s adversely affected the clergy and resulted in the breakdown of the alliance between the state and the clergy. But the clergy's response to the state was not unanimous. In fact, the highest religious leaders pursued a moderate political line and preferred to avoid political confrontation. More significantly, because of their moderation, the mosque retained some measure of immunity from the state, in part because it did not present any serious threat to the government. As a result, mosques remained open and available as places for assemblies and religious ceremonies. Indeed, the mosque was the only institution with a national network that was relatively immune from the power of the state, and by the time of the revolution, it represented the only option available for mobilization. Mosques were ideal places in which to convene because they were relatively safe from violent attacks. Yet it should be emphasized that political mobilization did not begin in the mosque, nor did the clergy initiate it. The mosque became a center for mobilization only after intense repression stifled opposition protests elsewhere. This situation greatly helped Ayatollah Khomeini and the small minority of militant clergy who supported him.

The Catholic Church and political conflicts in Nicaragua

The Nicaraguan Catholic Church likewise was active in the political conflicts of the 1970s, which culminated in a revolution. As in Iran, growing centralization of power and increased state intervention, particularly after the 1972 Managua earthquake, set the stage for conflict between the Church and the Somoza regime. Unlike in Iran, however, adverse state policies never fundamentally undermined the position of the Nicaraguan Church or the clergy. Although small in terms of numbers of personnel,[7] the Church's immunity from the state enabled it to take political stands against the government. Thus, from the beginning the

---

[7] In 1973 the Church had relatively limited personnel, numbering only 130 priests, some 500 nuns, and 40,000 lay workers (*La Prensa*, December 30, 1973). The scarcity of priests gave rise to the creation of the Delegates of the Word, known as DPs, who were chosen and trained to carry out the tasks of catechism, administration of the sacrament, and evangelization and community development. The DPs, whose training included health, literacy, agriculture and politics, in addition to biblical teachings, applied the consciousness-raising method developed by Paulo Fraire in Brazil. By 1979, there were approximately 5,000 DPs in Nicaragua (Sierra 1985:152).

Church was an important part of the opposition to the government. Its opposition contributed to the state's vulnerability and thus provided greater opportunities for some social groups to engage in collective action. During the revolutionary conflicts of the late 1970s, the Catholic hierarchy took a strong stand against the regime, in favor of the moderate opposition, while a small minority of priests allied themselves with the Sandinistas and actively promoted social revolution.

Until 1970, the highest echelon of the Nicaraguan Catholic Church either openly supported the Somoza regime or passively tolerated it. Many priests were on the government payroll, serving as ambassadors and public employees. The Church's conservatism and support for the government were explicitly expressed in a pastoral letter issued by Archbishop Mons. Gonzales y Robleto as late as 1959: "all authority comes from God . . . he who resists the authority resists God" (Williams 1989:21). In the late 1960s, Archbishop Gonzales y Robleto was himself very close to the Somoza family. He was always present at official ceremonies and celebrated numerous masses for the Somozas on different occasions (Foroohar 1989:67). Bishop Donald Chavez Nuñez publicly defended the government after the massacre of opposition in January 1967 (Berryman 1984:61). This conservatism led to a decline in the Church's public standing, however, as revealed in two public opinion surveys conducted by the Institute for Human Advancement in 1968 and 1969, which found that the Church's prestige had fallen to near zero (*La Prensa*, February 14, 1974).

Church politics began to diversify in the mid-1960s and remained divided throughout the next decade. A small faction continued to back Somoza Debayle, a sizable segment opposed the regime but were not supporters of the FSLN alternative, and a third, tiny minority was pro-Sandinista (Montgomery 1982/1983:210).

The politicization and radicalization of Nicaraguan priests began in the late 1960s as a result of the Second Vatican Council and the Catholic Church's conference in Medellin. In 1968, seven young priests issued a statement calling upon the Nicaraguan Church to generate a ministry of service and human development. They also demanded that the government halt repression and torture and free political prisoners (Berryman 1984:61). Their actions led the Somoza-owned newspaper *Novedades* to label these young priests "the seven priests of Marx" (Dodson and O'Shaughnessy 1990:125).[8] Soon, a small number of radicalized priests began to organize Ecclesiastical Base Communities (CEBs) among the marginalized populations in urban and rural Nicaragua (Foroohar

---

[8] In 1970, the government even arrested and tortured a priest who had intervened to reduce the violence between the National Guard and the FSLN (Berryman 1984:61).

1989:67; Kirk 1992:65; Sierra 1985:152). By 1979, more than 300 CEBs were estimated to be in operation (Sierra 1985:152).[9] The CEBs combined Bible study with critical reflection on existing social reality. Their evangelical activities were rooted in the Catholic Church's new "preferential option" on behalf of the poor. These priests and nuns working in the poor districts of Managua later became involved in mass mobilizations against the government during the revolutionary struggles. The CEBs became more radicalized after the earthquake when they came into direct contact with government agencies administering relief. Corruption and mismanagement of relief funds antagonized both the poor and the priests and nuns who were trying to help them (Foroohar 1989:124).

Some of these clergy, such as Father Ernesto Cardenal and Father Gaspar Garcia Laviana, even allied themselves with the Sandinistas during the revolutionary struggles in the late 1970s. Father Cardenal had organized a contemplative community in Solentiname where he preached revolutionary Christianity. Some members of his community were among the first to join the Sandinistas in armed struggle in October 1977 (Black 1981:102). Others, such as Garcia Laviana, a member of the Congregation of the Sacred Heart headquartered in Granada, left his parish to join FSLN guerrillas in the north of the country.[10] He justified his action thus:

Somocismo is sin, and to liberate ourselves from oppression is to get rid of sin. With rifle in hand, full of faith and love for the Nicaraguan people, I shall fight to my last breath for the advent of the kingdom of justice in our homeland, that kingdom of justice announced by the Messiah under the light of the star of Bethlehem (Sierra 1985:154–155).

Although their ideological shift was significant, these clergy initially did not exert a great impact on the political development of the country. They were small in numbers, located away from the Church's power center, and therefore unable to generate opportunities for national mobilization. Their contribution remained at the local level in grassroots organizing, which played an important role later when large-scale conflicts erupted.

The more significant change in Church–state relations occurred in early 1970 with the appointment of Archbishop Miguel Obando y Bravo. Although not a liberation theologian, the archbishop was influenced heavily by that theology. Nicaraguans often viewed his actions and statements as following the principles of the Second Vatican Council and the Medellin Conference (*La Prensa*, April 5, 1978). In April 1974, he criticized the Church's traditional role in avoiding social, eco-

[9] Many CEB members were victimized with the intensification of repression in 1974 (Sierra 1985:153).
[10] Father Gaspar Garcia Laviana was killed in battle in Rivas (*La Prensa*, December 11, 1978).

nomic, and political issues. "In our opinion it is both strange and ridiculous to see the interpretation of the Church's role assigned by the old capitalism. According to this interpretation, the Church should be content with its role in the sacristy, exercising its influence through individual conscience and in private life" (Kirk 1992:58). The archbishop even went so far as to acknowledge implicitly that when all peaceful means fail, the use of violence against an unjust government was justified (Foroohar 1989:85–86).

With Obando y Bravo at its helm, the Church gradually but dramatically reversed its role from upholder to outspoken critic of the Somoza government. Shortly after his appointment, the archbishop sold the Mercedes Benz that had been a gift from Somoza Debayle and gave the money to the poor (Williams 1989:27). Returning from a Synod of Bishops in Rome in 1971, Obando y Bravo declared that he would not dignify the upcoming election with his participation (Dodson and O'Shaughnessy 1990:120). In April 1972, the Nicaraguan Church issued a pastoral letter criticizing social conditions within the country. In a subsequent statement, Archbishop Obando y Bravo called the country's political situation "muddled" and declared, "The old system has too many faults" (Diederich 1981:90).

The principal factor that placed the Church on a collision course with the government was the earthquake in Managua at the end of 1972. For several weeks after the earthquake, Church organizations were the main distributors of relief materials on which most Managua residents depended for survival. Soon, however, the government assigned the responsibility for distributing relief materials to government agencies and associates of Somoza's Liberal Party. Their overt corruption and manipulation of human disaster for personal gain provoked strong criticism by the Church hierarchy and membership alike (Foroohar 1989:94). Nearly all of the twenty-seven parish churches in Managua were destroyed, yet the Church refused to solicit the government for funds to rebuild them, instead accepting aid from Italy and Germany (La Prensa, December 30, 1973). A few months later, the Nicaraguan bishops boycotted a state ceremony that transferred the powers of the executive office to a three-member junta, which Somoza had created to succeed him.

In the quake's aftermath the Church, as a collective, began criticizing the government, effectively using its relative immunity to challenge state policies and decisions through public statements. In 1973 and 1974, the Church issued eleven public statements. Seven of these protested against the government's political repression; two specifically condemned the state's repression of the Church; three statements declared that the government served narrow interests; one called for the reorganization of the National Guard; and one criticized the elections. In separate statements, Archbishop Obando y Bravo supported the demands of mothers of political prisoners, criticized the government's repression of journalists under the Libel Law, and backed striking construction workers (*La Prensa*, May 24 and September 29, 1973). More importantly, as the earthquake's devastation quickened conflicts among various social groups and between some of these groups and the government, the Church adopted political positions not only against the government but also against employers. For example, on May Day in a mass attended by hundreds of workers and their families to commemorate workers fallen in the earthquake, the archbishop stated, "I know that you, dear workers, are men of action, and if you halt your labors it is in order to protest, in order to go out in defense of your rights, in order to demand a just salary . . . a salary that permits [the worker] a level of life that is dignified and human" (*La Prensa*, May 1, 1973). When leftist labor leader Domingo Sanchez Salgado declared a hunger strike to protest against his continued detention after his prison sentence had expired, Obando y Bravo urged his release (*La Prensa*, July 5, 1973).

Issues of social justice remained in the forefront of the Church concerns. Addressing the Social Club of Masaya, the archbishop insisted that there could be neither peace nor tranquillity in a country where authentic social justice did not exist (*La Prensa*, September 29, 1973). Again in a statement the Church expressed its concern for the suffering of the Nicaraguan people: "the national church represented by Mons. Obando, had maintained an undiminished position confronting the abuses and errors of public power, and thus it will continue while misery and injustice continue adding to the prostration and anguish of the grand majority of marginal people" (*La Prensa*, December 29, 1973). In a circular letter, the bishops of Nicaragua admonished:

Temporal governments are not complying with their mission when they tyrannize and abuse the rights of citizens, when they restrict the exercise of legitimate freedoms, when they absorb what belongs to all in favor of particular factions, when they impede the search and formation of new options for the more complete development of the nation. The same could be said about an economy that monopolizes businesses for the exclusive advantage of a few, condemning to hunger the rest of the population; efforts to improve the condition of the worker turn out to be useless and false when there are no limits imposed on the detestable hunger for money. (*La Prensa*, November 18, 1973)

In 1974, seven bishops, including the archbishop of Managua, released a pastoral letter that was highly critical of the upcoming presidential elections. It asserted that when the government was engaged in legal warfare against its citizens, they had the right to dissent. The letter declared that while the Church had an obligation to promote political duty, it was not obliged to support political power; and that Christians could not be forced to vote against the principles of freedom that their faith demanded of them. The letter further observed that a single-party system was contradictory to human nature and recommended that if the vote was solely a formality, individuals should abstain from voting. The bishops insisted that peace could not be based on repressive force and mentioned the duty of moral resistance, noting that the right to dissent exists even among the military ranks (*La Prensa*, August 8, 1974).

During this period the Church's active opposition to the government made it a target of attack and repression. The government approached the Vatican in an effort to have the archbishop removed, but the Vatican conveyed its firm decision to maintain Obando y Bravo in his post (*La Prensa*, December 29, 1973). To intimidate Church authorities, the government erected obstacles to the entry and departure of foreign priests (*La Prensa*, December 5, 1973). On one occasion, a National Guard unit burst into the church of Fatima in Managua and dispersed a meeting of 200 SCAAS construction workers, an attack that provoked the archbishop's protest (*La Prensa*, July 13, 1973). The government also levied a fine of 1,000 córdobas, plus 333.33 córdobas for interests and costs, against the directors of *La Prensa* for publishing the poem, "Trip to New York" by Father Ernesto Cardenal, a well-known opponent of the government (*La Prensa*, November 17, 1973). In 1974, the General Tax Office, in a move that violated the Nicaraguan constitution, notified the archbishop that the Church owed the sum of 5,000 córdobas plus fines for property taxes dating back to 1970, the year he was appointed. The tax notification was issued on the heels of a strong statement by Obando y Bravo and the Archdiocese of Managua denouncing state censorship of the media (*La Prensa*, May 11, 1974). The government stopped short of taking even harsher measures against the Church in large part because of the Church's relative immunity.

The Catholic Church and the revolutionary conflicts in Nicaragua

Although silent during the state of siege imposed at the end of 1974, the Church continued to challenge Somoza once martial law was lifted in September 1977. The day after martial law was revoked, the Church published a statement it had issued months earlier about social justice and human rights in Nicaragua. In the statement, the Church condemned the state of terror that forced countless peasants to flee their homes and lands in the mountains of Zelaya, Matagalpa, and Las Segovias:

many settlements have been practically abandoned: houses and personal effects burned, and the people flee desperately and without assistance . . . On the one hand, the accumulation of lands and riches in the hands of the few increases. And on the other, humble peasants are evicted from their cultivated lands by threats and by taking advantage of the emergency situation. (*La Prensa*, September 20, 1977)

The statement denounced arbitrary arrests, imprisonment, and various other violations of human rights. The bishops further observed that the military commanders of some settlements insisted on requiring special permission for each religious meeting, while in other places, military patrols occupied Catholic chapels, converting them to military headquarters. Some lay Delegates of the Word (DPs) were pressured to suspend their work with missionary priests, others were arrested by the military and tortured, while still others simply disappeared (*La Prensa*, September 20, 1977).

This statement was soon followed by other proclamations issued by the Nicaraguan Catholic Church. During the final three months of 1977, the Church issued eleven public statements after press censorship was lifted. Its principal concern was government repression, mentioned in seven of these statements. In one statement the Church even criticized the narrow social base of the government, which it charged served particular interests. Four statements called for a national dialogue. In October, as conflicts between the Sandinistas and the government intensified, Archbishop Obando y Bravo issued a plea for a "national dialogue" to bring about peace and reconciliation. The statement, which received a great deal of attention and was widely supported by diverse groups and organizations, did not condemn any specific group or individual, but called for an end to bloodshed and suffering and "an end to the triumph of the barbarians" (*La Prensa*, October 18, 1977). The Church's political activities, particularly within the context of FSLN actions in the countryside and the occupation of churches by students, brought down government reprisals. At least two priests were arrested (*La Prensa*, November 6, 1977), and a number of priests and nuns were beaten by National Guard troops, who were attacking students in churches (*La Prensa*, December 19 and 21, 1977).

The Church's political involvement intensified during 1978 when it issued twenty-five statements against the Somoza regime. Seventeen of the statements condemned government repression, and five demanded Somoza's resignation. In four statements the Church called for amnesty for political prisoners, reflecting their growing numbers. Finally, in one of the statements, it denounced the government as both corrupt and serving only narrow interests.

Even before Chamorro's assassination in January 1978, the Catholic Church forcefully condemned government-sponsored violence and repression and the general social and economic conditions in Nicaragua. At the annual procession of the Catholic faithful on New Year's Day, Archbishop Obando y Bravo declared, "Christians cannot distance themselves from those social, political, and economic conflicts that damage and hinder peace" (*La Prensa*, January 2, 1978). The bishops, too, issued a statement decrying the unjust distribution of wealth, repression, the absence of free labor organizations, and corruption of public functionaries; the statement noted that one-half of the population lacked decent housing, health, adequate nutrition, and employment (*La Prensa*, January 9, 1978).

In the wake of the assassination of Chamorro, churches held masses and, like Iranian mosques, emerged as centers for mobilization and collective action. For example, when the state imposed tight censorship on the print and broadcast media during the general strike of January 1978, Catholic churches throughout Managua became loci for journalists to read out loud the news they could not publish or announce on the air. Nicaraguan churches became important places where Christian groups could mobilize to act collectively and protest against Chamorro's murder.

In response to the political activities of clergy and the mobilization of collective action through the churches, the government again resorted to repressive measures. During 1978, the government expelled two foreign priests, arrested at least four Nicaraguan priests, and insulted and physically abused others (*La Prensa*, August, 14, 1978). National Guard troops occupied at least five churches for varying lengths of time. Government repression led Church authorities to attempt to reduce the growing use of churches for political mobilization and collective action. The Catholic Episcopal Conference of Nicaragua, for example, released a statement in February deploring the use of churches for nonreligious ends such as protests or the dissemination of journalistic information (*La Prensa*, February 25, 1978). The Catholic hierarchy itself was unusually quiet from the end of February until August, though churches continued to be used as centers of anti-government protests with ever-greater frequency.

As conflicts intensified following the formation of the moderate political organization, FAO, the ecclesiastical hierarchy intensified its opposition activities. The Nicaraguan Episcopal Conference issued a new pastoral letter, denouncing the rising number of persons wounded, imprisoned, or missing as the result of repression. In a statement, the clergy declared that the Church must raise its voice against all injustice. The Catholic bishops called for a new socio-political order to provide humane conditions for the majority of the people, specifically, health, education, land, work and salaries, civil liberties including the right to form political associations, trade unions, an independent judiciary, agrarian and tax reform to redistribute wealth, honest and capable public officials, and the reorganization of the armed forces (*La Prensa*, August 3, 1978).

The single most important Catholic initiative came in the form of a statement issued in August by the Presbyterian Council of the Catholic Archdioceses of Nicaragua, which proposed a solution to the "national crisis." In the statement, the council called for Somoza Debayle to resign and a national government to be formed to prevent Nicaragua from falling into a vacuum of power and anarchy (*La Prensa*, August 4, 1978).[11] This proposal marked the onset of a new phase in anti-government opposition led by the moderate political organization FAO.

In the end, the Church failed in its efforts to remove Somoza through nonviolent means. The last general strike in 1978 faltered, resulting in many deaths and massive destruction. During the mediation efforts that followed, Somoza's intransigence blocked any resolution of conflicts through nonviolent means. As a result, the Catholic Church was unable to play any significant role in the months leading up to the revolution. Some clerics joined the Sandinista armed struggle and many priests and nuns signed a crucial document in 1979 protesting against the state of terror in Nicaragua and condemning hunger, malnutrition, unemployment, and government repression (*La Prensa*, February 19, 1979). In the absence of an acceptable alternative, however, the Church hierarchy remained largely inactive in politics during the final few months of Somoza's rule. The archbishop never threw his support behind the Sandinistas, even though he did go so far as to assert that the majority of the FSLN were not communist (*La Prensa*, September 29, 1978).

The Catholic Church and political conflicts in the Philippines

Unlike the Catholic Church in Nicaragua, the Philippine Church hierarchy was very restrained in its political activities and it did not play a leading role during much of the insurgency against the Marcos regime. In contrast to Iran, where the position of the clergy had been undermined by state policies, the general status of the Catholic Church in the Philippines was not adversely affected by the state. Like in Iran and Nicaragua, the Church in the Philippines enjoyed some measure of immunity from the

---

[11] In the final days of the revolution, the Catholic hierarchy reportedly still sought to reform the government in order to avoid a revolution (Dodson and O'Shaughnessy 1990: 129–131).

power of the state. In addition, it had substantial resources, which could be used to pursue an independent political course, especially after martial law, imposed in 1972, closed off most options for mobilization to the opposition. For example, the Church owned hundreds of hectares of prime land, sixteen radio stations, publishing houses, 2,000 church-affiliated schools, and held tax-exempt status (Tiglao 1988:59). It also possessed banking investments, including 60 percent of the Monte de Piedad Mortgage and Saving Bank (*Malaya*, March 2, 1985). Yet, Church conservatism prevailed throughout much of the twentieth century, as it had in the past when the Philippine Church legitimized the power of the colonizers and the elite. In the 1970s and 1980s, although certain segments of the clergy became increasingly critical of the government, the church leadership did not formally break with Marcos until the final days of his rule.

The prevailing conservatism was responsible for two developments within the Catholic Church. Church conservatism and inaction impelled "progressive" members of the clergy to leave the Church (Wurfel 1988:219). As a result, the Philippine Church had one of the lowest ratios of clergy to population in any Catholic country, with only 4,500 priests and 7,500 nuns in a country with a population of nearly 50 million (ibid.:215). In addition, the conservatism of the ecclesiastical leadership provoked a reaction on the part of many clerics who, responding to the Second Vatican Council, embraced liberation theology, thus diversifying Church politics in the late 1960s.

The imposition of martial law, elimination of all options for legitimate political activities, and socio-economic crisis for the working classes and the poor provided additional causes for the rise of a radical group of clergy that became allied with the revolutionary left. These radical clerics, in compliance with Vatican II, formed various religious organizations to assist the poor (Youngblood 1990:66–71). A growing number of priests and nuns began to live in poor urban neighborhoods in the 1970s. Sister Christine Tan and five other nuns moved to the slums in 1979 with the intention of helping the poor to be more critical of the root causes of their poverty. Radical clerics formed Christian base communities in rural areas as well. By the early 1980s they had changed the focus and purpose of the Church's activities. These base communities discussed not only spiritual matters, but also everyday problems such as the illegal expropriation of land and resources by foreign and domestic businesses, military terrorism, and forced evacuations (Wurfel 1988:261).

Some radical clerics also joined secular, communist-led organizations. One priest arrested in Samar in 1982 revealed the extent of communist infiltration within the Church (ibid.:279). In one case, radical clerics led by Father Edicio de la Torre and a small number of Catholic and Protestant priests, ministers, nuns, pastors, seminarians, and young lay people formed Christians for National Liberation (CNL) in February 1972. By 1985, the CNL consisted of 1,200 Catholic priests and nuns organized in secret cells (Youngblood 1990:82). In April 1973, CNL joined the National Democratic Front (ibid.:81), a coalition of groups led by the Communist Party.

Although the Church leadership was relatively silent during the early 1970s, radical clerics initiated some activities against the existing social, political, and religious structures. One such group was the Philippine Priests, Inc. (PPI), which had 1,400 members in 1972. They were highly critical of "foreign imperialism, local landlordism, and bureaucrat-capitalism" (ibid.:79). In one instance, they issued a public statement criticizing the corruption of politicians and the rich who exploited the people. They denounced apathy and inaction by the Archbishop of Ilocos Sur who, they alleged, did nothing to alleviate the sorry lot of the region's populace. They declared that bishops and priests had a duty to preach against social injustice, and that bishops who took money from politicians and the rich would not be able to defend abused workers and tenants (*Manila Times*, June 21, 1970).

As social conflicts intensified during martial law, some radical priests advocated the use of armed struggle to overthrow the government. Others even took up arms and joined the communist NPA (New People's Army) in their armed campaign to topple the government. Father Conrado Balweg, for example, led an army of 700 communists in the Cordilleras mountains north of Manila. He was quoted as calling the gun, "an instrument for a higher value, the value of justice, the value of the dignity of man" (*Malaya*, July 14, 1984).

During the final stages of the conflicts, radical clerics denounced Marcos and US policies in the Philippines, and advocated fundamental change. They issued several statements condemning government repression, urging an election boycott, and protesting against the "US–Marcos dictatorship." For example, one group of clerics, the Ecumenical Movement for Justice and Peace, issued a statement in February 1986 calling for an election boycott and continued militant struggle against this dictatorship: "The best interest of the Filipino people can only be achieved through the continuation and intensification of the militant struggle to dismantle the US–Marcos dictatorship. The regime has attempted to block this by confusing the issues and calling for a snap election." Condemning Marcos' "rabid red-baiting," these clerics also castigated the election platform of his opponents (the Aquino camp) as barely containing solutions to the country's basic problems (*Malaya*, February 4, 1986).

The activism and political involvement of these radical clerics made them the target of government repression. From the outset of martial law in 1972 until September 1983, sixty-two priests were arrested, two of whom were summarily executed. Father Edicio de la Torre, the leader of the Christians for National Liberation, was imprisoned for five years (Wurfel 1988:217), and nine foreigners were deported. Eleven Protestant pastors, nine nuns, and fifty church workers were also apprehended during the same period (*Malaya*, March 6, 1984). Between 1972 and 1982 religious institutions were the targets of twenty-two military raids to capture "subversives," halt "subversive" activities, or confiscate "subversive" documents (Youngblood 1990:115).

In contrast to this radical faction, the Church leadership played a very different role in Philippine politics. The leadership was very conservative and remained so during the conflicts of the early 1970s. As government repression escalated, the Church hierarchy issued only one public criticism when habeas corpus was suspended and took several months to make even a relatively mild appeal to Marcos to restore it (*Manila Times*, December 7, 1971). The ecclesiastical leadership opposed the student movement, criticized student demonstrators, and defended the Church against allegations of corruption. In 1972, when Marcos imposed martial law and abolished democratic institutions, the Catholic leadership, in general, reacted positively (Youngblood 1990:172). Their silence in the face of the breakdown of Philippine democratic institutions, massive repression, and violations of human rights revealed the basic conservatism of the leadership of both Catholic and Protestant churches in the Philippines in the early 1970s.

As social conflicts intensified later in the 1970s, the politics of the Church leadership also diversified. According to data from 1979, the Catholic Bishops' Conference of the Philippines, the major Catholic organization with ninety-four members, was divided along three lines. Forty-six bishops (58 percent) were conservative, eighteen (23 percent) were moderate, and fifteen (19 percent) were progressive (Youngblood 1990:72–73). As a group, the bishops never called for Marcos' ouster. Most of the Catholic bishops opposed only certain aspects of the current situation, in particular, three things that violated "the sanctity of life": the oppression of secret marshals and Amendment Six, and the economic crisis (*Malaya*, July 18, 1984). The Church leadership, of course, opposed armed struggle or the use of violent means. While the Catholic Bishops' Conference of the Philippines declared their respect for the decision of those priests who joined the communist insurgents, they emphasized that the Church approved only of nonviolent means to achieve change (*Malaya*, July 23, 1984).

Although the Catholic Church became the most significant institution outside the government once martial law was imposed, it failed to break with the Marcos regime. Instead, throughout the period, the Church adopted a political stance of "critical collaboration." Initially, this led to greater collaboration with the government than criticism of it (Thompson 1995:118). The architect of this political position was Archbishop Jaime Sin, who was appointed Archbishop of Manila and the country's second cardinal in 1976. A moderate, he was determined to protect Church institutions. In his view, too close identification with Marcos would damage the Church just as much as ignoring the country's social and political ills.

Throughout martial law, Cardinal Sin did not protest against the deportation of foreign missionaries who had been engaged in social justice work among the urban poor and rural peasants. Nor did he respond publicly to the expulsion of Father Edward Gerlock, an American Maryknoll priest. The cardinal defended his inaction by saying that had he "chosen to engage the government in a direct confrontation . . . [t]he Government could have ordered all Churches closed and all priests arrested . . . Thus, for the sake of the Church in the Philippines . . . I chose to keep silence" (Youngblood 1990:176).

When martial law was lifted in 1981, the government increased its attacks on the Church, leading the ecclesiastical leadership to modify its stand against Marcos. Following Marcos' reelection in June, Church–state relations deteriorated markedly as the government accused the churches of being thoroughly infiltrated by communists (ibid.:196). In 1982, one year after Pope John Paul II lectured priests against political activity, Cardinal Sin advised Filipino clergy that they had a moral obligation to engage in political action (Chapman 1987:212). In January 1983, the Catholic Bishops' Conference of the Philippines withdrew from the Church–Military Liaison Committee that was established a decade earlier to resolve Church–state controversies; the withdrawal was in protest against stepped-up raids on churches and arrests of priests and nuns during 1982 (Muego 1983:1168). The following month, the bishops circulated a blistering pastoral letter denouncing government repression, corruption, and economic mismanagement (Youngblood 1990:197). The statement warned that if the president and the moderate opposition were not reconciled, bloody revolution might be the result (Thompson 1995:118).

The assassination of Aquino in 1983 intensified political conflicts and provided a greater opportunity for the Church to oppose the government. Reacting to Aquino's slaying, the Catholic leadership released six formal statements calling for reconciliation, even though many priests were demanding Marcos' resignation and expressing solidarity with the poor and the exploited (*Malaya*, October 17, 1983). Cardinal Sin was the leading advocate of reconciliation, although he criticized the government's over-centralization, restrictions, and unreceptiveness (*Malaya*, September 1, 1983). A telling example of the lengths to which Cardinal Sin was prepared to go to bring about reconciliation is the fact that he obligingly celebrated mass to honor Marcos' birthday just one month after the assassination, even though the memory of Aquino's death brought tears to his eyes (Chapman 1987:213; Rush 1986c:6). A month later, Cardinal Sin nominated Aquino for the Nobel Peace Prize (*Malaya*, November 30, 1983).

In the final phase of the conflicts, Cardinal Sin pursued a very cautious policy of increasing his distance from Marcos and assisting the moderate opposition often through institutional politics. While some bishops called for a boycott of the elections to the National Assembly, the cardinal exhorted people to keep their options open (*Malaya*, May 2 and March 13, 1984). In January, he urged Marcos to ensure that the May elections would be "clean and honest" in order to avert a bloody confrontation with the people. He also called upon people to pray for the "conversion" of the president (*Malaya*, January 16, 1984). Witnessing Marcos' manipulation to defeat moderate candidates, Cardinal Sin castigated the president as "an oppressor," accusing him of using "candy and brass knuckles" to ensure that his party would remain in power even if it did not gain a majority in the elections (*Malaya*, February 13, 1984). Following the elections, the cardinal called for larger anti-government demonstrations as a "parliament of the streets," adding, "it is time that the leadership is made to realize that the discontent and the disenchantment are not confined to the students and the workers" (*Malaya*, October 4, 1984).

In the last months of the conflicts, Cardinal Sin became more active in assisting the moderate opposition. He helped Cory Aquino and Laurel to agree to form a united opposition ticket, which was publicly supported by a substantial number of clergy, including bishops. In the end, when it became clear that Marcos intended to remain in office after the election of February 1986, the official Catholic Bishops' Conference of the Philippines formally broke with Marcos. They characterized the polls as "unparalleled in . . . fraudulence" (Goodno 1991:89; Youngblood 1990:200), and declared that "a government that assumes or retains power through fraudulent means has no moral basis" (Thompson 1995:152). At last, the Catholic Bishops' Conference of the Philippines formally joined the opposition.

In the final four days of protests that forced Marcos out, Cardinal Sin played an important role in mobilizing the public to support the defecting segments of the military. The Catholic radio station, Veritas, broadcast the news and urged the people to defend the defectors (Johnson 1987:75). Thousands of people, including nuns, responded to the call and protected the rebels. The call was a significant move that contributed greatly to the removal of Marcos from power.

Conclusion

In all three countries, large segments of the religious clergy became politicized and took an active interest in social conflicts. The interests of clergy and their constituencies were adversely affected by exclusive rule, centralization of power, and the weakening or breakdown of historic alliances between the clergy and the state. In comparative terms, the breakdown of the clergy–state alliance and the erosion of the clergy's status were greatest in Iran, where the state pursued deliberate policies to undermine the clergy's position. In Nicaragua, adverse effects of the 1972 earthquake on Church–state relations, combined with the government's repressive measures against the population, generated conditions for conflict. Church–state relations deteriorated in the aftermath of the assassination of Chamorro. In the Philippines, increased arbitrariness and acts of repression against the Church and the population heightened the clergy's involvement in politics, particularly following Aquino's murder.

Ideologically, the clergy were divided along two or three tendencies. They were often divided among conservatives, moderates, and militants or radicals. In general, while the higher-ranking clerics usually advocated conservative and moderate policies, lower-ranking clergy subscribed to radical or militant positions. While the ecclesiastical leadership controlled the important organizations and the national religious networks, the lower-ranking clergy were more closely involved in the mobilization of local communities and less-advantaged social groups and classes, who were adversely affected by the development process. Given the greater power and visibility of the religious leadership, they had greater impact on national politics. In contrast, lower-ranking clergy lacked national visibility and, given their politics and their constituency, were less immune from government repression. In comparative terms, the Philippine Church had very intense divisions: it had the most conservative ecclesiastical leadership and the most radical clergy in the lower ranks. In both the Philippines and Nicaragua, the lower-ranking clergy adopted radical political ideologies and favored some form of socialism. But in Iran, Islamic socialism never gained much strength among the clergy, with the exceptions of a few clerics such as Ayatollahs Golzadeh-Ghafouri and Ashouri. Although not a socialist, Ayatollah Taleghani, too, defended the interests of the poor and the working classes. The minority of the militant clergy who followed Ayatollah Khomeini's brand of Islam never called for Islamic socialism or the fundamental restructuring of class relations.

The clergy's participation in the political conflicts was significant because it reduced the social bases of support for the government, rendering the rulers more vulnerable to challenge during periods of conflict. The clergy were able to oppose the state and even help mobilize the population because religious institutions possessed some degree of immunity from state repression. Religious institutions also possessed independent networks and resources, which enabled them to mobilize and engage in some measure of political opposition. Furthermore, religious spaces enjoyed sanctity, despite occasional intrusion in all three cases, which protected them from government repression and thus provided designated safe spaces for the population to gather, express their grievances, and mobilize for collective action. Despite relative impunity, the timing of clerical political activities coincided with large-scale social conflicts. Social and political pressures were central in the political mobilization of the clergy in all three countries, with the partial exception of Nicaragua in the early 1970s.

In all three cases, clerical politicization and opposition contributed differently to the mobilization process and the removal of the power-holders. In Iran, although they did not initiate the opposition nor break with the monarchy, the highest echelon of the clergy's leaders in Qom contributed to the anti-Shah mobilization by opening the mosques for gathering and mourning ceremonies, which produced the forty-day cycles of protest. The participation of the highest was significant because the opposition lacked other options for mobilization. Thus, the highest religious authority contributed to the dynamics of a process over which they lost control. The pro-Khomeini clergy, in particular, had neither the resources nor the national visibility to take political action. These clerics were not among the high-ranking clerics in the country. They were few in number and lacked a following among the population. This was evidenced in June 1975 when the rebellion of clerical students in Qom went largely unnoticed by broad segments of the Iranian population.

At the other extreme was the Philippines, where the conservatism of the Catholic leadership, together with the existence of opposition political organizations, reduced the relative significance of religious organizations and clergy in the political conflicts. The Catholic bishops' conservatism prevented them from breaking with Marcos and calling for his resignation until the final moments of the conflict. Yet even in the Philippines, Cardinal Sin and the resources of the Catholic Church were important in uniting the moderate opposition and calling upon the people to defend the rebellious military in the last four days of the insurgency.

In Nicaragua, the Catholic leadership was of central importance initially, providing an opportunity for other social groups to mobilize through the Church. The Church was also important during much of the conflict, playing a significant role in the process. At the end, however, the Church was unable to affect the final outcome largely because Somoza's intransigence relegated the Church leadership to a position of insignificance.

Despite their significance and contributions, however, the ecclesiastical leadership could not attain their goals in the final outcomes in Iran and Nicaragua where revolutionaries succeeded in seizing power. Yet the outcomes of the revolutions in those countries could not be explained by the strength of the militant and radical clerics who favored social revolutions and called for the overthrow of those regimes, for in both cases these clerical segments were initially quite small and politically marginal. Only in the Philippines did the Catholic leadership succeed in achieving its goal in the outcome of the conflict in a situation that no one could have predicted. Hence, a complete analysis of the conflicts and their outcomes must include the participation of other collectivities in the struggles. The next two chapters will focus on the roles of two major social classes, that is, workers and capitalists.

6   Workers: rebels with dual targets

Urban workers also participated in the insurgencies against the state in Iran, Nicaragua, and the Philippines. Any analysis of workers in revolutionary conflicts must take into account Karl Marx's theory of revolution. Marx's analysis focused primarily on class conflict and class struggle. He argued that workers' economic exploitation under advanced, industrial capitalism generated a common interest among the proletariat to oppose the capitalist system. Industrial workers, who were concentrated in large factories, Marx argued, would develop class consciousness and adopt radical political ideology. He maintained that with increased solidarity and organization, workers would, in time, rise up against capitalism, seize state power, and establish socialism. Although none of the three cases in this study can be considered advanced capitalist countries, the conflicts and struggles of workers were critical in the insurgencies and political developments of these countries. But Marx's class analysis could not accurately predict the outcome of the conflicts in the three cases studied here. As will be seen, workers' ideological transformation and radicalism may threaten privileged social classes and prevent coalition formation, which is significant to revolutions in the absence of military defeat or breakdown.

Located near the bottom rung of the stratification system in all three countries, workers saw their interests adversely affected by both the state and employers. As a result, workers had the potential to target both the state and the capitalist class. Workers' political demands were directed against the state because they were excluded from the polity and repressed by the government, which pursued policies geared toward rapid capital accumulation. At the same time, workers' economic conflicts induced them to target employers and demand higher wages, benefits, or other work-related improvements. Furthermore, workers' target of attack was affected by the level of state intervention. Workers attacked the government where state intervention was high and the government was the principal employer. On the other hand, workers attacked the capitalists where state intervention was lower and private entrepreneurs were the principal employers and holders of economic assets.

As a result of these dual conflicts, workers were potentially likely to press for a social revolution that would transform both the political and economic structures. This dual conflict also had the potential of leading workers to accept radical ideologies, as Marx emphasized in his analysis of revolutions. Less ideologically driven than students, workers nevertheless had a greater propensity than other social classes to shift their support to revolutionary challengers advocating fundamental changes in the social structure.

But, by themselves, workers' ideology and interest could not determine the timing of insurgency because unlike privileged social groups, which enjoyed some measure of immunity, workers were often vulnerable to adverse decisions by both the state and their employers. Furthermore, workers' economic interest could not predict the timing of workers' collective actions and insurgency, inasmuch as workers' interests in each country were adversely affected over a long time. Of course, workers' immediate economic conditions did play an important role in their mobilization because much of their collective action under ordinary conditions dealt with economic issues. In addition, at times, workers undertook collective action in response to sudden new violations of their established interests. But, on the whole, workers initiated large-scale mobilization primarily when favorable opportunities emerged, that is when state repression declined, or when governments became vulnerable due to national political crises and the rise of strong new allies.

Workers' collective actions and politics could potentially have a significant impact on the outcome of social conflicts. In contrast to students who did not contribute directly to the productive process, workers were central in the production of goods and services and, consequently, could significantly disrupt the social structure by withholding their contributions through strikes. Thus, workers' collective actions could potentially intensify economic difficulties and trigger political crisis and instability. In addition, workers' ideology had a direct bearing on the politics of the capitalist class, especially when workers supported radical political challengers. Hence, workers had the potential to affect the course and outcome of political development in these countries.

In the three countries, working-class mobilization interacted differently with the actions of capitalists and other actors. Workers' contributions to the conflicts differed in each country, depending on their capacity for collective action, mobilization options, and available allies. In different ways, workers in Iran and Nicaragua joined the anti-government coalitions and contributed to the revolutions' success by striking and disrupting the productive processes. In these two countries, workers' alliances with different challengers contributed to the formation of two very different kinds of regimes. Iranian workers were most hampered by repression and thus were the least organized. In addition, Iranian workers were least ideologically oriented. Lacking solidarity structures, they could not initiate collective action in the early stages of the conflicts. But, once opportunities emerged, Iranian workers mobilized and targeted the state because, as a hyperactive state, it was the principal employer. In the end, Iranian workers joined in the coalition with capitalists and other collectivities to overthrow the government. Their participation in the coalition was important in the overthrow of the monarchy which was the immediate outcome of the conflicts.

In contrast, Nicaraguan workers were more organized and able to mobilize early on. Additionally they had developed ideological orientations that affected their politics. Because the level of state intervention was lower in Nicaragua, workers, along with their radical student allies, attacked both the state and the capitalists in the initial stage of the conflicts following the 1972 earthquake. The result was the absence of class coalition and failure of the struggles. But, during the revolutionary conflicts, Nicaraguan workers coalesced with capitalists and other actors by primarily targeting the state. As the state became increasingly vulnerable and the moderates failed to remove Somoza from power, Nicaraguan workers shifted their support to the Sandinistas. Thus, workers directly contributed to the victory of the Sandinistas and the outcome of the Nicaraguan revolution.

In the Philippines, in a sharp contrast to Iran, a low level of state intervention and the existence of formal democratic institutions had generated working-class organizations that largely pursued collective bargaining and avoided political and ideological orientations. But, as a result of the repression during martial law, a segment of organized labor became increasingly radical in the mid-1980s and attacked both the state and capitalist employers. At the same time, economic deterioration heightened class conflict and thus prevented the formation of a class coalition. The absence of this coalition resulted in the failure of the insurgency that immediately followed the assassination of Aquino.

Workers in the Iranian revolution

Although scholars of the Iranian revolution have ignored or downplayed the participation and contribution of workers (Arjomand 1988:107–108), Iranian workers played an important role in the revolutionary conflicts. Iranian workers had a great potential for politicization and opposition to the government because of the high level of state intervention in capital accumulation and the nature of exclusive polity. In the first place, workers experienced a great deal of repression because the government intensely intervened in labor relations and industrial conflicts. Second, large segments of industrial workers were employed by the state, which became the principal employer in the country and was interested in rapid capital accumulation. As a result, workers' industrial disputes were immediately directed against the state with a high potential for politicization. Third, workers had no access to the polity and could not find representation in the political system as it was under the exclusive control of the Shah. Finally, Iranian workers' potential for collective action grew as the size of the urban workforce enlarged due to rapid economic development and industrialization.

Workers were unable, however, to develop sufficient solidarity structures to mobilize and independently influence the political process because severe repression undermined their organizations and ability to engage in collective action. As a result, workers' political action had to wait for appropriate opportunities, either when government repression declined and the state became vulnerable, or when powerful allies became available. Hence, workers, unable to initiate collective action independently, followed the lead of others rather than leading the events that culminated in the revolution.[1] Nevertheless, it is important to note that oil workers were critical during the final stage of the conflicts as they disrupted the flow of oil, intensified the economic crisis, and contributed to the paralysis of the state.

The revolutionary conflicts of 1977–1979 were preceded by two decades of industrial development, which greatly expanded the industrial labor force. In 1956, the manufacturing sector employed 815,699 workers out of a total workforce of 8,907,666. Two decades later, this sector numbered 1,672,059 workers, more than a two-fold increase. Nearly half a million of these workers were located in factories employing ten people or more.[2] Between 1956 and 1976, employment in the construction sector rose by 254 percent. Mining and quarrying operations, conducted almost exclusively by the state, employed roughly 90,000 persons, an increase of 264 percent.

The state was the largest industrial employer in Iran. By 1976, the state owned 130 large factories and workshops, excluding government-owned

---

[1] A reduction of repression in the 1940s and the formation of the Tudeh Party (Iranian Communist Party) enabled workers to mobilize and engage in some measure of collective action. Prime Minister Mosaddegh's liberalization in the early 1950s contributed to workers' mobilization and at that time, during the conflicts between the liberals, nationalists and monarchists, workers demonstrated a number of times in favor of the liberals.

[2] SCI (1981a:16). A 1977 survey indicated that large factories employed approximately 404,000 workers. This survey, however, excluded the rug industry.

carpet factories (SCI 1981a:30). The state was a major investor in 55 additional joint ventures with private sector and multinational corporations. The state employed 24 percent of the urban manufacturing and mining workforce (SCI 1976a:85). State industries were highly sophisticated and employed large numbers of skilled and semi-skilled workers who were concentrated in factories.

Despite its positive impact on the earnings of most workers, economic development had uneven consequences for the working class: highly skilled workers benefited most, while the majority of workers suffered the adverse consequences of rising inflation. The state's development strategy favoring large, modern industries widened the gap between highly skilled and unskilled segments of the working class. A 1974 survey covering 224,000 workers in 2,779 different enterprises reported the existence of a labor aristocracy: "while more than half of the families have a weekly income per head of less than 100 rials, 34.5 percent of them receive more than 501 rials each." Of even more importance was the report's conclusion that 73 percent of the working population received an income below the statutory minimum living wage.[3]

Workers' capacity to mobilize was expanded as a result of economic development and industrialization. The expansion of large state-owned enterprises facilitated their communication and increased their potential for mobilization. But workers' capacity for collective action did not expand in other enterprises because most other factories were small (Moaddel 1993:239), and thus prevented large-scale mobilization and collective action.

More importantly, like the rest of the population, workers were not permitted to develop their own political or ideological organizations. In 1971, shortly after the Marxist Feda'iyan launched their armed struggle, the government arrested and imprisoned approximately 400 members of SAKA (Sazman-e Enghelabi-e Kargaran-e Iran), an independent socialist labor organization (Moghadam, interview, March 1999). In addition, specific state policies kept workers' organizations highly fragmented and thereby prevented them from becoming autonomous. Furthermore, unions were restricted to individual factories, and no industry-wide unions were allowed to emerge. By 1978, 1,023 such unions had been formed (Halliday 1979:203), but because of their lack of autonomy and inefficacy, workers had little interest in joining them. In 1973, only 22.3 percent of factory workers were union members according to a secret government survey, while one-third of workers either thought the union was of no use or else had no idea of its positive functions (Bayat 1987:62).

[3] *Le Monde Diplomatique* (1975), quoted in Halliday (1979:190) and in Ghotbi (1978:32). At that time, a rial was worth approximately 1.4 cents.

Labor strikes were outlawed by the government. A leading industrial-ist suggested to the Shah in 1970 that workers should be allowed to strike so that they could feel they had won something through their own efforts, but the Shah rejected the idea (Taheri 1986:213). The SAVAK regularly intervened in labor activities (Ladjevardi 1985:213–214). Nevertheless, wildcat strikes increased during the 1970s, and the state responded by expanding and intensifying its repressive activities. In April 1974, a law was passed punishing "industrial saboteurs." The law created the Office of Security Affairs to supervise all activities in ten major industries, including steel, petrochemicals, gas, aluminum refin-ing, machine tool factories in Tabriz and Arak, and helicopter and air-plane manufacturing. Under the law, industrial saboteurs could be sen-tenced to fifteen years in prison or even be put to death (Ivanov n.d.: 299). This security office was staffed mostly by ex-military officers in direct contact with SAVAK.

Although adversely affected by such repression, workers were unable to act collectively in pursuit of their interests because they lacked both solidarity structures and favorable opportunities. As a result, from au-tumn of 1977 to autumn of 1978, the first full year of the revolutionary conflicts, workers held only thirty-nine strikes. Unlike the bazaaris' shut-downs, these workers' strikes were unrelated to each other and involved primarily economic rather than political demands.

There were exceptions, of course. Workers in large state enterprises at times articulated important political demands. For example, a workers' strike in the state-owned Machine Tool Factory in Tabriz in mid-April 1978 clearly targeted the state and contained political demands.[4] In their demand for higher wages, the factory workers declared that because of economic unevenness and the Iranian state's dependence on the United States, living expenses had risen to the point where their families were deprived even of the minimal living conditions necessary for survival. These workers issued a number of notable political demands, including prohibiting forced attendance by workers at government rallies; the re-lease of all political prisoners, and the return of all exiles, especially Ayatollah Khomeini; and the dissolution of SAVAK and expulsion of its agents from factories, universities, and other social institutions. The workers also denied the government's allegation that Iranian workers had participated in rallies against the International Labor Office (Abouzar 1978:27; *Zamimeh*, 1978, no. 20:35).

In the fall of 1978, a fresh opportunity for mobilization emerged with the appointment of a new prime minister, Sharif-Emami, who promised

---

[4] Bayat (1987:86–87) presents data that suggest a higher politicization of workers during the first few months of 1978, but the difference is not large.

liberalization and political freedom for all political groups except communists. But the proposed reforms offered nothing to the working classes. As a consequence, workers seized the opportunity and began to mobilize and demand change. Workers who had previously been involved in strikes or had been arrested and imprisoned used their informal networks in the workplace, formed secret cells and committees with trusted coworkers, and took the initiative to organize collective actions (Bayat 1987:91).

It is important to emphasize that workers did not participate in political conflicts at the outset, but joined in only after the struggles were already well underway. The industrial working class had taken no part in the cycle of mourning ceremonies during which bazaaris shut down their shops. The delayed mobilization of workers is an indication that their interests, conflicts against the state, and resources differed significantly from those of bazaaris and clergy. Nevertheless, as employees of the state, workers faced some similar problems and grievances and confronted a common enemy. Once they entered the fray, industrial workers directly targeted the state – their employer – for attack.

Given the context of mounting inflation and a declining standard of living, workers' initial demands, unlike those of bazaaris, were mainly economic, and strikers pressed to relieve their immediate grievances. Thus, the early demands of workers were primarily defensive in orientation; only later were their grievances expressed in political terms. An analysis of strikers' demands during this period reveals that with few exceptions economic issues were paramount, with job-related problems a close second. All strikers demanded higher wages; most also insisted on allowances or loans for housing expenses and medical insurance. Many complained of pay inequities, especially in sectors where foreign workers were employed. Some protested against arbitrary promotion rules and secret "rewards" by heads of bureaucracies.

As the number of strikes increased, the regime initially chose to deal with them on a national level and proceed with concessions, rather than repression. Repression was not used at the beginning because the scale of the strikes was vast and rapidly expanding. Thus, on October 10, the government announced that within six months, salaries of all state employees would be raised by 25 percent in two stages (*Ettelaat*, October 10, 1978). Five days later, the state promised housing loans to 20,000 government employees (*Ettelaat*, October 15, 1978).

Workers' responses varied. While some returned to their jobs, others were skeptical of the government's promises. Some strikers complained that although they had been on strike for days, the authorities had not even investigated their grievances. Most strikers were dissatisfied with the state's concessions, which they regarded as insufficient. Many state employees demanded 50 to 100 percent salary increases along with additional benefits (*Tehran Journal*, October 11, 1978).

As the strikes continued, those segments of the working classes that were more concentrated in large state enterprises and possessed greater skills and greater solidarity structures began issuing political demands as well. In a few cases, strikers pressed for the dismissal of directors of corporations or government offices. Striking oil workers and employees of a steel mill in Isfahan, a mine in the central Alborz mountains, a railway in Zahedan, and Iran General Motors in Tehran, all demanded the expulsion of various department chiefs. On September 2, workers in the Tabriz Machine Tool Factory struck and demanded the dissolution of government-sponsored unions and the lifting of martial law. On November 4, workers in Tabriz Tractor and Tabriz Machine Tool organized a joint strike, condemned government repression, and demanded lifting of martial law, freedom for all political prisoners, dissolution of government-sponsored unions, and proclaimed support for the political demands of students, teachers, workers, and government employees. More importantly, oil workers in Abadan and Ahvaz demanded freedom for all political prisoners, the dissolution of SAVAK, lifting of martial law, dissolution of government-sponsored unions and the formation of independent labor unions, freedom for all political parties, and other political concessions.

Although workers were becoming increasingly political, the nature of their demands was neither revolutionary nor Islamic; they were not clamoring for the overthrow of the state or the dominant classes, nor were they endorsing the Islamic movement or Ayatollah Khomeini. Nevertheless, within the Iranian context, the reforms demanded by workers were radical. A number of factors accounted for this growing politicization, the most obvious being the structural fact that most strikers were employed by the state, which increased the potential for politicizing conflicts. Another factor was the growing solidarity among strikers made possible by relaxed repression and prolonged strikes. Previously, repression had severely restricted the ability of workers to form networks and solidarity structures; now, strikers could communicate freely, express grievances, and plan their action. The partial lifting of media censorship, especially in radio and television, allowed the broadcast of strike news and their demands. Diverse groups of strikers were able to develop some solidarity structures because of the enhanced communication. This was evident especially during the oil workers' strikes, when numerous groups expressed support for their demands. Knowing that other large groups were on strike at the same time allowed strikers to realize that the regime was vulnerable and that, because the pressure on any single group was reduced, the effect of repression could not be too severe.

As a result of the rapid increase of politicization among the working classes and the spiraling social conflicts, a military government was declared on November 6, 1978. In a return to repressive measures, the army attempted to coerce striking workers to return to their jobs by occupying all strategic institutions, including oil installations, radio and television stations, and newspapers, which had just successfully concluded a strike. Most strikers went back to work, though some did not. The military government briefly succeeded in reducing the number of strikes by means of repressive measures, but the order imposed by the army could not be maintained. The few weeks of political opening and increased popular mobilization had enabled workers and white-collar employees to act collectively and form solidarity structures. To halt all strikes decisively, the military forces would have had to escalate repression on a massive scale, which they did not choose to do. Consequently, in response to military rule, bazaaris initiated protracted shutdowns in major cities. Their unprecedented actions electrified the conflicts by disrupting trade and highlighting the government's vulnerability, which, in turn, provided an opportunity for workers to resume their strikes. Within weeks of the military government's installation, extended politicized strikes erupted anew in many parts of the country. Strike committees sprang up everywhere to coordinate strike activities and demand political change. Striking workers issued statements denouncing state-sponsored violence and repression.

The impact of oil workers' strikes during this time was distinct from that of other industrial workers, in part because oil workers controlled the nation's most vital economic asset. They also shared certain characteristics, which increased the likelihood that their actions would become politicized. Oil workers numbered more than 30,000 and were heavily concentrated in specific oil-producing regions, which added to their ability to communicate, mobilize, and act collectively. Moreover, because oil workers were employed by the state, a greater potential existed for them to become politicized during times of conflict. A core of political experience existed among oil workers as a result of their participation in oil strikes of the early 1950s. Aware that they controlled the state's primary source of revenue, oil workers rapidly became more militant in the fall of 1978. Eventually, their politicization and conflicts served to mobilize other workers.

Industrial workers were keenly aware of the significance of oil workers' politics. During the intense struggles in the final stage of the monarchy, striking workers in Tehran looked to oil workers for leadership. In a number of demonstrations, these workers shouted the slogan, "Our oil worker, our determined leader."

For two weeks the striking oil workers resisted efforts by the military to force them back to work. Then on November 19, oil workers in the south returned to their jobs, determined to establish a national oil workers' organization to coordinate strikes and prevent their collapse. Once such an organization was formed, oil workers quickly walked out again on December 2. This time, they announced that they would fight until victory, by which they meant the overthrow of the government. It is important to note that this declaration was issued eight days before the impressive Tasoua march during which the opposition demanded the overthrow of the Pahlavi regime.

As the oil workers' strikes spread throughout the southern oil-producing region, oil exports plummeted to zero, severely aggravating the country's economic situation. Transportation systems in major cities were disrupted, and even military vehicles lacked fuel. The oil workers refused to bargain with government emissaries and insisted instead on negotiating directly with Ayatollah Khomeini's envoys, thereby generating a situation of dual sovereignty. In the end, oil workers allied themselves with other social groups behind Khomeini.

These strikes deepened the country's financial crisis and led to the dismissal of thousands of workers (*Kayhan*, January 14, 1979). By January 20, 1979, according to the Chamber of Commerce, 3.5 million workers were out of work, including 1.5 million industrial workers. By this time, the vast majority of workers had become fully politicized supporting the revolution.

Although the vast majority of Iranian workers supported the leadership of Ayatollah Khomeini, they did not display any ideological support for the formation of an Islamic theocracy. Unlike the early 1950s when workers had supported Prime Minister Mosaddegh, workers did not initiate any collective actions in 1963 in support of Ayatollah Khomeini. Neither did they engage in any collective action during the protests of clerical students in June 1975, despite Khomeini's support for the students. Thus, clearly workers' support for Ayatollah Khomeini in 1979 derived from political rather than ideological considerations.

But a small segment of Iranian workers did display clear ideological orientation. Despite repression of revolutionary organizations, a minority of workers who embraced some form of socialism quickly emerged in the final stage of the revolutionary struggles and played a leadership role. For example, all ten of the leaders of the strike committee in Tabriz Tractor Company were socialist (Shahrak, interview, February 1999). Similarly, the leadership of striking workers in the Machine Tool Factory in Tabriz were leftist (Moghadam 1987:167). Much of the leadership of workers' councils in the Sazman-e Gostaresh Va Nousazi Sanaye-e Iran

(Organization of Development and Renewal of Iranian Industries) that employed some 40,000 workers were socialist (Jalal Majidi, interview, March 1999). Marxists and socialists were very active among oil workers. Although the Ahvaz strike committee had a 35 percent avowedly Marxist leadership (*Washington Post*, February 26, 1979), the oil workers' national council was overwhelmingly Marxist. A member of the oil workers' council revealed that nine of the fourteen members were Marxist and four others advocated Islamic socialism (Yadollah Khosrow-Shahi, interview, March 1999). Their mobilization and collective actions, however, were initiated independently of any political organization or group, including the religious clergy.[5] Many of these workers had learned about socialism and Marxism either through their own informal networks or as a result of imprisonment where they met members and supporters of Marxist or Islamic socialist organizations. For example, Yadollah Khosrow-Shahi, a member of the oil workers' council, became familiar with the Marxist Feda'iyan following his arrest in a labor strike that resulted in his imprisonment.

Oil workers' strikes had a pronounced political, rather than religious, character; friction existed between the leaders of oil workers' strike committees and local clerics (*Ayandegan*, February 1, 1979). Although Ahvaz oil workers respected Ayatollah Khomeini, their backing for him was principally the result of his political opposition to the Shah, rather than his religious dictates (*New York Times*, November 19, 1978). One oil worker declared that he was unconcerned about the financial losses to Iran that could ensue from decreased oil exports: "We never saw any of that money anyway. It was all going in the pockets of Ali Baba and his 40 thieves." Another worker observed that Ayatollah Khomeini "has brought the eyes of the world on our problem here and made them see that the Shah is a puppet of the foreigners who are stealing our money" (*New York Times*, November 19, 1978). Oil workers considered their movement and the leadership of Ayatollah Khomeini to be "anti-despotic, anti-imperialist" struggles (*Kayhan*, January 16, 1979). After the overthrow of the monarchy, these workers formed the workers' councils to run the factories, but they were repressed by the government. While many of the leaders and activists of workers' councils were arrested and imprisoned, more than 600 of them were executed or killed in armed confrontation with the government between 1981 and 1985.

In sum, Iranian workers, excluded and long repressed by the highly interventionist state, lacked autonomous organizations to mobilize and

---

[5] A report in *Le Monde* of November 16, 1978 noted that in Abadan: "The workers we meet use the same words. Who has given them instructions to strike? No one in particular. Everyone agrees. There is really no organization." Quoted in Turner (1980:279).

engage in collective action. Organizational weaknesses prevented these workers from joining the forty-day cycles of mourning ceremonies organized by other social groups over several months. Thus, the timing of workers' entry into the conflicts was tied to the government's proclamation of reform and the consequent reduction of repression, rather than to ideological conversion or clerical exhortation. Most workers began mobilizing when the government announced liberal reforms and reconciliation in August 1978 and promised reduced repression.

As the evidence presented above indicates, with the exception of oil and a few advanced industrial enterprises, initially most statements issued by workers expressed neither political nor revolutionary concerns. Rather, for many of the early conflicts, the workers' demands were primarily economic and work-related. Given the high level of state intervention, however, and that the state was the largest industrial owner and employer in the country, workers in large enterprises soon targeted the state and demanded political changes. Yet the politicization of workers and their support for the formation of an Islamic republic did not emerge until quite late, at which time they contributed extensively to the monarchy's collapse. Significantly, the leadership of workers' struggles and the strike committees in large industrial establishments were in the hands of leftists who advocated some form of socialism.

Mobilization and collective action by workers in state-owned enterprises were crucial to the outcome of the conflicts. Workers' strikes succeeded in disrupting production, distribution and services in all sectors of the economy. Oil workers' strikes were especially significant because they intensified the state's fiscal crisis and encouraged workers in other sectors of the economy to mobilize and oppose the government. In combination, workers' disruptive actions intensified political instability, contributed to the rise of dual sovereignty, and paved the way for the overthrow of the state.

Nicaraguan workers and the revolutionary conflicts

The conflicts and mobilization of Nicaraguan workers were fundamentally different from those of Iranian workers, in large part because they were not primarily employed by the state and because they were able to maintain some degree of organization. Although the level of state intervention in the form of state-owned enterprises was lower in Nicaragua than in Iran, still Nicaraguan workers suffered from government repression. As a result, Nicaraguan workers targeted both the state and the capitalist class in their collective actions. While they targeted employers for economic conflicts, workers' collective actions were often politicized and became directed against the state. This dual attack often threatened the capitalist and thus prevented the formation of class coalition. The fragmentation of conflicts in turn resulted in the failure of workers' insurgency. This was the case in the early 1970s when workers, along with their student allies, attacked both the state and the capitalists and failed to effect any changes in the state structure. In the late 1970s, however, workers primarily targeted the government, coalesced with the capitalists at least for some time in the initial stages of the conflicts, and thus contributed positively to the outcome of the Nicaraguan revolution.

Although Vilas (1985:122) has downplayed the role of workers in the Nicaraguan revolution, organized labor in Nicaragua was consistently in the forefront of the political conflicts, unlike Iranian workers who followed the lead of other social groups in the revolutionary struggles. Long before capitalists protested against the assassination of Pedro Chamorro, organized workers became highly politicized and engaged in collective action against the Somoza regime. Leftist workers on a number of occasions organized joint demonstrations and rallies with radical students. These workers also formed coalitions with moderate political organizations that opposed the Somoza regime. When economic conditions deteriorated in 1973–1974, workers targeted capitalists as well with their economic demands. Workers were among the first to protest against the government during the revolutionary struggles. Initially organized workers had joined the coalition of moderate political organizations. But, in the summer of 1978 as state vulnerability increased and the moderate opposition failed to remove Somoza from power, workers shifted their support towards the Sandinistas.

Organized segments of Nicaraguan workers were highly visible in the political conflicts throughout the 1970s. Nicaraguan labor produced highly visible leaders at the national level. Many union leaders were always included in the major opposition organizations that emerged after the earthquake. For example, of the twenty-seven political figures who signed a well-publicized statement declaring, "there is no one to vote for" in the 1974 presidential election, six were labor leaders, and one was a mechanic (La Prensa, June 26, 1974). Domingo ("Chagüitillo") Sanchez Salgado was one of these twenty-seven political figures who called for a boycott of the 1974 election. One of CGT-I's most dynamic leaders, Domingo Sanchez was a well-known, politically influential figure in Nicaragua. By 1973 at the age of fifty-eight, he had been jailed 104 times for his political activities (La Prensa, July 22, 1973). Shortly after the earthquake, Sanchez Salgado was arrested for insisting that authorities provide food for the disaster victims. His imprisonment, which lasted more than six months, provoked widespread protests by popular groups, the working class, and the Catholic Church. Even the pro-government union, CGT-O, demanded his release (*La Prensa*, July 10, 1973). Later that year, he helped organize UDEL (Democratic Union of Liberation), one of the most active opposition entities, and was elected to its executive council (*La Prensa*, December 19, 1974).

Labor activism and struggle were made possible in part because of the government's economic development strategy, which expanded the labor force and workers' potential for mobilization. By the early 1970s, there were more than 70,000 industrial wage earners in manufacturing, construction, and transportation. By the end of the decade, the working class consisted of between 230,000 and 240,000 workers, or slightly less than 30 percent of the economically active population, which was estimated at nearly 800,000 (Vilas 1985:122). The expansion of the workforce and its concentration in a few centers, such as Managua, León, and Chinandega, enhanced the workers' capacity to mobilize and act collectively.

Although small, segments of Nicaraguan workers were able to organize and adopt clear political and ideological positions.[6] Five trade union organizations existed in the 1970s, representing approximately 10 percent of the workforce. The General Confederation of Workers-Independent, or CGT-I, was tied to the Socialist Party, which maintained a base among urban workers, especially in the construction sector. The Workers' Federation of Nicaragua (CTN) had connections with the Social Christian Party. CGT-I was the strongest organization, with more than 30,000 members in construction, manufacturing, and transportation, while CTN claimed approximately 20,000 members (*La Prensa*, July 18, 1978). There were three smaller labor organizations: the Council of Trade Union Unification (CUS) was associated with the American Institute for Free Labor Development; the Federation of Trade Union Action and Unity (CAUS) was tied to the Nicaraguan Communist Party; and the General Confederation of Workers-Official (CGT-O) remained loyal to the Somoza government (Ruchwarger 1987:42–45). It is important to note that none of the labor organizations was tied to the FSLN, despite attempts by the Sandinistas to penetrate the labor movement.

These divisions did not prevent workers from joint action at times of crisis. The combined forces of government repression and worsening economic conditions often unified the organized labor. For example, in March 1973, nearly ninety representatives from a variety of labor

---

[6] Vilas downplays the significance of the working class and its role in the revolution. According to his analysis, the urban workforce is estimated to have been between 75,000 and 80,000, or roughly 20 percent of the non-agricultural economically active population. In July 1979, only 138 unions, claiming a membership of only 27,000 affiliated workers, were registered in Nicaragua. This figure represented approximately 11–12 percent of the salaried population (Vilas, 1985:122).

organizations, including CGT-O, which was loyal to the government, met in Masaya and agreed on a common agenda. It called for higher wages and price controls, an end to speculation in urban land, participation of marginal classes in land redistribution within the new Managua, defense of renters' interests, solidarity with news media threatened by censorship, and support for striking medical doctors (*La Prensa*, March 12, 1973).

Workers' efforts to act collectively were restricted by the power of the state, which largely rendered their organizations ineffective. Despite its high degree of autonomy from the capitalist class, the Nicaraguan government historically pursued a policy of repressing labor in favor of capital accumulation. Although the Labor Code of 1944 recognized the legality of labor strikes, from 1944 to 1977 only three strikes were declared legal (Cardenal 1976:24). Between 1967 and 1973, Nicaraguan labor organizations were successful in obtaining only fifty-nine labor agreements (*La Prensa*, January 3, 1974).

Workers manifested a high degree of politicization. The leftist labor federation, CGT-I, declared the need to form an alternative, democratic government long before capitalists spoke up about social and economic issues. When the Grand Convention of Private Enterprise met in March 1974 but failed to address the central political issues, CGT-I bluntly announced that the first step in confronting the country's socio-economic problems consisted of "radically solving the political problem through the installation of a regime of democratic government." Its statement went on to call for fundamental changes such as land reform, nationalization of foreign businesses and banks, honest administration, income redistribution, an end to the use of state institutions for personal, familial, or group ends, and the establishment of mutually beneficial and independent relations with other countries (*La Prensa*, March 5, 1974).

Another example occurred on May Day, 1973, when CGT-I, SCAAS of Managua, the Independent Federation of Teachers of Nicaragua, and various other labor organizations met at the University Club of León where they had strong student allies. Speakers pointed to the widely disparate distribution of income in Nicaragua, noting that no more than 2 percent of the population controlled land, capital, and resources, while the working classes suffered. Other speakers denounced the 60-hour workweek and called on workers to unite in opposition to it. The assembly also sent a telegram to Somoza, then president of the Emergency Committee, demanding the release from prison of Domingo Sanchez Salgado and other labor leaders (*La Prensa*, May 2, 1973). In August, representatives from seventeen labor organizations belonging to CGT-I met to discuss the country's problems. They identified inflation as one of the most critical issues facing the population and laid the blame for rising prices squarely on Nicaragua's dependence on US imperialism, which "subjugates and oppresses the people of Latin America" (*La Prensa*, August, 27, 1973). Manufacturing workers also were highly politicized and held several demonstrations jointly with students during the early conflicts of 1973.

Workers' politicization intensified when repressive or unfavorable actions were taken by the government during strikes. This is precisely what happened immediately after the 1972 earthquake. The state intervened and used repressive mechanisms to demobilize the workers and, as a result, economic conflicts quickly assumed a political character, targeting both the state and the capitalist class. For example, when six unions struck the textile and metal industries, workers formed a coordinating committee to strengthen their solidarity and capacity to continue their struggles. When the sister of one of the union leaders was arrested for leafleting about the strike, they refused to negotiate as long as she remained in prison. Offering a class analysis of the nature of the state, they roundly denounced the Ministry of Labor for "acting on behalf of the owning class, being themselves directly responsible for the recent strikes" (*La Prensa*, August 15, 1973).

The timing of labor insurgency coincided with the devastating Managua earthquake of December 1972, which set the stage for the conflicts in the first phase. The earthquake enhanced the bargaining capacity of workers who were of central importance in the reconstruction of the capital. Skilled construction workers, already well organized, were in the forefront of labor mobilization in Nicaragua. They were doubly affected by the earthquake: its economic devastation set off rampant inflation, which eroded the workers' buying power, but also provided job opportunities for them. At the same time, workers were adversely affected by the government's reconstruction policies, which extended the workweek for construction workers from forty-eight to sixty hours and suspended two days of the customary Holy Week holiday. In response, construction workers, whose bargaining position had been strengthened by the rebuilding boom, declared widespread strikes. Their primary aim was to protect their economic and working conditions, but they soon made political demands as well.

During these struggles, construction workers expanded their organizational capacities. To protect themselves against government repression, they moved to fortify their solidarity structures by organizing SCAAS, a syndicate of carpenters, bricklayers, and pipe fitters. SCAAS drew some 15,000 workers in Managua and five other provinces into a single federation to pursue common interests and obtain unified collective bargaining agreements (*La Prensa*, August 12, 1974).

Although economic and work-related issues were the initial causes of the strikes, government repression quickly led to the politicization of workers. SCAAS construction workers held 195 strikes, which represented more than 70 percent of all workers' strikes between March and December 1973. Of these, 189 strikes demanded higher wages and improved working conditions.[7] Although workers' strikes featured an obvious emphasis on economic issues, the majority also contained significant political elements. A critical factor politicizing and radicalizing the working class was state repression. In 173 of the 195 strikes, construction workers protested against arrests. In 139 strikes, construction workers condemned the state's repression of political organizations and opponents, specifically the newly passed Libel Law, which prohibited the publication or broadcasting of news critical of the government. At least once, striking construction workers even announced that for every construction worker who was imprisoned, their strike would be extended for an additional week (*La Prensa*, April 24, 1973). Thus, workers' strikes quickly assumed a dual target.

Although workers' strike activities declined in 1974, largely due to the concessions won from employers and continued government repression, most of the seventy-nine strikes initiated by construction workers that year featured significant political dimensions. Thirty-two strikes protested against government repression, while twenty-two others were undertaken in solidarity with other strikers, such as medical doctors and nurses who demanded better salaries and improved working conditions.

During these strikes, the government continuously used repression to demobilize workers. In June 1974, CGT-I reported that government repression in four northern provinces had virtually eliminated all union activities there and was responsible for the deaths of several labor leaders. In Matagalpa, the president of CTN was jailed. Union leaders in Jinotega were arrested simply for being seen together in the street or at meetings in their own homes. In Estelí the military commander banned meetings held without a permit, even though martial law was no longer in effect. The Syndicate of Construction Workers in Rivas was notified that they must not accept any financial assistance or they would be liable to drastic sanctions (*La Prensa*, June 24, 1974).

The government also resorted to union busting. After striking workers demanding salary increases and protesting against firings occupied the Fabritex clothing factory, the Ministry of Labor and Fabritex management acted jointly to dissolve the Syndicate of Workers in the Textile

---

[7] Another important demand, in 144 of the walkouts, was that employers should turn over to the government the money deducted from workers' salaries for social security, thereby making workers eligible for the health benefits due them under the law.

Industry (*La Prensa*, January 18, 1974). The workers' syndicate of Metasa, a company owned by Somoza, was dissolved in a joint action by the company and the Labor Court after a two-month-long strike over higher wages (*La Prensa*, October 26, 1973). The state also sought to dissolve SCAAS, claiming that the construction workers' union was meddling in politics and did not represent the interests of its constituent workers. At a hearing held at the Labor Judge's office, some 1,000 workers appeared along with SCAAS leaders to defend the union (*La Prensa*, February 10, 1974). Construction workers' high degree of mobilization and central importance in Managua's reconstruction prevented the government from disbanding the union.

Government repression against workers intensified following the FSLN's attack on the Minister of Agriculture's home at the end of 1974. The government declared martial law and imposed a state of siege for thirty-three months, during which workers' organizations and activities were severely repressed. A number of union leaders, including Domingo Sanchez Salgado, were arrested repeatedly and often held in solitary confinement (Cardenal 1976:24). Such measures were successful in temporarily demobilizing the trade unions.

Assassination of Chamorro and revolutionary struggles

Once the state of siege was lifted in August 1977 as a result of President Carter's pressures, workers resumed their collective actions. Although the eight workers' strikes held in the last three months of 1977 were called to redress economic and work-related grievances, workers joined students to demonstrate and address political issues. Two of the strikes also protested against government corruption. Significantly, the major labor organizations continued to comment and act on political issues and formed a coalition with moderate/reformist political organizations. The largest labor syndicates, CGT-I and CTN, joined the other members of the moderate, revitalized political coalition, UDEL, in demanding a "national dialogue" to address the country's problems. Various labor leaders also met with journalists and endorsed a campaign to repeal the "Black Code" of radio and TV censorship (*La Prensa*, November 14, 1977). One group of workers, CAUS,[8] the Committee of Syndical Action and Unity, which had ties to the Communist Party, rejected any national dialogue and instead announced a gathering to celebrate the anniversary of the Russian Revolution (*La Prensa*, November 5, 1977).

---

[8] According to a United States Embassy report, this organization had 2,000 members in 1988–1989 and was traditionally strong in the Managua textile industry (American Embassy, Managua 1989:13).

As political conflicts intensified, 1978 became a fateful year for Nicaraguan workers. During the eighteen months that immediately preceded the ouster of the Somoza regime, the workers' economic situation rapidly deteriorated. Wages declined, and unemployment began to rise sharply by the end of 1977, while the following year conditions grew even more desperate. A study carried out by the Center for Socio-Economic Research revealed that real wages fell from an average of 2.93 córdobas per hour in 1965 to 2.45 córdobas in 1977. Similarly, adequate employment declined from 24.2 percent in 1975 to 20.6 percent in 1977, while underemployment rose from 57.8 percent to 67.9 percent during the same period (*La Prensa*, February 4, 1979).

Workers' mobilization and collective action intensified after the assassination of Pedro Chamorro in January 1978 that spurred popular mobilization and increased state vulnerability. Organized workers were the first social class to protest the murder of Chamorro, who was very popular among workers. Organized labor had worked closely with Chamorro during the conflicts that unfolded after the 1972 earthquake. Workers had participated in the UDEL coalition that he led. In 1974, thousands of SCAAS workers in Managua and Masaya went on a twenty-four-hour strike in support of Pedro Chamorro and Amada Pineda de Arauz who were sued by a National Guard sergeant alleging personal injury after his acquittal in a suit charging him with repeatedly raping Amada Pineda de Arauz while she was in custody (*La Prensa*, October 22 and 23, 1974). After the assassination, workers were in the forefront of a number of politically significant protests and played a pivotal role in the political process. On January 13, the two largest labor organizations, CGT-I and CTN, declared an indefinite walkout to mourn and protest about Chamorro's murder and the imprisonment of a large number of their leaders and affiliates. The construction workers' union, SCAAS, also joined the strike (*La Prensa*, January 13, 1978). This walkout was announced fully twelve days before the first of two highly publicized strikes by business.

Soon, workers expanded their collective action as state vulnerability after the assassination facilitated their mobilization and collective action. Workers organized 221 strikes in 1978, led by the organized, skilled construction workers who declared 84 walkouts. These construction workers' strikes were significant for their shift toward the FSLN. Forty-four of the strikes were organized in solidarity with Sandinista political prisoners. Construction workers also formed coalitions with other workers and undertook twenty-five strikes in solidarity with other strikers. They also organized three strikes to commemorate the forty-fourth anniversary of the assassination of Sandino, the "General of Free Men." In contrast to the burgeoning political aspect of workers' strikes, the number of economic and work-related strikes declined, with only twelve declared by construction workers to protest against the repression of unions by employers, and only four walkouts over wages and economic benefits.

Along with construction workers' strikes, workers in factories and workshops declared thirty-nine walkouts in 1978 in which the predominant issues were political: government repression (twenty-three), solidarity with Sandinista political prisoners (eleven), and firings and repression of unions (five). Only four strikes demanded economic improvements.

Workers also issued forty-five formal statements, most of which dealt with political matters. Government repression was mentioned in seventeen, followed by fourteen demands for the resignation of Somoza and the establishment of a democratic government. Six published statements protested about Chamorro's assassination, two deplored injustice and poverty in Nicaragua, and one demanded the reorganization of the National Guard. Workers' published statements devoted considerably less attention to purely economic issues. Two statements demanded higher salaries and work-related changes, one protested against tax increases, and three repression of unions by business.

Politicization of workers is also evidenced by the fact that they formed political coalitions with students and organized twenty-eight joint demonstrations during 1978. This radical coalition ultimately helped the cause of the FSLN. These joint actions protested against dictatorship and called for the establishment of democracy (eleven), condemned Chamorro's assassination (eight) and government repression (six), expressed solidarity with Sandinista political prisoners or slain guerrillas (four), supported land invasions by peasants (two), and protested higher taxes (one).

Workers consistently used strikes to express their opposition to repression by the state. At the end of February, CGT-I, CTN, and the Association of Steel Industries, along with UDEL, declared a nationwide strike for March 1 to protest against institutional terror, the repression of students and journalists, and to demand freedom and justice. A large number of workers in various factories and construction sites in Managua responded by walking off the job (*La Prensa*, March 1 and 2, 1978). In April, CGT-I announced a general strike for forty-eight hours in solidarity with hunger strikers led by the mother of Marcio Jaen, a Sandinista political prisoner; the strike also denounced the closing of the School of Agriculture and Cattle-Raising and the eviction of students from the school buildings they had occupied (*La Prensa*, April 18, 1978). Joining in this strike were construction workers at thirty job sites in Managua; 5,000 hospital workers in Managua, Masaya, Jinotepe, and Corinto; a few

Managua factories; and construction workers and more than 500 steel workers in Masaya. CTN and CGT-I joined other groups for a twenty-four-hour nationwide strike to protest against government repression in July when the National Guard killed three students and a worker in Jinotepe (*La Prensa*, July 10 and 18, 1978).

A combination of the state's vulnerability and the ineffectiveness of the moderate opposition without Chamorro, who had been highly respected by workers, led workers to search for an alternative option (Everingham 1996:143). The leading workers' organizations, including CTN, CGT-I, CUS, and CAUS, initially joined FAO, the broad, elite-led coalition, despite pro-Sandinista tendencies among some workers. Beginning in July 1978 with the departure of CGT-I, these organizations gradually withdrew from FAO, the Broad Opposition Front, and joined the FSLN-led coalition, MPU. The two largest labor organizations also supplied combatants for the FSLN in the fall (ibid.:153). By the end of 1978, workers in various sectors displayed a high degree of radicalization. One worker, employed at the anti-government daily, *La Prensa*, declared: "Those guys with the neckties have been running this country for years, since before Somoza. Five thousand of us haven't died over the last two months just for a change of faces in the bunker" (Kinzer 1979:8). Another worker stated: "they were perfectly happy with Somoza until they started to lose business. The old families have been in bed with him for years. Now we are fighting to take this country away from all of them. The FAO is not for us. We are Sandinistas!" (ibid.).

In sum, Nicaraguan workers were better organized than their Iranian counterparts. Because of the lower level of state ownership of enterprises, most workers were employed in the private sector. Thus, the target of workers' economic conflicts was the capitalist employer rather than the state. Workers targeted the state, however, because of the high level of repression. Although divided along political and ideological lines, Nicaraguan workers possessed some preexisting organizations that, when opportunities permitted, were critical in the mobilization of workers. For a long time, however, workers' organizations were rendered ineffective by government repression. In the first round of conflicts in the early 1970s, workers organized in response to both increased work demands by employers to reconstruct Managua and adverse conditions following the earthquake. Led by the organized, skilled construction workers, workers initially mobilized to improve their economic and working conditions. At the start, their collective action targeted the employers. Soon, government intervention and repression politicized workers who, along with their student allies, targeted the state as well, thus becoming involved in a dual conflict. Workers' mobilization, strikes, and coalition with radical students reduced the likelihood of coalition formation with the capitalists and thus failed to generate any change.

Later in 1978, workers' conflicts quickly became politicized as they focused their attacks directly against the state. The assassination of Chamorro, a popular ally of organized labor, generated intense workers' mobilization. Significantly, the political collective actions of workers in 1978 preceded those of entrepreneurs. With economic demands of secondary importance, class coalition, rather than conflict, prevailed and paved the way for the overthrow of the Somoza regime. Mobilization and politicization of the working class, however, did not lead to an immediate shift toward the FSLN. Even the socialist CGT-I remained within moderate political coalitions such as UDEL and FAO. The weaknesses of the moderate opposition and, ultimately, its failure to remove Somoza, together with increased state vulnerability caused by growing popular mobilization, provided the key conditions in which segments of workers shifted their support to the FSLN. Despite ideological divisions, organized labor finally joined with the Sandinistas and contributed to the government's overthrow.

Workers and political conflicts in the Philippines

Philippine workers' conditions differed from those in Iran and Nicaragua in two respects. In contrast to Iran, Filipino workers were employed largely in the private sector because state intervention was lower in the Philippines. As a result, workers did not target the state for economic gain. Unlike workers in Iran and Nicaragua, who had experienced varying degrees of repression for a long time, workers in the Philippines were able to organize and engage in collective bargaining because of the existence of formal democratic institutions. This condition generated labor unions that worked within the existing social structure, pursued reformist politics and generally demanded economic and work-related benefits. In the context of the low level of state intervention, workers' mobilization tended to generate some class conflict in the Philippines.

However, the imposition of martial law and the repression of independent labor in 1972 changed workers' relations with the state and their politics. Although the government initially succeeded in demobilizing the workers, soon a group of militant workers formed a new organization that advocated radical changes in the Philippine social structure. Militant labor organizations gained rapid momentum with Aquino's assassination in 1983, as the state became increasingly vulnerable and, as in Nicaragua, moderate challengers failed to dislodge the regime. More important, the militant labor movement produced leaders who, like those in Nicaragua, played a visible role in national politics. At times even the moderate opposition called upon these leaders for support and cooperation. But growing labor radicalism in the 1980s resulted in Filipino workers attacking both the government and the capitalist class. As a result, workers' radicalism prevented the formation of class coalition and contributed to the fragmentation of the opposition in the Philippines. Thus, workers' politics contributed to a different outcome in the Philippines than in Iran or Nicaragua. Let us examine the mobilization and conflicts of workers in two different periods: the early 1970s before martial law was imposed, and the 1980s.

In contrast to other developing countries, the government's intervention in Philippine labor conflicts diminished because of reform of the labor laws in the early 1950s. Prior to this policy change, independent action by organized labor was severely constrained by the fact that the Secretary of Labor was also president of the largest national union federation, and because the government resolved most labor–management disputes in a near compulsory fashion. One factor that depoliticized labor–management relations was the Industrial Peace Act of 1953. With the institutionalization of collective bargaining permitted under this Act, labor organizations were effectively freed from extensive government meddling. Although collective bargaining was supported by some independent union leaders, the real aim of the Act was to depoliticize the union movement, and it succeeded insofar as most unions restricted their demands to essentially economic and work-related issues[9] and avoided ideological conflicts with employers. As a result, large segments of Filipino workers pursued reformist politics, which included accepting the existing social structure and the idea of working within the system.

Under these conditions, Filipino workers mobilized and formed unions, which enhanced their capacity for collective action. The number of registered unions climbed steadily from the mid-1960s to 1970, when one million workers (Wurfel 1988:64) or 23 percent of the labor force was unionized, according to the Department of Labor (*Manila Times*, November 6, 1970). As industry expanded, unionization also increased until, by 1985, the Philippines had 2,000 registered labor organizations (American Embassy 1988/1989:13). The Trade Union Congress of the Philippines (TUCP), the only labor organization recognized by the government, was the largest, with 1.3 million members by the early 1980s (American Embassy 1982:11). The Trade Unions of the Philippines and Allied Services, linked to the communist World Federation of Trade Unions, had a membership of 250,000, while the radical KMU, Kilusang Mayo

---

[9] Ironically, depoliticization of the unions enabled a few labor leaders to become politicians and, eventually, coopted (Wurfel 1988:64).

Uno founded in 1980, had some 100,000 members by 1982 (ibid.:15). By the mid-1980s, this organization had expanded its membership to 600,000. The largest number of union members was employed in the manufacturing sector, which was concentrated in the Metro Manila area.

Despite the existence of formal democratic institutions and legally established unions, the economic situation of workers failed to improve. By the late 1960s and early 1970s, Filipino workers found collective bargaining to be inadequate and increasingly resorted to unauthorized collective action to improve their economic position. The conflicts also resulted in politicization among segments of the labor force.

The Philippine economy was laboring under the adverse effects of the islands' postwar economic development. Real wages for the industrial labor force did not improve between 1955 and 1971 and actually declined by more than 28 percent for skilled, nonagricultural workers (Baldwin 1975:148).[10] From 1960 to 1971, the wages for common laborers declined by 8 percent in real terms, while the earnings of skilled and semi-skilled workers declined even more, according to official statistics (ILO 1974:9–11). A devaluation of the peso in February 1969 and other IMF-imposed economic reforms created higher unemployment and a 10 percent reduction in wages over the next two years (Wurfel 1988:61). A Philippine Senate committee report in 1969 noted that of a labor force totaling 12 million, 1 million were without jobs. One labor leader estimated the number of unemployed workers in 1970 to be 3 million (Daroy 1988:12). Inflation, caused by devaluations in 1962 and 1970 (ibid.), also adversely affected the working class by eroding their purchasing power. According to a Philippine Department of Labor report in 1970, only 3–4 percent of the entire labor force received the minimum wage of 6 pesos (*Manila Times*, April 4, 1970). By 1972, wage laborers' real income was slightly below its level of twenty years earlier (Wurfel 1988:54).

Organized, skilled workers, who were the principal losers from an economic standpoint, mobilized to change their situation. Industrialization and rising employment in the manufacturing sector enhanced the capacity of this segment of the workforce and led to increased unionization. In 1970, workers participated in 104 strikes and 15 demonstrations. Their strike demands revolved primarily around economic issues, followed by union-related conflicts. In their demonstrations workers raised more political issues and protested about more diverse issues, such as low minimum wage, corporate capitalist policies, political repression, and fascism. Other demands included labor rights, bureaucratic reforms,

---

[10] Another source indicates that real wages dropped by 8 percent between 1962 and 1964 and by 30 percent between 1970 and 1974 (Daroy 1988:12).

and an end to feudalism and corruption. Although initially most workers' essential demands were economic, not political, increasingly their conflicts became politicized in response to government repression designed to demobilize their protests.

In 1971, the number of workers' strikes rose by 50 percent to 157. As conditions steadily worsened, the primary source of conflict remained unchanged, and workers continued to mobilize for greater economic gain. Although the government had boosted the minimum daily wage from 6 to 8 pesos in June 1970, workers now demanded 10 pesos. They also participated in thirteen demonstrations that displayed a political side, as workers demanded higher wages, greater labor rights, and relief from rising inflation and repression. In at least one demonstration, workers even called for Marcos to be impeached as a puppet of imperialism.

A significant development in 1970 was the rise of a small but active segment of workers who advocated a radical position. Increased government repression and failure of the moderates to gain concessions played a major role in the formation of this radical worker faction. As occurred in Nicaragua, these workers joined radical students for demonstrations against political conditions in the Philippines on forty-nine occasions in 1970 and 1971. These workers joined the Movement for a Democratic Philippines, a radical leftist coalition. The radical workers and their leftist allies organized a week-long "Workers' March for Justice" in May 1970. The march was intended "to dramatize the plight of Filipino labor suffering under the combined exploitation and suppression of the fascist Marcos regime and local and foreign capitals" (*Manila Times*, May 19, 1970). During one event, a spokesman stated that President Marcos "has ceased to be a leader of the Filipinos and has declared war on his own people by his repeated threats to impose martial law. Marcos is the puppet of American and vested interests that exploit the masses of suffering Filipino workers and peasants" (*Manila Times*, May 24, 1970). In a "People's Congress" organized during the week, labor activists called for revolutionary changes in society. They denounced military and police violence at picket lines. Finally, they shouted for the resignation or impeachment of Marcos. They chanted "Ibagsak si Marcos," or "Take Marcos down!" (*Manila Times*, May 25, 1970).

In 1971, these radical workers continued their political activities. On a number of occasions, the radical workers were attacked by the security forces. In the May Day celebration in 1971, three demonstrators were killed. In response to the killings, these radical workers and their allies organized various protest rallies and marches against Marcos. They stated that the massacre was simply a sign of the "total pattern of military suppression perpetrated by the Marcos regime in behalf of its imperialist, feudal and bureaucrat capitalist masters" (*Manila Times*, May 2, 1971).

Clearly, by the early 1970s, a segment of Philippine workers had become radicalized and formed an alliance with leftist students. Although these radical workers joined with moderates in some economic conflicts, such as that over the minimum wage (*Manila Times*, April 14, 1970), they held separate May Day rallies and articulated different demands. Despite generating divisiveness,[11] this ideologically driven labor movement became significant during the next phase of the conflicts in the 1980s.

However, their mobilization and collective action came to an abrupt halt when martial law was imposed in 1972. Martial law virtually demobilized organized labor and its allies, leftist students and intellectuals. The leaders of militant unions were harassed, imprisoned, and even killed (Nemenzo 1988:237). Under martial law, the state was autonomous but it had a decidedly negative impact on workers. Policy changes implemented under martial law aimed to stimulate investments by reducing workers' power and wages, restricting their right to strike,[12] and putting labor unions under surveillance. Wages and the unions' power to organize, bargain collectively, and strike were repressed as the government favored export-led industrialization. Organized labor included roughly 25 percent of all wage and salary workers in urban areas, but only 15 percent of all workers succeeded in obtaining collective bargaining agreements. In a speech at the Central Bank in January 1974, Marcos declared his determination to keep wages low: "Our country has one of the lowest average wage levels in this part of the world. We intend to see to it that our export program is not placed in jeopardy at an early stage by a rapid increase in the general wage level" (Wurfel 1988:264). In July the Philippines government placed an advertisement in the business section of the *New York Times* listing "Seven Good Reasons" for investing in the Philippines, among which was that labor costs were 35 to 50 percent lower than in Hong Kong or Singapore. The government also specifically banned strikes in the Export Processing Zones to ensure continued foreign investment.

The government's economic policies, its demobilization of labor unions, and the devaluation of the peso combined to cause a slide in the real wages of Philippine workers from 1969 until Marcos' ouster in

[11] One example was the struggle to gain management recognition by two rival labor groups in the National Waterworks and Sewage Authority, which led to five strikes over the issue (*Manila Times*, February 19, 1970).

[12] Despite the restrictions, militant workers made some attempts to redress their grievances in the industrial sector. Beginning in 1975, workers in a number of factories announced strikes. That year, more than two dozen such strikes were held (Tiglao 1988:62).

1986.[13] From 1972 to 1978, unskilled laborers' real wages plummeted 30.6 percent, while the wages of skilled workers in Manila fell by 23.8 percent (Steinberg 1990:128). By 1986, the wage decline had reached an alarming dimension: "a fall of 50 percent or more from the peak reached in the early 1960s to a level below that of the 1930s and only a little higher than those of 1897–1903 and 1944–1946" (Hooley 1991:203).

Although the minimum wage of nonagricultural workers in Metro Manila was raised to compensate for inflation, even the Department of Labor admitted that the raise was not adequate for a family of six. Still worse, 65 percent of employers violated the minimum wage standards, according to the government-sponsored Trade Union Congress of the Philippines. To honor the minimum wage became the most common demand of workers' strikes, almost all of which were declared illegal (Wurfel 1988:265).

Assassination of Aquino and workers' mobilization

Worsening economic conditions together with new political conditions gave rise to workers' mobilization in the 1980s, which can be considered the second phase of the labor conflicts. In the context of polarization, the assassination of Benigno Aquino and the popular mobilization it produced rendered the state vulnerable to challenge and attack, and generated a great deal of labor mobilization and collective action. Again, as in the earlier round of conflicts, organized labor divided along organizational and political lines. This time, however, the capacity of the radical faction of organized labor to mobilize was enhanced. These militant workers clearly demonstrated that they wanted fundamental changes. Thus, they targeted both their employers and the state. At the same time, economic deterioration generated conflicts between workers and capitalists throughout the country. As a result of these conflicts and the rise of the radical faction, a class coalition was not formed in the Philippines. Workers' attacks against employers forced the capitalists to seek the state's assistance in repressing the labor, particularly its radical faction. Thus, workers' mobilization in the Philippines contributed to a very different outcome from that in Iran or Nicaragua.

Although martial law and government repression demobilized the labor movement, they inadvertently strengthened the position of radical labor during this second round of conflicts. In contrast, during martial law, the position of the moderate labor organization declined. A significant segment of the labor movement was not affiliated with the TUCP,

---

[13] On the decline of wages from 1978 to 1982, see Bouis (1990:289–290).

the largest and officially recognized labor organization. Workers charged that the organization was too passive and susceptible to government control and manipulation (American Embassy 1982:11).

Radical labor began mobilizing in early 1980, even before martial law was lifted. Some industrial labor federations broke away from the ineffective government-controlled trade union and formed the Kilusang Mayo Uno, or First of May Movement. These federations organized a rally on May 1 in Quezon City at which 25,000 workers demanded an increase in the minimum wage, a return of the right to strike, and the "nationalization of all industries controlled by foreign monopoly capitalism" (Wurfel 1988:265). With the end of martial law in 1981, strikes more than quadrupled from 62 in 1980 to 260 in 1981, despite new decrees restricting them. At the same time, rising labor militancy and more frequent strikes were accompanied by heightened government repression. In 1982, for example, KMU's three national leaders, including its chairman, Felix Berto Olalia, and more than thirty trade union leaders, mostly from the KMU, were arrested on charges of "subversion and conspiracy to commit rebellion" (*Malaya*, December 7, 1983).

Workers' mobilization and collective action expanded after the assassination of Aquino in 1983 as popular mobilization rendered the government vulnerable to attacks. Workers organized seven demonstrations protesting about the assassination and engaged in 155 strikes in the final four months of 1983. They issued statements demanding additional labor rights and economic justice. Themes of the demonstrations clearly revealed the main political divisions within the labor movement. Although all workers demanded higher wages, the moderates protested about government corruption and the assassination of Aquino, while radicals mainly condemned repression, dictatorship, and imperialism. Radicals also attacked what they called the "US–Marcos dictatorship" and demanded the removal of US military bases from the Philippines.

The radical KMU was the most active labor organization during these political conflicts, but in 1983 it had not yet developed the capacity to mobilize on a large scale. The December funeral of KMU chairman, Felix Berto Olalia, was attended by only 5,000 workers, along with scores of students and churchmen (*Malaya*, December 14, 1983). Repression still contributed to the difficulties of Filipino radical labor. Labor disputes were frequently accompanied by violence, such as the death of a labor leader from the Butuan Logs Employees' Association who was murdered by two unidentified men in the wake of festering labor problems at the Butuan Logs company (*Malaya*, December 21, 1983). Radical labor made tremendous gains and achieved greater recognition in 1984 and 1985, however.

Workers' growing militancy was fueled, in part, by rising unemployment and inflation, which reduced real wages. During 1984, layoffs and retrenchment culminated in massive dismissals (*Malaya*, February 8 and November 6, 1984), sending the unemployment rate to a record high of 41.4 percent during the first six months of the year (*Malaya*, October 3, 1984). Workers called 282 strikes during 1984, issued 31 protest statements, and held 29 demonstrations, mostly led by the radical KMU. The workplace was still the most frequent arena of workers' mobilization, and conflicts with employers were overwhelmingly economic. The vast majority of the 282 strikes demanded higher wages, with new collective bargaining agreements a second issue of concern. Picket line violence multiplied during this period: in one instance, 126 persons, including 6 policemen, were injured (*Malaya*, March 19, 1984). Such fierce clashes occurred often, and militant labor blamed them on injunctions issued by the Ministry of Labor and Employment (*Malaya*, July 20, 1984).

These clashes, in turn, contributed to the politicization of labor and boosted its militancy. The increased militancy of these actions is mirrored in workers' statements, most of which addressed political concerns such as government repression, while economic issues were mentioned less frequently. Workers' statements also attacked the IMF and World Bank policies and the "US–Marcos dictatorship." Slogans aired during demonstrations also showed a preponderance of concern with political issues: repression of labor was the principal complaint followed by higher wages, union issues and collective bargaining, the US–Marcos dictatorship, and unemployment and poverty.

In 1985, workers widened their political activities, organizing 91 independent demonstrations and participating in 371 strikes, the highest number for each activity. Strikes also became longer in 1985. The largest category of labor protests, as in the previous year, centered on the workplace and targeted employers. The vast majority of workers' strikes demanded higher wages. As management fired workers and used "goons" to break up picket lines, strikers protested against management's "unfair labor practices," demanded collective bargaining, and denounced business's repression of labor, firings, and layoffs. Most of the strikes were disrupted by violent attacks by government forces, paramilitary troops, or agents hired by management, which led to further labor militancy (*Malaya*, May 1, 1985).

Workers joined forces to demonstrate alongside students, farmers, neighborhood residents, and professionals, and in events organized by popular groups. These highly political demonstrations often targeted both the state and employers. The most widely shouted slogans protested against the government's repression of labor organizations and jailing of labor leaders, lack of unemployment benefit for laid-off workers, and low wages. In addition, capitalists were targeted by slogans against firings, layoffs, and repression of labor by business. Similarly, workers published twenty-six statements, which primarily protested about the repression of labor by both the government and employers.

Most importantly, segments of Filipino workers began coordinated political general strikes in the south of the country. In February, some 140,000 workers throughout Mindanao took part in a general strike to protest about terrorism against labor in the region (*Malaya*, February 3, 1985). In August, more than 150,000 workers in the five southern islands launched a series of protests against militarization and military abuses (*Malaya*, August 9, 1985). A month later, roughly 90,000 workers belonging to 120 unions grouped under the umbrella organization, Center for Nationalist Trade Unions of Mindanao, walked off their jobs as a prelude to Welgang Bayan, a two-day gathering organized by Bayan, a militant coalition organization dominated by leftists (*Malaya*, September 21, 1985).

The radical KMU made important gains during these conflicts. It boosted its nationwide membership to 600,000 (Timberman 1991:133), as many workers favored the KMU because of its militant stance in the factories as a way to gain economic advantages (Goodno 1991:154). KMU-sponsored events such as the May Day celebrations in 1984 and 1985 attracted much larger crowds, despite President Marcos' presence at a rally held by the TUCP (*Malaya*, May 2, 1984 and May 2, 1985). KMU's position in the labor movement was recognized as preeminent even by the government-sponsored TUCP, which agreed for the first time to cooperate with KMU in protesting against Marcos' proposal to authorize the military to assume jurisdiction over labor disputes and certify them for compulsory arbitration (*Malaya*, June 28, 1985). KMU vigorously criticized the proposal, which would have permitted employers to replace strikers who violated government orders, and regarded it as essentially a ban against all strikes (*Malaya*, June 13, 1985). Opposition organizations recognized the significance of KMU during major political events. For example, the leader of the militant KMU, Rolando Olalia, along with other leading opposition figures, spoke at the commemoration of Aquino's death in 1984 (*Malaya*, August 22, 1984).

KMU relentlessly pursued a revolutionary ideology and thus attacked both the state and employers. It organized a second national congress, which condemned "the fascist attacks of capital and the state" and called for "further unity of the working class to militantly fight for union and democratic demands" (*Malaya*, February 27, 1984). In response to Marcos' call for equal sacrifices to hasten recovery, KMU leader,

Rolando Olalia, countered that the brunt of any belt-tightening measures should be borne by multinational and crony corporations, along with the government, all of which had brought about the economic crisis in the first place (*Malaya*, May 3, 1985). To prevent elite hegemony in the conflicts, KMU leaders criticized elite attempts to unify the opposition for a possible election, maintaining that unity cannot "truly free" the Filipino people, "especially the workers, from the claws of foreign exploitation in collaboration with its local cohorts." Instead of a snap election, KMU leaders called upon workers, together with the "exploited masses," to affirm their unity in a "congress of the streets" and change the repressive system (*Malaya*, March 11, 1985).

As the growth of militant labor began to threaten the entire social structure, workers became ever more repressed by both the government and employers. One report indicated that 1985 was "one of the bloodiest and most unstable years seen in the Philippine labor front" (*Malaya*, May 1, 1985). Unlike capitalists in Iran and Nicaragua, employers in the Philippines fired and laid off workers and closed their factories in response to labor militancy. In many instances, employers hired their own security agents, who imposed severe casualties on workers in picket lines. In one instance, even the Labor Minister warned the Employers' Confederation that the communist threat could be strengthened by the growing labor unrest sparked by bad working conditions (*Malaya*, April 12, 1985). At the same time, the government repeatedly jailed striking labor leaders (*Malaya*, March 26, 1984). Labor repression was so intense that the ILO severely rebuked the government for its anti-labor policies and arrests of labor leaders (*Malaya*, August 12, 1984). Repression of union leaders continued unchecked, despite rulings by the Supreme Court on at least two occasions, which ordered the military and police to produce missing labor leaders (*Malaya*, August 4 and 27, 1984).[14] Twenty-five deaths and fourteen abductions occurred in less than a decade, with forty labor leaders ending up in jails across the country for their organizing activities (*Malaya*, November 25, 1984). The total number of workers killed reached eighty-one in 1985. While most of the slain workers belonged to the militant labor groups, eleven were members of the moderate TUCP. The government detained 132 labor leaders and workers in detention camps nationwide, while twenty other unionists and organizers disappeared during 1985 (*Malaya*, December 22, 1985).

To summarize, unlike Iranian workers, workers in the Philippines had been permitted to organize and engage in collective bargaining through-

---

[14] On September 26, 1984, six labor leaders disappeared in Davao del Norte (*Malaya*, October 5, 1984). Members of the militant KMU, in particular, were targets of military repression (*Malaya*, July 27, 1984).

out the 1950s and 1960s. The institutionalization of industrial conflicts and absence of state intervention generated a reformist labor movement, which avoided political and ideological conflicts. During the economic decline and political conflicts of the early 1970s, the majority of Filipino workers initially demanded economic benefits, largely targeting the employers. But three factors led to the rise of a small radical segment within the Philippine labor movement. These factors included the failure of the moderates to gain concessions from employers and the state, increased government repression, and the rise of radical allies among students and intellectuals. As a result, a segment of labor was quickly politicized and targeted both the state and the capitalist class. The imposition of martial law in 1972 repressed the insurgents and halted social conflicts for several years. Under martial law, state intervention and repression expanded and provided further conditions for conflicts.

Although radical labor began mobilizing again in 1980, workers' large-scale collective action began after the assassination of Benigno Aquino in 1983 when the state became highly vulnerable to challenge and attack. At first, workers' demands were very diverse, as they protested about the assassination, government corruption, low wages, repression, and imperialism. Although divided along political and ideological lines, the radical segment of organized labor increasingly gained ground against other segments as a result of both the moderates' ineffectiveness and the state's increased repression. As occurred a decade earlier, militant workers, allied with leftist political forces, attacked both the state and their capitalist employers. This attack threatened the entire social structure and helped prevent the formation of a class coalition, as employers increasingly relied on government repression to pacify workers. The absence of such a coalition was, in part, responsible for the different outcome of the Philippines conflicts and insurgency.

Conclusion

Workers in all three countries were excluded from the polity and repressed by their governments. Although all three regimes formed exclusive rule and were autonomous of the capitalist class, workers in these countries were in varying degrees repressed as the governments were pursuing a course of rapid economic development and capital accumulation. Exclusion from the polity, combined with conflicts against the capitalist class, often resulted in dual conflicts. The conditions in turn led many workers to initiate insurgency and a shift in favor of ideologically driven challengers when opportunities permitted. Because workers played a central role in the productive process, they had the potential to play an important role in the conflicts and their outcomes in all three countries.

Workers' capacities for mobilization and collective action differed in each country because of different degrees of repression. The virtual absence of independent, preexisting labor organizations and the weaknesses of external allies in Iran constrained workers from mobilizing until the final phase of the revolutionary conflict. With the exception of oil workers, who played a significant role in the final stage of the Iranian conflicts, other workers were not as visible. On the other hand, better-organized Nicaraguan workers quickly took advantage of opportunities in the 1970s to mobilize against the government. Nicaraguan workers' greater organization and mobilization also meant that they played a more important political role in national politics. In the Philippines, greater organizational resources enabled workers to engage in a large number of collective actions before martial law and again during the 1980s. Labor organizations in both Nicaragua and the Philippines produced leaders who became highly visible nationally and played a role in national politics.

The timing of workers' mobilization and actions is best explained, not by ideological factors, but rather by favorable opportunities created by reduced repression and increased state vulnerability. These opportunities were especially important for the working class, which everywhere experienced varying degrees of repression. Favorable opportunities were most significant in Iran where workers lacked the basic solidarity structures for mobilization and had to rely on their own informal networks. Although workers in Nicaragua and the Philippines also needed favorable opportunities for mobilization, workers in both countries succeeded in launching collective action in the early 1970s without major changes in the political system. In each country, workers' mobilization also expanded during a period of state vulnerability following the assassination of a highly popular challenger who had threatened the existing ruler.

The targets of workers' collective actions were influenced by state intervention (including repression), the interest and ideological orientation of workers, and the appearance of coalition partners. Workers targeted the state when state intervention was relatively high. This occurred in Iran, where the state was the single largest employer, and state repression was most intense. Iranian workers inevitably targeted the state as soon as conflicts erupted. In contrast, workers targeted the capitalist class for economic action in the Philippines where state intervention was lowest and private entrepreneurs were the principal owners of the means of production. However, workers also targeted the state because of government repression. Thus, workers in Nicaragua and the Philippines targeted both the state and the capitalist class for economic and political reasons. Workers' collective actions also targeted the state when they found new allies. Ideological orientation, as well, affected workers' targets of collective action. In both Nicaragua and the Philippines ideological conversion to socialism among a segment of workers led to attacks on both the state and the capitalist class. The rise of leftist political allies in Nicaragua and the Philippines likewise influenced both ideological conversion and thus the target of collective action.

The timing of the workers' shift toward revolutionary challengers was affected by the extent of state vulnerability and the strength of alternative moderate or revolutionary challengers. In both Iran and Nicaragua, workers lacked preexisting organizational or political ties to the challengers who ultimately came to power. Neither one of these challengers had strong ideological support within the population in the initial stages of the revolutionary conflicts. With weak solidarity structures and organizations, Iranian workers did not shift their support to Khomeini until the final stage of the revolution, when the state became extremely vulnerable. At that point, oil workers, many of whom were socialist, led the working class in overthrowing the monarchy. Similarly, in Nicaragua organized workers were not allied with the Sandinistas. The largest labor federation, the socialist CGT-I, had allied itself with the moderates for a long time. But the CGT-I shifted its support to the FSLN in July 1978, as the state became increasingly vulnerable. Other segments of Nicaraguan organized labor also gradually shifted to the FSLN as the government intensified its repressive policies in the fall of 1978, and it became increasingly evident that the elite opposition lacked the capacity to remove Somoza from power.

In the Philippines, however, the ineffectiveness of the moderate opposition also affected the politics of the radicals in the labor movement. Unlike Nicaragua, where workers had formed a coalition with the moderates, in the Philippines no such alliance actually emerged. Perhaps the rising strength of revolutionary challengers also discouraged such a coalition between the radical labor and the moderates. As a result, the radical segment of the working class pressed for a social rather than political revolution.

Workers' mobilization, target of attack, and politics played a significant role in the outcome of the insurgency in all three countries. In Iran, where workers' collective actions were primarily directed against the state because it was both the employer and the instrument of repression, workers did not have any other major target of attack to reduce the likelihood of coalition formation. Workers' strikes and disruption of production and distribution played a major role in the overthrow of the monarchy. In contrast, in the early 1970s workers in both Nicaragua and the Philippines targeted both the capitalists and the government, and as a result reduced the likelihood that broad coalitions would arise. In Nicaragua, in 1978 and 1979, however, workers primarily targeted the state and thus facilitated the formation of class coalitions. As a result, their disruptive actions and their shift to favor revolutionaries significantly contributed to the outcome of the conflicts.

Workers' politics and target of attack also strongly affected the outcome of insurgency in the Philippines. In the final stage of the conflicts there, workers directed their collective actions against both the state and the capitalist class. While workers' political conflicts were directed against the government, workers' economic demands were directed against the capitalists who controlled the vast majority of the economic assets. Although rising labor militancy in the Philippines had prepared the ground for a shift in favor of revolutionary challengers, workers' collective action against capitalists prevented the formation of broad coalitions. As a result, workers' politics and targets of attack strongly affected the politics of the capitalists and thus contributed to the outcome of the conflicts in the Philippines. Now, it is time to analyze the conflicts and politics of the capitalist class in the three countries.

7   Capitalists: reluctant rebels

Recent structural theories have underlined the significance of schisms and divisions between the capitalist class and the state in revolutions. Indeed, the defection of capitalists from the state has been crucial to revolutions in contemporary developing countries. Yet, as will be argued, the mere existence of conflict between the capitalist class and the state and the former's defection from the state is not sufficient for revolutions to occur. The capitalist class must take an active role in the conflicts, pursue disruptive tactics, and join other classes and challengers to overthrow the government. But, despite their conflicts with the state, capitalists may not play an active role in its overthrow because of organizational weaknesses or more importantly because of the existence of radical threats. In particular, capitalists may not join the struggles against the government if rising class conflict and strong revolutionary challengers threaten the entire capitalist system. In such conditions, capitalists may become increasingly dependent on the state to contain the radicals and may thus attempt to steer the outcome of the conflicts in nonrevolutionary directions.

In general, the nature of capitalist politics in developing countries has been affected by the relations of this class, or its fractions, with the state, and the politics of the working classes and revolutionary challengers. Capitalist access to the polity and economic advantages or disadvantages have strongly affected the politics of this class. The nature of the relationship between capitalists and interventionist states in developing countries has often sharply divided this class between those who supported and those who opposed the government. A small segment of the capitalist class will have been allied with and dependent on the state for resources, and protection from the vagaries of the market and competition. Because it benefited from government intervention, this segment of the capitalist class will not have mobilized against the state during political conflicts. In contrast, another fraction, the majority, will have been excluded from the polity and lacked access to decision-makers who affected the economy and thus their interests. These capitalists have been excluded from the ruling coalition and have not benefited from government resources. They have received no economic assistance, interest-free loans, subsidies, or tax breaks from the government, nor have they been protected from competition or market forces during times of adversity. As a result, these capitalists have been the principal fractions of this class who have had an interest in opposing the government during times of crisis.

But the intensity of capitalist interest in opposing the state has often been mitigated somewhat by the threats of workers and their radical allies who advocate the transformation of the social order. In the presence of such threats, capitalists have had to rely on the state for protection and resolution of the conflicts. Capitalists' reliance on the state has increased where class conflicts have intensified and revolutionary challengers posed a real threat to the entire capitalist system. As a result, in such conditions, the intensity of the capitalists' conflict against the state has diminished, thus producing reluctant rebels.[1]

Ideologically, capitalists, excluded from the ruling coalition, have tended to favor nationalism and some form of democracy that provides them with access to the polity. When capitalists are under pressure from foreign capital and multilateral agencies, they are more likely to advocate nationalism. In such situations, capitalists have mobilized to change the polity that failed to protect them from the vagaries of the world market and the intrusion of foreign capital. When they are excluded from the polity and adversely affected by the state, capitalists demand greater democracy and expansion of the polity. Beyond these changes, capitalists may favor moderate social reforms, which benefit the middle and working classes. Their call for reforms may attract allies and enhance stability in the long run because capitalists need allies to achieve their goal of removing powerholders. Although capitalists do not subscribe to revolutionary ideologies and oppose social revolutions, which require a fundamental transformation of the system, they may sometimes be obliged to join in coalitions with radical and revolutionary organizations. Such coalitions in no way involve conversion to radical, revolutionary ideologies, but are merely tactical alliances entered into for the purpose of removing authoritarian, repressive state regimes.

Of course, capitalists' conflict of interest with the state has never been sufficient for insurgency. Like other actors, capitalists' organization and capacity for collective action have also affected their politics and tendency towards insurgency. Social, economic, and political divisions have often reduced their capacity for mobilization and collective action. Favorable opportunities and state vulnerabilities, too, have played an important role

---

[1] I have borrowed this term from the title of John Walton's book, *Reluctant Rebels* (1984).

in capitalist mobilization. Although capitalists have greater resources for mobilization than other social groups they, too, have had to wait for favorable conditions to engage in collective action. They have mobilized for collective action in at least two conditions: in response to a decline of government repression and when states became vulnerable during popular mobilization and formation of broad temporary coalitions.

Capitalists' defection from the state and their participation in opposition politics can be crucial, both at the onset of the conflicts and in the outcome. Because capitalists occupy a privileged position in the stratification system, they may be relatively insulated from violent repression. In addition, the capitalist class possesses resources that can be used for offensive mobilization in times of conflict. Their structural position gives capitalists the potential to disrupt the production processes and, thus, either generate or intensify economic crises or downturns. At the same time, the defection of the capitalist class from the state may drastically reduce the government's social bases of support, thereby increasing the state's vulnerability. The mobilization and collective actions of the capitalist class may also be crucial in providing favorable opportunities for other, less resourceful social groups and classes to mobilize and engage in collective action. Finally, capitalist resources can potentially assist groups and collectivities with fewer resources for mobilization.

Adversely affected by state intervention and the formation of exclusive rule, major segments of the capitalist class in all three countries opposed the governments during the crucial political conflicts. To be sure, capitalists' interests were generally served by state development strategies that promoted capital accumulation. Furthermore, the general interests of the capitalist class were protected by the state against the working classes and their revolutionary allies. But in all three countries the majority of these capitalists opposed the existing regimes because they had no access to the polity and received no favorable treatment from state intervention. They obtained no subsidies, low-interest loans, lucrative government contracts, or protection from competition and the vagaries of the world market. In fact, under certain conditions these capitalists became scapegoats for inappropriate government policies. As a result, large segments of the capitalist class in these countries developed an interest in opposing the government. This class, which includes both employers and the self-employed, was large, accounting for nearly one-third of the labor force in Iran and Nicaragua, and more than 36 percent in the Philippines. Their numbers provided them with substantial resources for political mobilization.

Although capitalists participated in the opposition in all three countries in this study, they played different roles in the conflicts, which had different outcomes. In the two cases of Iran and Nicaragua, where social revolutions overthrew the states, capitalists participated to a significant extent in the opposition and undermined the position of the existing regimes. In both cases, the capitalists resorted to disruptive activities such as business shutdowns and general strikes to bring down these regimes. In Iran, in particular, capitalists were very important throughout the struggles that ultimately overthrew the monarchy. Yet, in the end, they could not determine the nature of the postrevolutionary state. In Nicaragua, capitalists joined other groups and classes to overthrow Somoza, but they failed to affect the outcome in their own favor. In the Philippines, social divisions together with rising labor militancy and the threat of leftist forces prevented capitalists from playing a major role in the collective actions that unfolded after the assassination of Aquino in 1983. Although they did not use disruptive collective action and tactics, they were the beneficiaries of the outcome of the conflicts because in the end the Philippines did not experience a social revolution.

Capitalists and the state in Iran

Iran's capitalist class was divided between those who operated in the modern sector and were in some ways tied to the state and those who worked in traditional bazaars. Although the two fractions were linked through trade, they did not pursue similar politics because of their different relations to the state. The modern sector emerged largely as a result of Iran's state-sponsored economic development. This fraction of the capitalist class invested heavily in the modern sectors of industry and finance and was highly dependent on the state. Although the size of this fraction grew by the time of the revolution, they still remained a minority, comprising less than 10,000 individuals (Ladjevardian 1982:3). These entrepreneurs operated within a monopolistic, oligopolistic market, protected by the state through limited licensing and high tariffs (Mohtadi 1987:54). Most of these capitalists received considerable direct and indirect resources from the state, especially in the form of credit at favorable rates and tax holidays. They also received credit subsidies, which amounted to an estimated $.73 billion in 1975/1976 and $1.27 billion in 1977/1978. The latter amount was approximately equal to two-thirds of all private profits in the manufacturing sector (Salehi-Isfahani 1989:359).

Politically, these capitalists did not oppose the monarchy because they had been largely dependent on the state for their capital and were among the principal beneficiaries of state development policies. In addition, they were mostly unaffected by the government's price controls and anti-profiteering campaign, which generated conflicts for other segments of the capitalist class. Furthermore, these entrepreneurs had no independent organizations to mobilize and engage in collective action. Although they were granted permission by the state to form a chamber of commerce, this organization was hardly independent because the composition of the chamber's representatives was determined, in part, by the state, in line with its policy of checking the rise of independent organizations (Ladjevardian 1982:5–6). As a result, once conflicts erupted, many of these wealthy capitalists transferred their capital to Europe and the United States. By the end of October 1978, $50 million was leaving the country every day. Soon, many of these capitalists themselves also chose to depart.

In contrast to these capitalists, bazaaris – a term referring to merchants, shopkeepers, and artisans – were very active and significant during Iran's revolutionary conflicts. Bazaaris did not represent a single economic stratum. Although some bazaaris possessed small and medium-sized capital, many also represented very large commercial, financial, and industrial capital. Despite economic divisions, bazaaris often acted as a single social force during political crises and consequently their opposition to the state was crucial in widening insurgency against the regime. Significantly, bazaaris' shutdowns of their businesses disrupted commerce and trade, deepened the economic decline, and played an important role in the overthrow of the government. Bazaaris were also important in the mobilization of other social groups because they often provided resources for such groups during large-scale political conflicts.

The size, resources, and physical layout of the bazaars were significant factors enabling bazaaris to assume a critical position in Iran's political conflicts. By the time of the revolution Tehran's central bazaar, the heart of the nation's trade, encompassed six square miles and contained nearly 20,000 shops and workshops. Although a small segment of bazaar was involved in international trade, approximately half of these bazaaris were engaged in wholesale commerce. Roughly 100,000 people worked in the Tehran bazaar before the revolution. There were also approximately 20,000 more shops in the immediate vicinity of the bazaar that often followed bazaaris' politics even though their shops were not part of the bazaar proper.

Despite a relative decline in their control over commerce, bazaaris still dominated most of the national trade during the 1970s, accounting for more than two-thirds of the nation's domestic wholesale trade and more than 30 percent of all imports (Graham 1979:221). Bazaar moneylenders, comprising several hundred individuals,[2] controlled approximately

---

[2] This estimate is for the mid-1960s (Benedick 1964:66).

15 percent of all private sector credit, which amounted to billions of rials every year (*Kayhan International,* October 2, 1978; Graham 1979:221). Unlike the industrial and financial upper class, bazaaris were not dependent on the state for economic resources, nor did they depend on the state to control labor because their production was primarily carried out in small shops. Their independent resources and lack of close ties to the state enabled bazaaris to engage in collective action without risking either their capital or their immediate livelihood.

Another factor contributing to bazaaris' importance in Iran's political conflicts is the unique structure of the central bazaar, which served to facilitate mobilization and collective action during times of conflict. In most of Iran's major cities, the central bazaar is concentrated within a single location, in narrow alleys under covered roofs. Such concentration of shops and proximity of working conditions facilitate communication. Bazaaris deal in very specialized commodities, buying, selling, or producing a single line of goods only. All those who deal in that specific product work in the same street or alley, although the entire bazaar is interconnected. Proximity and dependence on single commodities can generate intense competition for customers. At the same time, however, these identical factors can also create a common fate with respect to market conditions, changes in technology, appearance of new competitors, and external factors of production such as the role of the state in business. These conditions can produce strong solidarity during periods of crisis and conflicts, especially when the diverse segments of the bazaar are faced with a common enemy.

Bazaaris' ideology and politics have often been misunderstood and misinterpreted. Bazaaris are often viewed as a traditional social class who often follow the leadership of the clergy. This traditionalism is supposedly evidenced by bazaaris' strong alliance with the clergy or willingness to follow clerical leadership in political matters (Arjomand 1981, 1986; Bashiriyeh 1984:61; Farhi 1990:92; Skocpol 1982). While it is true that many bazaaris, particularly the older generation, were religious and their religious contributions had long been important in maintaining Islamic mosques, functions, and ceremonies, bazaaris' religious orientation did not determine their ideology. Their contributions and participation in mosque activities, including prayers, had declined dramatically in the 1970s.[3] With the exception of a small minority,[4] most bazaaris never

---

[3] Personal interviews with a number of bazaaris.
[4] The leading supporters of Khomeini in the bazaar included Khamoushi, Pour-Ostad, Amani, Shafi'i, and Asgar-Oladi. The hard-core, activist segment of this group consisted of approximately thirty bazaaris who worked closely with the clergy during the monarchy's final days to coordinate strikes.

pursued religion as a political ideology (Lebaschi 1983, tape 3:15). In fact, a closer examination indicates that bazaaris' politics and financial resources have played an important role in influencing the clergy's politics. Some bazaari activists have even claimed that it has always been bazaaris who dictated clergy's politics, rather than vice versa.[5]

Bazaaris' politics and collective actions can best be explained not in terms of their ties to the clergy, but by the mobilization model used in this research. In fact, bazaaris' collective action in the past few decades has followed the politics of liberal-nationalists, rather than the clergy's authority. For example, in contrast to the vast majority of the clergy who supported the monarchy during the political conflicts of the early 1950s, bazaaris backed the liberal National Front led by Prime Minister Mosaddegh and mobilized against the Pahlavi state. Mosaddegh's liberal policies in 1951 reduced political repression and enabled the bazaar organization, Society of Merchants, Guilds, and Artisans (SMGA), to mobilize for collective action. Between 1951 and 1953, they repeatedly demonstrated their support for the prime minister by closing down the bazaar on at least fifty separate occasions (Lebaschi 1983, tape 1:9). After the prime minister's arrest, and in the face of public expression of support for the Shah by the highest clerical leaders including the most preeminent Marja'a Taghlid, Ayatollah Boroujerdi (*Ettelaat*, August 25 and September 1, 1953; Nategh 1982), bazaaris' loyalty to Mosaddegh was unswerving. They closed their shops to protest against his arrest (*New York Times*, August 21 and 22, 1953) and, despite government assurances that they would not be jailed, refused to open their doors out of loyalty to the prime minister. They were eventually obliged to reopen under duress by the government (*New York Times*, August 25, 1953).

While Mosaddegh was in prison, bazaaris formed a secret committee with a capital of 40 million rials in a vain effort to secure his release (Chehabi 1990:131). During his imprisonment, bazaaris went on strike twice more on his behalf and in opposition to the Shah. On October 8, the Tehran bazaar closed down to protest against the state prosecutor's demand that Mosaddegh be executed. Some 100 people, according to the state's own estimate, were arrested during the strike and accompanying demonstration (*Ettelaat*, October 8, 1953). Four days into Mosaddegh's trial, bazaaris struck again (*Ettelaat*, November 12, 1953). On this second occasion, more than 300 people, mostly bazaaris and students, were arrested. Of these, 218 were exiled to Khark Island in the south (*Ettelaat*, November 14, 1953). The roof of the bazaar was destroyed in several places by the government, and the new prime minister threatened to

---

[5] Interviews with Lebaschi and Shanehchi. See also *Kayhan International*, October 2, 1978.

demolish the entire roof if the strikes were repeated (*Ettelaat*, November 14, 1953; Binder 1962:295).

A decade later when another round of political conflicts erupted, bazaaris had their own set of conflicts against the state. Bazaaris were adversely affected by the government's stabilization policies, reduced credit and loans to bazaaris, and tight controls imposed on certain imports (*Ettelaat*, May 20, 1963). In addition, bazaaris protested strenuously against the state's new rate of taxation for the bazaar, designed with the assistance of pro-government merchant guilds. According to shopkeepers and artisans, the burden of taxation was being transferred to poorer elements within the bazaar, while the leaders of the merchants' guilds were assessed little in taxes (*Ettelaat*, April 30, 1963). In protest, they refused to pay taxes for more than three years and complained that the state did nothing to promote commerce (*Ettelaat*, May 21, 1963). In Tehran alone, 300,000 cases of refusal to pay taxes were discovered, the majority of which involved merchants, artisans, and small shopkeepers (*Ettelaat*, May 19, 1963). As a result of these policies and the economic recession, increasing numbers of bazaaris were forced into bankruptcy (*Ettelaat*, May 7, 1961).

Because of these conditions, bazaaris opposed the government in the conflicts of the early 1960s and supported the National Front once again. Bazaaris joined the anti-government protests led by clerics in June 1963 because the repression and imprisonment of most of the National Front's leaders and activists left no alternative option for mobilization (Parsa 1994:135). As the conflict between bazaaris and the state intensified, many bazaaris participated in the anti-government uprising that erupted in June 1963. They were unorganized, however, and failed to respond in a unified fashion to the state's economic threats. Shopkeepers and artisans actively protested against the state's actions, but merchants refrained from voicing open opposition. In a sample of 579 individuals arrested or killed in the protests, shopkeepers and artisans constituted the largest group, while only one was a merchant.[6] When street demonstrations turned violent and shots were fired, the bazaaris among the protesters rapidly withdrew (Jazani 1979:144).

[6] Moaddel (1986:544). According to a sample of 579 individuals in Tehran who participated in the uprising of June 1963, 22.1 percent were workers (9 percent were industrial workers, but only 2.9 percent of these were factory workers), 12.4 percent were students, 9 percent were clergy, 3.8 percent were peasants, 2.8 percent were unemployed, 0.9 percent were housewives, and 0.2 percent were merchants. The largest group consisted of those whom Moaddel labeled the "petty bourgeoisie," which comprised 43 percent and included ice-cream sellers, vegetable sellers, shoemakers, blacksmiths, grocers, and tailors. Their apprentices comprised an additional 5.9 percent. In terms of the occupational structure of the population of Tehran, virtually all groups except these were underrepresented.

Empirical data concerning bazaaris' politics and collective actions in the 1970s do not indicate that a large-scale ideological conversion occurred in favor of an Islamic theocracy. For example, let us consider the response of bazaaris to the revolt and massacre of clerical students in Qm in June 1975, when the students commemorated the uprising of 1963. Bazaaris did not participate in these protests, which culminated in a massacre of protesters, despite the fact that Ayatollah Khomeini, then in exile in Iraq, swiftly endorsed the clerical students' actions. The clerical students' protest on June 5 seems to have passed completely unnoticed by most of the population, including bazaaris. Bazaaris, who have often been assumed to be traditional followers of religious leaders, did not initiate a single shutdown, protest, or mourning ceremony anywhere in the country.

The explanation for the bazaaris' quiescence lies in the fact that the context of the clerical students' protests was not conducive to bazaari mobilization. In June 1975, the economy was still functioning, and the state's policies did not yet threaten bazaaris as a whole. True, the state's development strategies had generated competitive pressures that affected some segments of the bazaar: the rise of department stores, for example, produced unequal competition and posed a threat to some shopkeepers. On the other hand, the oil boom of the early 1970s had created a unique occasion for bazaaris to expand their assets, and many did so.[7] Some bazaaris even transferred a portion of their capital into the burgeoning construction sector and reaped additional profits. Most significantly, until the time of the clerical students' uprising, there had not been any major conflicts between the state and most bazaaris for more than a decade.

Bazaaris and revolutionary struggles

To understand bazaaris' eventual opposition to the state two years later, we must examine the changes that occurred after June 1975, which generated conflict and mobilization. Conditions began changing for bazaaris toward the end of 1975. After 1975, segments of the bazaar faced economic pressures and difficulties. In particular, the small artisans and shopkeepers in the carpet sector, which was the single most important industry after oil, were adversely affected by rising costs due to inflation and the higher prices they had to pay for imported wool to replace declining domestic supplies. The prohibition of child labor, historically the main producer of Persian rugs, also added to the cost of production.

[7] In personal communications with the author, several bazaaris from Tehran and Tabriz affirmed that during the initial stages of the oil boom, the economic condition of merchants and shopkeepers in most sectors began to improve.

In combination, these factors made Persian rugs less competitive on the world market. At the same time, the increased importation of machine-made carpets reduced the sale of rugs within the country. The result was that some bazaaris in the rug business were forced to move to other sectors. In just one example, in 1976 there were eighty shops selling Persian rugs in Ahvaz, capital of the oil-rich province of Khuzestan. During the last nine months of 1977, thirty-six of these shops closed down (*Kayhan*, December 24, 1977).

Bazaaris were also negatively affected by the government's fiscal policies. As lower oil revenues reduced the state's resources, the government imposed higher taxes on bazaaris while cutting back on bank loans to shopkeepers (*Ettelaat*, August 23 and 29, 1977). In addition, the state established minimum wage levels for workers in the bazaar and insisted that bazaaris contribute to the Social Insurance Fund.

Of all the state's policies affecting shopkeepers, the most damaging were price controls and the anti-profiteering campaign initiated in August 1975. The state fixed the profit rate at 14 percent even though inflation, according to the regime's own reports, was at least twice that figure. Prices were controlled at the retail market level where merchants and shopkeepers operated, but no serious controls were imposed on the factories that produced and priced commodities; nor were restrictions placed on the small number of large importers. Throughout this unevenly enforced campaign, very few big industrialists were arrested for violating price restrictions.

For bazaaris, the impact of price controls was staggering. In the first few days of the campaign, 7,750 shopkeepers were arrested (*Kayhan International*, August 8, 1975). By October 1977, approximately 109,800 Tehran shopkeepers, out of a total of 200,000, had been investigated for price control violations (*Ettelaat*, October 27, 1977). In the month of April 1977 alone, the state imposed 600 million rials in fines for profiteering, mostly against bazaar shopkeepers (Bashiriyeh 1984:103). According to the Ministry of the Interior, 20,000 shopkeepers had been jailed by the end of 1977. Another source stated that by 1978, an estimated 23,000 bazaaris from large cities were deported to remote areas for periods of from three months to five years (*Kayhan International*, August 8, 1975). By the fall of 1978, the nationwide total of shopkeepers in violation of the controls was 220,000 (*Ettelaat*, September 26, 1978).

In short, beginning in August 1975, the situation for bazaaris was radically altered by the state's policies. The ensuing years of widespread arrests and sanctions created conditions for an unprecedented conflict between the bazaar and the state. Never before had so many bazaaris experienced so many fines and arrests. By the end of the summer of 1977,

Tehran's bazaar merchants had met at least twice with officials of the Rastakhiz Party, the country's only political party, to express their dissatisfaction with the Chamber of Guilds, with the state's credit policy, and the new taxation plan (*Ettelaat*, August 23 and 29, 1977). The regime remained unresponsive and altered none of its policies. By refusing to meet at least some of the bazaaris' demands, the state eliminated the option of compromise and opened the door to conflict and confrontation.

To act collectively, however, bazaaris needed solidarity structures, which had been undermined by repression and economic differentiation. Political repression and economic development depoliticized many bazaaris. After years of repression and economic prosperity, the vast majority of shopkeepers throughout the country had become nonpolitical and withdrawn from political activities, especially during the oil boom. Hundreds of the more successful merchants whose operations grew too large left the bazaars and established businesses elsewhere. When well-known bazaari activists began to mobilize and distribute leaflets opposing the government, many bazaaris initially distrusted them, believing them to be SAVAK agents because they dared act so openly against the regime without apparent fear of reprisal (Lebaschi 1983, tape 3:19).

Furthermore, economic stratification and organizational weaknesses within the bazaars generated conflicts and reduced solidarity. Among the wealthier merchants who stayed in the bazaar, a minority still supported the Shah. This was true even among rug dealers, the most traditional sector of the bazaar.[8] The Merchants' Guild had been reduced to a mere formal organization after the *coup d'état* of 1953 and never regained its independence. Most of the leaders of the new guilds backed the government. Thus, in contrast to the 1950s, when most bazaaris were united behind Mosaddegh, bazaaris in the 1970s were not politically unified. As a prominent bazaari stated, disagreements verging on hostility existed throughout the bazaars between wealthy bazaaris and those who were less well off, as well as between bazaar employers and employees (Shanehchi 1983, tape 3:18).

Depoliticization and divisions among those bazaaris who opposed the regime were partially overcome for a time by the state's anti-profiteering campaign and price control policy, which politicized bazaaris and impelled them to mobilize. Struggle against the government, rather than ideological disagreements, assumed priority for bazaaris.

The principal activists in the bazaars were supporters of Prime Minister Mosaddegh and the liberal National Front. These activists illegally rees-

[8] In a statement issued during the summer of 1978, rug dealers in the Tehran bazaar condemned this minority, whom they labeled sellouts; see Organization of Iranian Moslem Students (1978:62).

tablished the Society of Merchants, Guilds, and Artisans of the Tehran Bazaar (SMGATB) in October 1977. The SMGATB played an important role in organizing bazaar shutdowns and strikes throughout the revolutionary struggles. The SMGATB had the support of Azerbijanis, who constituted the single largest group in the Tehran bazaar.[9] SMGATB's central committee was heavily staffed by Azerbijanis, who had been supporters of Prime Minister Mosaddegh. The leaders of the SMGATB enjoyed the respect of the bazaaris and had some recognition because of their long involvement in politics and repeated imprisonment. The SMGATB leaders also had important political skills honed during their decades of political activism.

Activists of the SMGATB were always in the forefront of the political struggles and helped others to expand their struggles. They were very resourceful, owned their own printing machines, encouraged religious bazaaris to issue public statements and printed their leaflets (Lebaschi 1983, tape 3:5, 15). They even distributed Khomeini's statements and tapes through their trading networks, and leaders of the SMGATB were responsible for providing space for special prayers at the end of the fasting month of Ramadan on September 4, 1978. These activities also expressed support for other anti-government groups. When workers' strikes erupted, they collected money for their support. When Khomeini was expelled from Iraq and went to France, leaders of the SMGATB brought a hundred baskets of flowers to the French embassy to appeal for Khomeini's freedom to carry out political activities. When Ayatollah Taleghani, a liberal cleric and an ally of Mosaddegh, was released from prison in November 1978, SMGATB leaders called for a march to his residence. In response, the bazaar closed down and more than 250,000 people participated in the march. Most importantly, when Khomeini met with leading members of the SMGATB in France in the fall of 1978, he asked them to resist pressures to reopen the bazaar, thereby tacitly acknowledging the importance of these activists in the bazaar (Lebaschi 1983, tape 3:15).

Because of their political activities, leaders and activists of the SMGATB were targeted for government repression. Lebaschi was arrested in the summer of 1977 for possessing political leaflets (Lebaschi 1983, tape 2:14–16), long before any clerics had initiated any mobilization against the government. Manian's house was bombed in the spring of 1978 (*Zamimeh* 1978, no. 14:33). On June 5, 1978, on the anniversary of the June 1963 uprising, when bazaaris closed their shops, it was the

---

[9] For example, after the massacre at Qm, Azerbijanis in the Tehran bazaar issued a public statement supporting the SMGATB's mobilization and shutdowns (*The Freedom Movement* [Abroad] 1978, 1:136–137).

supporters of the SMGATB who were arrested by the government (*Zamimeh* 1978, no. 16:54). Manian was arrested in September 1978, while Lebaschi managed to avoid arrest by going into hiding as soldiers searched his house to arrest him (Lebaschi, personal interview, February 1977).

A great deal of evidence indicates that these activists supported Ayatollah Khomeini not because of ideological reasons, but rather out of political considerations. In fact, these bazaaris knew little about Khomeini's ideology. When Lebaschi and Manian met with Khomeini in Paris, they were favorably impressed with his ideas on political matters. Lebaschi, in particular, has stated that in his two meetings with Khomeini in Paris, he did not receive the impression that the Ayatollah had any political aspirations to rule Iran (Lebaschi 1983, tape 3:15). Other bazaaris who knew Khomeini prior to his exile were impressed that he, unlike other religious leaders, was modest and sought neither rank, honor, power, nor influence (Shanehchi 1983, tape 3:12).

Furthermore, the timing of bazaaris' collective actions coincided not with exhortations by Khomeini or other religious leaders, but with the rise of favorable opportunities. The leading actors in the bazaar were activists who had long supported Mosaddegh and the National Front, such as Lebaschi and Manian. When the SMGATB was reestablished in October 1977, the clergy had not yet become involved in the conflicts. Even Khomeini commented at the end of December 1977 on the slow pace of clerical mobilization and encouraged clergy to take advantage of the opportunity to oppose the government as others had done (Khomeini 1983, vol. I:265).

Bazaaris' mobilization initially was not channeled through the mosque. Instead, bazaaris mobilized alongside modern, secular groups who also opposed the government from early on. In March 1977, for example, bazaaris joined students to establish funds to pay striking university professors whose salaries were suspended by the government (Nategh 1982). Later that year, in the fall, when students called for a day of mourning to protest about the death of a student killed in an anti-government demonstration following Soltanpour's poetry night, Tehran bazaaris responded by completely shutting down the bazaar (*Zamimeh* 1978, no. 8:12–13). But bazaaris and others soon found it difficult to mobilize because of state repression. For example, when bazaaris and leaders of the National Front gathered in an orchard in Karvansara Sangi in mid-November 1978 to celebrate Aid-e Ghorban, a religious holiday, SAVAK, aware that the assembly was in reality a political gathering, dispatched 750 agents to break it up, which resulted in a large number of injuries (*Zamimeh* 1978, no. 8:9–11). To insulate themselves from repression bazaaris needed a space, and mosques were the only safe spaces.

Bazaaris played an important role in affecting the politics of the clergy. Although in the early conflicts the clergy could not agree on whether or how to respond to political developments, bazaaris displayed little hesitation in mobilizing against the government. For example, when bazaaris were planning to strike after the massacre of students in Qm, Tehran's highest religious leader and one of most prominent ayatollahs in the country, Ayatollah Khonsari, advised bazaaris not to strike. Nevertheless, the SMGATB called for a strike. Soon, bazaaris from Azerbijan, Shiraz, and Isfahan who had businesses in the Tehran bazaar followed the SMGATB and called for a strike to protest against the deaths of Qm clerical student demonstrators in January 1978. Thus bazaaris defied the highest religious leader in Tehran and closed down their shops for the day. When the strike was concluded, Khonsari had to protect himself with police bodyguards whenever he attended prayer (*The Freedom Movement* [Abroad]1978, 1:139).

In the religious city of Qm, in January 1978, bazaaris independently closed down their shops on the second day of student protests against an anti-Khomeini article in a national newspaper, even though up to that point there had been no deaths or arrests. After bazaaris went on strike, the country's religious leaders met but could not agree on a course of action. One preeminent cleric argued that the bazaar should reopen, but angry bazaaris countered that they were willing to pay the fine of 150 tomans for each day they remained closed (*The Freedom Movement* [Abroad] 1978, 1:54). They stayed closed for four days while the preeminent Qm ayatollahs refused to endorse their strike. On the second day of the strike, after arrests and deaths had occurred, several bazaar leaders who had assisted families of the victims were also arrested and exiled to different parts of the country (*Kayhan*, October 26, 1978).

In the months that followed, bazaaris were the most important social group participating in the cycles of mourning ceremonies. To mark the fortieth day following the Qm massacre, shopkeepers in more than thirty cities shut down and joined in mourning ceremonies. Forty days later, another mourning ceremony was held to honor the martyrs of Tabriz. The anniversary of the uprising of June 5, 1963, was also widely observed; in Tehran, 70 percent of all shops closed, according to opposition sources. Most bazaaris in other large and medium-sized cities also shut down in memory of the event (*Zamimeh* 1978, No. 16:52). Bazaaris also financed mosque activities and, as a result, some shopkeepers who actively promoted mourning ceremonies and other mosque gatherings were arrested.

In response to these mourning cycles, the government softened repression in 1978. In late August, Sharif-Emami was appointed as the new prime minister and introduced a number of reforms. He embarked upon a strategy to appease shopkeepers and merchants by dismissing fifteen regional heads of the Chamber of Guilds and arresting some of them. Charges were also filed against the chamber's deputy who promptly went underground (*Ettelaat*, September 20 and 21, 1978). In an attempt to mitigate conflicts with bazaaris, the new prime minister announced that charges would be dropped against thousands of shopkeepers who were under court investigation, provided they pledged to honor price controls. This position proved unacceptable to bazaaris, however, because a major reason for their conflicts was precisely the imposition of price controls. Furthermore, bazaaris, along with other political leaders, interpreted the reforms as signs of vulnerability.

Thus, they expanded their mobilization and collective action in the fall of 1978. When Khomeini was expelled to France from Iraq for inciting opposition to the Shah, shopkeepers in more than a hundred cities went on strike on October 1, in a protest of an unprecedented scale. No comparable action had occurred when Khomeini had been initially exiled from his homeland fourteen years earlier. Tehran bazaaris threatened to boycott French goods if France did not lift the restrictions placed on his political activities. At this stage of the conflicts, bazaaris collected large sums of money for Khomeini's cause. They also supported the struggles of other social groups. For example, on October 10, when journalists at the three national newspapers walked off the job to protest against government censorship, bazaaris sent them flowers and publicly supported their strike. Manian, head of the SMGATB, telephoned representatives of the press and promised assistance (*Ettelaat*, October 15, 1978). Bazaaris also continued to support students and faculty in their struggle for autonomy and democracy within the universities. In early November, bazaaris closed down and joined a large demonstration at Tehran University to support students and faculty who had called for a week of solidarity against the government (*Kayhan*, November 5, 1978).

Bazaaris played an important role in the struggles against the imposition of the military government in November 1978. As the military broke some of the strikes and succeeded in sending some strikers back to work, bazaaris themselves struck. Their strikes disrupted production and distribution in much of the country and strongly contributed to the existing crisis.

In the final months of the struggles, bazaaris became a target of attack. When the government imposed martial law in twelve major cities, the repressive measures generated a hitherto unprecedented anarchic situation. Hooligans hired by SAVAK attacked, looted, and burned stores and shops where mobilization was occurring. By the first week of November 1978, shops in more than forty cities had been attacked by hooligans.

In combination, the imposition of the military government and hooligan attacks resulted in large-scale collective action by bazaaris throughout the country. While some responded by evacuating their goods to safe locations, most bazaaris closed down and demonstrated to demand that hooligans and their organizers be punished. Shopkeepers and merchants in many cities shut down the bazaars for long periods of time because of hooligan violence. Once a military administration was imposed, bazaar closings intensified. The bazaar in Yazd went on strike for three weeks; at the end of the second week, city residents began to raise funds for the shopkeepers' support (*Akhbar* 1978, no. 1 and no. 3). The Isfahan bazaar closed down for more than seventy-five days, while the central bazaar in Shiraz was closed for over two months. Bazaars in Znjan, Arak, and Qm shut down for more than forty- five days. Merchants in the central bazaar in Kashan went on strike shortly after the military came to power on November 6; on January 13, they announced that they would not reopen their shops until the final victory (*Kayhan*, January 13, 1979). The central bazaars in Ghazvin and Kazroun were closed for more than fifty days each, while the Abadan bazaar was closed for weeks in December and January (*Ayandegan*, January 7, 1979). In Tabriz, the central bazaar closed two weeks before the military administration took over and remained on strike for more than four months. Shops throughout Khomein, birthplace of Ayatollah Khomeini, also were closed for more than four months. In that city, a committee supervised by the clergy distributed basic goods (*Kayhan*, January 17, 1979). The central bazaar in Tehran also struck for more than four months, finally reopening on February 17, six days after the collapse of the regime.

Throughout their mobilization during this period, bazaaris' protests were primarily political in nature and directed against the state, although they also spoke out against various elements of the government's economic policies. Table 9 summarizes the contents of the fifteen protest statements issued by bazaaris from January to December 1978. All fifteen statements protested about government repression, evidencing a high degree of consensus among bazaaris against this negative feature of the government. The next most frequently mentioned topic was the despotic nature of the state, which was condemned by 53 percent of the bazaaris' protest statements. An equal number of statements condemned imperialist influence and the government's dependence on foreign powers.

Table 9   *Protest statements by bazaaris, September 21, 1977 to September 21, 1978*

Demand/protest	Frequency	Percentage
Political violence and repression	15	100
Despotism and its removal	8	53
Imperialism and independence	7	47
Corruption/government pillage	4	27
Imperialist pillage	3	20
Poverty/inequality	3	20
Civil liberties	2	13
Taxes	2	13
Repression/fines against bazaaris	2	13
Inflation	1	7
Health/housing	1	7
Formation of an Islamic government	1	7

N =5.
Source: author's compilation.

These issues were very similar to the ones bazaaris had protested about in the 1960s and earlier still in the 1950s. In the 1950s, bazaaris fought against the same problems under Mosaddegh's nationalist banner, including the Shah's dictatorial tendencies and British control of Iranian oil. Thus, the main focus of bazaaris' protests had changed little over the course of two-and-a-half decades. A few of the statements made by bazaaris in 1978 even referred back to the removal of Prime Minister Mosaddegh and the Shah's subsequent "usurpation" of power. Other issues mentioned in these statements included corruption, governmental and international "pillaging" of national resources, and growing poverty and inequality.

From the outset, bazaaris' statements were political and unanimously opposed to repression. In addition, an ideological shift by bazaaris did occur in favor of supporting an alternative government and was significant in the overthrow of the regime. That such a shift occurred is evident from subsequent statements, some of which were issued during the forty-day mourning cycles, while most were not released until months later. The ideological shift toward supporting an "Islamic movement" was not unanimous among all segments of the bazaar, however. Although three statements specifically supported the Islamic movement and two backed the clerical community and its struggles, only one statement, by Isfahan bazaaris, explicitly called for the establishment of an Islamic government. Two statements issued late in the year acknowledged

Khomeini as the leader of the opposition movement, which was consist-ent with the fact that during the forty-day mourning cycles Khomeini was increasingly emerging as a widely respected leader.

Yet, although bazaaris supported Khomeini and acknowledged his leadership in the struggle against the state, nowhere in their statements was any mention made of the Islamicization of laws or clerical supervision of the government, nor did their statements manifest any interest in establishing a theocratic Islamic state in Iran. Instead, bazaaris' backing for Khomeini was derived from his indomitable stance against "despot-ism." They supported his political opposition to the monarch. A well-known bazaari activist who was a devout Muslim and had raised a great deal of money for Khomeini stated that "had bazaaris known about Khomeini's ideas on theocracy, they would have never supported him" (Shanehchi, personal communication, April 1998).

An analysis of the post-revolutionary conflicts also bears out the point that bazaaris' support for Islamic leaders was based, not on ideological conversion, but on a political coalition. As a prominent pro-Khomeini bazaari and an important government official stated, after the revolution bazaars were not under the control of the "Hezb-ollah" (*Kayhan*, April 14, 1983). In fact, as late as January 1981, Khameneh-i, the successor of Khomeini, met with Lebaschi, one of the leaders of the SMGATB, and invited him to cooperate (Lebaschi 1983, tape 3:18). But most bazaaris, despite internal political divisions, opposed the fundamentalist clergy and favored the rule of organizations other than religious ones. Although Khomeini ordered the formation of a treasury to help needy bazaaris (*Ettelaat*, March 29, 1979), bazaaris' opposition to the new rulers did not cease.

The most striking example of this rejection of the fundamentalists occurred in Isfahan, where bazaaris supported their liberal politician, and caused Ayatollah Taheri to depart from the city. These were the very same bazaaris who, during the revolutionary conflicts, had called for the formation of an Islamic government and, in fact, had even closed down to protest against Taheri's arrest by the Shah's government. Thus, al-though in the final stage of their struggle against the monarchy, broad segments of the bazaar shifted to favor the formation of an Islamic government, their post-revolutionary conflicts with the ruling clerics reveal that many of them opposed the establishment of a theocratic state as promoted by Khomeini. Moreover, bazaaris' actions were incompat-ible with the clerical faction of the Islamic government, further support-ing the analysis that the need to form coalitions, rather than ideological conversion, was the force behind their earlier support for the fundament-alist clergy.

As a result of political and ideological conflicts, many bazaaris suffered harsh repression by the Islamic government on an unprecedented scale. Prominent bazaari activists, such as Lebaschi and Shanehchi, were forced to flee the country during the period of intense repression in 1981. Mahmoud Manyan withdrew from politics and public life, but was killed in a traffic "accident" in front of his house. In the wake of the conflicts that emerged under the new regime, more than a hundred bazaaris were killed or executed (Parsa 1989:282).

To summarize, bazaaris participated overwhelmingly in support of the nationalists in the conflicts of the early 1950s and again in the early 1960s. Although segments of the bazaar were economically squeezed during the early 1970s, many bazaaris took advantage of favorable economic conditions during the oil boom of 1973. The bazaar still controlled more than two-thirds of the domestic trade and more than one-third of the foreign trade and was in an advantageous position to benefit from the economic upswing. Accordingly, bazaaris throughout the country did not respond to Khomeini's call to support rebellious clerical students in Qm in June 1975, despite numerous arrests, injuries, and even deaths. Not until the government inaugurated its anti-profiteering campaign a few months later did bazaaris' political stance begin to change.

Bazaaris' mobilization and collective actions from 1977 to 1979 were in response to the state's infringement of their established rights and interests. State policies promoting capital accumulation passed over the bazaar and instead systematically benefited modern industrial and commercial sectors, thus generating a basis for conflict. In August 1975, the state actively intervened in the market mechanism by instituting price controls and an anti-profiteering campaign in an attempt to control inflation. The following year, a decline in oil revenues prompted the state to raise bazaar taxes. In the midst of the prevailing economic adversity brought on by these policies, bazaaris' capacity for mobilization was weakened by the lack of any autonomous organization, by their internal political divisions, and by the depoliticization of most bazaaris during the years of repression. Although bazaaris had been given an impetus to mobilize by the government's anti-profiteering campaign of 1975, their own organizational weaknesses forced them to wait for favorable opportunities to mobilize and act collectively. In 1977 that opportunity came with the state's adoption of a policy of limited liberalization. Bazaaris increasingly located their mobilizing activities within mosques, which were relatively safe locations for gathering, communicating, broadcasting the government's repression, and organizing the opposition nationally through the mosque network.

Political coalition, rather than ideological conversion, explains the participation of capitalists in Iran. In the 1970s bazaaris did not follow a single ideology, but as the conflicts unfolded and mosques proved the only effective option for mobilization, broad segments of the bazaar came to support the anti-Shah movement. Without doubt, the bazaar underwent a significant shift away from the existing government and toward an alternative regime that excluded the Pahlavis. Bazaaris publicly acknowledged their support for Ayatollah Khomeini in the early fall of 1978 when the government's reforms reduced repression and popular mobilization heightened the state's vulnerability. Although bazaaris' statements indicated support for the formation of an Islamic movement, they made no mention of a theocratic state. The fact that bazaaris shared Khomeini's anti-dictatorial and anti-imperialist orientation cannot be interpreted as connoting an ideological conversion in favor of Khomeini because bazaaris had used the same slogans when they rallied in the nationalist movement during the 1950s and 1960s. Finally, the upsurge of post-revolutionary conflicts between sizable fractions of the bazaar and fundamentalist clerics attests to ideological incompatibility. The unprecedented post-revolutionary repression levied against segments of the bazaar contradicts any suggestion that bazaaris' earlier shift was in support of establishing a theocratic state.

Capitalists and the state in Nicaragua

Historically, the Nicaraguan capitalist class was economically weak, regionally and politically divided, and often unable to unite to pursue a coherent political agenda (Wickham-Crowley 1991:219–220). Although the economic development of the 1950s and 1960s generated a new class of agro-industrialists with considerable economic resources (Paige 1997:90–95), many of these capitalists were highly dependent on the state, and consequently avoided political confrontation with the government. The capitalist class found the Somozas to be attractive allies because of increased state intervention, US economic assistance to the Somoza regime, and the creation of the Central American Common Market. In fact, the lure of such vast economic and political resources, coupled with the regulative powers and labor policies of the Somoza regime, coopted some segments of the economic elite. Thus, the largest Nicaraguan capitalists bargained and competed with each other to gain concessions and favors from the state (Spalding 1994:43). Although this capitalist class, in contrast to Iranian bazaaris, were permitted and even encouraged by the Somozas to mobilize and form associations, their organizations were often in competition with each other and successfully manipulated by the state, which made them politically ineffective (ibid.:33, 43–47).

The financial conglomerates, BANIC and BANAMERICA, did not join with the excluded segment of the capitalist class because they were dependent on the state, and, as a result, they failed to play a leading role in the revolutionary conflicts. These two giants among Nicaraguan capitalists were not included in COSIP, an umbrella organization representing medium-sized businesses (Gilbert 1985:165; 1990:107), although some of their representatives were active among the opposition (Paige 1997:39, 381). The politics of big capital in the important cotton and coffee sectors was also conservative. A majority of the coffee elite and many large cotton growers stayed with the Somoza regime to the end and, consequently, had their properties confiscated after the revolution (Paige 1997:33, 39), although many had already sent hundreds of millions of dollars abroad (Vilas 1986:136–137).

During intense popular mobilizations after the assassination of Chamorro in 1978, capitalists in the financial sector did join some of the shutdowns against Somoza, but they did not take the lead and participated only when the strikes were already underway. The moderate opposition lacked confidence that big business would join the struggles in the summer of 1978, during the crucial period when moderates were organizing a nationwide strike to remove Somoza from power. In August Los Doce expressed doubt over the politics of "big capital." Even FAO issued a statement condemning any deal that might be struck between "big capital" and Somoza behind the backs of the people (*La Prensa*, August 3, 1978), although the President of BANIC[10] had publicly and unexpectedly criticized Somoza's government in April (*La Prensa*, April, 28, 1978).

Because of its favored relationship with the state, big capital in Nicaragua was often targeted for attack by other segments of the capitalist class. For example, small cattle producers charged that the Association of Cattle Ranchers of Nicaragua and INFONAC together constituted a monopoly that bought their meat at exaggeratedly reduced prices below the international benchmark, thereby reaping fabulous profits (*La Prensa*, March 22, 1973). Small coffee producers complained of exploitation by intermediaries who refused to pay a fair price for their coffee (*La Prensa*, March 16, 1973). Small businesses also complained that large businesses were responsible for price inflation.

[10] Somoza Debayle charged that Dr. Eduardo Montealegre, president of BANIC, made sizable cash contributions to the FSLN. Montealegre reputedly told Somoza, "We can control them" (Somoza 1980:262).

Small and medium-sized capitalists, excluded from state resources, were especially affected after the Managua earthquake and increasingly opposed the Somoza regime. The earthquake's profound effects were exacerbated by the state's policies, which often had the effect of restricting, rather than assisting, the financial recovery of many segments of the business community. Approximately 90 percent of entrepreneurs suffered at least some earthquake damage, while the greatest losses were sustained by small businesses, which constituted the vast majority of the private sector. This segment, which possessed inadequate resources, received no state aid and was forced to compete against Somoza's cronies, who were readily supplied with government assistance.

The Somoza regime repeatedly violated the competitive bidding process in Managua's post-earthquake construction boom by awarding contracts to companies with ties to the government and, in the process, expanding corruption and cronyism. As mentioned in chapter 3, between March and December 1973, *La Prensa* reported at least twenty-five major cases of government corruption. These incidents included government contracts awarded to businesses owned by high-ranking officials without public bidding or through other questionable procedures. Furthermore, the government imposed a very mild price on items of basic consumption and largely did not enforce price controls that adversely affected small businesses. Small businesspeople protested that price controls were unevenly applied. They claimed that the state should target big merchants and large businesses for price controls, instead of imposing sanctions on small businesses, which only pass on the prices set by the former (*La Prensa*, July 13, 1973).

Even more detrimental to the business community were other state tax policies, export/import regulations, and, to a lesser extent, pricing. Small producers were particularly affected by the government's taxation policies. Cattle producers complained that they, not the exporting firms, ended up paying the government's 10 percent export tax on meat (*La Prensa*, March 22, 1973). In a similar vein, 7,000 small coffee producers protested against the 10 percent surtax and exploitation by middlemen, as well as the fact that the National Institute of Foreign and Domestic Commerce (or INCEI), which was supposed to regulate coffee prices, failed to act on their behalf (*La Prensa*, May 14 and August 6 and 24, 1973). Milk producers, too, expressed dissatisfaction over the new surcharge imposed by the government (*La Prensa*, April 4, 1973).

Business interests were also negatively affected by the state's export/import regulations, which were designed to obtain foreign exchange through exports. For example, despite appeals to the state by the Chamber of Construction and other industrial sectors to halt raw lumber exports in order to assure adequate supplies for domestic rebuilding, the government granted concessions to foreign corporations to export lumber (*La Prensa*, January 7, 1974). Similarly, large quantities of hides were exported by associates of the regime, causing shortages in the domestic market and forcing a number of shoe factories to shut down. The Chamber of Industry charged that the government raised taxes on shoe factories in 1974 from 5 percent to 16 percent (*La Prensa*, November 29, 1974). Domestic shoe factories were placed at a competitive disadvantage compared with cheaper imports because taxes on imported shoes remained stable (*La Prensa*, November 21, 1974). Three large shoe factories in Managua decided to close their operations at the end of 1974 (*La Prensa*, December 11, 1974). In Masaya, 90 of the city's 160 shoe manufacturers closed in 1973 (*La Prensa*, August 28, 1973).

As a result of these conditions, Nicaraguan capitalists issued a number of statements expressing their grievances, but did not make any major political demands. In all their statements, capitalists primarily challenged the government's economic policies, but failed to call for any democratization of the government. Associations, mostly representing producers of the country's main export crops of cotton, coffee, and cattle, issued twelve public statements. Their principal concerns involved the government's economic policies (seven statements), and the fact that the government served narrow interests (four statements). Other concerns involved government corruption, tax increases, government regulations, and rising inflation. In addition, various business chambers released nine statements protesting about government corruption, utility rate hikes, increased taxes, the government's economic policies, regulation, and inflation. Unlike the producers' statements, which specifically mentioned exclusion from favorable resources, the chambers' statements made no such complaint.

The lack of any serious challenge from the capitalists was evident in the first Grand Convention of Private Enterprise held in March 1974. Nearly two thousand representatives from all the country's provinces attended the convention, organized by COSIP, to discuss the private sector's concerns. Among those present were former ministers and vice-ministers in the Somoza regime (*La Prensa*, March 3, 1974). Somoza also attended the meeting briefly, but reacted by calling the participants "school children" (Everingham 1996:114). The convention produced a document detailing a number of recommendations about economic and administrative matters, but failed to address significant political issues. The document recommended that the government change some economic policies, eliminate restrictive regulations, expand the operation of market forces, and eliminate cartels and monopolies that were hindering free competition and the equitable distribution of the benefits of development. They also recommended that the system of public bidding be strengthened to guarantee the correct use of public funds and state resources. Except for demanding free speech, the document failed to address the central political problems of Nicaragua (*La Prensa*, March 2, 1974).[11]

The nature, recommendations, and demands of this statement demonstrate that private enterprise's organized segment was not yet interested in mounting a challenge to the state. The capitalists did have opportunities to join the opposition, but did not do so. In June 1974, for example, when seven major political groups and two large labor organizations announced a boycott of the upcoming presidential elections, the private sector failed to take a stand. Two individual retailers signed the boycott statement but they did so as members of political parties, not as representatives of private enterprise. Six months later, when these same nine organizations joined forces to form UDEL, a broad coalition advocating social reform, the various business chambers again remained on the sidelines. Chamorro, a UDEL founder and leading member of the opposition, complained that businessmen were only interested in economic issues (Everingham 1996:119). The majority of COSIP members were silent between 1974 and Chamorro's death in 1978 (ibid.:140).

Assassination of Chamorro and capitalist mobilization

Economic and political conditions changed in 1977 and 1978 and drastically altered capitalist attitudes toward Somoza. The country's economic conditions began to deteriorate, and sales declined to alarming levels. One report in 1977 characterized the economic situation of Managua's shopping centers as "desperate." According to the Chamber of Commerce, a number of businesses had already closed down, and others were on the point of shutting their doors if the situation continued. Although the economic decline affected mainly small businesses, some large companies such as Fabritex and Tienda Vanity were also forced to cut back their operations (*La Prensa*, August 11, 1977).

In the political arena, removing martial law in the early fall of 1977 provided an opportunity for capitalists to mobilize. Antagonism between COSIP and the state, fueled by the government's economic policies and

---

[11] Other recommendations included the following: eliminate restrictive regulations on financing, prices, sales, and exports in the cattle-producing industries; eliminate the current system of licensing; guarantee the correct and efficient use of state resources; initiate state intervention in private enterprise only when absolutely necessary for the common good; and establish mechanisms for private sector participation in decisions regarding national reconstruction.

the surtax, became increasingly open by the end of 1977. In a meeting between representatives of the Chamber of Industries and the General Director of Revenue, the businessmen were cursed by the director. COSIP responded by protesting this "violent and shameful" incident in a telegram to Somoza (*La Prensa*, December 16, 1977).

Although capitalists were becoming increasingly politicized and determined to bring about some changes, they did not join in the political coalition that comprised the UDEL, the moderate political organization. Instead, capitalists limited their actions to issuing a number of statements in the last few months of 1977.[12] Of sixteen statements issued by various chambers, ten supported the national dialogue called for by the Catholic Church, four protested surtaxes, and two denounced government repression. Business groups and producers' associations also issued six protest statements aimed at the introduction of certain social reforms. Two of the statements attacked government cronyism and the narrow interests it served, and two supported a national dialogue. Other issues noted in the statements were the surtaxes, government corruption and repression, and the reorganization of the National Guard. Although none of these statements called for the removal of Somoza, certain segments of the capitalist class had begun demanding some social reforms.

The assassination of Chamorro proved to be the catalyst that mobilized the business sector for insurgency. After this event, for the first time in Nicaraguan history, various private sector organizations participated in a number of business shutdowns, including three nationwide general strikes. Businesses shut down in ten cities and towns on separate occasions, primarily to protest about specific local incidents of repression. More importantly, by the time of the third strike, most of the capitalist class in Nicaragua had broken away from the regime and used their ultimate disruptive powers to oppose Somoza. Businesses and their organizations issued seventy-seven political statements during 1978. In contrast to the protests of the early 1970s, capitalists were now fully politicized and their demands were primarily noneconomic. In fact, the largest number of demands, twenty-seven, now called for Somoza's resignation and the formation of a democratic government; twenty-two of the statements condemned government repression and fourteen protested against higher taxes.

The first general strike began on January 23 to protest about Chamorro's murder. Although businesses in sixteen cities closed down in support of the strike, it is important to note the reluctance of the

---

[12] With one exception, private entrepreneurs did not engage in any business shutdowns. The sole exception was initiated by thirty traders in the town of Matigüas who demonstrated against municipal tax fraud (*La Prensa*, October 14, 1977).

Nicaraguan capitalists to initiate insurgency. They did not initiate their strikes until ten days after the largest labor organizations, CGT-I, CTN, and SCAAS, had declared an indefinite strike. Several days after workers initiated their strikes, a National General Strike Committee, composed of different political parties and business organizations, issued a statement calling upon workers, employees, students, and entrepreneurs to stop working in protest against Chamorro's assassination and the increasing scale of official terrorism. The strike demanded that those responsible for the assassination be brought to justice. A few days later, the committee released another statement, which, like the first, contained no mention of resignation by Somoza (*La Prensa*, January 23, 1978). On the morning of the second day of the strike, chambers and other business organizations, including the financial sector, met but did not issue any statement. That afternoon, various groups belonging to COSIP and INDE (Nicaraguan Development Institute) released a statement pledging their support to the strike. The most powerful economic entity, the financial sector, did not sign this statement, although employees of financial institutions were already on strike, and the public was staying away from banks. The financial organizations finally joined the strike that afternoon, prompting the government to threaten sanctions.[13] Ironically, one of the companies obliged to close its doors because of absenteeism by employees and clientele was Interfinanciera, owned by Somoza (*La Prensa*, January 25, 1978).

A statement in early February supporting the strike and signed by sixteen business groups, including various chambers and producers of export crops, reveals the nature of the capitalists' demands at this time. Their political demands were for an independent judiciary, an apolitical National Guard, respect for human rights, amnesty for political crimes, political pluralism and democratization, and freedom from censorship. A number of economic and social issues were raised as well, as the businessmen demanded an end to the government's unfair competition with private enterprise, more administrative honesty and punishment of infractions, improved conditions for peasants and rural dwellers, free labor unions, and a politically independent civil service (*La Prensa*, February 5, 1978). It should be noted that, although by this time a number of political organizations such as UDEL were openly calling for Somoza's resignation, the business sector did not yet go that far. Nor did private enterprise completely cut off all options for compromise. Although the Chamber of Commerce declined two invitations to meet with Somoza, saying they

[13] On January 27, the Superintendent of Banks threatened to inspect daily each banking or financial company to determine whether they were open for business during the strike and to levy fines of 100,000 córdobas per day and possibly close them down if they were not working (*La Prensa*, January 27, 1978).

were confronting problems of national breadth, they left the door open for a future meeting (*La Prensa*, January 24, 1978). In fact, three days later, the nine major organizations representing private enterprise released a statement asking Somoza to search for a constitutional solution to bring about a permanent climate of peace, freedom, and democracy (*La Prensa*, January 27, 1978).

A second round of nationwide strikes, not investigated by most scholars of the Nicaraguan revolution, was called by FAO in July to protest against rising repression against the country's youth and judicial corruption (*La Prensa*, July 12, 1978). Although not announced by the private sector, the strike was observed by businesses in twenty cities and towns across the country.

The context of the third business strike was the return of Los Doce in July. Los Doce, who had long called for Somoza's ouster, returned to Nicaragua and openly mobilized the population through their anti-government rallies in a number of cities (*La Prensa*, July 6, 1978). An additional factor was the package of new taxes, ranging from 15 to 45 percent on different items, approved by the Nicaraguan Senate in August (*La Prensa*, August 8, 1978). Private enterprise reacted swiftly to the state's decision to raise taxes by declaring a campaign of passive resistance and abstention from paying taxes. The Chamber of Commerce issued a statement suggesting alternative measures that the government could adopt to increase revenues and finance the deficit (*La Prensa*, August 4, 1978). In the context of rising popular protests and Los Doce activities, FAO announced the third nationwide strike for the last week of August. This strike demanded the immediate separation of Somoza from the presidency and from his post as head of the National Guard, and the creation of a national government (*La Prensa*, August 25, 1978). In response, businesses in fourteen cities and towns closed down.

Although capitalist mobilization and strikes reduced social support for the government and helped to isolate the regime, the role of the capitalist class diminished in the final stage of the conflicts as strikes failed to force Somoza out of office. Capitalist divisions and disagreements increased in early September when the Central Bank severed lines of credit to all businesses that closed during the third strike (Everingham 1996:152). The business sector also suffered damages due to political violence, which destroyed 616 commercial establishments and 19 factories (*La Prensa*, December 31, 1978). Unable to change the conditions, businesses responded with massive capital flight. Honduran sources reported that at the end of October, various Nicaraguan businesses were applying to move to Tegucigalpa (*La Prensa*, October 27, 1978).

In the final phase of the Nicaraguan revolution, capitalists participated in the general strikes that were called by the FSLN, in a transmission from Radio Sandino, their clandestine radio station. A survey of businesses in Managua's largest commercial center on June 3 revealed that 88 percent of them would remain closed for the strike (*La Prensa*, June 3, 1979). During the weeks that followed, the strike was observed by the vast majority of businesses. On June 6, 1979, COSEP (former COSIP, now expanded) issued a statement calling for the immediate resignation of Somoza. On June 24, eleven days after a revolutionary junta was formed in Costa Rica, COSEP issued a formal statement recognizing it as the new government of Nicaragua.

Capitalists' support for the FSLN was based on tactical coalition, rather than ideological conversion. The basic vision held by the Nicaraguan capitalists of an alternative social structure was primarily reformist and consisted of recasting certain aspects of society and government, rather than introducing broad social transformations. Specifically, they sought to reduce state intervention in the economy, expand the polity, reduce corruption, reform the National Guard and eliminate its repressive aspects, and introduce some reforms to ameliorate the conditions of the working classes. This vision was hardly compatible with that of the FSLN, and, as a result, capitalists did not shift their support to them until the final days of the revolution when it became clear that no other option existed. As one business leader remarked, "The businessmen thought of the Sandinistas as their people. They thought they could put [the Sandinistas] in the   field to take care of the guard. Then they would step in and take over when Somoza fell. If there was a problem, the United States would stop the Sandinistas from taking power" (Spalding 1994:61).

In summary, historical divisions and weaknesses of the capitalist class prevented the business sector from playing an important political role in Nicaraguan politics. Despite rising conflicts, Nicaraguan capitalists were slow to join the opposition and challenge the regime. Although broad segments of the entrepreneurial sector were adversely affected by the earthquake and certain state policies in the early 1970s, and even though they possessed some measure of organization, capitalists failed to play a significant political role immediately after the earthquake. But the assassination of Chamorro and the political and economic crisis resulted in capitalist mobilization and defection from the state. By August 1978, the capitalists ultimately broke away from Somoza and demanded his resignation. Although the third capitalist strike failed to accomplish its goal, capitalists' defection from Somoza was crucial in isolating the state and rendering it vulnerable to challenge.

The capitalist class and Marcos in the Philippines

Squeezed by Marcos from above and threatened by labor militancy and the radical left from below, Filipino capitalists, in marked contrast to Iranian and Nicaraguan entrepreneurs, did not, as a class, engage in a high level of collective action. Although the core of the Filipino capitalists opposed the Marcos regime by the early 1980s, they became increasingly concerned about deteriorating economic conditions and political instability in the aftermath of the assassination of Aquino. More importantly, the business sector made no effort to use their disruptive powers to remove Marcos from power. Faced with uncertain conditions, while some attempted to mobilize for elections and a "smooth transition," others chose alternative options such as capital flight. Between 1972 and 1986, Filipino entrepreneurs divested more than $12 billion of their assets out of the Philippines (Boyce 1993:295), an amount constituting more than 44 percent of the national debt.

As in Iran and Nicaragua, Filipino capitalists were divided economically and lacked class cohesion. After independence, economic development in the Philippines gradually differentiated the Philippine entrepreneurs, which reduced elite cohesion in the early 1970s (Hawes 1987:36, 136–142; Wurfel 1979:233). Toward the end of Marcos' rule, Philippine entrepreneurs included a group of "crony" capitalists created by and tied to the Marcos regime: large, independent capitalists who produced raw materials, agricultural goods, and manufactured products for the world market, and medium-sized and small producers operating within the local market. These capitalists were highly dependent on the state and remained loyal to Marcos (Hutchcroft 1991:436). They amassed large fortunes because of their close ties to the Marcos family, and all of them held high-level posts in Marcos' political machine. Through their government connections, these individuals engaged in highly profitable dealings, often reaping billions of pesos in profits (*Malaya*, February 15, 1985). They also owed huge debts to the government: failed crony enterprises borrowed $4 billion, or roughly 20 percent of the state's foreign debt, from the government (*Malaya*, April 23, 1985).

Relations with foreign corporations also diversified the politics of Filipino capitalists. Large Filipino capital, for example, was linked to foreign capital and thus favored transnational investment in the Philippines. Small and medium-sized businesses, in contrast, opposed transnational corporate investment, which could generate stiff competition and a loss of market for some of these producers (Broad 1988:105; Stauffer 1980: 35–39). Since most small and medium-sized producers operated within the domestic market, they favored tariff protections and subsidies. Thus, they objected to the Structural Adjustment Program and liberalization policies prescribed by the IMF and World Bank, although these programs were favored by large capital (Hawes 1987:142).

Ethnic divisions also reduced the cohesion of the capitalist class. In particular, a significant group of capitalists, those of Chinese origin, not only benefited from government policies but remained unintegrated into the Filipino entrepreneurial community.[14] Overall, the Chinese, who constituted less than 1 million of the Philippine population of 60 million, controlled perhaps one-third of the country's national wealth (*Chicago Tribune*, December 19, 1993). By 1981, nine of the ten leading Philippine banks were under Chinese control (Overholt 1986:1152). Chinese economic prosperity generated some antagonism between Chinese and Filipinos. To overcome Filipino economic nationalism, the Chinese were obliged to rely on the political system (Wurfel 1988:58). Marcos' policies made the Chinese a major economic power, thereby not only insuring ethnic tension, but also reducing the capitalist community's cohesion. Filipinos' resentment of the Chinese role in the country's economy surfaced in the early 1980s when Dewey Dee, a Chinese-Filipino textile tycoon, fled the country after his financial empire collapsed, causing a crisis. Although the government's crackdown on Chinese currency transactions led some of them to contribute money secretly to the opposition at the end of Marcos' rule (Thompson 1995:120), these capitalists did not actively join the anti-Marcos opposition (Ambassador Ordones, interview, May 1999).

Deep organizational and political differences also existed among Filipino capitalists. Unlike Iranian bazaaris who were prevented by the state from organizing, Filipino capitalists were divided into many separate constituencies. These constituencies were weak and poorly organized, riddled by diverse tendencies, rivalries, factionalism, and often unable to reach agreement on major issues (Hutchcroft 1991:426–427). Although some joined the "parliament of the streets" that followed the assassination of opposition leader, Benigno Aquino, others recommended patience and reconciliation, as did the Businessmen's Committee for Reconciliation (Diokno 1988:139–141).

During the first phase of the political conflicts, in the early 1970s, Filipino capitalists remained aloof from the anti-government protesters. Attacked and criticized by protesting students and workers, Filipino capitalists issued several statements condemning the demonstrations

---

[14] By 1975, at least 600,000 people in the Philippines were entirely or partly of Chinese descent, spoke a Chinese dialect at home and observed Chinese cultural patterns (McCarthy, 1975:348).

(*Manila Times*, February 26, 1970), and sought a more cordial relationship with the government. On January 12, 1970, just two weeks before
bloody student demonstrations demanding social reforms and greater
government intervention, the Philippine Council of the International
Chamber of Commerce directed an open letter to Marcos, in which they
reiterated their willingness to work with the government to strengthen the
recession-weakened economy, reduce income inequalities, and fortify the
middle class to head off social instability. The Council declared, "We
trust that you will see to it that, as partners, the government will not
compete with the private sector but will provide equal opportunities for
all, and that you will extend government benefits to so many instead of to
so few" (*Manila Times*, January 18, 1970). Also targeted by militant
students, the National Federation of Sugarcane Planters sent a statement
to Marcos defending their own policies as well as the honor of the
government: "We are making these facts public, Your Excellency, so that
the militant youth and all other vigilant elements of the citizenry may not
be misled and your administration be not unjustly maligned" (*Manila
Times*, January 26, 1970).

As social conflicts intensified and segments of labor and students
became more radicalized, Filipino capitalists became even more dependent on the state. As a result, when Marcos dismissed the writ of *habeas
corpus*, Filipino capitalists failed to condemn the beginning of the end of
Philippine democracy. Most Filipino capitalists actually supported the
imposition of martial law (Lande 1986:116; Overholt 1986:1142;
Thompson 1995:9).

Although martial law generated an economic boom in the early years,
state intervention soon antagonized broad segments of the capitalist class.
While Philippine state intervention was not as extensive as in Iran, it rose
dramatically during the period of martial law. Although the state did not
launch any sector-wide assault comparable to the price controls and
anti-profiteering campaign in Iran, state policies adversely affected the
interests of segments of the capitalist class. In particular, state intervention in two of the most important industries in the Philippines economy,
coconuts and sugar, expanded, with producers adversely affected by the
creation of government monopolies to control their export. These monopolies, consigned to presidential cronies, diverted accumulation from
the regional to the national level (Hawes 1987:127). State regulation of
businesses and industries increased dramatically and finally the Marcos
government initiated ambitious projects by extorting funds from business
(Tiglao 1988:41–48).

Increased state intervention also adversely affected the interests of
other segments of the capitalist class. For example, landed wealth in rice

and corn areas underwent a land reform designed by Marcos to curb the power of landlords who posed threats to his power (Hutchcroft 1991:444). Wealthy opponents of Marcos such as the Lopez family, the Cojuangcos (Aquino's in-laws), and the Jacintos lost some of their properties to Marcos' cronies. The Lopez family, in particular, were singled out because they were a threat to Marcos' continued rule. Before martial law, the Lopezes were regarded as the wealthiest family in the country, and Fernando Lopez served as Marcos' vice-president. After martial law, he was discarded along with the Congress and the old constitution, and the Lopez family's economic assets were seized by the government and given to various Marcos cronies. The family's media holdings were appropriated by Roberto Benedicto, a Marcos crony. The family's electrical generating plants, which supplied most of Manila's electricity, were secured by the First Philippine Holding Company, which represented the investment interests of the family of Imelda Romualdez Marcos (Hawes 1987:127). Eugenio Lopez, Jr., was arrested and charged with plotting to assassinate Marcos.

Still worse, state policies contributed to a sharp economic downturn, which adversely affected all segments of the capitalist class. By 1980, the Philippine economy was in dire straits. The second oil shock struck in 1979, increasing government debt, inflation, and interest rates. Bankruptcies soon proliferated, with some 21,000 officially acknowledged in 1980 (Wurfel 1988:239). The departure of Dewey Dee caused a bank run that forced the Central Bank of the Philippines to provide support to the twenty-eight banks and insurance companies that were absorbing his debts, which totaled $83 million (Steinberg 1990:129).

Major sectors of the Philippine economy, particularly sugar, were in crisis by the mid-1980s. Fourteen sugar mills built in the heady early years of Marcos' rule had gone bankrupt and closed down (ibid.:130). Ten of the fifteen new sugar mills under the control of the Philippine Sugar Corporation lost more than 695.6 million pesos in 1984 alone (*Malaya*, September 29, 1985). Producers of sugar experienced losses calculated at between 11 billion and 14 billion pesos from 1974 to 1983, brought on by the government's sugar monopoly, the National Sugar Trading Corporation (Villegas 1986b:165).[15] Coconut exports declined by 38 percent in 1986, following export values that plummeted nearly 40 percent in 1985. In addition, currency devaluation had such a negative impact on manufacturing in the Bataan Export Processing Zone that between 1981 and 1984, nine of fifty-three firms closed down operations, and the number of workers in the BEPZ dropped from 25,000 to 16,000.

---

[15] Another source estimates the producers' net loss from 1977 to 1983 to have been 2.6 billion pesos (De Dios 1988:100).

Twenty of the companies that remained were also hurt by the poor economic situation (*Malaya*, January 13 and June 6, 1984), and in other sectors as well, the decline was marked.

During 1984 and 1985, the economic skid worsened because of political conflicts, currency devaluation, and the lack of foreign exchange. In early 1984, the business community grew alarmed over a proposed presidential decree that would have forced the opening of bank accounts to Internal Revenue investigators inquiring into the bank deposits of alleged tax evaders. Businessmen feared that such a decree might cause the banking system to collapse by scaring off depositors (*Malaya*, February 3 and 6, 1984), although this threat by the government against the business sector was eventually called off. During 1985, most established businesses experienced sales slumps of 10 to 15 percent for non-durable consumer goods and as much as 70 to 90 percent for consumer durables (Villegas 1986a:137). Market interest rates climbed above 50 percent in 1985, nudging many firms to the brink of bankruptcy (ibid.).

Despite these adverse conditions, Filipino capitalists did not initiate large-scale, disruptive collective action to overthrow the regime following Aquino's assassination. From the time of the murder in August until the end of the year, business and professional groups issued only one statement and organized only two independent demonstrations out of a total of 147 such events held during the period. Although Aquino was assassinated on August 21, the business community was able to hold its first independent rally ever in the Makati business district on September 16.

But most importantly, as conflicts unfolded, Filipino capitalists failed to use their most fundamental weapon. Never did they close down to challenge the regime, as did capitalists in Iran and Nicaragua. When the opposition organization, the August Twenty-One Movement, headed by Agapito "Butz" Aquino, brother of the slain opposition leader, called for a general strike on November 28, the announcement was ignored by most people, who went to work as usual (*Malaya*, November 30, 1983). Significantly, no business shutdown took place anywhere in the country on that day.

Capitalist divisions can be seen from their political positions during the final stage of the conflicts. One organization, the Businessmen's Committee, noted in October 1983 that the country's problems resulted from a decade of one-man rule, but they did not demand the president's ouster. A few months later, they declared that the demand for Marcos' resignation was an extreme measure and should be considered "only as a last resort." They warned, however, that "The patience of the people will not last forever, and it is time for Mr. Marcos to heed our simple message:

LEAD US OR LEAVE US!" (Javate-de Dios, et al. 1988:577). Another group of capitalists organized the Association of Businessmen for Aquino, and in 1983 called for a campaign to boycott products and services from businesses owned by Marcos' cronies (*Malaya*, October 10, 1983).

The most powerful organization representing businessmen was the Makati Business Club. Formed in the early 1980s when economic conditions began deteriorating, the Makati Business Club represented the core of the Philippine capitalist class and included the top 1,000 Philippine corporations. It soon became the most articulate organization representing business interests. In 1981, when billions of pesos of funds were openly transferred from government banks to crony corporations, the business elite criticized Marcos. In August 1982, the Makati Business Club issued a statement of demands, including honesty, integrity, peace, and greater confidence in government; a curb on military abuse and government corruption; an end to red tape and cronyism; reduction of government intervention in the private sector; removal of lopsided competition by the government; and protection of the media in its crusade against injustice and the curtailment of human freedoms (De Dios 1988:103).

The assassination of Aquino and rising political protests encouraged the Makati Business Club to mobilize in September of 1983. Makati businessmen, bankers, brokers and real estate executives and members of manufacturing and insurance companies, along with professionals and students, organized a demonstration of 15,000. Their chants included, "Marcos, Marcos, resign" (*Malaya*, November 27, 1983). Although it was the largest protest in Makati's history up to that time, by Filipino standards the size of the demonstration was not impressive.

Unlike Iran, most business organizations were highly concerned about economic crisis and political instability. In contrast to both Iran and Nicaragua, business leaders tried to pressure Marcos in meetings or through letters to bring about social and political change. The Philippine Chamber of Commerce and Industry, the nation's largest and broadest business group, which was rarely critical of the government, sent a letter to Marcos declaring that the widespread fear of instability was an obstacle to renewing credit lines and made foreign banks reluctant to grant new loans. The letter urged Marcos to take steps to improve conditions; specifically they urged him to revamp the commission he had appointed to investigate Aquino's slaying (*Los Angeles Times*, September 19, 1983). Although the statement expressed grave concern for the economic problems of the country, it did not demand that the president resign.

Similarly, the Philippine Business Conference, following a three-day conference, sent a report to Marcos noting that the country was facing the most critical period in its economic history. Although the report expressed concern about political stability, it did not call for Marcos' resignation (*New York Times*, November 11, 1983). The report called for political changes, including an independent and honest judiciary, restoration of public constitutional rights, relief from pervasive militarism, and clear, legal provisions for presidential succession in order to restore domestic and international confidence in the Philippine economy (Silliman 1984:155). On the final day of the conference, an angry Marcos met with the 350 participants, accusing them of contributing to the country's economic ills by evading taxes, hoarding foreign currency, overpricing, smuggling, dealing in stolen goods, and other illegal practices. Marcos declared that only 29,000 of the 2.96 million income tax returns filed in 1982 came from the corporate sector (*New York Times*, November 11, 1983).

Another example of capitalist pressure on Marcos occurred in November 1983. Thirty-three top officials, middle-level executives, and key employees of eight local textile and garment companies met with Marcos to urge a resolution of the country's political and economic crisis through major reforms, including an end to government corruption. Incensed, Marcos ordered that smuggling and currency charges be filed against the businessmen (*Los Angeles Times*, November 15, 1983).

As economic and political conditions worsened in 1984, capitalists did not undertake any large-scale collective action. Some businessmen organized three independent demonstrations, compared with the total number of 266 demonstrations held that year.[16] On one occasion, some 300 businessmen and professionals staged a protest against Marcos by standing at a Makati street corner for one hour with no fanfare or banners. Makati residents and office employees were invited to join in the event (*Malaya*, September 14, 1984). In another demonstration, 800 professionals and businessmen led by Corazon and "Butz" Aquino held an "indignation rally" and called for Marcos' resignation (*Malaya*, November 10, 1984). Despite rising political conflicts, business entrepreneurs issued seven statements during 1984, most of which were concerned with various economic issues. Politically, business urged unity among opposition political groups and a common team for the presidency and vice-presidency in the event of an election. One statement called for a "smooth

---

[16] In one instance, 5,000 sugar plantation owners and their workers rallied in Bacolod City to protest the government's monopoly over the sugar industry. The protesters denounced the Philippine Sugar Commission and the National Sugar Trading Corporation (*Malaya*, February 8, 1984).

transition" of power after Marcos' exit (*Malaya*, December 21, 1984). None of the statements made any reference to major reforms of social and political structures.

Significantly, as class conflict intensified in the context of deteriorating economic conditions, capitalists became increasingly concerned about threats from the radical left. Large producers organized in the Employers Confederation of the Philippines, or ECOP, were especially concerned about the impact of workers' strikes. While many employers locked out workers, others hired strikebreakers to resolve labor disputes. At the same time, they attempted to enlist government assistance. For example, in September 1984, hundreds of businessmen from ECOP met with the defense minister to warn that some unions were being infiltrated by subversive elements (*Malaya*, September 20, 1984). In a conference with the labor minister several months later, ECOP members again expressed concern over labor's unrest and infiltration by communists, which threatened the free enterprise system (*Malaya*, April 1, 1985). These were important issues for the business sector because, according to a ranking constabulary intelligence officer, 53 percent of the country's labor strikes and protests were engineered by communists (*Malaya*, July 18, 1985).

Filipino capitalists in the agricultural sector were also concerned about rising insurgency and the communist New People's Army (NPA) expanding activity in the countryside, most notably on sugar plantations. A statement by sugar producers warned of possible widespread unrest following layoffs of nearly 150,000 regular and casual sugar workers in Negros Occidental (*Malaya*, May 5, 1985). Officials and managers of companies in this sugar-producing region expressed apprehension over the infiltration of the island's farms by "subversives" (*Malaya*, May 5, 1985).

Soon, better working relations emerged between the capitalists and the government. Initially, Marcos had responded angrily to political mobilization organized by the Makati businessmen, calling them "traitors" (Diokno 1988:141). He had even threatened to arrest businessmen who participated in anti-government rallies and demonstrations (*Malaya*, September 29, 1983). But two factors pressured Marcos to change his policy towards the capitalist class. First, the rising strength of the revolutionary challengers and their armed wing threatened the government and the privileged. More importantly, the United States also became increasingly concerned about the strength of revolutionaries and pressured Marcos to hold an election to gain legitimacy. Thus, by 1985, the government had turned an attentive ear to business grievances. In response to ECOP concerns, the labor minister announced that the government would vigorously pursue the fight against subversive infiltration in certain industries (*Malaya*, April 26, 1985). Some measures were adopted by the government to improve economic conditions (*Malaya*, June 30, 1984). Marcos assured businessmen and investors of the government's undiminished support to enable them to meet stiff competition from multinational business firms: "As long as I am President, I am going to protect the legitimate local investors and factory owners" (*Malaya*, August 17, 1985). He even announced his intention to foster the economic recovery of small and medium-scale businesses by simplifying the maze of business taxes and extending government assistance to small businessmen (*Malaya*, September 20, 1985). As a result, in 1985, despite the fact that the total number of demonstrations reached an all-time high of 393, capitalists did not undertake a single independent collective action against the government.

In the final stage of the conflicts, some Filipino capitalists, often as individuals, attempted to promote presidential elections and the campaign of Corazon Aquino, and some even contributed financially to the small number of underground military rebels who had defected from Marcos. Capitalists did not organize any disruptive action during the final four days of popular mobilization that contributed to the removal of Marcos from power. Indeed, Filipino capitalists played a very different role in the conflicts than did capitalists in Iran and Nicaragua in the conflicts of their countries.

In sum, although broad segments of the capitalists were excluded from the polity and adversely affected by state policies, capitalist mobilization in the Philippines was significantly less intense than in Iran and Nicaragua. Economic, political, ethnic, and organizational divisions in part explained part of the mobilization problem for the Filipino capitalists. Even though individual capitalists did play significant roles in the anti-Marcos activities of certain political organizations, the capitalist class did not organize sustained independent anti-government demonstrations or even a single general strike to protest Aquino's assassination. In contrast to bazaaris, Filipino capitalists were very concerned about economic issues and political instability. Rising labor militancy and radicalism, along with the growing strength of the left in the countryside, challenged the capitalists and rendered them dependent on the state for containing those forces. As a result of these conditions, capitalists were reluctant to engage in disruptive collective action to remove Marcos from power.

Conclusion

Capitalists' politics were differentiated in all three countries on the basis of their relationship to the state, which primarily served the interests of a small segment of this class. Excluded from the polity, large segments of the capitalist class did not benefit from state intervention, although state intervention promoted capital accumulation. The majority of these capitalists were obliged to work through the market mechanism, while the cronies, often in the highest echelons of this class, received state protection and resources. This bifurcation of interests was important in determining the nature of capitalist conflicts against the state; everywhere, it was the excluded segments of the capitalist class that took part in the collective actions against the government. The intensity of the conflicts differed in the three cases. Capitalist exclusion from the polity was most prolonged in Iran and Nicaragua where the two dynasties had ruled for decades. The conflicts were most intense in Iran where state intervention in the market through price controls and an anti-profiteering campaign adversely affected large segments of the bazaaris. In both Iran and Nicaragua, capitalists participated actively in collective action against the state and used their disruptive powers against those regimes.

Capitalists' tendency to participate in the insurgency was also affected by the extent of class conflict and the threat from leftist revolutionary challengers. Filipino capitalists were most threatened by rising class conflict and a strong, well-organized revolutionary left. As a result, Filipino capitalists relied increasingly on the state to control the working class and eliminate the threat of a powerful communist movement. In contrast, the working class posed the least threat in Iran, where bazaaris were able to engage in a high level of collective action, while their statements were least concerned with economic issues. Nicaraguan capitalists were not threatened by the radical segment of the labor movement during the revolutionary conflicts because workers directed their attacks against Somoza. Nor did the Sandinistas pose a threat to Nicaraguan capitalists because moderate opposition organizations, not the FSLN, were in the forefront of the anti-Somoza struggles in the early stages of the conflicts in 1978.

In all three countries, organization and solidarity, along with state vulnerability, and opportunities for mobilization, rather than ideological changes affected capitalist insurgency. In all three countries economic and social divisions reduced the capacity of this class for collective action. The social divisions were particularly pronounced in the Philippines and affected the capacity of the capitalists to act collectively. The rise of favorable opportunities or state vulnerability was crucial for capitalist insurgency in all three countries. In both Iran and Nicaragua, President Carter's human rights campaign was instrumental in creating an initial aperture in the political arena. In Nicaragua, the assassination of Chamorro in the context of national polarization rendered the state vulnerable and contributed greatly to mobilization and disruptive collective action by businesses. Similarly, in the Philippines, the assassination of Aquino in the context of heightened polarization generated popular insurgency and rendered the state vulnerable, and contributed to business mobilization.

In Iran and Nicaragua, where revolutionary challengers came to power, capitalist support for these challengers was based on tactical coalition, rather than ideological conversion. In both countries, capitalists demanded a more democratic state, which would include them in the polity. They favored reduced state intervention and elimination of government corruption. Although they did not support a radical transformation of the entire social structure, in the end they supported radical organizations because of tactical, not ideological, considerations. Everywhere, capitalists were reluctant rebels.

Finally, the participation of capitalists in insurgency strongly affected the outcome of the political struggles in all three countries. In both Iran and Nicaragua, the capitalist opposition against the state was essential to the success of revolutionary challengers. In Iran, without the participation of bazaaris, the clergy and other social groups and classes could not have carried out the revolutionary struggles. In Nicaragua, the defection of the capitalists from the state and their strikes isolated the regime and rendered the state vulnerable to challenge and attack. In the Philippines, the defection of capitalists from the government also reduced the social base of support for the regime, but in the end their failure to use general strikes to disrupt the social order affected the outcome of the conflicts. Yet, despite their significance, by themselves capitalists were unable to determine the specific outcomes. In both Iran and Nicaragua, where social revolutions took place and ideologically driven challengers came to power, large segments of the capitalist class ended up with regimes that they would not have favored ideologically. Thus, to understand the final outcomes, other factors such as the nature of the coalitions, the strength of the various challengers, the character of the armed forces, and external pressures all must be analyzed. These topics are the focus of the next chapter.

Part III

Outcomes and conclusions

8 Coalitions, challengers, and political outcomes

The emergence of a revolutionary situation depends at a minimum on the formation of broad coalitions against the state and the rise of new contenders, or a coalition of contenders, who advance exclusive competing claims to control the state (Tilly 1994:10). Such coalitions emerge only infrequently, despite the fact that social conflicts are prevalent throughout developing countries, and that, from time to time, revolutionary challengers rise to transform the social order. In the absence of prior state breakdown or military victory by insurgents, broad coalitions increase the likelihood of a transfer of power and a revolution for four reasons. First, broad coalitions tend to isolate the government and reduce or eliminate the social basis of support of the regime. Second, such coalitions increase the likelihood that factionalism, defection, or paralysis will beset the armed forces. Third, broad coalitions are essential to initiate large-scale disruptive activities, such as general strikes, in order to dislodge the powerholders. Finally, in the case of government intransigence, broad coalitions may encourage greater social support for armed struggle, as the last resort, to defeat military forces.

Although structural factors such as exclusive rule, levels of state intervention and economic crises affect the likelihood of coalition formation, so too do political factors and processes. The probability that broad coalitions will be formed depends, in part, on the strength of the alternative challengers, the extent of class conflict, and the available mobilization options. Coalitions are unlikely to be formed in the presence of powerful, ideologically driven challengers that make exclusive claim to state power. Coalitions are also unlikely when workers shift to radical ideologies and intensify class conflict that threatens the capitalist class and the entire social structure. Under such conditions, the strength of ideologically driven challengers together with the radicalization of the working classes threaten the capitalist class and make it increasingly dependent on the state for stability, thereby reducing the likelihood of broad coalitions. The result may be elite compromise and electoral contest, which often exclude the revolutionary challengers from the contest. In contrast, the likelihood

239

of coalition formation is high where ideologically driven challengers are weak, and class conflict is limited or non-existent. Under these conditions, revolutionary challengers do not threaten the moderate opposition and the capitalist class. Thus, a broad coalition may emerge once favorable opportunities open up. Such coalitions may enable ideologically driven challengers to seize power particularly in situations where moderate challengers are unable to remove the rulers from power.

The strength and solidarity of the armed forces and external pressures are also factors that affect the outcome of the conflicts. Incomplete government control over the armed forces may render the military ineffective and even result in state breakdown in times of crisis. In addition, armies that lack cohesion and are internally divided may be vulnerable to disintegration at times of popular insurgency. Finally, powerful external forces may also play a role in influencing the outcome of the conflicts. Regimes that are highly dependent on external support are very vulnerable to external pressures and withdrawal of support.

All three countries examined in the current research experienced periods of prior political turmoil in which no revolution occurred because of the absence of broad coalitions. As long as the opposition was limited to students, intellectuals, segments of workers, or the clergy, the regimes in these countries could repress them. For example, repression prevailed in Iran in June 1963 in part because students, workers, and white-collar employees did not join bazaaris and clergy in the conflicts. In the Philippines, capitalists did not form a coalition with students and workers in the conflicts of the early 1970s, and as a result, Marcos declared martial law and succeeded in repressing all his opponents. In Nicaragua, the capitalists remained apart from the mobilization of students and workers in the conflicts of 1973–1974, and the government was able to repress the opponents and put an end to insurgency.

Subsequently, all three countries experienced large-scale mobilization, which succeeded in effecting social revolutions in Iran and Nicaragua and the removal of the Marcos regime in the Philippines. In Iran, the formation of a broad coalition, coupled with large-scale disruptions and western pressures, forced the Shah into exile and resulted in the formation of an Islamic government. In Nicaragua, an elite-led coalition along with disruptive collective action and international pressures were insufficient to dislodge Somoza, leaving no other option but armed struggle, which defeated the National Guard and swept in a Sandinista-led coalition. But in the Philippines, two years of protests and demonstrations failed to remove Marcos from power because of the absence of class coalitions and large-scale disruptions. The intensification of class conflict accompanied by the rising strength of a powerful revolutionary left prevented coalition

formation and disruptions of the social structure. The result was a stalemate, which was eventually broken by the defection of a faction of the
military after a disputed election. The ensuing crisis generated massive
popular insurgency that prevented the government from deploying loyal
troops to repress the rebellious faction. In the end, pressures from the
USA led to Marcos' departure from the country. Power was eventually
transferred to a reformist faction of the elite.

Coalition formation, disruptive action, and revolution in Iran

The mobilization of students and bazaaris along with leftist and nationalist intellectuals eventually forced the regime to change tactics and promise some basic reforms. The promise of reforms and relaxation of repression in late August 1978 quickly expanded the scale of the mobilization.
Prior to the appointment of the new prime minister, some seventy cities
had experienced political protests. During Sharif-Emami's reform government, an additional one hundred cities experienced political protests,
and the demonstrations in all major cities became larger than ever (Parsa
1989:57).

Equally significant, the promised reforms largely ignored working- and
middle-class interests, and provoked mobilization among these classes.
White-collar employees and professionals who had not participated in the
conflicts of the early 1960s now mobilized for collective action. Large
segments of the new middle class had been adversely affected by the
state's policy of consistently benefiting the upper echelons of industry and
the bureaucracy at the expense of the middle- and lower-level workers. In
some cases, white-collar employees resented the presence of highly paid
foreign experts who occupied positions of authority. Teachers, university
professors and employees, journalists, bank employees, and employees of
various government ministries went on strike. The newly formed National Organization of University Professors organized the "Solidarity Week"
that attracted a great deal of attention and was supported by students and
the public. Even physicians in various cities demonstrated against government brutality. In Shiraz 200 doctors went on hunger strike to protest
against nighttime shootings by the army and the arrest of three physicians. The National Organization of Physicians in Tehran denounced
military attacks on hospitals and called for the "overthrow of the illegal
and oppressive regime" (Parsa 1989:156).

In the final stage of the revolutionary struggles, even the Iranian peasantry joined the insurgencies. Iranian peasants and farmers, who lacked a
history of revolutionary struggles (Kazemi and Abrahamian 1978), had

remained passive throughout much of revolutionary conflicts. Perhaps the large-scale migration of the younger generation had reduced the capacity of the rural population to mobilize for collective action. The lack of internal organization and weaknesses of leftist challengers and allies also perhaps contributed to the absence of peasants in the earlier parts of the struggles. But, in the final weeks of the monarchy, once the state became very vulnerable, peasants and farmers who lived close to large urban areas also joined the anti-government forces.

Strikes by oil workers and bazaar closings soon disrupted all social and economic activities, paralyzing the government. At the end of December 1978, representatives from twenty-three state ministries and private sector organizations formed a central council to coordinate the strikes. Another twenty organizations soon joined the council. The council formally recognized Khomeini as the leader of the people's "anti-imperialist, anti-despotic" movement, and simultaneously rejected any compromise with Bakhtiar, the Shah's last prime minister, who they claimed represented "imperialism and dictatorship" (*Hambastegi*, 1979, nos. 9 and 10). On February 3, 1979, parliamentary employees went on strike, followed the next day by employees in the prime minister's office. These state employees declared their solidarity with the popular struggles and denounced violence and bloodshed by the state (*Kayhan*, February 4, 1979). On February 7, employees of eleven other government ministries announced that they would obey only the government of Bazargan, Khomeini's nominee. The broad coalition eventually created a revolutionary situation, which led to instability in the armed forces and eventually the ouster of the monarchy.

The armed forces became unstable and eventually collapsed as a result of structural weakness. The military had been organized in such a way as to insure that it remained subordinate to the Shah (Afshar 1985:186–189). Thus, no army commander had any real power; the slightest decision had to be made by the Shah himself (Katouzian 1998:195). The Shah insured that the armed forces never formed a cohesive organization capable of initiating political action. As a result of lack of power and leadership, the Shah's departure in January 1979 generated large-scale discipline problems in the military. These weaknesses were compounded by the military recruitment pattern that further reduced the cohesion of the armed forces. Approximately one-half of the infantry comprised conscripts with close ties to the civilian population. As a result of these weaknesses, the armed forces began to display signs of instability and disintegration precisely when popular mobilization and struggles expanded and forced the government to use the army extensively. In the fall of 1978, the army had to be spread thinly throughout the country to

only Shah
could make
decisions

contain the massive disruptions, demonstrations, and strikes. Soon, lack of cohesion in the armed forces proved to be a problem. Increased utilization of soldiers to repress the population inevitably resulted in widespread defection (Amuzegar 1991:161). Approximately one thousand soldiers were deserting the army per day by the time Bakhtiar was appointed as the Shah's last prime minister (Ghara-Baghi 1984:138). Soon, the desertion rate increased rapidly. Eventually a number of military trucks in Tehran even displayed pictures of Khomeini the day before the Shah left the country. In the end, the structural weaknesses of the military and large-scale disruptions, combined with two days of armed struggle, paralyzed the armed forces and led its leaders to declare neutrality on February 11, 1979.

The failure of secular challengers

In contrast to other twentieth-century revolutions, secular forces in Iran did not succeed in gaining state power, although they played an important role in the opening stages of the insurgency. Secular organizations had been drastically weakened by government repression, which for all practical purposes had reduced their capacity for large-scale mobilization. At the time of the revolution, two secular organizations existed, each espousing a different political program. One was the National Front, which was revived in early 1977 by liberal-nationalists; the other was the Organization of the Iranian People's Fedayee Guerrillas, also known as the Feda'iyan. Both organizations were repressed and declared illegal during the 1960s and 1970s. For different reasons, the two organizations did not form a coalition, and neither group was able to play a significant role during the revolutionary struggles. As a result, the secular forces could not present themselves as viable options to seize state power.

The National Front, a moderate political organization, failed to gain control over the state power despite the fact that it, along with other secular organizations such as the Writers' Association, played a significant role in the initial stage of the insurgency. The National Front's failure was in large part due to the lack of organized networks and to its policies, which caused it to follow events rather than lead them. The Front had flourished during the political apertures of the early 1950s and early 1960s, but had been weakened by the political repression that followed the *coup d'état* in 1953, which resulted in the arrest and imprisonment of Dr. Mosaddegh, its highly popular and charismatic leader. The Front was able to revive somewhat in the early 1960s as political opportunities expanded. With the virtual elimination of the Tudeh Party, the National Front was the only challenging organization that could mobilize broad segments of the population in the early 1960s. In May 1961, the first legal gathering of the Front in Tehran since the overtures of Prime Minister Mosaddegh in 1953 attracted 80,000 people.

The repression of 1963, however, combined with the National Front's own internal policies, demobilized the Front and weakened its support bases. Even before the June 1963 uprising, support among university students for the Front was weakened because its conservative faction expelled ninety leftist students on charges that they favored communism. After the June insurgency, when some of its leaders were released from jail, the Front prevented students from holding demonstrations in September (Jazani 1979:132). Although the students called off their demonstrations, they broke away from the National Front, never to follow its lead again. This loss of student support drastically weakened the Front. A few of its leaders attempted to establish a third National Front in 1965, but SAVAK promptly arrested and jailed the organizers, who were later released after signing statements agreeing not to engage in political activities. In combination, these developments and policies prevented the National Front from playing any role in politics until 1977, when a new political opening provided an opportunity to mobilize.

Although Front leaders were among the first to mobilize and challenge the monarchy in 1977, they had few networks for activating political action. Most of the Front's support came from the ranks of teachers, professors, journalists, lawyers, and segments of the bazaaris. But, unlike in the 1950s, the National Front in 1977 had no access to the media and lacked a specific, safe location where members and supporters could discuss political issues, communicate decisions, coordinate activities, and mobilize for collective action. The Front's leadership had been drastically weakened. By 1978, nine of the twenty founders of the original National Front, including Mosaddegh, had either died, abandoned politics, or left the country (*Ettelaat*, October 31, 1978). Of the remainder, only one was actually active. Without Mosaddegh and other such prominent figures, the Front lacked widely recognized leaders. Moreover, the Front's programs did not address issues of social justice, which might have attracted students and workers. As a result, it had very limited support among students and other members of the younger generation who had little familiarity with it.

For all these reasons, the National Front failed to take the initiative to form a broad coalition and lead the conflicts once popular mobilization began to spread. In fact, the Front never presented an exclusive claim to power. As late as November 1978, it had not called for the overthrow of the monarchy. As a result, it lagged behind the pace of popular uprising as Sanjabi, its leader, admitted (*Kayhan*, November 1, 1978).

Under growing popular mobilization and pressure from Khomeini, the National Front eventually changed its politics and called for the overthrow of the monarchy. As anti-Shah struggles widened and Prime Minister Sharif-Emami resigned, Sanjabi met Khomeini in Paris and under pressure from him agreed to reject the monarchy. Sanjabi signed a declaration, on November 6, stating that the Shah's regime lacked any legal basis for violating Islamic laws; that the nationalist Islamic movement would not compromise with any form of government as long as the monarchy remained; and finally, that the government must be both democratic, that is determined by popular vote, and based on Islamic rules. In the following few months, the leaders of the National Front were involved in many of the major political events that led to the overthrow of the monarchy. Because of their rejection of the monarchy and cooperation during the revolutionary struggles, once the monarchy was overthrown, a number of members and leaders of the National Front were appointed to high-level positions in the Provisional Revolutionary Government, headed by Mehdi Bazargan, another ally of Dr. Mosaddegh.

In contrast to the moderate National Front, which was at least present at many of the events of collective action, the radical Feda'iyan was conspicuously absent in the popular collective actions. Although the repression and weakening of the National Front in 1963 expanded support for the Feda'iyan, the organization was unable to play a major role in the revolutionary conflicts. Formed in 1964, the Feda'iyan, a Marxist-Leninist organization, attempted to overthrow the regime through armed struggle. It lacked the advantage of the National Front, which was able to operate legally during the early 1950s. The timing of the Feda'iyan's armed struggle was unfavorable because it coincided with the oil boom of the first half of the 1970s, as opposed to the earlier period of economic decline. In addition, its Marxist-Leninist ideology and radical revolutionary vision precluded the possibility of attracting support from the middle and upper classes. This limited most of its support to university students and intellectuals, particularly because repression prevented it from establishing links to the working classes.

Moreover, the Feda'iyan's commitment to armed struggle provoked relentless state repression, which made operations more difficult. Its struggles, however, attracted the attention of university and college students, where the Feda'iyan initially emerged and gathered support. It certainly impressed the Shah who observed, "The determination with which they fight is quite unbelievable. Even the women keep battling on to their very last gasp. The men carry cyanide tablets in their mouths and commit suicide rather than face capture" (Alam 1991:461).

Despite its uncompromising dedication to overthrowing the monarchy, the Feda'iyan organization was marked by a serious structural weakness: its membership was relatively small and drawn primarily from the intelligentsia; its operation was geographically limited. On the eve of the revolution in late 1977, the organization experienced heavy losses and its membership was down to only about twenty-five to thirty-five members.[1] The organization was largely composed of intellectuals and students. In a sample of 125 Feda'iyan members killed in the 1960s and 1970s in battle, under torture, or by execution, 60 percent were university students or college graduates, and only 10 percent were industrial workers. Although by early 1978 the Feda'iyan was able to establish ties with the larger body of student supporters, it had little connection to the working class. Geographically, the organization's activities were limited. Nearly 85 percent of the Feda'iyan were located in the capital, which reduced their impact in the rest of the country.[2] The organization was also limited in its operations. In the twelve months prior to the ouster of the monarchy, the Feda'iyan launched sixteen armed raids on the police, the army, and SAVAK, all of which were carried out in a few major cities, with seven of these in Tehran (OIPFG 1978). These data illustrate their lack of bases or networks outside a few major cities.

Finally, the dynamics of political development did not favor the cause of the Feda'iyan. Government concessions offered in the autumn of 1978 were not extended to the Feda'iyan, and its members were not released from jail or allowed to return from abroad until just a few weeks before the monarchy's final collapse. Government repression was not the only obstacle encountered by the Feda'iyan. Religious groups also occasionally hampered its efforts to mobilize and act collectively. On December 11, 1978, on Ashoura, an important Shia day of mourning, a pro-Feda'iyan demonstration by 2,000 students, teachers, and workers in Tabriz was disrupted by a group of religious protesters and a leftist demonstration in Tehran was also broken up by an Islamic group (*Kayhan*, January 16, 1979).

In the final days of the monarchy, as political prisoners were released from prisons, the Feda'iyan gained greater momentum and demonstrated its mobilization capacity. The day before power was transferred to the new rulers, the Feda'iyan organized a rally at Tehran University that attracted more than 50,000 people. A few days later, the Feda'iyan

[1] The figure of twenty-five was estimated by a Fedayee leader (Mirsepassi-Ashtiani and Moghadam 1991:34). The figure of thirty-five was given to me by Farrokh Negahdar, the top leader of the organization in 1979.

[2] The sample of Feda'iyan members was collected from various issues of their publication *Kar*.

organized another rally at the university, which drew more than 150,000 people (*Ayandegan*, February 24, 1979). Some members of the Feda'iyan also participated in the final two days of armed battle against the Immortal Guard, but, at that time, they were not in a position to influence the course of the revolution.

Ayatollah Khomeini's leadership

The weaknesses of the secular challengers forced the opponents to mobilize through the mosque, which enabled Ayatollah Khomeini to lead the insurgency. But Khomeini's rise to the position of paramount leader of the Iranian revolution was due primarily to political rather than ideological reasons. Perhaps because he was very interested in forging a broad coalition, Khomeini never publicly told the Iranian people about his radical, theocratic ideology. He never mentioned doctrinal issues, such as the concept of *Velayat-e fagih*, or jurist's guardianship, in his public statements addressed to the Iranian people in the years prior to the revolution. Even clerics and clerical students who supported Khomeini did not know anything about such concepts and plans (Tahmaseb Pour, interview, February 1999). Even some of Khomeini's closest political allies and advisors who had been in Paris with him were completely bewildered after the revolution when they first heard this concept (Abrahamian 1993:30). Although he expressed concern over the decline of the status of the clergy and erosion of Islam, Khomeini repeatedly claimed to have no aspiration to political position. At the end of 1977 while still in Iraq, Khomeini instructed his clerical supporters to respect and work with students and intellectuals. "Tomorrow we will not become government ministers; our work is different. These are the ones who become ministers and representatives" (Khomeini 1983, vol. I:436). While in France he noted that, as in the past, he would be merely a guide to the people (*Ayandegan*, January 10, 1979).

At the same time, Khomeini borrowed the basic tenets of the liberal-nationalist movement, which were freedom from dictatorship and imperialism, and condemnation of pillaging of the country's national resources. The only concern that Khomeini added to the nationalist demands was the government's violation of Islamic principles. He steadfastly maintained that an Islamic government would guarantee national independence and provide political freedom for all Iranians. In the final weeks of the revolutionary conflicts, Khomeini repeatedly declared that independence and freedom would be the essence of any Islamic republic (Khomeini 1983, vol. IV:252). In Paris, he suggested that even Marxists would be free to express themselves under an Islamic republic.

Women, too, would be free "to govern their fate and choose their activities." The Shah's dictatorial regime, he asserted, reduced women to objects of consumption, while Islam opposed such treatment of women (*Ayandegan*, January 17, 1979). Thus, Khomeini received the backing of the vast majority of the Iranian population because of his opposition to dictatorship and his defense of freedom and national interests, not because of his theocratic ideology, which was unknown to the majority of Iranians.

More importantly, Khomeini had certain political advantages that helped place him in a position of leadership. Although his position within the clerical community as one of the preeminent ayatollahs made him relatively immune from government repression, as evidenced by the fact that he was exiled rather than executed in 1964, it was Khomeini's political stand that distinguished him from others. In addition, his exile enabled him to continue opposition against the Shah. As a result, while all other political leaders capitulated to repression, Khomeini was the only religious or political leader who for years called for the overthrow of the regime. While in Iraq Khomeini was able to meet with his followers and, through them, send messages back to Iran. Khomeini also received funds from religious contributions, which he used for political purposes, including assisting families of political prisoners (Shanehchi 1983, tape 3:15). No other political leader enjoyed such advantages. Equally important, unlike moderate political leaders, Khomeini took an uncompromising stand against the Shah, which made him popular among segments of the population.

Although the 1977 openings were not of his making, Khomeini took full advantage of political opportunities. He quickly seized the opportunity and prodded people, especially the clergy, to mobilize: "Other parties have been writing and signing petitions, and we notice that nothing has happened to them. This is a unique opportunity that, if it is lost and this man's position is somewhat stabilized, he would cause serious damage, which would hurt the clergy first" (Khomeini 1983, vol. I:265). Whereas he had issued only eight statements to the Iranian people, including an open letter to Prime Minister Hoveyda, over a period of thirteen years, once conflicts erupted, he expanded his activities and issued regular statements during or after every major political event. Between the fall of 1977 and his departure from Paris in early 1979, Khomeini sent forty-three messages to the Iranian people. In comparative terms, the number of Khomeini's statements was greater than that of any individual or organization inside Iran.

Khomeini's ability to influence the political process in Iran increased with his expulsion from Iraq and relocation to Paris in early October

1978. This coincided with the government's retreat from repression and formation of a government of "national reconciliation," which led to an upsurge in popular collective action. In his messages Khomeini called for unity and building coalitions. He appealed to intellectuals and clerics to cooperate, urging intellectuals to refrain from calling the clerics backward, and the clergy to cease accusing university people of not believing in God. Khomeini also used his new opportunities to reject any compromise with the Shah, thereby preventing the moderate opposition accepting the continuation of the monarchy.

In the fall of 1978, as the regime's vulnerability became increasingly apparent, support for Khomeini widened. Some bazaaris and a few wealthy capitalists contributed substantial sums of money to Khomeini for political purposes.

After the overthrow of the monarchy, as the coalitions broke apart, Khomeini and his fundamentalist supporters maintained power because of complex factors and processes. To mitigate the intensity of rising domestic conflicts and discredit their opponents, Khomeini promoted or took advantage of external conflicts, first through the hostage crisis and later the war with Iraq, to ban strikes, close the universities, and repress dissidents. Khomeini and his supporters quickly monopolized the mosques, brushing aside their opponents and thereby blocking other social groups from mobilizing through this channel. A great deal of money was distributed to sympathetic clerics to ensure their support, while clerics who opposed their rule were isolated and repressed. As a result, the most important location for pre-revolutionary mobilization was closed to dissidents.

More importantly, rising class conflict along with the growing strength of the left, both secular and religious, forced Khomeini to introduce new ideological elements into the revolution. This time he was forced to borrow some of the basic tenets of the radical left. Khomeini's ideological shift was significant in the survival of the Islamic Republic and the clergy's rise to political supremacy. He met the challenge posed by the left by shifting his pre-revolutionary focus on independence from foreign powers and freedom from dictatorship to a resolute concentration on social justice. Khomeini declared that the Islamic Republic was established to serve the interests of the poor and the oppressed. This political shift placed Khomeini farther to the left than any established Iranian politician in the twentieth century, including Dr. Mosaddegh. By making such a shift, Khomeini was able to prevail over liberals who had no plans to restructure the social order or redress social inequality. Khomeini's shift was also intended to reduce the left's ability to mobilize students, workers, and peasants around the issues of social justice and equality. He stated repeatedly that Islam served the interests of the mostazafin, the oppressed and deprived, noting that the feast of the oppressed is when the oppressors are eliminated (Khomeini 1983, vol. IX:246). "God was determined to cleanse the earth of the oppressors and put the oppressed in power. Islam had come for this purpose" (Khomeini 1983, vol. VI:71). He insisted that Islam intended that people should have both a material and spiritual life (Khomeini 1983, vol. V:127). To attract working-class support, Khomeini even sounded more radical than Karl Marx when on May Day, 1979, he declared that "Every day should be considered Workers' Day for labor is the source of all things, even of heaven and hell as well as of the atom particle" (Abrahamian 1993:71). Although several times he noted that the revolution was for Islam, not for "the stomach" or for "grapes and melon," he warned the new Islamic government, "If we cannot reduce economic polarization and reduce the inequalities between the rich and the poor, and if consequently people get disappointed in Islam, nothing can prevent the resulting explosion; and we will all be destroyed" (Khomeini 1983, vol. X:50).

Khomeini also pressured the state to adopt policies favoring the lower socio-economic classes. Shortly after his return, he ordered the expropriation of the Pahlavi dynasty's assets and their use for housing and employment for the poor. Khomeini himself opened a bank account and asked people to contribute money to build housing for the poor. He also established a committee to help bazaaris in economic distress and ordered the provisional government to provide free water and electricity for the poor who had been deprived by the monarchy (Khomeini 1983, vol. V:120).

Most importantly, Khomeini relied heavily on the Revolutionary Guard and the informal Hezb-ollah, or God's Party, to effectively demobilize the opposition. During the conflicts and power struggle, the Guard, along with the revolutionary committees, carried out an unprecedented level of repression against the opposition. Between the summers of 1981 and 1985, approximately 12,000 opponents of the state were either executed or killed in armed struggle (*Mojahed*, Appendix to no. 261, September 6, 1985).

National insurgency and failure of the Nicaraguan moderates

The final phase of the Nicaraguan conflicts began when Somoza lifted martial law in September 1977, under pressure from the US President Jimmy Carter. During the state of siege that lasted for thirty-three months, major segments of the Nicaraguan population were adversely affected by government policies and were prepared for some changes. Once martial law was lifted, various social groups organized at least twenty-two demonstrations against the government. Furthermore, various political organizations and social groups also issued eighty-one protest statements. By the end of the year, Nicaraguan society had become increasingly polarized. On one side stood the Somocistas and the National Guard; on the other, stood the vast majority of the population, including the working classes, students, the middle class, some segments of the private enterprise, the Catholic Church, moderate political organizations and the Sandinistas. Obviously, a broad opposition had begun to emerge within Nicaraguan society, although no consensus existed among the various groups and collectivities over the nature of changes.

At this stage of the struggles, the moderate opposition took the initiative to work with the government to effect change in Nicaragua. At the end of 1977, moderate opposition organizations together with the Catholic Church reached an agreement to meet with Somoza after the February municipal elections to discuss the mounting political crisis facing the country. The Coordinating Commission for the National Dialogue[3] issued a statement in the first week of January 1978, outlining the prerequisites for opening a dialogue with the government. These included a broad investigation into the numerous disappearances of persons, with participants to include the National Commission of Human Rights, the Commission of Human Rights of the OAS, and Amnesty International; a speedy trial in the Common Courts for the many prisoners held without trial, and liberty for those against whom no charges had been filed; an exhaustive inquiry into the squandering and misuse of public money by diverse governmental organizations and autonomous entities; suspension of censorship and freedom of political activities for opposition political groups; approval by the Labor Ministry for numerous labor syndicates to become formally incorporated; and the dropping of all charges against Los Doce (*La Prensa*, January 6, 1978), a leadership group of twelve well-known citizens that had been formed by the FSLN.

The murder, four days later, of Pedro Chamorro, co-founder of UDEL and editor of *La Prensa*, abruptly and decisively cut short any possibility of compromise between the opposition and the government. More importantly, in the context of heightened polarization, the assassination ignited political mobilization by all major social groups and classes in urban Nicaragua. In contrast to 1973 and 1974, when only ten cities and towns had experienced demonstrations, in 1978, at least forty-four cities

---

[3] The statement was signed by representatives of the following organizations: UDEL, the Social Christian Party, the Authentic Conservative Party, and the Conservative Party-minority (*La Prensa*, January 6, 1978).

and towns were rocked by demonstrations. Following Chamorro's murder, various social groups and classes organized 648 demonstrations, which was unprecedented. Various social groups and political organizations also issued 484 political statements against the government. The number of popular demonstrations representing a coalition of students, workers, urban poor, and the middle class skyrocketed in 1978 to a high of 374.

In addition to students, workers, and capitalists, Nicaraguan professionals and middle-class organizations also mobilized against the regime. Nicaraguan women became very active in the political conflicts. In 1978, women's groups organized thirty-five demonstrations, five occupations, and four hunger strikes. The majority of their actions protested against political repression and demanded that Somoza resign. AMPRONAC (Association of Women Against the National Problem), in particular, established a vigorous campaign against the government. Following Chamorro's death in January, hundreds of AMPRONAC members occupied the United Nations' development office in Managua for twelve days and hung a banner over the entrance proclaiming: "We take this place demanding an answer to our disappeared relatives and freedom for political prisoners" (La Prensa, January 26, 1978).

Even the Nicaraguan peasants who had been harshly repressed for a long time mobilized and initiated collective action. Over the years, peasants had attempted to organize but always faced government repression. As early as May 1974, peasant organizers in Matagalpa had tried to form an agricultural cooperative and school. The government response was the arrest and torture of a large number of peasants in the region. In one instance, the National Guard arrested five peasants suspected of subversive activities. The peasants later charged that while in detention, they were bound, beaten, starved, and deprived of water. One of the arrested peasants was Amada Pineda de Arauz, the wife of a peasant leader. The Guard took her to Santa Rita and repeatedly raped her during the thirteen days she was in custody. After her release, she filed charges against the lieutenant in charge of the patrol. Although a military tribunal acquitted the lieutenant of any wrongdoing, Amada Pineda de Arauz received tremendous sympathy throughout Nicaragua for several months (La Prensa, May 28, 1974). Government repression of peasants intensified during the state of siege and inevitably reduced peasant mobilization.

But, after the assassination, Nicaraguan peasants expanded their mobilization. In 1978, Nicaraguan peasants organized in part by Catholic priests and in part by Sandinistas mobilized and engaged in two demonstrations, two occupations, and ten land invasions despite massive government repression. The Rural Workers' Association, formed in 1977 partly under FSLN auspices and staffed, in part, by former organizers of the Agrarian Promotion and Educational Center (CEPA), organized a "hunger march" in Diriamba on April 9 to protest against the conditions endured by the peasantry. The National Guard prevented peasants arriving from surrounding communities from entering Diriamba and arrested several peasant leaders. Nevertheless, 1,200 members and rural supporters joined the march, which chose as its theme, "we have hunger; we don't have jobs or health." They issued a statement, declaring, "The Nicaraguan peasantry is tired of living in exploitation and hunger, without having a piece of earth to cultivate; and out of this situation of misery and injustice, today lifts and unites its voice and force with the workers and the people in general to emit its protest" (*La Prensa*, April 9, 1978).

More importantly, the assassination of Chamorro activated political organizations that pressed for change. Political organizations issued a large number of political statements after Chamorro's assassination with the central themes a demand for Somoza to resign and a protest against government repression.[4] Furthermore, the moderate opposition expanded its organizing capacity to demand change. The most important initiative by these diverse political organizations was the formation in May of the Broad Opposition Front, or FAO, a coalition comprising UDEL, the Independent Liberal Party, National Conservative Action, the Nicaraguan Social Christian Party, the two leading labor organizations CGT-I and CTN, both factions of the Conservative Party of Nicaragua, the Authentic Conservative Party, and the Nicaraguan Democratic Movement. Subsequently, FAO issued twenty-eight statements, most of which demanded some measure of social and political reforms and an end to repression.

But FAO lacked a cohesive structure and remained fairly weak until August 1978, when it was bolstered by the incorporation of Los Doce and other smaller groups such as the Confederation of Syndical Unification (CUS) (*La Prensa*, January 2, 1979). Los Doce, in particular, provided a measure of dynamism with their energetic campaigning against the regime. Their addition, together with the Catholic Church's call for a transitional government, emboldened FAO to press for Somoza's removal. Toward the end of August, FAO issued a statement supporting both the Episcopal Conference's pastoral letter and the statement by the Catholic Archbishop's Presbyterian Council appealing for a "national government to dismantle the dictatorship and open the country to an authentic, progressive, and pluralistic democracy" (*La Prensa*, August 7, 1978). Two weeks later, FAO released another statement to serve as a

---

[4] Among these statements were twenty-eight issued by FAO, twelve by Los Doce, eight from MPU, and a total of eleven from all other political organizations.

basis for a national transitional government. This statement stipulated a number of measures, such as democratic freedoms, release of all political prisoners, elimination of corruption, agrarian reform, and resolution of the problems of inflation, health, and illiteracy (*La Prensa*, August 21, 1978). Significantly, the statement made no mention of the FSLN.

Perhaps FAO's most notable achievement was to mobilize and announce the indefinite nationwide strike begun on August 25. The demands put forth by FAO included the immediate removal of Somoza as president and head of the National Guard, as well as from any other governmental office; and the separation of his son, Major Anastasio Somoza Portocarrero, and half-brother, General José Rodriguez Somoza from the Armed Forces and their other official positions. FAO's statement also urged the creation of a national government by capable, honest persons backed by all sectors of society (*La Prensa*, August 25, 1978). The strike lasted thirty-one days but finally came to an end without accomplishing its intentions. Nevertheless, FAO hailed it as a successful demonstration of "the patriotism of workers, the consumer public, and honest traders and businessmen" (*La Prensa*, October 5, 1978).

With the failure of the strike's goal, FAO proceeded with its attempts to remove Somoza through institutional measures. When a multinational negotiating team arrived in Nicaragua on October 6, FAO called for a plebiscite to be accompanied by, among other things, the confinement of National Guard units to their barracks and the departure of Somoza and his family from Nicaragua during the voting. This proposal was rejected outright by Somoza, who labeled it ridiculous (Somoza 1980:223).

The futility of negotiating, given Somoza's intransigence, together with FAO's own indecision as to whether or not the National Guard should be dissolved, weakened the moderate political opposition's leading organization. FAO was further weakened by the withdrawal on October 26 of Los Doce and two assistants to its Political Commission. Three weeks later, the labor organization CTN also left, explaining in a statement that it feared certain members of FAO were preparing to cut a deal with the multinational mediating commission to accept less than FAO's full demands for the total expulsion of the Somoza family and the restructuring of the National Guard (*La Prensa*, November 19, 1978).

In a final bid to regain the leadership momentum, FAO issued an ultimatum declaring that it would withdraw from negotiations if Somoza did not resign and leave the country with his family by November 21. The deadline passed unheeded, and on November 22, FAO withdrew from the international mediating commission (*La Prensa*, November 22, 1978). From then on, FAO's role in the opposition was limited to issuing statements and pursuing a course of events led by others.

At the end of December, the United States recalled its ambassador to Nicaragua, its representative to the international mediating commission, and the head of the US Army's Southern Command in Panama. The State Department characterized Somoza's refusal to accept the "fair and workable" proposal of the mediators as "a serious snag." The failure of both FAO and the international negotiating team left the Nicaraguan opposition no other option but to dislodge the Somoza regime through armed struggle, which was already underway by the Sandinista Front for National Liberation.

Sandinista struggles and social revolution in Nicaragua

In 1979, the Sandinista Front for National Liberation, or FSLN, succeeded in seizing power in Nicaragua because of a complex set of factors. Although the Sandinistas had long enjoyed the support of the vast majority of Nicaraguan students, they had been unable to develop support among other segments of the urban population. In fact, in the fall of 1977 when political opposition was resumed, the Sandinistas did not have any support even among the socialist faction of organized labor. But soon the dynamics of political development greatly favored the Sandinistas. They certainly benefited from Somoza's intransigence and the failure of the moderate opposition to remove him from office. More importantly, the Sandinistas reduced threats against the capitalist class by adopting an ideological stance that promised a mixed economy and moved away from a strictly socialist platform. In addition to forming an alliance with the middle class and professionals through Los Doce, in the final stage of the insurgency, the Sandinistas accepted the inclusion of two members of the moderate opposition in their junta. The Sandinistas transferred their combatants from rural to urban areas where much of the insurgency was located. Finally, they succeeded in overthrowing the Somoza regime through a combination of armed struggle and general strikes that disrupted the entire social structure.

Formed in 1961, the Sandinistas were a Marxist guerrilla organization whose members, like the Iranian Feda'iyan, were drawn overwhelmingly from the ranks of the intelligentsia (Cruz 1989:61; Wickham-Crowley 1992:213, 335–336). The Sandinistas also launched their struggles as an avowedly guerrilla organization in rural areas (Hodges 1986:218). In the process, they gained support among certain segments of the peasantry, particularly those with high rates of sharecropping, squatting, and migratory labor (Wickham-Crowley 1989:143–150). But the organization was forced to change its tactics after the severe military defeat in the mountains of Pancasan in 1967 (Ruchwarger 1987:14–16). After this defeat, the FSLN attempted to expand its urban support base into neighbor-hoods, universities, and factories. At that time, the Sandinistas won little support among organized workers or in the neighborhoods, and their gains were primarily limited to students (Ruchwarger 1985:90). The FSLN also contacted a few "progressive" clerics, forging a tactical al-liance and acquiring the backing of some Catholic priests (Foroohar 1989:117–118). In 1974 the FSLN had some success in organizing peasants, when a Sandinista leader of peasant origin established a peasant guerrilla unit in the north-central region of the country (Ruchwarger 1987:38). But the FSLN's organizing activities in rural areas once again provoked heavy government repression aimed at preventing the guerrilla organization from establishing large-scale bases among the peasantry.[5]

Despite their efforts to mobilize support, by the end of 1974 the organization was still only a "vanguard" entity with a membership of less than a hundred (Kinzer 1979:12) and insufficient social support to influ-ence political processes. Although mobilization and collective action by urban inhabitants provided an opportunity for the FSLN to step up its own guerrilla attacks against the state, its actions in the early stage of the conflicts were relatively insignificant. Thus, by 1974, the FSLN's guer-rilla activities in both rural and urban areas had been largely unsuccessful. It had failed to mobilize either the working classes or the peasants, had been defeated in guerrilla actions, and instead had invited harsh repres-sion, which had resulted in considerable losses for the organization.

Yet two actions initiated by the FSLN did provide a great deal of national exposure. The first was the largest hunger strike in Nicaraguan history. In December 1973, eight FSLN prisoners, including Daniel Ortega Saavedra, declared a hunger strike to protest against the con-tinued detention of an ex-National Guardsman who had sold his rifle to the FSLN (*La Prensa*, December 11, 1973). Mothers of imprisoned FSLN members and the mother of the ex-Guardsman soon joined the hunger strike, generating numerous popular demands for the release of the ex-Guardsman, who had been detained in jail twenty-one months beyond his sentence. The hunger strike, which lasted one month, ended after the ex-Guardsman was released from prison (*La Prensa*, January 16, 1974).

The second FSLN event attracted even greater attention. At the end of 1974, with the deepening political crisis, the Sandinistas seized the op-portunity to gain national exposure. In an audacious raid on December 27, they invaded a reception for the US ambassador at the mansion of the

---

[5] Peasants were the main victims as the National Guard, in search of guerrillas, union organizers, and bandits, initiated an extensive sweep in the north, causing many peasants to flee their lands and homes, which were often destroyed (*La Prensa*, May 28, 1974).

Nicaraguan Minister of Agriculture and took hostage a number of politicians and close friends of the Somoza family. To free the hostages, Somoza paid $2 million in ransom, released a number of Sandinista prisoners, and broadcast guerrilla communiqués on all the country's media outlets.

The phenomenal success of this attack brought with it unexpected complications. First, the action attracted to the FSLN a large number of intellectuals from diverse academic backgrounds. As a result, divisions began to materialize within the organization. In 1975, the first major organizational partition emerged with the formation of the Proletarian Tendency, whose adherents differed from those belonging to the faction known as the Prolonged People's War, which had carried out FSLN actions in the countryside. At the end of 1975, a third faction emerged, the Insurrectional, which advocated a combined strategy of rural–urban warfare together with massive popular resistance in the cities fomented by mobilizing Nicaragua's middle sectors (Hodges 1986:218–255). For a time, these internal divisions weakened the FSLN by reducing its capacity to act collectively. A second major complication was continued government repression, which led to the deaths of many of the FSLN members, including its co-founder, Carlos Fonseca Amador, in 1976.

Sandinista coalition and armed struggle

With martial law still effectively blocking all traditional options for implementing change, armed struggle gradually gained support within segments of the civilian population as the only route through which they might bring about a transformation in Nicaragua. Under heavy repression, the Insurrectional faction made a fateful move and formed a coalition with a leadership group of twelve well-known citizens who collectively became known as Los Doce in June 1977. Los Doce comprised mostly intellectuals and highly educated individuals including two Catholic priests, six professionals (a writer, dental surgeon, the former rector of the National Autonomous University, an agronomist, a lawyer, and an architect), three businessmen, and one lawyer-businessman. Los Doce began issuing statements in October 1977 in support of the Sandinistas and continued their activities until Somoza's ouster. Their pronouncements and actions helped to mobilize support for the FSLN. On October 14, for example, Los Doce released a statement demanding substantial changes and the creation of a democratic system with the participation of the FSLN.

More importantly, Los Doce became relatively insulated from government repression despite advocating the cause of the FSLN. When the

Nicaraguan government filed charges against Los Doce for conducting "subversive activities" in Costa Rica, the US embassy in Managua objected and compelled Somoza to withdraw the charges (Somoza 1980:105). After their return to Nicaragua, Los Doce were able to travel to most of the country's major cities, where they held rallies and called openly for the regime's overthrow with virtual impunity. The endorsement of these twelve leading citizens enhanced the FSLN's credibility, both at home and abroad.

In addition to forming this significant coalition, Sandinistas shifted their struggle from rural to urban areas where much of the insurgency was to occur. Thus, beginning roughly in May 1977, the FSLN inaugurated a strategy of insurrection aimed at widening its attacks on the regime (Hodges 1986:218). Thus, once the state of siege was lifted, in the last three months of 1977, the FSLN engaged in at least fourteen armed clashes and carried out eight anti-government activities. In a series of attacks beginning on October 12, in Ocotal, Sandinistas attacked police stations and government forces. The next day, they struck at the National Guard barracks in San Carlos. In the next few days, they assaulted a number of targets in different parts of the country, including Managua. As a result, the FSLN attracted ever-increasing popular backing and resources from segments of the population that had completely broken away from the regime.

Sandinista rise to leadership

In contrast to other sectors of the opposition, whose positions evidenced a gradual but inevitable shift toward calling for Somoza's removal, the FSLN from the beginning announced its intention to oust the Somoza regime and consistently rejected any compromise with the government. The day before Chamorro was murdered, when a national dialogue with Somoza was still being organized by other opposition groups, the FSLN issued a statement rejecting any such dialogue and calling it a lie against the people. Only the fall of the Somoza regime and the establishment of a popular democracy, the FSLN reiterated, could save Nicaragua (*La Prensa*, January 9, 1978).

As each alternative attempt to resolve the political crisis ended in failure, support for the FSLN grew. In 1978, there were unmistakable signs that a number of social groups, notably workers, students, women, and white-collar employees, had begun to side with the FSLN. On April 11, representatives from several groups in Leon staged a progressive hunger strike, with two representatives from each group fasting for twenty-four hours, to demonstrate solidarity with Sandinista political prisoners. These groups represented a broad spectrum of labor, professional, political, and women's organizations, including AM-PRONAC, CGT-I, UDEL, the University Center at UNAN (CUUN), the Association of Professors of UNAN, the Medical Society of León, SCAAS, the Syndicate of Workers of San Vincente Hospital, the Democratic Movement of Nicaragua, gasoline distributors, and the Institute of Syndical Capacitation. Their demands included better treatment for two FSLN prisoners, Marcio Jaén and Tomás Borge; the transfer of all FSLN political prisoners from Managua Police Headquarters to the Model Prison in Tipitapa; and accelerated judicial hearings for political prisoners (*La Prensa*, April 11, 1978). On April 19, the leftist labor organizations CGT-I and SCAAS, and hospital workers organized a 48-hour strike in solidarity with Sandinista political prisoners. Large numbers of students and workers observed the strike. In April and July, both the Rural Workers' Association and the women's organization, AMPRONAC, aligned themselves with the FSLN (Ruchwarger 1987:40–41, 50).

With increased social support in July, the FSLN organized a gathering at UNAN of 2,000 students, workers, white-collar employees and professionals, teachers and professors, and women, along with representatives of CGT-I and the socialist and communist parties to organize the United People's Movement, or MPU.[6] MPU had three broad objectives: to mobilize the population to overthrow the Somocista dictatorship; to enhance the organization and unification of the broad popular sectors; and to unify the revolutionary forces (*La Prensa*, July 28, 1978). In August, MPU established a network of underground neighborhood cells, known as Civil Defense Committees, or CDCs. During the final year of the struggle against the Somoza regime, these cells provided urban residents with an autonomous power structure. The CDCs carried out many tasks: they stockpiled food, medicine, and weapons; built air-raid shelters; and trained people in first aid, military strategy, barricade-building, and the use of weapons (Ruchwarger 1985:92).

[6] The twenty-two organizations that comprised MPU included: the Association of Professors of the Ruben Dario University Center; Working People; the National Union of Employees; Committee of Struggle for Syndical Freedom; Union of Progressive Intellectuals and Artists of Central America; Association of Democratic Lawyers of Nicaragua; Federation of Youth Movements of Managua; Committee of Mothers and Relatives of Political Prisoners; Communist Party of Nicaragua; Nicaraguan Socialist Party; Revolutionary Student Front; Revolutionary Worker Movement; Revolutionary Student Movement-Marxist-Leninist; General Confederation of Workers-Independent; University Center of UNAN; Association of Secondary Students; Secondary Student Movement; Student Center of Polytechnic University; and the Organization of Democratic Women of Nicaragua (*La Prensa*, July 28, 1978).

The FSLN garnered even greater resources and support during the nationwide general strike in August and September of 1978, when the National Guard relentlessly bombed, burned, and destroyed private homes and business establishments in five major cities in an effort to crush urban insurgency. In León, a conservative estimate of the damage to homes and commercial establishments was 500 million córdobas (*La Prensa*, September 19, 1978); in Masaya, damage to commercial establishments alone reached 100 million córdobas (*La Prensa*, October 15, 1978). In the country as a whole, some 3,000 persons lost employment because their workplaces were damaged, and 170,681 family housing units were damaged or lost (*La Prensa*, November 27, 1978). The massive, indiscriminate, destruction of urban Nicaragua rendered the civilian population vulnerable and forced ever greater numbers of people to seek alternative means both of protecting themselves and of removing Somoza. As a result, greater segments of the population threw their support behind the FSLN. Consequently, popular support for the Sandinistas surged, with sixteen recorded incidents of pro-FSLN actions carried out by the populace in different parts of the country.

Building on the foundation of its growing social support, the FSLN dramatically expanded its mobilization and multiplied its attacks against the government. Once again it captured national and international attention when on August 22, the FSLN's third faction, the Insurrectionalists, executed a bold operation that further enhanced the organization's position. Attacking the National Palace in broad daylight, Sandinista commandos took between 2,500 and 3,000 hostages, including congressional deputies, government officials such as the Minister of the Home Office, visitors, and journalists. This stunning raid netted some $500,000 in ransom, freedom for some fifty political prisoners, and enormous media publicity, with their statement published in all newspapers and broadcast over radio and television three times in a single day, all of which garnered more support for the FSLN.

As a result of these successes, membership in the FSLN grew from fewer than 100 in 1974 to approximately 700 by September 1978. The FSLN merged with another armed group, known as the Eleventh of November, and the three Sandinista factions announced that they had united in order to bring about the final overthrow of the Somoza regime. Furthermore, the Sandinistas' daring attacks enabled them for the first time to establish temporary control over parts of Nicaragua. In September, during a widespread insurgency against urban centers, FSLN guerrillas succeeded in occupying and controlling parts of seven cities, including León and Chinandega, the second and fourth largest cities in Nicaragua, thus briefly creating a situation of *de facto* dual sovereignty.

Sandinista seizure of power

During 1979, Nicaragua's economic and political situation deteriorated precipitously, with a corresponding slump in investment and employment.[7] The economy's rapid disintegration within the context of widespread political mobilization generated massive collective action in the form of general insurrection and enhanced support for the FSLN. The Sandinistas expanded their efforts to form still broader coalitions against the Somoza regime in the final months of the revolutionary conflicts. In February 1979, the FSLN organized the National Patriotic Front (FPN), which comprised the MPU, Los Doce, the Independent Liberal Party (PLI), CGT-I, CTN, the Workers' Front, the Popular Social Christian Party (PPSC), and the Union of Radio Journalists of Managua (*La Prensa*, February 13, 1979). This coalition, established to direct the anti-Somoza opposition, was deemed more likely to succeed where FAO had failed. Just one month before Somoza was finally driven from power, the Sandinistas proposed a 33-member quasi-legislative Council of State, which would include representatives from all political groups that opposed the regime.[8]

As evidence of the popular backing for the FSLN grew, symbols of support for the guerrilla organization proliferated in 1979. In January and February, the red and black flags of the FSLN began appearing in León, Jinotega, Matagalpa, and Boaco. On the morning of the forty-fifth anniversary of the death of Sandino, red and black flags materialized in different sections of León, Jinotega, and Corinto. In León, FSLN flags were even suspended from the light posts at intersections (*La Prensa*, February 21–23, 1979). On the first anniversary of an insurrection in Monimbó, an Indian neighborhood of Masaya, hundreds of FSLN flags were displayed by spectators assembled to hear speakers from MPU, FPN, and Archbishop Obando y Bravo, who presided over an afternoon mass (*La Prensa*, February 26, 1979). When five young FSLN supporters were killed by the National Guard in a church in León, delegates from more than twenty diverse organizations, including the Chamber of Commerce, occupied the church in protest (*La Prensa*, February 22, 1979).[9]

---

[7] For closings, see *La Prensa*, February 8, March 18, May 23, 1979; for divestiture, see *La Prensa*, May 10, 1979.

[8] The FSLN even admitted two business representatives to its five-member Government of National Reconstruction (Gorman 1986:15).

[9] These organizations were CUUN, the Commission of Human Rights of CUUN, Association of Professors of UNAN, Medical Society of León, Permanent Commission of Human Rights-León, Syndicate of Employees and Workers of UNAN, Syndicate of Hospital Workers, Association of Lawyers of León, Association of Independent Journalists, the Chamber of Commerce, UDEL, ANDEN, MDN, MPU, AMPRONAC, Interns and Residents of San Vincente Hospital, the Liberal Constitutional Movement, the Social Christian Party, SCAAS-León, and Religious Communities of León.

In Managua, a group of UNAN professors, students, and workers occupied the Ecclesiastical Curia for forty-eight hours to protest about these killings and request the Catholic Church to excommunicate Somoza (*La Prensa*, February 20, 1979).

Backed by a groundswell of popular support, the FSLN assumed indisputable control of the anti-government struggles. By early June, the Sandinistas controlled twenty-five towns and villages in the north of the country alone (Black 1981:155). With increased popular support, in a broadcast from Radio Sandino, the Sandinistas called upon business owners and workers to observe a nationwide general strike on June 4. FPN, MPU, and FAO all followed the FSLN's lead and supported the walkout (*La Prensa*, June 3, 1979). The strike, which lasted for six weeks, was observed by most businesses, workers, and students. The FSLN led armed insurrection in numerous communities and neighborhoods, and even some priests[10] and ministers joined the struggle.[11] FAO declared its support for the Sandinista-led Junta of the Government of National Reconstruction on June 24, and COSEP, representing business, followed suit three days later. With such broad support, the FSLN was in a realistic position to defeat the National Guard, which had remained fully loyal to Somoza.[12] On July 19, two days after Somoza departed from Nicaragua, FSLN troops entered Managua in triumph. The dynasty was finally overthrown.

Aquino assassination and the failure of the moderate opposition in the Philippines

More than a decade of exclusive rule and deteriorating economic conditions in the Philippines resulted in the polarization of the population and isolation of the Marcos regime. In the context of heightened polarization, the assassination of Benigno Aquino, a leading and popular opponent of Marcos, in late August 1983, resulted in popular mobilization and collective action. Although the initial reaction of the traditional opposition leaders had been to panic and search for sanctuary in guerrilla zones (Pimentel 1991:333), a broad array of opposition emerged shortly after news of the murder. Various social groups and classes mobilized and

---

[10] Father Gaspar Garcia Laviana, member of the Congregation of the Sacred Heart headquartered in Granada, left his parish to join FSLN guerrillas in the north of Nicaragua. He was killed in battle in Rivas (*La Prensa*, December 11, 1978).

[11] At least ten Protestant ministers either joined the FSLN in combat or organized on their behalf among their parishioners during the final insurrection (Dodson and O'Shaughnessy 1990:129; Montgomery 1982/1983:217).

[12] In 1978, there were fourteen cases, and in 1979 there were only five cases of desertions in the National Guard, as reported in *La Prensa*.

engaged in collective action. In contrast to the conflicts of the early 1970s when the principal protesters were students and workers, the protests and demonstrations that followed Aquino's assassination were largely undertaken by "popular groups," consisting of various segments of the population.

From the assassination in late August 1983 until the end of the year, various groups organized 149 demonstrations; popular groups, representing various actors, engaged in 103 demonstrations, more than any single social group. The main slogans of the demonstrators were political and directly targeted Marcos. The principal demands of the demonstrators included: justice for Aquino and freedom (102 demonstrations), an end to government repression (26 demonstrations) and Marcos' resignation (14 demonstrations). Two important facts emerge from the analysis of these demands. First, the predominant demand in the demonstrations revolved around the compelling but narrow issue of Aquino's assassination. Second, although demonstrators in seven demonstrations protested US imperialism and US military bases in the Philippines, these more radical demands were in the distinct minority. The inescapable conclusion is that most of these protests were led by moderate and conservative opposition forces who were protesting about the assassination, but who were not seeking major social transformation.

An unusual aspect of these protests was the mobilization of unlikely groups. Even professionals who generally remained nonpolitical joined the street demonstrations demanding that Marcos resign. In Makati's largest demonstration to date, some 20,000 professionals, including doctors, lawyers, dentists, and nurses, together with some students and Makati employees, staged a march for freedom and human rights. Two former Supreme Court justices joined the processional. One group of doctors carried signs proclaiming, "Doctors' advice: resign," while a physician toted a sign reading "More power to lupus erythematosus! Get him at once," and a dentist marched with a placard saying, "Fight truth decay." As the marchers passed by the Manila Bank building, a group of employees serenaded them with a popular children's song that ran, "Mother, Mother, I am sick/Call a doctor very quick/Doctor, Doctor, shall I die?/No, no, no, just resign." One banner read, "Galman is dead, but the gunman is alive"[13] (*Malaya*, November 14, 1983). In another event, professionals and students marched through the Makati financial district, shouting "Marcos, Marcos, resign" (*Malaya*, November 27, 1983).

[13] Rolando Galman, the alleged assassin, was gunned down by government troops at the airport immediately following Aquino's murder.

Another new development during this period was the mobilization of farmers and peasants. In 1984, they organized thirteen demonstrations demanding land reform, protesting against repression and, in one case, calling for a boycott of elections. In one demonstration, they issued a statement that condemned the government's land reform policies, which led to rising debt among farmers and forced them to join farmers' organizations (*Malaya*, October 6, 1984). Farmers and peasants organized twenty demonstrations the following year, issued nine statements, and organized one strike. Again they called for land reform and protested against government repression, which had resulted in the detention of more peasants than any other single group in the country (*Malaya*, August 3, 1985). As their economic situation deteriorated, they protested about high interest rates and foreign influences in agricultural policies. Their statements also protested against the high cost of farm production, demanded the abolition of the Rice Institute, and deplored the lack of land reform.

The large-scale, anti-government protests had rendered the regime vulnerable and, in the absence of any resolution, protests in the next two years intensified and became increasingly radical. The number of demonstrations increased from 149 in the last four months of 1983, to 266 in 1984 and a high of 389 in 1985. Demonstrators protested against government repression in at least 290 events during 1984 and 1985. More importantly, the moderate opposition's failure to remove Marcos from power resulted in a greater shift in favor of radicals. Nationalist and leftist radicals expanded their mobilization and attacked both Marcos and the United States. As a result, attacks against what was labeled the US–Marcos dictatorship increased to at least sixty-five events, while the issue of justice for Aquino and freedom declined drastically to only fourteen events. Demonstrators turned to broader political issues. Protestors opposed the US–Marcos dictatorship and attacked Marcos' economic system of crony businesses and their foreign investments. With the radicalization of protestors, the final stage of the Philippine political struggles became increasingly anti-American, much more than in Iran and Nicaragua.

Ultimately, the widespread mobilization and collective actions proved fruitless as a means of removing Marcos from power because of political divisions and absence of broad coalitions. One important factor responsible for this failure was the existence of unbridgeable divisions within the elite opposition. Moderate, cause-oriented political organizations were deeply divided and unable to exert hegemony. Justice for Aquino, Justice for All (JAJA) comprised dozens of organizations, which united to demand the resignation of Marcos, his entire cabinet, the Executive Committee, members of the National Assembly, and the top military generals; the release of all political prisoners; and the restoration of democracy and constitutional rights. But the components of JAJA were split over the nature of a transition government and the issue of foreign intervention (Diokno 1988:135). JAJA's inability to lead resulted in the formation of another organization: Coalition of Organizations for Restoration of Democracy (CORD). CORD, which included fifty-seven cause-oriented organizations pledged to oppose Marcos (*Malaya*, June 25, 1984), was no more successful in agreeing on goals and approaches. The August Twenty-One Movement (ATOM), headed by Agapito "Butz" Aquino, was also divided within itself. In 1985 Aquino was unable to convince other members of ATOM to join Bandila (*Malaya*, July 22, 1985), yet another umbrella group formed by some seventy organizations under the auspices of liberal democrats, mostly businessmen and professionals.

Schisms within and between political parties and social movement organizations made it impossible for the opposition to present a single front against Marcos. For example, the August Twenty-One Movement was the only organization that called for a general strike on November 28; other organizations did not endorse the call and most people ignored the announcement (*Malaya*, November 30, 1983). Similarly, attempts to unite the opposition prior to the May elections for the National Assembly were rather unsuccessful. In January 1984, social democratic groups joined Makati-based organizations in convening a Congress of the Filipino People (Kompil). The Congress presented a list of demands to Marcos to serve as a basis for participating in the election. When Marcos rejected the demands, the opposition groups and parties could not agree on whether to campaign or boycott the election. Some fifty organizations belonging to various coalitions whose members included the radical left, most social democrats, and the old nationalists, chose to boycott the election. The left wing of the old Liberal Party also boycotted. PDP-Laban (Philippine Democratic Party–People Power) faced an internal crisis with its younger, more ideologically oriented faction favoring a boycott of the election, while its traditional politicians preferred to participate. Eventually, a compromise was reached that allowed local party units of the PDP-Laban to act independently, even though the party itself was officially pro-boycott. Despite some alliances, the opposition remained highly fragmented as a total of forty-three distinct political parties took part in the elections for the National Assembly (*Malaya*, May 14, 1984).

Most importantly, a deep division existed between the two major social classes that prevented the formation of a class coalition. Such a coalition would have been essential for disruptive tactics, such as general strikes, to paralyze the social structure and government functioning. Threatened by rising radicalism and militancy among workers and students in cities and the NPA in the countryside, Filipino capitalists failed or refused to initiate national strikes, which would have escalated the conflicts and disrupted the production and distribution process. Instead, rising labor militancy and the increased power of the radical left resulted in the fact that capitalists became increasingly dependent on the state for protection. As a result, Filipino capitalists did not embrace the use of disruptive tactics to remove Marcos from power.

Existing divisions only benefited Marcos. With the opposition rendered virtually impotent by extreme factionalism, Marcos moved to widen their divisions and encourage the population to choose the traditional, nonrevolutionary means of protesting by ballot, where he had greater control, and to repress those who favored more radical options. That he succeeded in this effort was shown in the high voter turn-out of 89 percent (Timberman 1991:147), even though the election was marred by massive fraud, according to the National Citizens' Movement for a Free Election (*Malaya*, May 15, 1984). With the organization and assistance of 290,000 members of his KBL Party (New Society Movement), serving as councilmen and captains of barangays (the basic political unit of the Philippines) in more than 21,000 citizens' assemblies, Marcos was able to influence the election results. Opponents charged that 613 ballot boxes were "carted off," and that voting conditions in two-thirds of the country were "intolerable" (Rush 1986b:7). Marcos also attempted to buy votes by announcing salary increases for government employees and paying people to take part in a pre-election rally (Kessler 1984:1221). Despite manipulation and fraud, the opposition won fifteen of twenty-one seats in Metro Manila (ibid.:1209). Nationwide, Marcos was successful at using fraud to insure that only 64 of the 183 seats went to the least threatening, most conservative segments of the opposition.[14] In so doing, Marcos was able to coopt the traditional politicians and political organizations, which posed less of a threat to his rule, rather than the more militant groups and parties that had boycotted the election.

Existing divisions also enabled Marcos to use repression against the more radical organizations to prevent them from mobilizing. From 1977 to 1985, 17,723 people were arrested, 599 political prisoners were incarcerated in 110 detention camps, and 383 prisoners were tortured (*Malaya*, November 28, 1985). The stepped-up mobilization by leftist

[14] The opposition won 64 seats (including 4 for Roy's wing of the Nacionalista Party, which had broken from Marcos). Most of the victorious candidates belonged either to UNIDO, with 49 seats, or PDP-Laban with 6. KBL won 112 of the seats, and 7 went to independents (Kessler 1984:1223; Kimura 1991:216).

and militant groups in 1985 was met with intensified government repression, with 7,253 persons arrested, 43 disappeared, and 517 slain (Kessler 1989:137). Some demonstrations even ended in wholesale massacres. During a "people's strike" in the town of Escalante, for example, 27 sugar workers were killed by the military (*Malaya*, September 25, 1985). Like Iran and Nicaragua, the government also used an unidentified gang of vicious killers to eliminate opponents. This unofficial repression was responsible for the deaths of at least 172 people in Manila during a period of six weeks in 1984 (*Malaya*, March 22, 1984). The Philippine Conference for Human Rights denounced the Marcos dictatorship's intensified campaign of military terrorism (*Malaya*, August 19, 1984), in which more than 100 people were slain. But similar killings continued.

Failure of the powerful revolutionary challengers

Unlike Iran and Nicaragua, the Philippines had a thriving, armed radical left, which represented a viable, revolutionary alternative to the existing regime by 1986. The imposition of martial law in 1972 and repression of the moderates expanded the influence of the radical left in the Philippines. In fact, concerned about the rising strength of the left, Ninoy Aquino had decided to go back to the Philippines to prevent the communists from taking advantage of the political vacuum in case of Marcos' death (Ambassador Sedfrey Ordonez, interview, May 1999). After his assassination, the failure of the elite to remove Marcos from power opened a more favorable condition for revolutionary challengers to overthrow the regime. As the influence of moderate political organizations in popular collective actions declined, radical challengers and organizations did expand and increase their mobilization against Marcos.

Although the Communist Party of the Philippines (CPP) was relatively small in the early 1970s, the imposition of martial law, massive government repression, military brutality, and the absence of alternative options contributed to the party's expansion. In particular, government repression of the student movement in the early 1970s converted and impelled some nationalist students into the radical camp. This trend was furthered under martial law (Chapman 1987: 83–84, 100), when many of these students became interested in pursuing armed struggle against the regime. The New People's Army (NPA), the armed wing of the Communist Party, was obliged to turn away some of these members because it lacked sufficient arms (Timberman 1991:88). By early 1986, CPP leaders claimed more than 30,000 members with a nationwide "mass base" of 1 million (Chapman 1987:14). Local party cadres had infiltrated one-quarter of the country's 41,600 barrios where, in many places, underground committees of the National Democratic Front had become the *de facto* government (ibid.:238).

More than a decade earlier, the Communist Party had also expanded its activities among various segments of the urban population by establishing the National Democratic Front (NDF) in 1973. Intended to unite all those opposed to the "US–Marcos dictatorship," the NDF embraced teachers, workers, women's groups, and students, as well as Christians for National Liberation (CNL). Most of the organization's rank-and-file members were students, poor farmers, and workers; its largest components were the Revolutionary Workers, the Revolutionary Movement of Peasants, Kabataang Makabayan, and CNL. The NDF also embraced religious organizations and clergy. By the late 1970s, CNL had become an open participant in the NDF (Wurfel 1988:217), and even two bishops were open supporters. Significantly, no less than 53 percent of all labor strikes and protests in 1985 were attributed to the communists by a ranking constabulary intelligence officer (*Malaya*, July 18, 1985).[15]

To expand its capacity in the struggle, in 1985 the NDF formed Bayan, or New Nationalist Alliance, a broad coalition of about five hundred leftist and nationalist forces. By 1986, Bayan claimed more than 1 million members (*Manila Times*, February 12, 1986).[16] Major organizations within Bayan included the KMU, the League of Filipino Students, the Nationalist Alliance for Justice, Freedom, and Democracy – itself composed of a dozen or so organizations – the Alliance of Concerned Teachers, the Movement of Farmers of the Philippines, and the NDF. Bayan quickly became dominated by left-leaning factions, notably the NDF, which won 29 of 132 seats in the Filipino National Assembly (Villegas 1986a:130). The radicals and militants, under the umbrella of Bayan, were always better organized and launched larger demonstrations than the moderates. For example, on August 21, 1985, for the commemoration of Aquino's murder, Bayan organized a demonstration of 40,000, which marched on the Mendiola bridge and confronted police at the entrance to Malacañang, the presidential residence. The same day, the moderate opposition, consisting of Bandila, UNIDO (United Nationalist Democratic Opposition), and others, observed the anniversary of Aquino's murder with a rally at Makati's central plaza, which was attended by only 20,000 people (Rush 1986c:6).

---

[15] My data indicate that in 1985, 43 percent of popular collective actions in the form of demonstrations were led by Bayan (see below).

[16] Bayan was formed through the efforts of Tanada, Diokno, and "Butz" Aquino. Diokno was president, Tanada served as chairman, and Bayan's elected council of "national leaders" included militant labor leader, Rolando Olalia.

More impressive for the left were the gains of their armed wing, the NPA, which was influential in the countryside. In September 1972, the NPA's troop strength was estimated between 1,000 and 2,000, according to government officials; by February 1986, the estimate had grown to 20,000 (Kessler 1989:56), with perhaps half that number in armed, local militia units (Chapman 1987:14). The NPA took advantage of a vacuum created by absentee landlordism and the concentration of elites in Manila to extend its influence in the countryside (Kessler 1989:20). NPA operations in such areas provoked the military and drew the rural population into a new set of conflicts. To root out the NPA, the armed forces resorted to detaining citizens without charges, to torture, murder, illegal wholesale searches of entire barrios, and even a form of "strategic hamletting," i.e., total destruction of villages (ibid.:180), used also by Somoza in Nicaragua during martial law. The NPA benefited from the resultant erosion of support for the military among peasants and farmers.

By 1985 the NPA was active in sixty-two of the country's seventy-three provinces and controlled or influenced at least 20 percent of the barangays. Although the NPA did not control any part of the country in the strict sense, in many villages it collected taxes, exacted sanctions, directed communal work, and provided medical and municipal services such as health and sanitation (ibid.:14). The NPA also used its coercive powers to obtain higher wages for rural workers and lower land rents and interest payments for tenants (ibid.127). According to Filipino officials, the NPA also stepped up its operations against the government. According to Deputy Chief of Staff, Fidel Ramos, insurgency-related incidents by the NPA rose by 25 percent during the year, to an average of thirteen incidents each day, compared with ten during the first three months of 1984. Ramos also reported that an average of seven guerrillas a day were being killed, compared with three in 1984, along with an average of three government personnel and four civilians slain. The NPA further expanded its operations in 1985. It even dared to organize events close to Manila. In a provocative move in September 1985, the NPA even organized a funeral for one of its slain members in Bulacan, a mere forty-five minutes' drive from Manila. Some 1,000 members and supporters participated in the funeral and sang "The Internationale" (*Malaya*, September 30, 1985).

The growing strength of the NPA became a source of concern for both the United States and Filipino capitalists. Officials and managers of private sugar-producing firms in Negros Occidental expressed concern over the infiltration of the island's farms by "subversives" (*Malaya*, May 5, 1985). The American ambassador Stephen Bosworth (interview, August 1998) noted that the growing strength of the NPA became a matter of concern in the final years of the Marcos regime. The USA was also concerned about Marcos' inability to deal effectively with the insurgents. In 1985, US State Department analysts predicted a strategic stalemate between the NPA and the Philippine armed forces was likely in three years (Chapman 1987:232–233). Alarmed by NPA operations in 1985, Marcos even threatened to use foreign troops if the infiltration and subversion by communist insurgents proved overwhelming (*Malaya*, June 2, 1985).

Despite the NPA's growing presence, the leftists, militants, and the NPA were not in position to overthrow the government by themselves. By itself armed struggle in the countryside would have been inadequate to overthrow Marcos. By the mid-1980s, the NPA still had only some 12,000 modern automatic rifles, a grossly inadequate supply compared with Marcos' army of 250,000 (Chapman 1987:121). In addition, most of the NPA's estimated 1 million-plus backers were farmers (ibid.130). Furthermore, although the leaders of the NPA and NDF were educated middle-class men and women, the organization did not enjoy much support from the middle class. As late as 1986, the NDF's leaders estimated that 90 percent of its members in Manila, where the country's middle class was concentrated, were workers and urban poor (ibid.:218). Thus, the revolutionaries had to form a coalition with other challengers.

These revolutionaries did attempt to enter into a broader coalition with the moderate opposition in 1985, but this effort soon failed. A number of leading opposition figures, including Tanada, Diokno, "Butz" Aquino, Jaime Ongpin – a leading businessman and advisor to Corazon Aquino – and the labor leader, Rolando Olalia, all promoted such a coalition. The coalition actually came together, but quickly fell apart when most of the moderates withdrew because the leftist NDF insisted upon a larger number of seats than its coalition partners. This demand was rejected by moderates Aquino, Ongpin, and Diokno (ibid.:223), who left the organization and instead organized Bandila, or Banner. Thereafter, moderates and radicals rarely cooperated (Goodno 1991:87). Even during major events, such as the second anniversary of Aquino's murder on August 21, moderates and radicals could not hold joint actions (*Malaya*, August 22, 1985). Though the two groups did demonstrate side by side to protest against the acquittal of Armed Forces chief, General Fabian Ver, and twenty-five others accused of Aquino's murder, a formal coalition never emerged (*Malaya*, December 4, 1985).

The revolutionaries, by themselves, initiated a new repertoire of collective action in the final stage of the conflicts. These were several *welgang bayan*, or people's strikes, organized by Bayan, in highly militarized areas in the south, in August and September 1985. The simultaneous strikes undertaken by transportation and manufacturing workers, and students paralyzed an entire city or region. These general strikes were held in the south of the country initially as part of an experiment that was to be introduced throughout the country. Participants made primarily political demands, such as for the dismantling of the Marcos dictatorship, an end to repression, and genuine land reform, together with condemnation of the militarization of the region.

Had general strikes spread to the rest of the country, they could have had a decisive impact on the outcome of the conflicts. Combined with armed uprising, as occurred in Nicaragua, the *welgang bayan* had the potential to influence the outcome in the direction of a social revolution. But, under pressure from the United States, Marcos announced a snap presidential election in early November 1985, which proved to be a major setback for the leftist challengers. The election narrowed the options to two elite candidates, virtually excluding the left, which could not have benefited from any presidential election where Marcos was in charge. Predictably, Bayan called for a boycott of the election, which in the end had the effect of reducing popular support for the organization (Chapman 1987:242; Goodno 1991:91). Although Bayan remained one of the most powerful organizations in the country, it lost the momentum in the conflict once the options were reduced by the electoral contest between two elite factions .

Election stalemate, military split, and popular uprising

The militant gains, worsening economic conditions, and Marcos' deteriorating health were factors impelling the USA to ensure a stable succession, even though Marcos' term was set until 1987. But, for the first time since he imposed martial law, Marcos could not fully control the processes that began to unfold after his announcement of the special election. He secretly attempted to manipulate the Supreme Court, which he had long been able to control, into invalidating the election (Chapman 1987:236). Now, however, that body was more autonomous as a result of popular mobilization and US pressure. Marcos' control failed, and the court rejected his plan. Marcos' own coalitions were clearly weakening, and his forces were so disorganized that they were unable to secure his victory in this election with the ease of previous occasions.

As in earlier elections, the opposition, too, was disorganized and divided along political and ideological lines: UNIDO and PDP-Laban, led by Corazon Aquino, represented the conservative reformists; CORD, the successor to JAJA, represented the liberal democrats. Radical forces, which chose to boycott the election, included the Communist Party of the Philippines, the NPA, the NDF, and Bayan (Lande 1986:125). The moderates and conservatives chose to participate in the election, but as before, they were divided over the selection of a presidential candidate. As early as 1984, a group of businessmen and professionals had begun to devise a plan to choose a candidate in case of a sudden presidential election.[17] Despite much effort, they were unable to decide on a single candidate. The divisions within the opposition were so intense that ten opposition members of the National Assembly announced a fast to protest against disunity among the opposition and the lack of a candidate in case of a special election (*Malaya*, April 25, 1985).

As the possibility grew that a special election would be held, a new organization, the Cory Aquino for President Movement, emerged on October 15 with the purpose of drafting Aquino's widow as a candidate. By November 25, scarcely three weeks after Marcos officially announced the early election, the Cory Aquino for President Movement had gathered 1 million signatures on petitions urging her candidacy (*Malaya*, November 26, 1985). She and the other leading opposition candidate, Salvador Laurel, although competitors, were eventually united on a single ticket, partly as the result of the mediation of Cardinal Sin and partly out of their own family ties. The sudden, unexpected solidification of the opposition stunned Marcos (Almendral 1988: 189).

Aware of the diverse demands and claims of different social groups and classes, Corazon Aquino proposed a number of reforms in order to build a broad coalition and win the election. She promised the Makati business community that she would reduce government intervention in the economy. She also outlined eight principal areas of concern: equitable distribution of land to solve the problems of farmers and the rural poor; elimination of repression directed against labor; solution of the housing problem by creating employment for the urban poor; government aid to assist Muslims and tribal minorities to develop autonomously; health; and education; a cease fire, halt to insurgency and the release of political prisoners; and attention to women's issues (Schirmer and Shalom 1987:338–343).

As usual, the election was marred by fraud and violence. On election day, despite the presence of international observers, at least 3.3 million

---

[17] In November of 1984, Tanada, Corazon Aquino, and Ongpin became the convenors to implement the plan. At the same time, UNIDO organized the National Unification Committee to select candidates for local and presidential elections scheduled for 1986 and 1987. Although the two groups were critical of each other (Kimura 1991:216–217), a breakthrough occurred in April 1985 when they agreed to narrow the choice to one candidate each from the Liberal Party, the Nacionalista Party, UNIDO, PDP-Laban, and Bayan.

people were disenfranchised by having their names removed from voters' rolls and by threats of violence (Villegas 1987:195). Fifty-six persons were killed in election-related violence (*Malaya*, February 8, 1986). After the polling was completed, both sides claimed victory. US President Reagan accused both sides of fraud and suggested that Aquino concede defeat and wait for the next election, despite the fact that Ambassador Bosworth and the US embassy in Manila favored Aquino (Almendral 1988:207). In the face of the Filipinos' strong negative reaction to its earlier position, the White House reversed itself and cast doubts upon the official election results, which showed Marcos to be the winner (Wurfel 1988:301).

At this point, the elite opposition had no option but to initiate disruptive collective action. They began planning a general strike, while Corazon Aquino's supporters in Davao City prepared to establish a provisional revolutionary government. The Catholic bishops issued one statement condemning government fraud and another calling for a "non-violent struggle for justice" to force the government to respect the people's mandate for change (*Malaya*, February 16, 1986). To force Marcos out, the opposition launched a campaign of non-cooperation by upper- and middle-class groups, including activities such as boycotting crony businesses, banks, the press, luxury stores, and utilities. As soon as the boycott went into effect, the stock exchange experienced a massive slump (Almendral 1988:209). The opposition drew up plans for a series of organized actions to further cripple the Marcos regime. Even Bayan, the NDF, and the KMU, all of which had boycotted the elections, offered to support these protests organized by the Aquino camp.

In the midst of feverish activity by the anti-Marcos forces, the last bastion of Marcos' support, the armed forces, suddenly fractured, setting in motion a process that quickly drove Marcos from the Philippines. The armed forces had played an increasingly significant role in the country since the imposition of martial law, enabling Marcos to consolidate his hold on power and carry out his plans. In the process, the size and expenditures of the armed forces had grown substantially.

As the military played a greater role in the Philippines, segments of it accumulated grievances over the years with regard to the way in which the armed forces were organized. An important division existed in the armed forces due to the alternative recruitment channels. About 50 percent of the officers were recruited from the graduates of the Philippine Military Academy. The rest were given Reserve Officer Training Corps commissions after finishing a university degree (Wurfel 1988:301). A new division emerged as a result of the politicization of promotions in the military. Many officers were adversely affected because of their inability to rise in rank, as senior ranks were monopolized by Marcos' supporters and loyalists. In 1981, General Fidel Ramos, a West Point-trained professional and favorite of academy graduates, was bypassed for Armed Forces Chief of Staff in favor of Ver, Marcos' cousin and former bodyguard, who came from the reserve officer corps that had been integrated into regular service (ibid.:240). In 1984, Ramos, the country's most respected military leader, offered to resign in protest against the fact that the military would be under the command of a crony who was universally resented (Overholt 1986:1159). Marcos and General Ver gutted the Constabulary, which had been run by Ramos, and throughout the armed forces they sidetracked the careers of professional officers in favor of pro-Marcos personnel (ibid.:1152). Some of the country's military officers were exiled in 1984 because Marcos wanted to insure military backing for his policies (ibid.:1142). As a result of these adverse policies, a number of military officers also defected from the Marcos camp and sought asylum in the United States (Almendral 1988:199).

Inevitably, military support for Marcos declined and he was obliged to rely increasingly on a small group of his most loyal generals. By 1985, twenty-seven of the armed forces' sixty generals were "overstaying," i.e., had reached the point of retirement but were remaining out of loyalty to Marcos (Timberman 1991:137).

Numerous grievances and low morale characterized the lower echelon of the armed forces. Low pay was one problem for the lower echelon. To boost soldiers' morale, Ramos announced a government plan to raise the pay of enlisted Constabulary personnel by 32 percent and officers by 17 percent (*Malaya*, October 31, 1985).

These adverse conditions impelled a group of "reformist" officers to form an organization known as RAM, or Reform the Armed Forces Movement. RAM, whose members came from the Philippine Military Academy (*Malaya*, May 16, 1985), initiated a process to bring about changes within the military and present a better image. Its members established contact with various sectors of society, including the Church, business, students, teachers, and social movements (Almendral 1988:193). A group of moderate officers even announced a plan to participate in a dialogue with pro-Aquino leaders in a move toward reconciliation (*Malaya*, December 30, 1984).

The leaders of RAM plotted a *coup d'état* to be pulled off on January 1, 1986, but the special election caused them to postpone their plans. During the electoral campaign, RAM held a series of prayer seminars around the country on campaign issues and, despite threat of punishment from Marcos, sent at least 40,000 letters to soldiers, government officials, and teachers to explain their objectives (Youngblood 1987:1246). During the presidential campaign, RAM leaders contacted Corazon Aquino and pledged their support, although their original plan had not included her in their new government.

Feuding within the Marcos regime was further deepened in the aftermath of the special election, particularly between those who backed General Ver and supporters of Defense Minister Juan Ponce Enrile. When Enrile discovered that he and other RAM members were slated to be arrested, he decided to revolt and was joined by Ramos. The number of rebels occupying two adjacent camps in Manila on Saturday, February 22, initially only 300, grew to some 500 by Sunday afternoon (Johnson 1987:14). The rebels were soon forced to seek help from Corazon Aquino's camp and the Church to protect themselves from forces loyal to Marcos. Troops dispatched by General Ver failed to destroy the rebellion, as an outpouring of massive popular opposition made it impossible for the officers to carry out their orders (Almendral 1988:218). By Monday night, most members of the armed forces had switched sides to join the rebels, and Ramos claimed that 90 percent of the country's 250,000 military troops were now under his control (Rush 1986d:6).

In open defiance of Marcos' orders, millions of civilians surged into the streets, troops deserted, and those who remained loyal to the president could not or would not carry out his orders. These four days of "people power" finally won the support of the USA, which appealed to Marcos to leave quickly and definitively. Marcos lost no time and fled the Philippines on February 25, 1986. An elite democracy was restored.

Conclusion

In the absence of prior state breakdown or military victory by insurgents, formation of a broad coalition was an important factor for the success of revolutionary challengers and removal of the powerholders. In particular, class coalition seems to have played an important role in the success of opposition. Absence of coalitions in Iran in the early 1960s and in Nicaragua and the Philippines in the early 1970s prevented the removal of these regimes from power. Broad coalitions were formed at a later point in both Iran and Nicaragua and were followed by disruptive collective action. In both countries, the low level of class conflict and weakness of ideologically driven challengers, especially in the initial stages of the conflicts, facilitated coalitions. In contrast, in the Philippines, rising class conflict and strength of revolutionary challengers prevented the formation of a class coalition for more than two years. Although workers and capitalists opposed Marcos, they failed to join a coalition to remove him from power. As capitalists became increasingly dependent on the state for stability and the maintenance of the social structure, they attempted to change the system through nondisruptive mechanisms. In the end, moderate challengers succeeded in seizing power because the military became paralyzed and was unable to repress the opposition.

In Iran, the organizational and political weaknesses of leftist challengers and the absence of class conflict among workers and bazaaris facilitated the formation of a broad coalition. The coalition succeeded in disrupting production, distribution, and services, and through the oil strikes paralyzed the economy and deprived the state of revenues. These disruptions were crucial inasmuch as they increased desertions in the armed forces and forced the West, especially the United States, to demand that the Shah leave. The departure of the Shah paralyzed the conscript-based military, which had been subject to increased defections and desertions. Eventually, two days of popular uprising sealed the fate of the monarchy and ushered in the transfer of power to an Islamic regime.

Khomeini became the acknowledged leader of the coalition because of government repression and the weaknesses of secular challengers. In his public statements to the Iranian people, Khomeini never stated his goal of establishing an Islamic theocracy. Instead, Khomeini's basic ideological pronouncements closely followed those of the National Front. Among the principles he advocated were freedom and independence while he was in exile, and greater social justice after his return to Iran.

Similarly, in Nicaragua, in 1978 a broad coalition was formed, which initiated disruptive collective action to remove Somoza from power. Unlike the early 1970s, when class conflict was substantial, the intensity of such conflict during the revolutionary struggles was reduced, as workers largely targeted the state rather than the capitalist class. As in Iran, the weaknesses of revolutionary challengers, the Sandinistas, in the early stages of the conflicts facilitated the formation of moderate-led coalitions. The moderates unequivocally broke away from the Somoza regime, but failed to remove him from power, despite launching disruptive collective action. Somoza's refusal to hold an electoral contest brushed aside the moderate opposition and encouraged the leadership of the FSLN to wage armed struggle.

The Sandinistas were swift in taking advantage of the situation, modifying their ideological claims and forming a fateful coalition with dissident intellectuals and middle-class professionals known as Los Doce, which played an important role for the advocacy of their cause in the country and abroad. Ultimately, armed struggle became the most important means of overthrowing the regime, because the National Guard remained loyal to Somoza until the end. Consequently, the Sandinistas, who had shifted their armed struggle from rural areas to urban areas toward the end of 1977, were in a good position to combine general strikes with armed struggle in the final phase of the conflicts. The ultimate outcome was the victory of social revolutionaries.

In the Philippines, the increasing threat from radical forces and rising class conflict prevented the formation of a broad coalition. In the meantime, US pressures led Marcos to hold a snap election, which narrowed the options in favor of elite candidates and inevitably excluded the revolutionary challengers. A stalemate resulted after a disputed election that was followed by defections within the highest echelons of the armed forces. In the end, popular mobilization in favor of Corazon Aquino disrupted transportation and prevented the movement of loyal troops to confront the defectors. The paralysis of the loyal forces and threat of further deterioration of conditions compelled the United States to ask Marcos to leave the country. The outcome was the success of the moderate political forces, the restoration of elite power, and little in the way of social change. Without the defection of some top leaders of the military, this outcome would not have been likely.

The effectiveness of the military and the solidarity structures of the armed forces also played a significant role in the outcome of the conflicts. Preexisting divisions and lack of complete control over the military may be a cause for defection, rebellion, or the breakdown of the armed forces. Solidarity within the armed forces and the relationship between the military and the civilian population clearly affected the effectiveness of the armed forces. Armies that are staffed by conscripts are particularly vulnerable to schisms and defection because the conscripts often maintain extensive contact with the civilian population. Such extensive contact between the conscripts and the civilians in the context of broad coalitions proved detrimental for the regime in Iran. In contrast, when the armed forces are kept isolated from the civilian population, they may be used more effectively in times of insurgency. The isolation of the National Guard from the population in Nicaragua proved beneficial to the regime as the Guard fought against the insurgents until the end. In the Philippines, incomplete control over the armed forces and preexisting divisions within the military proved fateful in the outcome. The divisions eventually resulted in rebellion and defections as popular struggles deepened the crisis.

Finally, external forces also played a role in the outcome of the conflicts. In all three cases, the United States, in an effort to avoid more extreme outcomes, prepared conditions for transfer of power and even urged the rulers to leave office. The United States was clearly successful in this regard in the case of Iran, but failed in the case of Nicaragua. In the Philippines, the United States finally succeeded in convincing Marcos to leave the country. Had the United States failed, the opposition would have had to resort to disruptive economic tactics, which were already in the planning stage during the stalemate. In that case, the outcome of the struggles would have been less predictable. Indeed, the Philippines might have followed the same route as Nicaragua.

9   Summary and conclusions

Social revolutions are very complex phenomena and are affected by various social, political, economic, and historical forces. No single theory or model can explain all the processes that result in revolutions. This research attempts to develop a model of Third World revolutions by linking structural and process approaches. This synthetic perspective is rooted in an analysis of state structures, process approaches that predict the eruption of social conflicts, and those variables that facilitate coalition formation and the disruption of the social structure. Each perspective contributed to our understanding of the very complex processes that culminate in large-scale social conflicts and revolutions in developing countries. Structural theories analyze the structures of the state and the economy in the context of the larger world system, the structure of the state and the polity, as well as the state's relation to various social classes. Variables that analyze the nature of the state are central to the study of revolutions. These variables help illuminate the extent of state vulnerabilities and the likelihood of the state being targeted for attack. These variables also enhance understanding of the extent of popular opposition to the state in times of social conflict. Resource mobilization variables help explain the timing and nature of social conflict and collective action. Political process theories analyze the likelihood of coalition formation and the disruption of the social structure. Finally, it is important to analyze the conditions that favor the ascendancy of radical challengers and lead to social revolutions. This multifaceted approach has proved a worthy, comprehensive guide throughout this research.

The three cases of Iran, Nicaragua, and the Philippines proved to be very useful for applying the theoretical model. All three experienced large-scale social conflicts in the 1970s and 1980s because they had generated many of the structural features that render states vulnerable to such conflicts. In addition, the three countries were useful for the study of revolution because they all had periods of insurgency that failed to effect changes in the economic or political structures. Powerholders simply succeeded in repressing the opposition and continued to stay in

279

power. These negative experiences proved valuable for measuring the validity of the model. Most importantly, the three cases diverged in the ultimate outcome of their conflicts, thereby allowing a useful comparative analysis of large-scale social conflicts. Table 10 highlights some of the findings.

The preceding analysis demonstrates that exclusive rule, centralization of power, and high level of intervention render states vulnerable to conflict and challenge. States in Iran, Nicaragua, and the Philippines became increasingly centralized, exclusive, and interventionist. In each of the cases, economic and political development interfaced in such a manner that the state came under the exclusive control of rulers who centralized power during periods of political crises, which involved nationalist, socialist, or reformist movements. These regimes established political systems that were unaccountable to any domestic social or political forces. The regimes in Iran and Nicaragua succeeded in establishing dynasties that lasted for decades. In these dynasties, power was transferred from father to son with no option for others to gain control over state power. Although autonomy and centralization also characterized the Marcos regime, he ruled under different historical and political conditions and could not establish a dynasty. But Marcos retained power well beyond his legitimate two terms and was ousted unwillingly from office.

As these cases demonstrate, exclusive rule has crucial consequences. Exclusive rule narrows the social base of support for the state. These conditions in turn force the state to rely on external support and coercive apparatus. With reduced social support, the rulers in all three countries managed to gain the backing of the United States, a willing ally that was also interested in weakening or repressing nationalist and socialist movements. Substantial American political, economic, and military support further enhanced the position of these rulers. To maintain power, these regimes also relied heavily on the armed forces. All three expanded the size, equipment, and salaries of the armed forces to ensure repression of the opposition.

But in the long run neither external support nor the armed forces succeeded in protecting these regimes. Reliance on the armed forces rendered these governments vulnerable particularly where the military had weak solidarity structures. Under popular insurgency, the regimes in both Iran and the Philippines could not continue to rely on the armed forces because preexisting divisions and incomplete control led to defections and rebellions. Although Somoza's National Guard, staffed by professionals and insulated from civilians, proved loyal, it failed to maintain power once large-scale disruptive actions were combined with popular armed insurrections.

Table 10   *The nature of the state, challengers, and outcomes in comparative perspective*

Variables and outcomes	Country		
	Iran	Nicaragua	Philippines
State power	Exclusive/ centralized	Exclusive/ centralized	Exclusive/ centralized
State repression of moderate opposition	Extreme	High	Moderate
State intervention	Extreme	Medium, expanded	Low, expanded
Popular opposition and collective action	Initially low	High	High
Class coalition	Present	Present	Absent
Revolutionary challengers	Initially weak	Initially weak	Initially strong
Transformations			
In the class structure	Medium	High	None
In the power structure	Radical theocrats	Revolutionary socialists	Reformist bourgeois
Outcomes	Social revolution	Social revolution	Political revolution

State repression of the elite and moderate opposition also had significant consequences. In particular, the weakening or elimination of moderate opposition provided an opportunity for radical and militant challengers to gain the leadership of the opposition. Extreme repression of moderate opposition weakened the capacity of the moderates for mobilization and could force them to accept the hegemony of the radicals. In the long term, repression also led to the radicalization of segments of the population, particularly students. Finally, repression clearly affected the mobilization options available in the next rounds of conflicts.

As table 10 demonstrates, the extent of the repression of the moderate opposition varied in the three cases. The variation helps explain a part of the variation in the outcome of the cases. The Iranian government used extreme repression and virtually eliminated the moderate opposition. The Shah repressed virtually every social organization, from independent political parties to the merchant guild to students' organizations and labor unions. The only institution able to retain an independent network and some measure of autonomy *vis-à-vis* the state was the mosque. This policy contributed to eventual social revolution in Iran. On the other hand, the Nicaraguan and the Philippines governments permitted the moderates to survive. But the moderate opposition experienced different fates in the latter two countries. During the revolutionary conflicts in 1978, the Nicaraguan government continued to repress and exclude the moderates from the polity. Somoza's intransigence in dealing with the moderate opposition also narrowed the mobilization options and prepared the ground for radical challengers to lead the insurgency. This situation contributed to the outcome of social revolution in Nicaragua. The Marcos regime, despite violating the constitution, did permit the existence of many social, economic, and political organizations. Most importantly, in the context of popular mobilization in 1984, Marcos even allowed the moderate opposition to participate and win some seats in elections for the National Assembly. While this policy deepened the schism between radicals and moderates, it practically isolated the radicals at least for a short period of time, but improved the position of the moderates for further mobilization. In the final weeks of the conflicts, Marcos even held a snap presidential election and allowed the moderates to run for the office. The election further enhanced the capacity of the moderates to mobilize and ultimately contributed to the absence of social revolution in the Philippines. *Moderates elected*

State intervention also affected the nature of economic development and eventually the conflicts. Despite impressive growth, increased state intervention in all three cases was also accompanied by development strategies that adversely affected certain social classes and set the stage for social conflicts, once again making the state the target of attack. Although autonomous and not accountable to any particular class, state intervention was often far from neutral and did not serve "national" or "societal" interests. As a result, state development strategies widened social inequalities. State intervention everywhere favored the interests of particular groups and a fraction of the capitalist class. Government policies provided favorable conditions and resources for capital accumulation to only a small fraction of the entrepreneurial class while leaving the rest to operate through the market mechanism, unprotected from its fluctuations and adverse conditions. Excluded from state resources, small and medium-sized capital were often forced to resort to bribery, which imposed an additional tax on entrepreneurs and generated a condition for conflict. Although these states were not dependent on the support of the capitalist class, they pursued unfavorable policies toward the working classes. Governmental regulative activities, coupled with state intervention in industrial conflicts, frequently led to the weakening or repression of working class organizations and, consequently, the politicization of economic conflicts.

Because government policies in all three countries served a narrow set of interests, economic conflicts were inevitably politicized and rendered the state vulnerable to challenge and attack. In times of economic crisis or decline, governments, rather than markets, were held responsible for mismanagement and inappropriate policies.

As table 10 demonstrates, the extent of state intervention varied in the three cases. Once again, Iran and the Philippines represented the two extremes. The Iranian government was the most hyperactive and interventionist in every respect. The Nicaraguan government was not a major economic actor in ownership of industrial assets, but beginning in the 1950s it expanded its intervention in the economy and in capital allocation. State intervention grew throughout the 1960s, and capital expenditure and allocation increased dramatically after the earthquake. Although state intervention also grew rapidly in the Philippines, it was the lowest in these cases, and not at all high compared with other developing countries.

The level of state intervention affected the nature and the outcome of the conflicts. While low state intervention encouraged disadvantaged collectivities to demand state intervention on their behalf, as happened in the Philippines in the early 1970s, a high level of intervention encouraged such collectivities to target the state for attack. Where state intervention was high, it reduced the range and operation of the market mechanism, politicized economic processes, and rendered the states as potential targets for challenge. In periods of economic decline or crisis, highly interventionist governments were directly blamed for economic mismanagement; disadvantaged and excluded collectivities targeted state power and acted collectively to change the situation when opportunities permitted. Where state intervention was lower and market forces predominated, as in the case of the Philippines especially before martial law, disadvantaged collectivities mobilized to demand that the government intervene in the economy on their behalf. The high level of state intervention in Iran rendered the state as the principal target of attack. In addition, level of state intervention affected the nature of class conflict and consequently the likelihood for coalition formation. The high level of state intervention in Iran reduced the intensity of class conflicts and contributed to the formation of class coalition. On the other hand, the lower level of state intervention in the Philippines contributed to the intensification of class conflict and thus reduced the likelihood of class coalitions.

Yet these macro-level characteristics such as the formation of exclusive rule, centralization of power, and state intervention by themselves would have been insufficient for the analysis and explanation of the conflicts and their outcomes. These variables largely set the stage for conflict by rendering the state potentially vulnerable to challenge and attack. Furthermore, structural variables affect the capacity of various actors through their repression and exclusion. But they do not determine the process and outcome of the conflicts. The inescapable conclusion is that structural variables only affect the likelihood of certain outcomes, but they are not the determinants of the actual outcome. Rather, to predict the outcome of the social conflicts, it is necessary to analyze variables that affect the process of these conflicts. These would include an analysis of the role of opportunity structures, the capacity for collective action and mobilization, ideology, and, in particular, the likelihood of coalition formation and the capacity of challengers to disrupt the social structure.

Opportunities, coalitions, and outcomes

Virtually all the major social conflicts in the three countries took place in the context of economic decline or economic crisis that adversely affected broad segments of the population. The Iranian social movements of the early 1950s and early 1960s, as well as the revolutionary upheavals of 1977–1979, took place within the context of economic downturn. In Nicaragua, the conflicts of 1973–1974 occurred following an earthquake, which generated massive economic difficulties for the working and middle classes. The mobilizations and conflicts of 1977–1979 also erupted during an economic downturn and difficulties for the population at large. In the Philippines, the insurgencies of the early 1970s and the collective actions of 1983–1985 both emerged within the context of economic decline.

However, favorable political opportunities and state vulnerabilities were important predictors of the actual timing of mobilization and conflict. Under highly repressive regimes, favorable opportunities for mobilization may occur once repression is reduced or the state is rendered vulnerable due to large-scale mobilization or outside pressures. Ordinarily, these states were so repressive as to block opportunities for the opposition to mobilize. In all three countries repression in an earlier era had, in fact, demobilized opponents of the regimes. In both Iran and Nicaragua, a reduction of repression was a prerequisite in bringing about favorable opportunities for collective action. In both cases, the rulers' dependence on the United States rendered them vulnerable to external pressures. The Iranian opposition, with the weakest organization capability, could not initiate large-scale mobilization until the limited liberalization of 1977, in response to the election of President Carter. In Nicaragua, reduction of repression in 1977 also provided an opportunity for opponents to mobilize. In the Philippines, external pressures played a part in leading Marcos to lift martial law in 1981. The lifting of martial law at least reduced some of the worst aspects of repression. Needless to say that once opportunities emerged, groups and collectivities that possessed preexisting organizations and greater resources were in an advantageous position to initiate collective action.

However, social theorists should also examine the impact of state vulnerabilities on collective action. In the context of national crises and political polarization, regimes that are threatened by well-established challengers may resort to repression to intimidate and demobilize the opposition. Ironically, such repressive measures in such contexts may render the government vulnerable by generating at least a temporary coalition among disparate actors. In both Nicaragua and the Philippines, the regimes were isolated and threatened by moderate challengers. The assassinations of Chamorro and Aquino quickly implicated the two regimes and rendered them vulnerable. In the context of national polarization, political repression may give rise to large-scale political mobilization and collective action.

For revolutions to occur, in the absence of prior state breakdown or military victory by insurgents, broad coalitions had to be formed and the social structure had to be disrupted. In the absence of prior state breakdown, such broad coalitions and the disruption of the social structure were often critical in neutralizing the government's coercive apparatus. The likelihood of revolution increased where large segments of the population, including students, workers, capitalists, and white-collar workers and professionals, formed coalitions and engaged in disruptive actions that paralyzed the central processes of production, distribution, and government services. The absence of such a coalition led to the failure of movements in all three countries in earlier conflicts. In Iran in 1963, industrial workers, students, and white-collar employees and professionals did not join the uprising, which was repressed. Similarly, entrepreneurs in Nicaragua and the Philippines held back from the collective actions of workers and students in the early 1970s and thus blocked revolution. The lack of a broad coalition among Filipino social classes and political organizations was a key factor behind the opposition's failure to bring down the Marcos regime before 1986.

The likelihood that coalitions will be formed is dependent on several broadly defined conditions. Both exclusive rule and interventionist states prepared the background and encouraged coalition formation. Regimes that are highly exclusive and block all options for social change and eliminate autonomous social organizations become, in the long run, susceptible to generating large-scale opposition that could coalesce. Exclusive rule tends to weaken the moderate opposition in favor of radicals. The weakening of moderates in turn increased the likelihood of coalition formation. The likelihood that coalitions will be formed is greater when the principal actors are weakly organized and have little option but to come together against the common enemy. In the context of preexisting conflicts and mobilization, a sudden outbreak of government repression against well-known, established challengers and public figures can ignite popular mobilization and the formation of broad coalitions. Thus, highly authoritarian regimes become very vulnerable in the long run. A high level of state intervention also may encourage coalition formation by directing all attacks against the state. Economic declines and crises also facilitate the formation of coalitions. Each of these countries experienced various degrees of economic downturn during periods of large-scale political conflicts, which provided the background for coalition formation.

Political and ideological factors such as the strength of revolutionary challengers affected the likelihood of coalition. The relative weakness of revolutionary challengers encouraged coalition formation because they did not threaten the privileged classes. In both Iran and Nicaragua, radical challengers were relatively weak in initial stages of the conflicts and did not pose a serious threat against the capitalist class. In contrast, the strength of revolutionary challengers may prevent the formation of coalitions. Under such conditions, elite and upper classes may become increasingly dependent on the state to check the radical threat. In the Philippines, the rising strength of revolutionary challengers threatened the privileged groups and thus reduced the likelihood of coalition formation.

Finally, the extent of class conflict also affected the likelihood of coalition formation. A low level of class conflict facilitates class coalition as the state, rather than capitalists, becomes the principal target of attack. A high level of class conflict, on the other hand, prevents coalition formation as workers attack the capitalists, rather than the state. Unlike theories that emphasize the role of class conflict in revolutions, the present analysis has emphasized class coalition, most notably, coalitions that target the state. A high level of state intervention in Iran reduced the intensity of class conflict and resulted in the fact that the major social classes and collectivities targeted the state for attack. In Nicaragua and the Philippines, the level of state intervention was lower than in Iran in the early 1970s and resulted in the fact that workers and students targeted both the state and the capitalists, thus preventing coalition formation. Capitalists did not join the mobilization of students and workers in the early 1970s in either Nicaragua or the Philippines, and as a result those prior movements failed in both countries. In Nicaragua, the target of attack shifted in the second phase of insurgency as students and workers principally targeted the state after the imposition of martial law and the assassination of Chamorro when capitalists also joined the insurgency. Thus, they succeeded in overthrowing the regime. In the Philippines, a lower level of state intervention resulted in the fact that radical workers, students, and their revolutionary allies targeted both the state and the capitalists and thus impeded the formation of class coalitions.

Unlike the work of some structural theorists (Skocpol 1979), who emphasize the upper classes' defection as a factor generating political opportunities, the present research has demonstrated that upper-class defection from the state was not the primary reason favorable opportunities emerged for others who then overthrew the state. Rather, opportunities emerged in the context of external pressures, government reforms, such as in Iran and Nicaragua, and economic decline or crisis. Because these states did not depend on support from the upper class, its loss did not create opportunities for others to rebel. More importantly, primacy cannot always be given to upper-class politics because their politics are not only affected by their relationship with the state, but are also affected by the politics of working classes. The present work has demonstrated that working-class politics was critical to the politics of the upper class and, thus, directly affected the likelihood of class coalitions and the outcome of the conflicts.

Working-class militancy and workers' alliances with ideologically driven challengers may hinder the formation of a broad coalition. Working-class militancy and an ideological shift in favor of radical challengers may force capitalists to rely on government repression in order to maintain the social structure. In the Philippines and Nicaragua, for example, workers' mobilization and alliance with radical students in the early 1970s targeted capitalists and thus impeded coalition formation. Similarly in the Philippines, rising militancy among segments of workers and their alliance with radical students, along with the growing strength of the left, prevented the capitalists from joining the opposition alliance with the result that the collective actions after Aquino's assassination failed to remove Marcos from power. The likelihood that workers will mobilize against capitalists increases where state intervention is lower and economic power lies in the private, rather than the public, sector as in the Philippines.

Ideology and revolutionary struggles

Recent scholarship has presented sweeping generalizations about the role of ideology in contemporary Third World social revolutions. Some analyses of revolutions have portrayed ideology as an independent actor with its own magical power and dynamic. As earlier analyses in this research demonstrated, the social structures of these countries were not constructed on the basis of broad ideological consensus. Indeed in all three countries, repression and external support played an important role in the formation and continuity of states. The rise of revolutionary ideology could not generate opportunities for popular collective action. But once favorable opportunities emerged, ideologically driven groups were in the forefront of the struggles. Thus, students and intellectuals were always in the forefront of political and ideological struggles.

In none of the cases did a single ideology dominate the entire opposition. Even in the case of Iran, where some claimed major ideological conversion, Islamic ideology and culture could not produce coordinated collective action as there was a great deal of variation in the timing of collective action and articulated demands of various social groups and classes. It is also significant to note that in spite of claims regarding the culture of martyrdom among Iranians, available evidence demonstrates that in both absolute and relative terms, a much greater number and proportion of people were actually killed during the Nicaraguan revolution in 1979.

Any analysis of ideology must examine its relationship to the existing social structure. Analyses that attribute sweeping powers to ideology tend to mystify it and isolate it from its social context and origin. Revolutionary ideology appealed differently to different groups in the social structure. Individual collectivities had different propensities toward different political ideologies, depending on their position in the social structure, regardless of the country or the culture. The reason was that collectivities that carried out the revolutionary processes were located in different positions in the social structure, represented disparate interests, and articulated different demands. The preceding chapters demonstrated that the principal social group readily available for an ideological shift toward a new social order was to be found among dissident intellectuals and students in all three countries. Engaged in producing and analyzing both ideas and alternative possibilities, intellectuals possessed the ability to challenge these regimes on ideological grounds. They enjoyed some measure of immunity from state power, in part because many of them were affiliated with institutions of higher education. Students remained in the vanguard of ideological and political struggles in every case as soon as opportunities permitted. They developed an interest in transforming the entire social structure. They staffed guerrilla organizations, and fought for ideals of democracy, social justice, and socialism. They also promoted the causes of workers, peasants, and small producers. A small minority of the clergy, often in the lower ecclesiastical ranks, also adopted ideological shifts and favored radical transformation of the social structure. Finally, segments of organized workers also favored revolutionary ideologies that would fundamentally transform the social order. These workers often constituted the principal ally of students and intellectuals, particularly where they possessed preexisting organizations and when radical allies emerged and presented alternative visions of the social order.

On the other hand, privileged social groups and classes were less susceptible to radical, revolutionary ideologies. In broad outline, the upper echelons of the clergy in all three countries favored moderate political courses of action and outcomes. Regardless of the country, the vast majority of these clerics did not support radical challengers who called for fundamental transformations in the social structure. Similarly, capitalists participated in the struggles primarily to transform the political system, not the entire social structure. The principal demands of the capitalists extended only as far as replacing the powerholders and expanding the polity that permitted them access to the state. Everywhere, they opposed cronyism, government regulations, and state intervention in the market and capital accumulation. Aside from their own interests, capitalists favored moderate reforms that often included some benefits for disadvantaged groups and classes. When capitalists did support ideologically driven challengers who favored radical changes, they did so out of a lack of alternative options, as in the case of the Nicaraguan capitalists, who shortly before the fall of Somoza declared their support for the FSLN. Similarly, bazaaris' support for Khomeini was due to political rather than ideological reasons. In fact, with the exception of a tiny minority of bazaaris, the majority never knew about Khomeini's vision of an Islamic theocracy, which he never proclaimed in his public statements to the Iranian people during the insurgency against the monarchy.

Revolutionary challengers and outcomes

The leadership of revolutionary challengers was essential for the success of social revolutions. Yet, while revolutionary ideologies and challengers were certainly popular among certain segments of the population, particularly students, analyses of social revolutions should not exaggerate the role of their ideologies in revolutions. These challengers could not and did not always present all aspects of their ideologies to the public either because of government repression or concern for broad political support and formation of coalitions. Thus, the success or failure of revolutionary challengers must also be analyzed in terms of the dynamics of the conflicts and availability of mobilization options especially in the final stage of insurgency.

Mainstream analysts of the Iranian revolution have explained the seizure of power by Ayatollah Khomeini and establishment of a theocracy in Iran in terms of the rise of a strong Islamic movement and the conversion of major segments of the population to this ideology. These scholars have provided few systematic, empirical data to support their analysis of the rise of an Islamic movement in the 1970s. If an ideological conversion occurred prior to the overthrow of the monarchy, it should be demonstrated by concrete evidence articulated by particular social actors in specific social positions. Although segments of students did favor Islamic socialism, the demands and slogans of the vast majority of Iranians during the revolutionary conflicts did not reveal a conversion to Islamic theocracy. In the absence of such evidence, some analysts have confused the massive political support manifested for Khomeini in the final phase of the revolutionary conflicts with ideological conversion in favor of Islamic theocracy or fundamentalism.

The substantial empirical data presented in this research have demonstrated that major segments of the Iranian population supported Khomeini, not because of his religious ideology or his goal of creating a theocracy, which they knew nothing about, but for political reasons. It is important to note that some opponents of the Shah had supported Khomeini when he was first arrested in June 1963, long before he had adopted a theocratic ideology. Although some students and intellectuals advocated Islamic socialism in the 1970s, the vast majority of Iranians ignored the 1975 rebellion of clerical students who supported Khomeini, just two years before the beginning of revolutionary conflicts. Most importantly, during the revolutionary struggles, various social groups and classes entered the struggles at different times and demanded different changes because they did not have similar interests and ideologies. Khomeini and his fundamentalist Islam had little support among students, a social group with intense ideological orientation. In the final stage of the revolutionary struggles, the broad coalition that supported Khomeini united because of their political opposition against the regime, not due to an ideological consensus over the nature of the future Islamic government. The unprecedented waves of repression and violence that unfolded after the overthrow of the monarchy demonstrated the lack of ideological consensus.

The outcome of the Iranian revolution was due, in the first place, to the fact that the Shah had closed all mobilization options for the moderate opposition. Government repression had eliminated or drastically weakened both the liberal-nationalists and the socialists. All options for mobilization were blocked except the mosque. Eventually, the clergy's monopoly over this mobilization option enabled a segment of the clergy to seize state power, expel their coalition partners from the polity, and repress all opponents. These militant clerics consisted of only a small fraction of the clergy.

In this context, Khomeini rose to a position of prominence not because of his theocratic ideology but because of his uncompromising stand against the Shah. Perhaps to ensure coalition formation, Khomeini never, in his public statements to the Iranian people, stated his intention to establish an Islamic theocracy. Although he regularly expressed concern about the erosion of Islam under the Pahlavis, Khomeini in his statements to the Iranian people did not articulate any new ideological claims. In fact, Khomeini's ideological pronouncements closely followed the central tenets of the nationalist movement as he attacked dictatorship and imperialism, and called for freedom and independence. It was after the overthrow of the monarchy that Khomeini revealed his goal of establishing a theocratic state. More importantly, to maintain power after the ouster, he adopted a major ideological shift. As popular mobilization expanded and increased the power of revolutionary leftist political organizations, Khomeini repeatedly claimed that the Islamic government was to serve the interests of the poor and the downtrodden. Thus, he borrowed the general egalitarian principles from the socialists and Marxists in order to gain the support of the poor and isolate the left. But even this major ideological shift was not sufficient to ensure the rule of the Islamic regime continued. In the end, Khomeini had to resort to an unprecedented wave of repression and violence to demobilize the population and silence the left. The continual use of ruthless repression demonstrates the absence of ideological support for an Islamic theocracy in Iran.

In Nicaragua, Somoza's intransigence and the moderate opposition's failure to effect changes in the state, coupled with unrelenting repression by the National Guard, narrowed mobilizations and left the field open for armed struggle under the direction of the Sandinistas. Initially, however, when popular mobilization expanded after the assassination of Chamorro, the Sandinistas were weak organizationally and politically. They were both divided and drastically weakened by repression. Although they had the support of students and segments of the peasantry in some parts of the countryside, the Sandinistas did not enjoy the support of any segment of organized labor, which comprised a sizable socialist faction.

But the Sandinistas actively pursued tactics that enhanced their capacity for coalition formation. They modified their ideological stance, reducing threats against the privileged segments of the population. Thus, they succeeded in gaining the support of a tiny segment of the bourgeoisie and professionals in 1977 when they formed Los Doce. Yet for months following the assassination of Chamorro, the Sandinistas did not have hegemony over popular struggles because the vast majority of the Nicaraguan population followed the moderate opposition. Gradually, as the state became increasingly vulnerable and resorted to greater repressive measures, the Sandinistas gained greater support from various segments of the population. By early 1979, the Sandinistas had the backing of the vast majority of the population. Eventually, capitalists and moderate political organizations had no choice but to support the Sandinistas. The failure of the moderate opposition to remove Somoza from power left one remaining option: armed struggle and popular uprising. Popular support combined with the Sandinistas' military victory made it possible for them to control the state and consolidate their own power at the expense of elite opposition.

In the Philippines, the revolutionary challengers were in a favorable position to seize state power and transform the social structure. They organized the National Democratic Front and the NPA that waged armed struggle in the countryside against the government. The position of the revolutionaries was greatly strengthened during the years after the imposition of martial law and the closure of the polity that repressed and weakened the moderate opposition. When popular mobilization erupted after the assassination of Aquino in 1983, revolutionary challengers were much more organized and more powerful than the moderate opposition. They garnered support among students, nationalist intellectuals, segments of the clergy, peasants and farmers, and growing numbers of the urban working class. The NPA operated widely and was able to exert power in growing parts of the countryside. Given the weaknesses of the moderate opposition and absence of alternative options, the radical left would have been the principal candidate for power in the Philippines.

Yet this powerful revolutionary challenger in the Philippines failed to seize power. The failure of the Filipino revolutionaries was in part due to their power position and the tactics they pursued. Ironically, their military strength and organizational capacity, along with rising class conflict, contributed to threats against the privileged classes and the extant social order and as a result prevented formation of coalitions. Unlike the Sandinistas, the Filipino revolutionaries attempted to gain the hegemony of the struggles at the negotiating table. Their demand to have a larger share of power in a likely coalition with the moderate opposition threatened the moderate forces and prevented the formation of coalitions because moderates refused to accept the hegemony of the revolutionaries.

Still, the revolutionaries might have succeeded in establishing themselves as the hegemonic power in the battleground, as did the Sandinistas, in urban areas where a great deal of the insurgency was located. The revolutionaries came close to such struggles in the final months of 1985 when they initiated large-scale collective actions by organizing general strikes and paralyzing entire cities or regions in the south. Had the general strikes gradually expanded throughout the rest of the country and been combined with armed struggle in the cities, the revolutionaries might have practically gained the hegemony of the struggles. But the revolutionaries failed to expand the regional strikes to the rest of the country before Marcos announced the snap presidential election. Furthermore, the NPA failed to transfer its armed forces to the cities throughout the country to combine with general strikes to force Marcos out of power.

Had Marcos succeeded in his intransigence, as did Somoza, mobilization options would have been reduced to the single channel of armed struggle. In that case, the armed NPA, which was more organized and powerful than the FSLN, would have been the sole candidate to seize power, and a social revolution would have been the likely outcome.

In the end, the snap election bypassed the revolutionaries and altered the outcome of the conflicts. The electoral contest naturally narrowed the options in favor of the moderate opposition as it shifted the arena of the conflicts away from disruptive collective action and armed struggle toward the elite-controlled political alternative. A top-down coalition comprising capitalists, the upper echelon of the Catholic Church, and some middle-class organizations succeeded in mobilizing the public against Marcos during the election campaign. Although Aquino claimed victory, Marcos was not about to give up power. In fact, the National Assembly declared Marcos winner of the election. As the Aquino camp prepared for disruptive tactics, defections in the armed forces paralyzed the government. Eventually, four days of popular mobilization against Marcos' loyal forces and the withdrawal of American support propelled the elite to the forefront.

In sum, the outcomes of the conflicts in the three countries were strongly affected by the dynamics of the political processes and the mobilization option that was available, particularly in the final stages of the conflicts. The availability of one particular option over an alternative was, in part, due to the state's policies, which closed certain avenues while opening others. Revolutionary challengers who ordinarily threatened the privileged segments of the population gained great strength and succeeded in seizing power where the moderate opposition was weakened by repression and intransigence of rulers. Thus, to understand social revolutions, it is important to combine the structural variables with an analysis of the dynamics of political processes and mobilization options.

Future implications

If this framework is valid, it should be relevant for the analysis of large-scale social conflicts and revolutions in the future. Applying some of the variables of this model to the current conditions in developing countries demonstrates that, at present, contradictory forces are at work pulling in different directions. While some changes point in the direction of reduced likelihood of social revolutions, others point to the continuation of revolutionary conflicts. To the extent that new political structures in developing countries are less marked by high levels of centralization and exclusive rule, they will reduce the likelihood of large-scale political conflicts and revolutions. The development of formal democratic institutions, which expand the polity and permit moderate political organizations access to the state, tends to reduce the likelihood of large-scale political conflicts. Democratic institutions may strengthen the position of moderate challengers and isolate and render ineffective revolutionary and radical challengers. Such conditions also diminish the likelihood of coalition formation among reformist and revolutionary challengers, and thus reduce the likelihood of the types of revolutions studied in this research.

Similarly, to the extent that governments become less hyperactive, less interventionist and allow market forces to determine capital allocation and accumulation, the state will be insulated from the type of challenges studied in this research. Thus, the state is unlikely to become the principal focus of conflict, although adversely affected collectivities and classes may organize and demand state intervention on their behalf. In such conditions, the target of social conflict tends to be other social groups and classes, rather than the state. As a result, social conflicts become more segmented and fail to generate broad coalitions. The absence of broad coalitions, in turn, reduces the likelihood of the kind of social revolutions that occurred in Iran and Nicaragua.

On the other hand, the current trend in reduced state intervention and expanding of market forces may generate contradictions and crises that intensify social conflicts. With increased globalization, economic decline or crisis in major industrial countries will affect developing countries more than ever before. As developing countries become increasingly integrated into the world economy, they remain vulnerable to the vagaries of the world market and decisions made by transnational corporations and financial institutions, as demonstrated in Brazil, Mexico, and South Korea. Market forces tend to generate economic swings that cannot be easily controlled, a trend that is likely to be intensified under conditions of greater integration into the world economy. Regional integration will also have broader implications in times of economic downturns, as was the case with the decline in Asian markets in 1998. The current trend toward greater economic integration may create new winners and losers across class lines and different economic sectors. These conditions may result in nationalist movements initiated by the losing sectors and classes that oppose powerful international actors, such as transnational corporations, the IMF, and the World Bank. Such coalitions may demand greater state intervention and protection from unfavorable global trends.

Furthermore, the expansion of free markets may continue to exacerbate class conflict and ethnic divisions and provide ample cause for conflict. Although reduced state intervention may cut down on crony capitalism and great accumulations of wealth, expanding market forces may also intensify inequalities among classes and regions in developing countries. Currently, with the expansion of market forces, economic disparities are on the rise virtually everywhere in the world. The gap between the rich and the poor of the world is widening at an alarming rate. Rising social and economic inequalities generate inevitable causes for social conflicts. They tend to impel students and workers to mobilize for collective action and social change. Finally, rising inequalities may intensify regional as well as ethnic conflicts.

While democratization tends to expand the capacity of social groups to mobilize, the weakening or absence of revolutionary challengers tends to reduce the likelihood of social revolutions. Yet rising social inequalities and the expansion of higher education in developing countries lead to the continued involvement of students and youth in politics. Students will also continue to produce dissident intellectuals and challengers as long as rising social inequalities continue to plague the developing countries. Whatever the future direction, many factors persist that produce large-scale social conflicts and violence. I hope this work has contributed to an understanding of the social causes of revolutions in developing countries where resides the vast majority of suffering humanity.

Bibliography

THEORY

Arjomand, S. 1981. "Shi'ite Islam and the Revolution in Iran." *Government and Opposition* 16:293–316.

    1986. "Iran's Islamic Revolution in Comparative Perspective." *World Politics* 38:383–414.

Aya, R. 1990. *Rethinking Revolutions and Collective Violence: Studies on Concept, Theory, and Method.* Amsterdam: Het Spinhuis.

Boswell, T. 1989. "World Revolutions and Revolutions in the World-System." In *Revolution in the World-System,* edited by T. Boswell. New York: Greenwood Press.

    1993. "Marx's Theory of Rebellion: A Cross-National Analysis of Class Exploitation, Economic Development and Violent Revolt." *American Sociological Review* 58:681–702.

Boswell, T., and W. J. Dixon. 1990. "Dependency and Rebellion: A Cross-National Analysis." *American Sociological Review* 55:540–559.

Burns, G. 1996. "Ideology, Culture, and Ambiguity: The Revolutionary Process in Iran." *Theory and Society* 25:349–388.

Calhoun, C. 1983. "The Radicalism of Tradition: Community Strength or Venerable Disguise and Borrowed Language?" *American Journal of Sociology* 88:886–914.

Chehabi, H., and J. Linz. 1998. *Sultanic Regimes.* Baltimore: The Johns Hopkins University Press.

Colburn, F. 1994. *The Vogue of Revolution in Poor Countries.* Princeton: Princeton University Press.

Eckstein, S. 1989. "Power and Popular Protest in Latin America." In *Power and Popular Protest: Latin American Social Movements,* edited by S. Eckstein. Berkeley: University of California Press.

Farhi, F. 1990. *States and Urban-Based Revolutions: Iran and Nicaragua.* Chicago: University of Illinois Press.

Foran, J. 1993. *Fragile Resistance: Social Transformation in Iran from 1500 to the Revolution.* Boulder: Westview Press.

    1997a. "The Comparative-Historical Sociology of Third World Revolutions: Why a Few Succeed, Why Most Fail." In *Theorizing Revolutions,* edited by J. Foran. New York: Routledge.

    ed. 1997b. *Theorizing Revolutions.* New York: Routledge.

Foran, J., and J. Goodwin. 1993. "Revolutionary Outcomes in Iran and Nicaragua: Coalition Fragmentation, War, and the Limits of Social Transformation." *Theory and Society* 22 (2).

Gamson, W. 1975. *Strategy of Social Protest*. Homewood, Ill.: Dorsey Press.

Gillis, M. 1980. "The Role of State Enterprises in Economic Development." *Social Research* 249–289.

Goldfrank, W. 1979. "Theories of Revolution and Revolution Without Theory: The Case of Mexico." *Theory and Society* 7:135–165.

Goldstone, J. 1980. "Theories of Revolution: The Third Generation." *World Politics* 32:425–453.

1982. "The Comparative and Historical Study of Revolutions." *Annual Review of Sociology* 8: 187–207.

1986. "The Comparative and Historical Study of Revolutions." In *Revolutions: Theoretical, Comparative, and Historical Studies*, edited by J. Goldstone. San Diego: Harcourt Brace Jovanovich.

1991a. "Ideology, Cultural Frameworks, and the Process of Revolution." *Theory and Society* 20:405–455.

1991b. *Revolution and Rebellion in the Early Modern World*. Berkeley: University of California Press.

Goodwin, J. 1994. "Toward a New Sociology of Revolutions." *Theory and Society* 23:731–766.

1997. "State-Centered Approaches To Social Revolutions: Strengths and Limitations of a Theoretical Tradition." In *Theorizing Revolutions*, edited by J. Foran. New York: Routledge.

Goodwin, J., and T. Skocpol. 1994. "Explaining Revolutions in the Contemporary Third World." In *Social Revolutions in the Modern World*, edited by T. Skocpol. Cambridge: Cambridge University Press.

Gould, R. 1995. *Insurgent Identities: Class, Community, and Protest in Paris from 1848 to the Commune*. Chicago: University of Chicago Press.

Haggard, S., and R. Kaufman. 1995. *The Political Economy of Democratic Transitions*. Princeton: Princeton University Press.

Hall, J., and G. Ikenberry. 1989. *The State*. Minneapolis: University of Minnesota Press.

Hobsbawm, E. 1973. "Peasants and Politics." *The Journal of Peasant Studies* 1:3–22.

1974. "Peasant Land Occupation." *Past and Present* 62:120–152.

Jenkins, J. C. 1983. "Resource Mobilization and the Study of Social Movements." *Annual Review of Sociology* 9:527–553.

1985. *The Politics of Insurgency: The Farm Worker Movement in the 1960s*. New York: Columbia University Press.

Jenkins, J. C., and C. Perrow. 1977. "Insurgency of the Powerless." *American Sociological Review* 42:249–268.

Jenkins, J. C., and K. Schock. 1992. "Global Structures and Political Processes in the Study of Domestic Political Conflict." *Annual Review of Sociology* 18:161–185.

Katz, M. 1997. *Revolutions and Revolutionary Waves*. St. Martin's Press: New York.

Kedde, N., ed. 1995a. *Debating Revolutions*. New York: New York University Press.

1995b. "Can Revolution Be Predicted; Can Their Causes Be Understood?" In *Debating Revolutions*, edited by N. Keddie. New York: New York University Press.

Kim, Q.-Y. 1991. "Paradigms and Revolution: The Societal and Statist Approaches Reconsidered." In *Revolutions in the Third World*, edited by Q.-Y. Kim. Leiden: E. J. Brill.

Kimmel, M. 1990. *Revolution: A Sociological Interpretation*. Philadelphia: Temple University Press.

Kirkpatrick, C. H. 1984. "Business Behavior in the Public Sector." In *Industrial Structure and Policy in Less Developed Countries*, edited by C. H. Kirkpatrick, N. Lee, and F. I. Nixon. London: George Allen & Unwin.

Koenker, D. P., and W. G. Rosenberg. 1989. *Strikes and Revolution in Russia, 1917*. Princeton: Princeton University Press.

Korpi, W. 1974. "Conflict, Power and Relative Deprivation." *American Political Science Review* 68:1569–1578.

Kurzman, C. 1996. "Structural Opportunity and Perceived Opportunity in Social-Movement Theory: The Iranian Revolution of 1979." *American Sociological Review* 61:153–170.

Linz, J. 1975. "Totalitarian and Authoritarian Regimes." In *Macropolitical Theory*, edited by F. Greenstein and N. Polsby. Reading, Mass.: Addison-Wesley.

Lupher, M. 1996. *Power Restructuring in China and Russia*. Boulder: Westview Press.

McAdam, D. 1982. *Political Process and the Development of Black Insurgency, 1930–1970*. Chicago: University of Chicago Press.

McAdam, D., and D. A. Snow. 1997. *Social Movements: Readings on their Emergence, Mobilization, and Dynamics*. Los Angeles: Roxbury Publishing Company.

McCarthy, J. D., and M. N. Zald. "Resource Mobilization and Social Movements: A Partial Theory." *American Journal of Sociology* 82:1212–1241.

McDaniel, T. 1991. *Autocracy, Modernization, and Revolution in Russia and Iran*. Princeton: Princeton University Press.

Midlarsky, M., and K. Roberts. 1986. "Inequality, the State, and Revolution in Central America." In *Inequality and Contemporary Revolutions*, edited by M. Midlarsky. Denver: University of Colorado Press.

Migdal, J. S. 1974. *Peasants, Politics, and Revolution: Pressures toward Political and Social Change in the Third World*. Princeton: Princeton University Press.

Moaddel, M. 1993. *Class, Politics, and Ideology in the Iranian Revolution*. New York: Columbia University Press.

Moore, Jr., B. 1966. *Social Origins of Dictatorship and Democracy: Lord and Peasant in the Making of the Modern World*. Boston: Beacon.

1978. *Injustice: The Social Bases of Obedience and Revolt*. New York: M. E. Sharpe.

Morris, A. 1981. "Black Southern Student Sit-in Movement: An Analysis of Internal Organization." *American Sociological Review* 46:744–767.

1984. *The Origins of the Civil Rights Movement: Black Communities Organizing for Change*. New York: The Free Press.

Oberschall, A. 1973. *Social Conflict and Social Movements*. Englewood Cliffs, N.J.: Prentice Hall.

O'Dea, T. 1966. *The Sociology of Religion*. Englewood Cliffs, N.J.: Prentice Hall.

Paige, J. 1975. *Agrarian Revolution: Social Movements and Export Agriculture in the Underdeveloped World*. New York: The Free Press.

1997. *Coffee and Power: Revolution and the Rise of Democracy in Central America*. Cambridge, Mass.: Harvard University Press.

Parsa, M. 1985. "Economic Development and Political Transformation: A Comparative Analysis of the United States, Russia, Nicaragua, and Iran." *Theory and Society* 14:623–675.

1989. *Social Origins of the Iranian Revolution*. New Brunswick: Rutgers University Press.

1995. "Conversion or Coalition? Ideology in the Iranian and Nicaraguan Revolutions." *Political Power and Social Theory* 9:23–60.

Piven, F. F., and R. A. Cloward. 1977. *Poor Peoples' Movements: Why They Succeed, How They Fail*. New York: Vintage Books.

Rice, E. 1991. *Revolution and Counter-Revolution*. Blackwell: Oxford.

Rueschemeyer, D., and P. Evans. 1985. "The State and Economic Transformation: Toward an Analysis of the Conditions Underlying Effective Intervention." In *Bringing the State Back In*, edited by P. Evans, D. Rueschemeyer, and T. Skocpol. Cambridge: Cambridge University Press.

Rueschemeyer, D., E. Stephens, and J. Stephens. 1992. *Capitalist Development and Democracy*. Chicago: University of Chicago Press.

Salert, B. 1976. *Revolutions and Revolutionaries*. New York: Elsevier.

Schutz, B., and R. Slater. 1990. "A Framework for Analysis." In *Revolution and Political Change in the Third World*, edited by B. Schutz and R. Slater. Boulder: Lynne Rienner.

Schwartz, M. 1976. *Radical Protest and Social Structure: The Southern Farmers' Alliance and Cotton Tenancy, 1880–1890*. Chicago: University of Chicago Press.

Scott, J. 1979. "Revolution in the Revolution: Peasants and Commissars." *Theory and Society* 7: 97–134.

1985. *Weapons of the Weak: Everyday Forms of Peasant Resistance*. New Haven: Yale University Press.

Selbin, Eric. 1993. *Modern Latin American Revolutions*. Boulder: Westview Press.

1997. "Revolution in the Real World: Bringing Agency Back In." In *Theorizing Revolutions*, edited by J. Foran. New York: Routledge.

Sewell, W. 1985. "Ideologies and Social Revolutions: Reflections on the French Case." *Journal of Modern History* 57:57–85.

Shepherd, W. 1976. *Public Enterprise: Economic Analysis of Theory and Practice*. Lexington, Mass.: Lexington Books.

Short, R. P. 1984. "The Role of Public Enterprises: An International Statistical Comparison." In *Public Enterprise in Mixed Economies*, edited by R. H. Floyd, C. S. Gary, and R. P. Short. Washington D.C.: IMF.

Shorter, E., and C. Tilly. 1974. *Strikes in France, 1830–1968*. London: Cambridge University Press.

Skocpol, T. 1979. *States and Social Revolutions: A Comparative Analysis of France, Russia, and China*. Cambridge: Cambridge University Press.

1982. "Rentier State and Shi'a Islam in the Iranian Revolution." *Theory and Society* 11:265–283.

Snyder, R. 1998. "Paths out of Sultanic Regimes: Combining Structural and Voluntarist Perspectives." In *Sultanic Regimes*, edited by H. Chehabi and J. Linz. Baltimore: The Johns Hopkins University Press.

Snyder, D., and C. Tilly. 1972. "Hardship and Collective Violence in France: 1830–1960." *American Sociological Review* 37:520–532.

Stinchcombe, A. 1965. "Social Structure and Organizations." In *Handbook of Organizations*, edited by J. March. Chicago: Rand McNally and Company.

Supple, B. 1980. "The State and the Industrial Revolution." In *The Fontana Economic History of Europe: The Industrial Revolution*, edited by C. Cipolla. Glasgow: Fontana.

Tarrow, S. 1994. *Power in Movement: Social Movements, Collective Action and Politics*. Cambridge: Cambridge University Press.

Tilly, C. 1963. "The Analysis of a Counter-Revolution." *History and Theory* 3:30–58.

1973. "Does Modernization Breed Revolution?" *Comparative Politics* 5:425–447.

1978. *From Mobilization to Revolution*. Reading, Mass.: Addison-Wesley.

1979. "Repertoires of Contention in America and Britain, 1750–1830." In *The Dynamics of Social Movements*, edited by M. Zald and J. D. McCarthy. Cambridge: Winthrop.

1990. *Coercion, Capital, and European States, AD990–1990*. Oxford: Basil Blackwell.

1994. *European Revolutions, 1492–1992*. Oxford: Blackwell.

US Department of Commerce. 1992. *Survey of Current Business*. Washington, D.C.

Walton, J. 1984. *Reluctant Rebels: Comparative Studies of Revolution and Underdevelopment*. New York: Columbia University Press.

1989. "Debt, Protest, and the State in Latin America." In *Power and Popular Protest: Latin American Social Movements*, edited by S. Eckstein. Berkeley: University of California Press.

Walton, J. and D. Seddon. 1994. *Free Markets and Food Riots: The Politics of Global Adjustment*. Oxford: Blackwell.

Weiss, L., and J. Hobson. 1995. *States and Economic Development: A Comparative Historical Analysis*. Malden, Mass.: Blackwell.

Wickham-Crowley, T. 1997. "Structural Theories of Revolution." In *Theorizing Revolutions*, edited by J. Foran. New York: Routledge.

Wolf, E. 1969. *Peasant Wars of the Twentieth Century*. New York: Harper Torchbooks.

World Bank. 1991. *DEC Analytical Database: Report on Methods and Data Sources*. International Economics Department, Analysis and Prospects Division.

Zagoria, D. 1976. "Asian Tenancy Systems and Communist Mobilization of the Peasantry." In *Peasant Revolution and Communist Revolutions in Asia*, edited by J. Lewis. Stanford: Stanford University Press.

Zagorin, P. 1982. *Rebels and Rulers, 1500–1660*. Cambridge: Cambridge University Press.

Zysman, J. 1983. *Governments, Markets, and Growth: Financial Systems and the Politics of Industrial Change*. Ithaca: Cornell University Press.

IRAN

Abouzar. 1978. *Asnad Va Tasaviri As Enghelab E khalgh-e Mosalman-e Iran*. Vol. I, parts 1 and 3. Tehran: Abouzar.

Abrahamian, E. 1968. "The Crowd in Iranian Politics." *Past and Present* 41:184–210.

1982. *Iran Between Two Revolutions*. Princeton: Princeton University Press.

1989. *The Iranian Mojahedin*. New Haven: Yale University Press.

1993. *Khomeinism: Essays on the Islamic Republic*. Berkeley: University of California Press.

Afshar, H. 1985. "The Army." In *Iran: A Revolution in Turmoil*, edited by H. Afshar. London: Macmillan.

Akhavi, S. 1980. *Religion and Politics in Contemporary Iran*. Albany: State University of New York Press.

Alam, A. 1991. *The Shah and I: The Confidential Diary of Iran's Royal Court, 1969–1977*. London: I. B. Tauris.

Alexander, Y., and A. Nanes, eds. 1980. *The United States and Iran: A Documentary History*. Frederick, Md.: University Publications of America.

Amirahmadi, H. 1990. *Revolution and Economic Transition: The Iranian Experience*. Albany: State University of New York Press.

Amuzegar, J. 1991. *The Dynamics of the Iranian Revolution: The Pahlavis' Triumph and Tragedy*. New York: State University of New York Press.

Arjomand, S. 1981. "Shi'ite Islam and the Revolution in Iran." *Government and Opposition* 16:293–316.

1986. "Iran's Islamic Revolution in Comparative Perspective." *World Politics* 38:383–414.

1988. *The Turban for the Crown: The Islamic Revolution in Iran*. New York: Oxford University Press.

Ashraf, A., and A. Banuazizi. 1985. "The State, Classes, and Modes of Mobilization in the Iranian Revolution." *State, Culture, and Society* 1:3–40.

1992. "Classes in the Pahlavi Period." In *Encyclopaedia Iranica*, edited by E. Yarshater, vol. 5, fascicle 7. Costa Mesa: Mazda Publishers.

Bakhash, S. 1984. *The Reign of the Ayatollahs: Iran and the Islamic Revolution*. New York: Basic Books.

Bakhtiar, S. 1982. *Yekrangi*. Paris: Albion Michel.

Bashiriyeh, H. 1984. *The State and the Revolution in Iran, 1962–1982*. New York: St. Martin's Press.

Bayat, A. 1983. "Workers' Control after the Revolution." *MERIP Reports* 13 (3):19–34.

1987. *Workers and Revolution in Iran*. London: Zed.

1997. *Street Politics: Poor People's Movements in Iran*. New York: Columbia University Press.

1998. "Revolution Without Movement, Movement Without Revolution: Comparing Islamic Activism in Iran and Egypt." *Comparative Studies in Society and History* 40 (1):136–169.

Bazargan, M. 1983a. *Moshkelat va Masael-e Avvalin Sal-e Enghelab.* Tehran: The Freedom Movement.

  1983b. *Shora-ye Enghelab Va Dolat-e Movaghat.* Tehran: The Freedom Movement.

  1984. *Enghelab-e Iran Dar Du Harkat.* Tehran: Mazaheri.

Benedick, R. 1964. *Industrial Finance in Iran: A Study of Financial Practice in an Underdeveloped Economy.* Boston, Mass.: Harvard University, Graduate School of Business Administration, Division of Research.

Bharier, J. 1971. *Economic Development in Iran, 1900–1970.* London: Oxford University Press.

Bill, J. 1988. *The Eagle and the Lion: The Tragedy of American Iranian Relations.* New Haven: Yale University Press.

Binder, L. 1962. *Iran: Political Development in a Changing Society.* Berkeley and Los Angeles: University of California Press.

Blair, J. 1976. *The Control of Oil.* New York: Vintage Books.

BMI (Bank Markazi Iran). Various years. *Bank Markazi of Iran: Annual Report and Balance Sheet.* Tehran: BMI.

Boroujerdi, M. 1996. *Iranian Intellectuals and the West: The Tormented Triumph of Nativism.* Syracuse: Syracuse University Press.

Burn, T., and R. Dumont. 1978. "Imperial Pretensions and Agricultural Dependence." *MERIP Reports* 8 (8):15–20.

Burns, G. 1996. "Ideology, Culture, and Ambiguity: The Revolutionary Process in Iran." *Theory and Society* 25:349–388.

Carter, J. 1978. *Public Papers of the Presidents of the United States: Jimmy Carter, 1977.* Washington, D.C.: GPO.

Chehabi, H.E. 1990. *Iranian Politics and Religious Modernism: The Liberation Movement of Iran under the Shah and Khomeini.* Ithaca: Cornell University Press.

Cottam, R. 1979. *Nationalism in Iran.* Pittsburgh: University of Pittsburgh Press.

Farhi, F. 1990. *States and Urban-Based Revolutions: Iran and Nicaragua.* Urbana: University of Illinois Press.

Fischer, M. 1980. *Iran: From Religious Dispute to Revolution.* Cambridge, Mass.: Harvard University Press.

The Freedom Movement. 1983. *Safehati As Tarikh-e Mo'asaer-e Iran.* Tehran: The Freedom Movement.

The Freedom Movement (abroad). 1978. *Dar Bareh-e Ghiam-e Hammaseh Afarinan-e Qom Va Tabriz Va Digar Shahr Haye Iran.* 3 vols.

Gamson, W. 1975. *The Strategy of Social Protest.* Homewood, Ill.: Dorsey Press.

Garthwaite, G. 1983. *Khans and Shahs: A Documentary Analysis of the Bakhtiyari in Iran.* Cambridge: Cambridge University Press.

Gasiorowski, M. 1991. *US Foreign Policy and the Shah: Building a Client State in Iran.* Ithaca: Cornell University Press.

Ghara-Baghi, A. 1984. *Haghayegh Dar Bare-he Bohran-e Iran.* Paris: Sohail.

Ghoreyshi, A., and C. Elahi. 1976. "Social Mobilization and Participation in Iran." In *Iran: Past, Present, and Future,* edited by J. Jacqz. New York: Aspen Institute for Humanisitic Studies.

Ghotbi, A. (T. Jalil). 1978. *Workers Say No to the Shah: Labour Law and Strikes in Iran.* London: CRTURI (Campaign for the Restoration of Trade Union Rights in Iran).

Graham, R. 1979. *Iran: The Illusion of Power.* New York: St. Martin's Press.

Green, J. 1980. "Pseudoparticipation and Counter-Mobilization: Roots of the Iranian Revolution." *Iranian Studies* 13:31–53.

———. 1986. "Countermobilization in the Iranian Revolution." In *Revolutions: Theoretical, Comparative, and Historical Studies,* edited by J. Goldstone. San Diego: Harcourt Brace Jovanovich.

Halliday, F. 1978a. "The Economic Contradiction." *MERIP Reports* 8 (6):9–19.

———. 1978b. "Trade Unions and the Working Class Opposition." *MERIP Reports* 8 (8):7–13.

———. 1979. *Iran: Dictatorship and Development.* New York: Penguin Books.

Hezar-Kani, M. 1982. "The Only Obstacle is Khomeini Himself." *MERIP Reports* 12 (3):33–34.

Hooglund, E. 1981. "Iran's Agricultural Inheritance." *MERIP Reports* 11 (7):15–20.

———. 1982. *Land and Revolution in Iran, 1962–1980.* Austin: University of Texas Press.

Hoveyda, F. 1980. *The Fall of the Shah.* London: Weidenfeld and Nicolson.

Huntington, S. 1968. *Political Order in Changing Societies.* New Haven: Yale University Press.

International Labor Office. 1972. *Employment and Income Policies in Iran.* Geneva: ILO.

International Monetary Fund (IMF). 1981. Government Finance Statistics Yearbook. Washington, D.C.: IMF.

Iranian Oil Worker. 1980. "How We Organized the Strike that Paralyzed Shah's Regime." In *Oil and Class Struggle,* edited by P. Nore and T. Turner. London: Zed.

Irfani, S. 1983. *Revolutionary Islam in Iran: Popular Liberation or Religious Dictatorship?* London: Zed.

Issawi, C. 1978. "The Iranian Economy 1925–75: Fifty Years of Economic Development." In *Iran Under the Pahlavis,* edited by G. Lenczowski. Stanford: Hoover Institution Press.

Ivanov, M. n.d. *Tarikh-e Novin-e Iran.* Stockholm: Tudeh Publication.

Jabbari, A., and R. Olson. 1981. *Iran: Essays on a Revolution in the Making.* Lexington, Ky: Mazda.

Jami [pseud.]. 1976. *Gozashteh Cheragh-e Rah-e Ayandeh Ast.* Paris: Jami.

Jazani, B. 1979. *Tarh-e Jame-eh Shenasi Va Mabani-e Strategy-e Jonbesh-e Enghelabi-e Khalgh-e Iran.* Tehran: Maziar.

Kambakhsh, A. 1972 and 1974. *Nazari Be Jonbeshe Kargari Va Komonisti Dar Iran.* 2 vols. Stockholm: Tudeh Publication.

Katouzian, H. 1978. "Oil versus Agriculture: A Case of Dual Resource Depletion in Iran." *Journal of Peasant Studies* 5:347–369.

———. 1981. *The Political Economy of Iran.* New York: New York University Press.

———. 1998. "The Pahlavi Regime in Iran." In *Sultanic Regimes,* edited by H. Chehabi and J. Linz. Baltimore: The Johns Hopkins University Press.

Kazemi, F. 1980. *Poverty and Revolution in Iran.* New York: New York University Press.

Kazemi, F. and E. Abrahamian. 1978. "The Nonrevolutionary Peasantry of Modern Iran." *Iranian Studies,* 11.

Keddie, N. 1981. *Roots of Revolution: An Interpretative History of Modern Iran.* New Haven: Yale University Press.

1983. "The Iranian Revolutions in Comparative Perspective." *American Historical Review* 88:579–598.

Khalili, A. 1981. *Gam be gam ba enghelab.* Tehran: Soroush.

Khomeini, R. 1976. *Avay-e Enghelab.* United States: Moslem Student Association.

1979. *Hokomat-e Eslami.* Tehran: Amir Ksbir.

1983. *Sahifeh-e Nour.* 16 vols. Tehran: Ministry of Science.

Kian, A. 1993. "The Politics of the New Middle Class in Iran and Egypt from the Nineteenth Century until 1979." Unpublished Ph.D. dissertation, University of California, Los Angeles.

Klare, M. 1979. "Arms and the Shah." *Institute for Policy Studies Bulletin* 43 (8).

Ladjevardi, H. 1985. *Labor Unions and Autocracy in Iran.* Syracuse: Syracuse University Press.

Lambton, A. 1969. *The Persian Land Reform.* Oxford: Clarendon Press.

McCarthy, J., and M. Zald. 1977. "Resource Mobilization and Social Movements: A Partial Theory." *American Journal of Sociology* 82:1212–1241.

McLahlan, K. 1968. "Land Reform in Iran." In *The Cambridge History of Iran: The Land of Iran,* vol. 1, edited by W. Fisher. Cambridge: Cambridge University Press.

Menashri, D. 1992. *Education and the Making of Modern Iran.* Ithaca: Cornell University Press.

Milani, M. 1988. *The Making of Iran's Islamic Revolution: From Monarchy to Islamic Republic.* Boulder: Westview Press.

Mirsepassi-Ashtiani, A., and V. Moghadam. 1991. "The Left and Political Islam in Iran: A Retrospect and Prospects." *Radical History Review* 51:27–62.

M.J. [pseud.]. 1979. *Vaghaye-a Enghelab-e Iran.* Tehran.

Moaddel, M. 1986. "The Shi'i Ulama and the State in Iran." *Theory and Society* 15:519–556.

1993. *Class, Politics, and Ideology in the Iranian Revolution.* New York: Columbia University Press.

Moghadam, V. 1987. "Industrial Development, Culture and Working-Class Politics: A Case Study of Tabriz Industrial Workers in the Iranian Revolution." *International Sociology* 2.

Mohtadi, H. 1987. "Industrialization and Urban Inequality in LDCs: A Theoretical Analysis with Evidence from Prerevolutionary Iran." *The Journal of Developing Areas* 22:41–58.

Momayezi, N. 1986. "Economic Correlates of Political Violence: The Case of Iran." *Middle East Journal* 40:68–81.

Najinabadi, A. 1987. *Land Reform and Social Change in Iran.* Salt Lake City: University of Utah Press.

Nategh, H. 1982. "The Clergy and Democratic Freedoms." *Jahan,* January,

March, and April, nos. 1, 3, and 4.

Omid, H. 1994. *Islam and the Post-Revolutionary State in Iran.* New York: St. Martin's Press.

Overseas Consultants. 1949. *Report on the Seven Year Development Plan for the Plan Organization of the Imperial Government of Iran, vol. 3.* New York: Overseas Consultants, Inc.

Pakdaman, N. 1995. "Ten Nights of Poetry Readings: A Review and Evaluation of an Event at the Beginning of the Iranian Revolution." *Kankash,* 12:125–206.

Parsa, M. 1988. "Theories of Collective Action and the Iranian Revolution." *Sociological Forum* 3:44–71.

 1989. *Social Origins of the Iranian Revolution.* New Brunswick: Rutgers University Press.

 1994. "Mosque of Last Resort: State Reform and Social Conflict in the Early 1960s." In *A Century of Revolution: Social Movements in Iran,* edited by J. A. Foran. Minneapolis: University of Minnesota Press.

 1995a. "Entrepreneurs and Democratization: Iran and the Philippines." *Comparative Studies in Society and History* 37:803–830.

 1995b. "Conversion or Coalition? Ideology in the Iranian and Nicaraguan Revolutions." *Political Power and Social Theory* 9:23–60.

Pesaran, H. 1976. "Income Distribution and its Major Determinants in Iran." In *Iran: Past, Present, and Future,* edited by J. Jacqz. New York: Aspen Institute for Humanistic Studies.

Pouyan, A. 1975. *On the Necessity of Armed Struggle.* New York: SCIPS (Support Committee for the Iranian People's Struggle).

The Public Relations of the Islamic Consultative Assembly. 1983. *Ashna'i Ba Majles-e Shora-ye Eslami.* Tehran: Islamic Consultative Assembly.

Ravasani, S. 1978. *Iran.* Stuttgart: Alektor Verlag.

Saikal, A. 1980. *The Rise and Fall of the Shah.* Princeton: Princeton University Press.

Salehi-Isfahani, D. 1989. "The Political Economy of Credit Subsidy in Iran, 1973–1978." *International Journal of Middle East Studies* 21, 359–379.

SCI (Statistical Center of Iran). 1956. *National Census of Population and Housing.* Tehran: SCI.

 1966a. *National Census of Population and Housing.* Tehran: SCI.

 1966b. *Statistical Yearbook.* Tehran: SCI.

 1976a. *National Census of Population and Housing.* Tehran: SCI.

 1976b. *Netayej-e Amar Giri-e As Bank Hay-e Keshvar.* Tehran: SCI.

 1976c. *Tehran Census.* Tehran: SCI.

 1977a. *Statistical Yearbook.* Tehran: SCI.

 1977b. *Fehrest-e Nam Va Neshan-e Kar Gah Haye Bozorg-e Sanati 2534.* Tehran: SCI.

 1980. *Netayej-e Amar Giri-e Keshavarzi-e Rousta'i 1354.* Tehran: SCI.

 1981a. *Amar-e Kargah Haye Bozorg-e Sanati 1355.* Tehran: SCI.

 1981b. *Tehran Census.* Tehran: SCI.

Shaji'i, Z. 1965. *Namayandegan-e Majles-e Shora-ye Melli dar Bisto-yek Doreh-e Ghanoon Gozari.* Tehran: Tehran University Press.

Shariati, A. 1979. *On the Sociology of Islam.* Berkeley: Mizan Press.

Siavoshi, S. 1990. *Liberal Nationalism in Iran: The Failure of a Movement.* Boulder: Westview Press.

Sick, G. 1985. *All Fall Down.* New York: Random House.

Skocpol, T. 1982. "Rentier State and Shi'a Islam in the Iranian Revolution." *Theory and Society* 11:265–283.

Stempel, J. 1981. *Inside the Iranian Revolution.* Bloomington: Indiana University Press.

Sullivan, W. 1981. *Mission to Iran.* New York: W. W. Norton.

Tabari, A. 1983. "Land, Politics, and Capital Accumulation." *MERIP Reports* 13 (3):26–30.

Tabari, E. 1977. *Jame'eh Iran Dar Doran-e Reza Shah.* Stockholm: Tudeh Publication.

Taheri, A. 1986. *The Spirit of Allah: Khomeini and the Islamic Revolution.* Bethesda, Maryland: Adler & Adler.

Tehrani, N. 1970. *Ranhaniat Dear Shia.* Tehran: Ketabkhaneh Melli.

Tehranian, M. 1980. "Communication and Revolution in Iran: The Passing of a Paradigm." *Iranian Studies* 13:5–30.

Turner, T. 1980. "Iranian Oilworkers in the 1978–79 Revolution." In *Oil and Class Struggle*, edited by P. Nore and T. Turner. London: Zed.

United Nations. 1953. *Review of Economic Conditions in the Middle East 1951–52.* Supplement to World Economic Report. New York: UN.

Vakil, F. 1976. "Iran's Basic Macroeconomic Problems: A 20-Year Horizon." In *Iran: Past, Present, and Future*, edited by J. Jacqz. New York: Aspen Institute for Humanistic Studies.

Walton, T. 1980. "Economic Development and Revolutionary Upheavals in Iran." *Cambridge Journal of Economics* 4:271–292.

Wilber, D. 1975. *Riza Shah Pahlavi: The Resurrection and Reconstruction of Iran.* New York: Exposition Press.

Zabih, S. 1982. *Iran Since the Revolution.* Baltimore: The Johns Hopkins University Press.

Zonis, M. 1971. *The Political Elite of Iran.* Princeton: Princeton University Press.

NEWSPAPERS AND PAMPHLETS

Akhbar-e Jonbesh-e Eslami. A series of newsletters published by the Freedom Movement in 1978 and 1979.

Ayandegan. A national newspaper.

Enghelab-e Eslami. A national newspaper published by Bani-Sadr and his supporters.

Ettelaat. A national newspaper.

Guilds. A newsletter published in Tehran in 1979 by bazaar shopkeepers.

Hambastegi. A series of newsletters published by the National Organization of the Iranian Universities, the Writers' Association, and the Committee for Defense of Political Prisoners in 1978 and 1979.

Iranshahr. A newspaper published in the United States.

Iran Times. A newspaper published in the United States.

Jumhuri Eslami. A national newspaper published by the Islamic Republican Party.

Kar. Weekly publication of the Organization of the Iranian People's Fedayee Guerillas (Fedayeen).

Kayhan. A national newspaper.

Kayhan International and *Kayhan Havaee. Kayhan* newspaper for Iranians abroad.

Mizan. A newspaper published by the Freedom Movement.

Mojahed. Newspaper published by the People's Mojahedeen Organization of Iran.

Oil Workers' Newsletter. 1979.

OIPFG. See The Organization of the Iranian People's Fedayee Guerillas.

Organization of Iranian Moslem Students. 1978. *Some of the Statements Published in Iran During July–August 1978.* Wilmette, Illinois.

The Organization of the Iranian People's Fedayee Guerillas (OIPFG). 1978. *Pareh-ie as Ealamieh Hay-e Sazman-e Cherikhay-e Fedayee-e Khalgh-e Iran.*
1979. *Gozareshatie as Mobarezat-e Kharej as Mahtoodeh.*

Payam-e Mojahed. Official organ of the Freedom Movement published in the United States.

Payman. A newspaper.

The People's Mojahedeen Organization of Iran. 1979. *Tahlile Jonbesh-e Khalgh-e Ghahraman-e Tabriz.* Tehran.

Rastakhiz. A national newspaper.

Shanzdah-e Azar. A newspaper.

Tehran Economist. A journal published in Tehran.

Tehran Journal. The English edition of the *Ettelaat* newspaper.

Zamimeh-e Khabar Nameh. 1978. A collection of newsletters published by the National Front (abroad).

Zobe-Ahan: Tahlily Bar E'atesab-e Mehr Mahe 1357. 1978. Pamphlet written by a group of anonymous steel mill employees.

ARCHIVAL MATERIAL

In addition to a number of my own interviews with bazaaris and members of various political organizations, I have used the following interviews conducted by Dr. H. Ladjevardi at the Middle Eastern Studies Center, Harvard University. Tape recordings can be found in the Iranian Oral History Collection, Houghton Library, Harvard University.

Ladjevardi, G. 1983 (January 29)
Ladjevardian, A. 1982 (October 11)
Lebaschi, A. 1983 (February 28)
Shanehchi, M. 1983 (March 4)

NICARAGUA

American Embassy, Managua. 1989. *Foreign Labor Trends.* Washington, D.C.: US Department of Labor, Bureau of International Labor Affairs.

Baumeister, E. 1985. "The Structure of Nicaraguan Agriculture and the Sandinista Agararian Reform." In *Nicaragua: A Revolution Under Siege*, edited by R. Harris and C. Vilas. London: Zed.

Berryman. P. 1984. *The Religious Roots of Rebellion: Christians in Central American Revolutions.* Maryknoll, NY: Orbis Books.

Biderman, J. 1983. "The Development of Capitalism in Nicaragua: A Political Economic History." *Latin American Perspectives,* Issue 36, 10(1) Winter.

Black, G. 1981. *Triumph of the People: The Sandinista Revolution in Nicaragua.* London: Zed.

Booth, J. 1982. *The End and the Beginning: The Nicaraguan Revolution.* Boulder: Westview.

1991. "Socioeconomic and Political Roots of National Revolts in Central America." *Latin American Research Review,* 26 (1).

1998. "The Somoza Regime in Nicaragua." In *Sultanistic Regimes,* edited by H. Chehabi and J. Linz. Baltimore: The Johns Hopkins University Press.

Booth, J., and T. Walker. 1989. *Understanding Central America.* Boulder: Westview Press.

Brooks, J. 1967. "The Impact of the Cotton Policy on El Salvador and Nicaragua." *Public and International Affairs,* 5 (1).

Cardenal, S. J. F. 1976. Testimony before the International Organizations Sub-Committee of the House Foreign Relations Committee, Washington, D.C., June 8–9, 1976.

Carl, B. M. 1984. "How Marxist is Nicaragua? A Look at New Laws." *Crime and Social Justice,* No. 21–22.

Christian, S. 1985. *Nicaragua: Revolution in the Family.* New York: Random House.

Close, D. 1988. *Nicaragua: Politics, Economics and Society.* London: Pinter.

Cruz, A. 1989. *Memoirs of a Counterrevolutionary.* New York: Doubleday.

Deere, C., and P. Marchetti. 1981. "The Worker–Peasant Alliance in the First Year of the Nicaraguan Agrarian Reform." *Latin America Perspectives* 8 (2):40–73.

Diederich, B. 1981. *Somoza: And the Legacy of US Involvement in Central America.* New York: E. P. Dutton.

Dodson, M., and L. N. O'Shaughnessy. 1990. *Nicaragua's Other Revolution.* Chapel Hill: The University of North Carolina Press.

Dorner, P., and R. Quiros. 1973. "Institutional Dualism in Central America's Agricultural Development." *Journal of Latin American Studies,* 5:217–232.

Enriquez, L., and R. Spalding. 1987. "Banking Systems and Revolutionary Change: The Politics of Agricultural Credit in Nicaragua." In *The Political Economy of Revolutionary Nicaragua,* edited by R. Spalding. Boston: Allen and Unwin.

Everingham, M. 1996. *Revolution and the Multiclass Coalition in Nicaragua.* Pittsburgh: University of Pittsburgh Press.

Farhi, F. 1990. *States and Urban-Based Revolutions: Iran and Nicaragua.* Urbana: University of Illinois Press.

Foran, J., and J. Goodwin. 1993. "Revolutionary Outcomes in Iran and Nicaragua: Coalition Fragmentation, War, and the Limits of Social Transformation." *Theory and Society,* 22 (2).

Foroohar, M. 1989. *The Catholic Church and Social Change in Nicaragua.* Albany: State University of New York Press.

Gibson, B. 1987. "A Structural Overview of the Nicaraguan Economy." In *The Political Economy of Revolutionary Nicaragua*, edited by R. Spalding. Boston: Allen and Unwin.

Gilbert, D. 1985. "The Bourgeoisie." In *Nicaragua: The First Five Years*, edited by T. Walker. New York: Praeger.

——. 1990. *Sandinistas: The Party and the Revolution*. Cambridge: Basil Blackwell.

Gorman, S. 1986. "Sandinista Chess: How the Left Took Control." *Caribbean Review* 10 (1).

Graham, L. S. 1987. "The Impact of the Revolution on the State Apparatus." In *Nicaragua: Profiles of the Revolutionary Public Sector*, edited by M. E. Conroy. Boulder: Westview.

Harris, R. 1985. "The Economic Transformation and Industrial Development of Nicaragua." In *Nicaragua: A Revolution Under Siege*, edited by R. Harris and C. Vilas. London: Zed.

Heriot, Jr., J. 1982. "The Economy." In *Nicaragua: A Country Study*. Washington D.C: US Department of the Army.

Hodges, D. 1986. *Intellectual Foundations of the Nicaraguan Revolution*. Austin: University of Texas Press.

International Bank for Reconstruction and Development. 1953. *The Economic Development of Nicaragua*. Baltimore: The Johns Hopkins University Press.

International Monetary Fund (IMF). 1982 and 1990. *Government Finance Statistics Yearbook*. Washington, D.C.: IMF.

Kaimowitz, D. 1986. "Nicaraguan Debates on Agrarian Structure and their Implications for Agricultural Policy and the Rural Poor." *Journal of Peasant Studies*, 14 (1).

Kinzer, S. 1979. "Nicaragua: Universal Revolt." *The Atlantic*, 243 (2).

Kirk, J. M. 1992. *Politics and the Catholic Church in Nicaragua*. Gainesville: University Press of Florida.

LaFeber, W. 1984. *Inevitable Revolutions: The United States in Central America*. New York: W. W. Norton.

Leiken, R., ed. 1984. *Central America: Anatomy of Conflict*. New York: Pergamon.

Lernoux, P. 1980. *Cry of the People*. New York: Doubleday & Company.

Midlarsky, M., and K. Roberts. 1985. "Class, State, and Revolution in Central America: Nicaragua and El Salvador Compared." *Journal of Conflict Resolution* 29:163–193.

Millett, R. 1977. *Guardians of the Dynasty*. Maryknoll, NY: Orbis Books.

——. 1982. "The Historical Setting." In *Nicaragua: A Country Study*. Washington, D.C.: US Department of the Army.

Montgomery, T. S. 1982/1983. "Cross and Rifle: El Salvador and Nicaragua." *Journal of International Affairs*, 36 (2).

Paige, J. 1985. "Cotton and Revolution in Nicaragua." In *States vs. Markets in the World-System*, edited by P. Evans, D. Rueschemeyer and E. Stephens. Beverly Hills: Sage.

——. 1989. "Revolution and the Agrarian Bourgeoisie in Nicaragua." In *Revolution in the World System*, edited by T. Boswell. New York: Greenwood.

——. 1997. *Coffee and Power: Revolution and the Rise of Democracy in Central America*. Cambridge, Mass.: Harvard University Press.

Parsa, M. 1995. "Conversion or Coalition? Ideology in the Iranian and Nicaraguan Revolutions." *Political Power and Social Theory* 9:23–60.

Rather, D. "Somoza." In *60 Minutes*, vol. 11 (14). CBS TV News Network.

Rosset, P., and J. Vandermeer. 1983. *The Nicaragua Reader: Documents of a Revolution under Fire*. New York: Grove.

Ruchwarger, G. 1985. "The Sandinista Mass Organizations and the Revolutionary Process." In *Nicaragua: A Revolution Under Siege*, edited by R. Harris and C. Vilas. London: Zed.

1987. *People in Power: Forging a Grassroots Democracy in Nicaragua*. South Hadley, Mass.: Bergin & Garvey.

Ryan, J. M. 1970. *Area Handbook for Nicaragua*. Washington, D.C.: The American University.

Sequeira, A. C. 1984. "The Origins of Sandinista Foreign Policy." In *Central America: Anatomy of Conflict*, edited by R. Leiken. New York: Pergamon.

Sierra, L. 1985. "Ideology, Religion, and Class Struggle in the Nicaraguan Revolution." In *Nicaragua: A Revolution Under Siege*, edited by R. Harris and C. Vilas. London: Zed.

Sholk, R. 1984. "The National Bourgeoisie in Post-Revolutionary Nicaragua." *Comparative Politics* 16:253–276.

Shugart, M. S. 1989. "Patterns of Revolution." *Theory and Society* 18:249–271.

Somoza, A. (as told to J. Cox). 1980. *Nicaragua Betrayed*. Boston: Western Island.

Spalding, R. 1994. *Capitalists and Revolution in Nicaragua*. Chapel Hill: The University of North Carolina Press.

Strachan, H. 1976. *Family and Other Business Groups in Economic Development: The Case of Nicaragua*. From *Praeger Special Studies in International Business, Finance, and Trade*. New York: Praeger.

United Nations. 1978. *Economic Survey of Latin America*. Santiago, Chile: United Nations.

1990. *National Accounts Statistics: Main Aggregates and Detailed Tables*, various years. New York: United Nations.

Vilas, C. M. 1985. "The Workers' Movement in the Sandinista Revolution." In *Nicaragua: A Revolution Under Siege*, edited by R. Harris and C. M. Vilas. London: Zed.

1986. *The Sandinista Revolution: National Liberation and Social Transformation in Central America*. New York: Monthly Review Press.

1995. *Between Earthquakes and Volcanoes: Market, State, and Revolutions in Central America*. New York: Monthly Review Press.

Walker, T. 1981. *Nicaragua: The Land of Sandino*. From *The Nations of Contemporary Latin America*. Boulder: Westview.

1985. "Revolution in General, Nicaragua to 1984." In *Nicaragua: The First Five Years*, edited by T. Walker. New York: Praeger.

Weber, H. (Trans. by P. Camiller). 1981. *Nicaragua: The Sandinist Revolution*. London: Verso Editions and NLB.

Weeks, J. 1985. *The Economies of Central America*. New York: Holmes and Meier.

Wheelock, J. R. 1978. *Imperialismo y Dictadura*. Mexico, D.F.: Siglo Veintiuno

Editores.

Wickham-Crowley, T. 1989. "Winners, Losers, and Also-Rans: Toward a Comparative Sociology of Latin American Guerrilla Movements." In *Power and Popular Protest: Latin American Social Movements*, edited by S. Eckstein. Berkeley: University of California Press.

1991. *Exploring Revolution: Essays on Latin American Insurgency and Revolutionary Theory*. New York: M. E. Sharpe, Inc.

1992. *Guerrillas and Revolution in Latin America: A Comparative Study of Insurgents and Regimes Since 1956*. Princeton: Princeton University Press.

Williams, P. 1989. *The Catholic Church and Politics in Nicaragua and Costa Rica*. Pittsburgh: University of Pittsburgh Press.

Williams, R. 1986. *Export Agriculture and the Crisis in Central America*. Chapel Hill: The University of North Carolina Press.

World Bank. 1979. *World Development Report 1979*. New York: Oxford University Press.

1980. *World Development Report 1980*. Oxford: Oxford University Press.

Zwerling, P., and Martin, C. 1985. *Nicaragua: A New Kind of Revolution*. Westport, Conn.: Lawrence Hill.

NEWSPAPERS

La Prensa. A national newspaper.

THE PHILIPPINES

Almendral, G. N. 1988. "The Fall of the Regime." In *Dictatorship and Revolution: Roots of People's Power*, edited by A. Javate-de Dios, P. Daroy, and L. Kalwa-Tirol. Metro Manila: Conspectus.

American Embassy, Manila. Various years. *Foreign Labor Trends, Philippines*. The US Department of Labor, Bureau of International Labor Affairs.

Baldwin, R. E. 1975. *Foreign Trade Regimes and Economic Development: The Philippines*. Vol. V. New York: Columbia University Press.

Bello, W., D. Kinley, and V. Bielski. 1982. "Containment in the Countryside." In *Development Debacle: The World Bank in the Philippines*, edited by W. Bello, D. Kinley, and E. Ellinson. San Francisco: Institute for Food and Development Policy.

Bouis, H. E. 1990. "Evaluating Demand for Calories for Urban and Rural Populations in the Philippines: Implications for Nutrition Policy Under Economic Recovery." *World Development* 18 (2):281–299.

Boyce, J. K. 1993. *The Philippines: The Political Economy of Growth and Impoverishment in the Marcos Era*. London: Macmillan.

Broad, R. 1988. *Unequal Alliance: The World Bank, the International Monetary Fund, and the Philippines*. Berkeley: University of California Press.

Canoy, R. R. 1984. *The Counterfeit Revolution: The Philippines from Martial Law to the Aquino Assassination*. Manila: Philippine Editions.

Carroll, J. J. 1965. *The Filipino Manufacturing Entrepeneur: Agent and Product of Change*. Ithaca: Cornell University Press.

Chapman, W. 1987. *Inside the Philippine Revolution*. New York: W. W. Norton.

Cheetham, R. J., and E. K. Hawkins. 1976. *The Philippines: Priorities and Prospects for Development.* Washington, D.C.: The World Bank.

Daroy, P. B. 1988. "On the Eve of Dictatorship and Revolution." In *Dictatorship and Revolution: Roots of People's Power,* edited by A. Javate-de Dios, P. Daroy, and L. Kalwa-Tirol. Metro Manila: Conspectus.

De Dios, E. 1988. "The Erosion of the Dictatorship." In *Dictatorship and Revolution: Roots of People's Power,* edited by A. Javate-de Dios, P. Daroy, and L. Kalwa-Tirol. Metro Manila: Conspectus.

Diokno, M. S. 1988. "Unity and Struggle." In *Dictatorship and Revolution: Roots of People's Power,* edited by A. Javate-de Dios, P. Daroy, and L. Kalwa-Tirol. Metro Manila: Conspectus.

Doronila, A. 1992. *The State, Economic Transformation, and Political Change in the Philippines, 1946–1972.* Singapore: Oxford University Press.

George, T. J. S. 1980. *Revolt in Mindanao: The Rise of Islam in Philippine Politics.* Kuala Lumpur: Oxford University Press.

Golay, F. H. 1961. *The Philippines: Public Policy and National Economic Development.* Ithaca: Cornell University Press.

———. 1983. "Manila Americans and Philippine Policy: The Voice of American Business." In *The Philippine Economy and the United States: Studies in Past and Present Interactions,* edited by N. G. Owen. Ann Arbor: The University of Michigan Center for South and Southeast Asian Studies.

Goodno, J. B. 1991. *The Philippines: Land of Broken Promises.* Atlantic Highlands, N.J.: Zed.

Hackenberg, R. A., and B. H. Hackenberg. 1987. "The Urban Working Class in the Philippines: A Casualty of the New Society." In *Rebuilding a Nation: Philippine Challenges and American Policy,* edited by C. H. Lande. Washington, D.C.: Washington Institute Press.

Hawes, G. 1987. *The Philippine State and the Marcos Regime: The Politics of Export.* Ithaca: Cornell University Press.

———. 1990. "Theories of Peasant Revolution: A Critique and Contribution from the Philippines." *World Politics* 42 (2):261–298.

Hooley, R. 1991. "Economic Developments in the Philippines." In *Democracy and Development in East Asia: Taiwan, South Korea, and the Philippines,* edited by T. W. Robinson. Washington, D.C.: The AEI Press.

Hutchcroft, P. 1991. "Oligarchs and Cronies in the Philippine State: the Politics of Plunder." *World Politics* 43 (3):414–40.

International Labour Office. 1974. *Sharing in Development: A Programme of Employment, Equity, and Growth for the Philippines.* Geneva: International Labour Office.

Jackson, R. T. 1989. "A Note on Income Distribution in the Philippines, 1956–88." *Malaysian Journal of Tropical Geography* 20 (December):12–19.

Javate-de Dios, A., P. Daroy, and L. Kalwa-Tirol, eds. 1988. *Dictatorship and Revolution: Roots of People's Power.* Metro Manila: Conspectus.

Johnson, B. 1987. *The Four Days of Courage: The Untold Story of the People Who Brought Marcos Down.* New York: The Free Press.

Kerkvliet, B. J. T. 1977. *The Huk Rebellion: A Study of Peasant Revolt in the Philippines.* Berkeley: University of California Press.

Kessler, R. J. 1984. "Politics Philippine Style, Circa 1984." *Asian Survey* 24

(12):1209–1228.

1989. *Rebellion and Repression in the Phillippines.* New Haven: Yale University Press.

Kimura, M. 1991. "Martial Law and the Realignment of Political Parties in the Philippines (September 1972–February 1986): With a Case in the Province of Batangas." *Southeast Asian Studies* 29 (2):205–226.

Koppel, B. M. 1987. "Agrarian Problems and Agrarian Reform: Opportunity or Irony?" In *Rebuilding a Nation: Philippine Challenges and American Policy,* edited by C. H. Lande. Washington, D.C.: Washington Institute Press.

Landé, C. H. 1964. *Leaders, Factions, and Parties: The Structure of Philippine Politics.* New Haven: Yale University Press.

1986. "The Political Crisis." In *Crisis in the Philippines: The Marcos Era and Beyond,* edited by J. Bresnan. Princeton: Princeton University Press.

1987. 'Introduction: Retrospect and Prospect." In *Rebuilding a Nation: Philippine Challenges and American Policy,* edited by C. H. Landé. Washington, D.C.: Washington Institute Press.

Lichauco, A. 1973. *The Lichauco Paper: Imperialism in the Philippines.* New York: Monthly Review.

Marcos, F. E. 1980. *An Ideology for Filipinos.* Philippines.

McCarthy, C. J. 1975. "The Chinese in the Philippines Today and Tomorrow." *Fookien Times Philippines Yearbook 1975* 348–351, 360.

Muego, B. N. 1983. "The Executive Committee in the Philippines: Successors, Power Brokers, and Dark Horses." *Asian Survey* 28 (11):1159–1170.

Nemenzo, F. 1988. "From Autocracy to Elite Democracy." In *Dictatorship and Revolution: Roots of People's Power,* edited by A. Javate-de Dios, P. Daroy, and L. Kalwa-Tirol. Metro Manila: Conspectus.

Noble, L. G. 1986. "Politics in the Marcos Era." In *Crisis in the Philippines: The Marcos Era and Beyond,* edited by J. Bresnan. Princeton: Princeton University Press.

Ordonez, V. M. 1983. "An Analysis of Reactions of Investors to the Recent Investment Climate in the Philippines." In *The Philippine Economy and the United States: Studies in Past and Present Interactions,* edited by N. G. Owen. Ann Arbor: The University of Michigan Center for South and Southeast Asian Studies.

Overholt, W. H. 1986. "The Rise and Fall of Ferdinand Marcos." *Asian Survey* 26 (11):1137–1163.

Parsa, M. 1995. "Entrepreneurs and Democratization: Iran and the Philippines." *Comparative Studies in Society and History* 37:803–830.

Paua, F. J. 1993. *Managing External Linkages: A Comparative Analysis of State-Led Development.* Senior Honors Thesis. Hanover: Dartmouth College.

Pimentel, B. 1991. *Rebolusyon: A Generation of Struggle in the Philippines.* New York: Monthly Review Press.

Poblador, N. S. 1971. *Foreign Investment in the Major Non-Financial Corporate Sector of the Philippines, 1964 and 1965.* Diliman, Quezon City: School of Economics, University of the Philippines.

Poole, F., and M. Vanzi. 1984. *Revolution in the Philippines: The United States in a Hall of Cracked Mirrors.* New York: McGraw-Hill.

Power, J. H., G. P. Sicat, and M. Hsing. 1971. *The Philippines and Taiwan:*

Industrialization and Trade Policies. New York: Oxford University Press.

Reinah, D. 1987. "Philippine Sugar Industry Market Considerations and United States Policy." In *Rebuilding a Nation: Philippine Challenges and American Policy,* edited by C. H. Lande. Washington, D.C.: Washington Institute Press.

Rosenberg, D. A. 1987. "The Changing Structure of the Philippine Government from Marcos to Aquino." In *Rebuilding the Nation: Philippine Challenges and American Policy,* edited by C. H. Lande. Washington, D.C.: Washington Institute Press.

Rush, J. R. 1986a. "Bringing Marcos Down: Part I: The Electoral Tradition." *UFSI Reports* (3):1–7.

1986b. "Bringing Marcos Down: Part II: The Opposition Divided." *UFSI Reports* (6):1–7.

1986c. "Bringing Marcos Down: Part III: Suspending Disbelief." *UFSI Reports* (7):1–11.

1986d. "Bringing Marcos Down: The Miracle of Edsa: Part IV: Conclusion." *UFSI Reports* (29):1–10.

Schirmer, D. B., and S. R. Shalom, eds. 1987. *The Philippines Reader: A History of Colonialism, Neocolonialism, Dictatorship, and Resistance.* Boston: South End Press.

Sicat, G. 1972. *Economic Policy and Philippine Development.* Philippines: University of the Philippines Press.

Silliman, G. S. 1984. "The Philippines in 1983: Authoritarianism Beleaguered." *Asian Survey* 24 (2):149–158.

Stauffer, R. 1975. *The Philippine Congress: Causes of Structural Change.* Beverly Hills: Sage Publications.

1980. *Transnational Corporations and the Political Economy of Development: The Continuing Philippine Debate.* Research Monograph No. 11, University of Sydney.

Steinberg, D. J. 1990. *The Philippines: A Singular and a Plural Place.* Boulder: Westview.

Sullivan, W. H. 1987. "The United States–Philippine Strategic Relationship." In *Rebuilding a Nation: Philippine Challenges and American Policy,* edited by C. H. Lande. Washington, D.C.: Washington Institute Press.

Thompson, M. 1995. *The Anti-Marcos Struggle: Personalistic Rule and Democratic Transition in the Philippines.* Hew Haven: Yale University Press.

Tiglao, R. 1988. "The Consolidation of the Dictatorship." In *Dictatorship and Revolution: Roots of People's Power,* edited by A. Javate-de Dios, P. Daroy, and L. Kalwa-Tirol. Metro Manila: Conspectus.

Timberman, D. G. 1991. *A Changeless Land: Continuity and Change in Philippine Politics.* Armonk, N.Y.: M. E. Sharpe.

Valdepenas, V. B., and G. M. Bautista. 1977. *The Emergence of the Philippine Economy.* Manila: Papyrus Press.

Villegas, B. 1986a. "The Philippines in 1985: Rolling With the Political Punches." *Asian Survey* 26 (2):127–140.

1986b. "The Economic Crisis." In *Crisis in the Philippines: The Marcos Era and Beyond,* edited by J. Bresnan. Princeton: Princeton University Press.

1987. "The Philippines in 1986: Democratic Reconstruction in the Post-Marcos Era." *Asian Survey* 27 (2):194–205.

Villegas, E. 1983. *Studies in Philippine Political Economy*. Manila: Silangan Publishers.

Walton, J. 1984. *Reluctant Rebels: Comparative Studies of Revolution and Underdevelopment*. New York: Columbia University Press.

Wolters, W. 1983. *Politics, Patronage, and Class Conflict in Central Luzon*. The Hague: Institute of Social Studies.

World Bank. 1991. *DEC Analytical Database: Report on Methods and Data Sources*. International Economics Department, Analysis and Prospects Division.

Wurfel, D. 1979. *Elites of Wealth and Elites of Power, the Changing Dynamic: A Philippines Case Study*. Singapore: Institute of Southeast Asian Studies.

1988. *Filipino Politics: Development and Decay*. Ithaca: Cornell University Press.

Youngblood, R. L. 1987. "The Corazon Aquino 'Miracle' and the Philippine Churches." *Asian Survey* 27 (12):1240–1255.

1990. *Marcos Against the Church: Economic Development and Political Repression in the Philippines*. Ithaca: Cornell University Press.

NEWSPAPERS AND PERIODICALS

Ang Pahayagang Malaya (cited as *Malaya*). A national newspaper.
IBON Fact and Figures, published by IBON Databank Philippines, Inc.
Manila Times. A national newspaper.

Index

316

CPSIA information can be obtained at www.ICGtesting.com
Printed in the USA
BVOW070354110112

280240BV00003B/10/A